A COMMUNITY OF EUROPEANS?

A COMMUNITY OF EUROPEANS?

Transnational Identities
and Public Spheres

Thomas Risse

CORNELL UNIVERSITY PRESS   **ITHACA AND LONDON**

First published 2010 by Cornell University Press
First printing, Cornell Paperbacks, 2010

Printed in the United States of America

Library of Congress Cataloging-in-Publication Data

Risse-Kappen, Thomas.
   A community of Europeans? : transnational identities and public spheres / Thomas Risse.
       p. cm.
   Includes bibliographical references and index.
   ISBN 978-0-8014-4663-4 (cloth : alk. paper) —
   ISBN 978-0-8014-7648-8 (pbk. : alk. paper)
   1. Group identity—Europe.   2. Transnationalism—Social aspects—Europe.
3. Social integration—Europe.   4. Nationalism—Europe.   5. European federation—Public opinion.   6. Public opinion—Europe.   I. Title.

   HM753.R57   2010
   305.80094—dc22   2009047395

Cornell University Press strives to use environmentally responsible suppliers and materials to the fullest extent possible in the publishing of its books. Such materials include vegetable-based, low-VOC inks and acid-free papers that are recycled, totally chlorine-free, or partly composed of nonwood fibers. For further information, visit our website at www.cornellpress.cornell.edu.

Cloth printing   10 9 8 7 6 5 4 3 2 1
Paperback printing   10 9 8 7 6 5 4 3 2

Contents

Figures

Acknowledgments

This book has been in the making for a long time. It documents a rather long journey from Konstanz, Germany, via Florence, Italy, to Berlin and also includes a stay in Cambridge, Massachusetts.

I first became interested in questions of European identity shortly after I had started teaching at the University of Konstanz in 1993. My first research project on "the idea of Europe" started in the mid-1990s and was originally funded by the state of Baden-Württemberg and subsequently by the German Research Foundation (Deutsche Forschungsgemeinschaft, or DFG). Members of this first team included Daniela Engelmann-Martin, Hans-Joachim Knopf, and Klaus Roscher. Martin Marcussen joined the group in 1997 when I moved to the European University Institute (EUI) in Florence, Italy. This group got me going on questions of European identity, for which I am extremely grateful.

In 1999, I served as codirector of the European Forum at the EUI's Robert Schuman Centre for Advanced Studies entitled "Between Europe and the Nation-State: The Reshaping of Interests, Identities and Political Representation," together with Stefano Bartolini, the political scientist, and Bo Strath, the historian. Shortly afterward, I coordinated IDNET, a thematic network funded by the European Commission's fifth framework program on socioeconomic research and focusing on "Europeanization, Collective Identities, and Public Discourses" (Risse and Maier 2003). This network brought together sociologists (Klaus Eder, Bernhard Giesen, Wilfried Spohn), political scientists (Jeffrey Checkel), and social psychologists (Laura Benigni and Anna Triandafyllidou). The debates and discussions of the European Forum and IDNET made me realize how poorly equipped political scientists are to tackle questions of collective identities and how much we can learn from interdisciplinary exchanges.

In 2000, Bernhard Giesen from the University of Konstanz talked me into a project on the Europeanization of public spheres, which was subsequently funded by the DFG. This was my first venture into media analysis and communication studies. We conducted a frame analysis of newspapers in five countries pertaining to the so-called Haider debate, the EU reaction to a right-wing populist party in Austria entering into government (Van de Steeg 2002, 2005; Risse and Van de Steeg 2008). The research team included Valentin Rauer, Sylvain Rivet, and Marianne Van de Steeg. I owe a lot of what I learned about public spheres and Öffentlichkeit to this group of wonderful and dedicated researchers, in particular Marianne.

At about the same time, I ran into Richard Herrmann of Ohio State University who was interested in examining the possibilities of transnational identities beyond the nation-state. This encounter resulted in an edited volume on European identity (Herrmann, Risse, and Brewer 2004) that brought together social psychologists (Marilyn Brewer and Emanuele Castano), sociologists (Jack Citrin), social anthropologists (Ulrike Meinhof), sociolinguists (Ruth Wodak), and others.

In the meantime, I had moved back to Germany, to Berlin's Freie Universität. Cathleen Kantner, who had written a superb PhD dissertation on the possibilities and limits of a European public sphere (Kantner 2004), and I teamed up to direct another DFG-funded project on "A European Public Sphere and European Foreign and Security Policy." Working with Cathleen as well as Amelie Kutter and Swantje Renfordt (Kantner 2009; Kutter 2009; Renfordt 2009) made me realize how much methodological progress we have made in recent years in the study of transnational public spheres. Thank you, Cathleen, Amelie, and Swantje!

Last but not least, I have to mention our DFG-funded Research College on the "Transformative Power of Europe," which started in 2008 and which Tanja A. Börzel and I codirect (www.transformeurope.eu). The Research College provides a wonderful opportunity to invite guest scholars and postdoctoral fellows to enter into intensive discussions about issues related to our research. I thank particularly Silke Adam, Jürgen Gerhards, Barbara Pfetsch, and Fritz W. Scharpf for extremely stimulating discussions.

I had originally planned to write this book while at the EUI. I am happy that I did not, since so much new work on the Europeanization of identities and public spheres has been published in the meantime. I finally used my sabbatical at Harvard University's Minda de Gunzburg Center for European Studies in 2006/2007 to get started on the book. I thank the CES for providing me with this opportunity. For research assistance on the book, I am very grateful to Claire Guehenno and Linnea Sundberg at Harvard as well as Gisela Hirschmann, Mirco Günther, and Jing Tian at the Freie Universität Berlin.

Over the past two years, I presented the main arguments at various places, among them Harvard University, Cornell University, the European University Institute, the University of Denver, the London School of Economics, and the Freie Universität Berlin. I thank the various audiences for their comments and criticisms. My own thinking on European identity got another boost when Jeffrey Checkel and Peter Katzenstein invited me to come to Oslo in the fall of 2007 to comment on their edited book project (Checkel and Katzenstein 2009a).

I also have to thank various readers: Gary Marks and an anonymous reviewer read the entire manuscript and commented on it. I am also very grateful to Silke Adam, Jürgen Gerhards, Cathleen Kantner, Amelie Kutter, Swantje Renfordt, and

Marianne Van de Steeg for their valuable comments on individual chapters. I also thank John Raymond for his meticulous copyediting, Kate Mertes for preparing the index, Alexandra Kuhles for help with the proofreading, as well as Susan C. Barnett, Ange Romeo-Hall, and Rachel Post at Cornell University Press for their help along the way of the book's production.

Last but not least, this book would probably not have been written had two people not constantly reminded me that there was a manuscript in my head that needed to get out. The first is Roger Haydon at Cornell University Press. Whenever I stopped at the Cornell booth during the American Political Science Association annual meetings of the past ten years or so, Roger reminded me that I had promised him a book on European identity. When I finally gave in and started writing, Roger read every single chapter and commented on it. I owe you one, big time, Roger!

The second person without whom I could not have written this book is my wife, Tanja Börzel, of course. Tanja constantly reminds me how little I actually know about the EU. Although Tanja "does not do identity," she nevertheless read the entire manuscript and commented on it in detail. She also asked all the right and critical questions that nobody else dared to ask. As a result, the book has improved tremendously. Finally, Tanja endured my constant mood changes, particularly during the final weeks of completing the manuscript. Danke, mein Schatz!

THOMAS RISSE

Berlin

Abbreviations

CAP	Common Agricultural Policy
CDU	Christlich Demokratische Union Deutschlands (German Christian Democratic Party)
CEEC	Central Eastern European Countries
CFSP	(European) Common Foreign and Security Policy
COREPER	Committee of Permanent Representatives (Committee of national "ambassadors" to the EU in Brussels)
EEC	European Economic Community (based on the Treaty of Rome)
EC	European Community (as the EU was called prior to the Maastricht Treaties)
ECB	European Central Bank
ECJ	European Court of Justice
ECSC	European Coal and Steel Community (predecessor of the European Economic Community)
EFTA	European Free Trade Association
EMU	(European) Economic and Monetary Union
EP	European Parliament
ESDP	European Security and Defense Policy
FPÖ	Freiheitliche Partei Österreichs (Austrian Liberal Party, a right-wing populist party)
GDR	German Democratic Republic (former East Germany)
IGC	Intergovernmental Conference (EU treaty-making conferences)
NATO	North Atlantic Treaty Organization
OSCE	Organization for Security and Cooperation in Europe
QMV	qualified majority voting (number of votes necessary in the Council of Ministers for a decision to pass)
RPR	Rassemblement pour la République (former French Gaullist party)
SPD	Sozialdemokratische Partei Deutschlands (German Social Democratic Party)
UK	United Kingdom
UMP	Union pour un Mouvement Populaire (French center-right party incorporating the former RPR)

A COMMUNITY OF EUROPEANS?

THE EUROPEANIZATION OF IDENTITIES AND PUBLIC SPHERES

DRAWING INSPIRATION from the cultural, religious and humanist inheritance of Europe, from which have developed the universal values of the inviolable and inalienable rights of the human person, freedom, democracy, equality and the rule of law, RECALLING the historic importance of the ending of the division of the European continent and the need to create firm bases for the construction of the future Europe...

—Council of the European Union 2008, 18

Turkey, that is, an Asian country, an Islamist government, an Extra-European civilization...Turkey does not have its place in Europe! Europe with Turkey, that is, the borders of Europe pushing toward Iran and Iraq, the free installment of 72 million Turks and Kurds in Europe, the subordination (*vassalisation*) of Europe to American interests, a Europe without borders—a step toward a world state!

—Front National 2007[1]

Once I was an Eastern European; then I was promoted to the rank of Central European....Then a few months ago, I became a New European. But before I had the chance to get used to this status— even before I could have refused it—I have now become a non-core European.

—Hungarian writer Péter Esterházy, quoted in Case 2009

These three quotations capture a range of identity constructions in Europe today. The first is from the preamble to the Lisbon Treaty as signed by the European Union's Heads of States and Governments on October 19, 2007. It presents the collective identity of the European Union (EU) as understood by its political

---

1. Here and in the following, all translations from the originals are mine.

leaders. It refers to Europe's cultural heritage, to universal values of human rights and democracy, and to the European past of the cold war. There is also a reference to the religious inheritance of Europe which, however, stops short of mentioning Christianity. In other words, this is the modern and cosmopolitan Europe with its roots in the age of Enlightenment, a Europe that is proud of its open borders.

In sharp contrast, the second quotation comes from a pamphlet of the French right-wing party Front National opposing Turkish membership in the EU. It shows us an exclusionary Europe with clear boundaries against Asia, Islam, and any "extra-European civilizations"—a nationalist Europe that is closed to strangers. What is remarkable is that a right-wing populist party would talk about Europe and its identity at all, thereby offering an alternative vision to the official cosmopolitan one.[2]

In the third quotation, Hungarian writer Péter Esterházy muses about his place in Europe, in the context of rows over the Iraq War in 2003. When Hungary belonged to the Warsaw Pact during the cold war, he was an East European. The end of the cold war "promoted" him to Central Europe. In early 2003, U.S. Secretary of Defense Donald Rumsfeld labeled those in Central Eastern Europe who supported the U.S. intervention in Iraq as "new Europe." Shortly thereafter, philosophers Jürgen Habermas and Jacques Derrida countered Rumsfeld's identity talk with their own, praising France and Germany, which had refused to support the United States, as "core Europe" (Habermas and Derrida 2005). As a result, Hungarians such as Esterházy were once again relegated to the status of "noncore Europeans."

As Esterházy shows, identities "do not float freely."[3] Rather, they become salient and are fought over in particular historical moments, especially in times of crisis. In this sense, identity crises represent the "normal" state of affairs insofar as they make identities visible and subject to debate. Europe is no exception. Ever since the end of the cold war ushered in two decades of EU "deepening" leading to ever increased integration and a strengthening of supranational institutions as well as of "widening," which more than doubled the EU's membership from twelve in 1990 to twenty-seven in 2007, Europe has been facing identity crises. The wars in the western Balkans of the 1990s further added to the sense of uncertainty with regard to the EU's purpose.

The EU's enlargement toward Central Eastern Europe in the 2000s, for example, sparked debates about Eastern Europe's place in the "new Europe" that were

---

2. For a very similar slogan, see the Austrian right-wing Freiheitliche Partei Österreichs: "Save Europe! Stop Turkish Accession" (http://www.stoppt-den-tuerkei-beitritt.at). I owe this point to discussions with Douglas R. Holmes. See Holmes 2009.

3. This is taken from Risse-Kappen 1994.

sharpened by the fight over European contributions to the U.S.-led "coalition of the willing" in Iraq. Controversies over Turkish membership in the EU and over immigration also expressed themselves in identity language, pitting a modern and enlightened Europe of open borders against a nationalist and closed fortress Europe. The latter debate often has religious undertones of a Christian Europe against Muslim Turkey, as in the following slogan by the Austrian populist right-wing party Freiheitliche Partei Österreichs (FPÖ): "Occident in the Hands of Christians! Day of Reckoning!"[4]

Moreover, and for the better part of the 2000s, the EU was preoccupied with constitutional issues. The European Constitutional Convention drafted a Constitutional Treaty for the European Union, which was rejected by French and Dutch public referenda in 2005, only to be resurrected in the 2007 Lisbon Treaty, which was rejected by the Irish in 2008 and then approved in a second referendum in 2009. Interestingly, the latter treaty which went into force at the end of 2009 strips the EU's foundational texts of all symbols such as the flag. Whereas the failed Constitutional Treaty was full of identity talk and symbols, the Lisbon Treaty delivers a European "identity lite" in order to make the document acceptable to a skeptical public.

Last but not least, when the world faced its most serious global economic and financial crisis since the Great Depression of the 1930s, it was—once again— "show time" for European solidarity. Would the wealthier EU members such as France, Germany, and the United Kingdom come to the rescue of their poor fellow European nations such as Ireland, the Baltic states, or Hungary when economic disaster hit? Or would the single market, the single currency, and borderless traffic in "Schengenland"[5] simply dissolve, leading to a remake of the "beggar thy neighbor" policies of the late 1920s and 1930s? How does the EU cope with such crises, which put its institutions under severe stress?

The controversies surrounding Eastern and Turkish enlargement, immigration, the Constitution, and the economic crisis add up to a new stage in the evolution of the European Union. Using gradual and functional integration below the radar screen of domestic politics, the EU has evolved into a multilevel polity that deeply affects the lives of its citizens. EU member states have ceded core features of national sovereignty to the union with regard to monetary policies (with the introduction of the euro) and to internal security (with the removal of internal border controls in Schengenland, which now encompasses twenty-two

---

4. Slogan for the 2009 elections to the European Parliament, quoted from http://www.tagesschau.de/ausland/euoesterreich100-magnifier_mtb-1_pos-1.html.

5. The "Schengen agreements" are named after a small town in Luxembourg in which the original treaty on borderless travel was signed in 1985.

EU member states as well as Norway and Switzerland). Even national security is no longer the sole preserve of national sovereignty, with EU-sponsored military missions in the western Balkans and elsewhere.

It was only a question of time before the EU public finally noticed what was happening in their midst. The so-called permissive consensus in public opinion, with approval rates for European integration above 60 percent on average, disappeared in the early 1990s,[6] but it took a while for European politics to become subject to public scrutiny. European affairs became more and more politicized in the early 2000s. European and domestic politics intersect in most member states. Out of these debates we are witnessing the emergence of transnational public spheres in Europe.[7]

The Argument

It's no wonder that issues of European identity, community, and democracy have assumed center stage in EU politics. Policymakers, scholars, and ordinary citizens increasingly ask several basic questions:

1. What are the prepolitical conditions of a supranational polity? Can the EU rely on a sense of community among its peoples and a collective identity? How does European identity relate to communication across borders? And how can we explain the emergence as well as the limits of a European sense of community and of a European public sphere?
2. How do a European sense of community and a European public sphere affect European integration and political change? Do European identity and a transnational European public sphere facilitate or hinder effective policymaking in the EU? Alternatively, can the EU work without a sense of community and without politicization?
3. What are the implications for the democratic legitimacy of the European project? How much collective identity and shared communicative space

---

6. Average support for EU membership dropped from an all-time high of about 70% during the early 1990s to an all-time low of about 45% in 1997 and has fluctuated since then between 48% and 58% (cf. European Commission 2009, 44). For data before 1995, see the Eurobarometer's Interactive Search System, http://ec.europa.eu/public_opinion/cf/index_en.cfm.

7. Throughout the book, I use the terms "EU" and "Europe" interchangeably in order to make the prose more readable. Of course, even an EU of twenty-seven-plus member states does not equal Europe as a whole. However, political Europe increasingly coincides with the EU insofar as the EU has managed to occupy the identity space of Europe as a political community (see chapter 4). In this sense, the EU has crowded out other European-wide organizations such as the Council of Europe or the Organization for Security and Cooperation in Europe (OSCE). Even nonmember states have to define themselves in terms of their relationship to the EU.

does the EU need as a multilevel governance system? And what are the conclusions for the EU's future of thirty-plus member states?

This book tackles each of these questions. It presents and evaluates the emerging knowledge about European identity and European public spheres from a variety of disciplinary and methodological approaches in the social sciences. I advance six main claims.

First, I reject the conventional wisdom that Europeans lack a sense of community. It is true that we do not observe the emergence of a uniform and shared European identity above and beyond the various national identities. Rather, the available data show the *Europeanization* of collective local, national, gender, and other identities. Europe and the EU are integrated in people's sense of belonging. Empirical analyses document that more than 50 percent of European citizens hold such Europeanized national identities, if only as a secondary identity. Those who incorporate Europe into their sense of identity tend to support European integration much more than individuals who adhere to exclusively nationalist identities (Hooghe and Marks 2005). Yet, support for European integration in general is not to be confused with backing for specific policies. Moreover, the Europeanization of collective identities varies widely across old and new EU member states, and the meanings attached to "Europe" are also diverse. In general, however, the Europeanization of identities is well advanced in continental Western and Southern Europe, while majorities in Scandinavia and—most important—Great Britain still hold exclusively nationalist identities. Interestingly enough, citizens of the new Central Eastern European member states are not that different from people in the older EU member states with regard to their identification levels.

Second, I also challenge the notion that the EU lacks common communicative spaces because of the absence of a common language and European-wide media. Instead of looking for a European public sphere above and beyond national public spheres, we can observe the Europeanization of public spheres whenever European issues are debated as questions of common concern using similar frames of reference and whenever fellow Europeans participate regularly in these national debates. Such Europeanization of public spheres is still segmented and varies across member states. Once again, continental Western and Southern Europe seems to be integrating into a transnational public sphere, while we know too little about Central Eastern Europe to reach firm conclusions (see, however, Kutter 2009 on Poland). Once again, Great Britain remains the odd one out.

Thus, we can see the gradual emergence of transnational European communities of communication through the interconnectedness of Europeanized public spheres. Europeanized identities and European public spheres are closely linked, since European public discourses constitute spaces where collective identities are constructed as well as contested. Finally, the increasing politicization of European affairs contributes to the Europeanization of public spheres. The main problem in the past was not so much that Europeans were unable to communicate across borders but that the EU lacked politicization. This is changing rapidly and will profoundly transform the European landscape in the years to come (see Checkel and Katzenstein 2009b).

Third, struggles over European identity involve at least two distinct substantive concepts of what "Europe" actually means. On the one hand, there is a modern EU Europe supported by the European elites (Fligstein 2008; Bruter 2005) and embracing modern, democratic, and humanistic values against a past of nationalism, militarism, or Communism. This modern and secular Europe resonates in the elite discourses of France, Germany, Spain, and Italy, but also to some extent in Poland, the Czech Republic, and other new member states. On the other hand, there is a Europe of white Christian peoples that sees itself as a distinct civilization (in the sense of Huntington 1996). This European identity construction is less open to strangers and entails boundaries against Islam as well as Asian or African "cultures." The extreme version of this antimodern and antisecular identity construction is nationalist, xenophobic, and racist. This "nationalist Europe" is increasingly politicized by Euroskeptical populist parties particularly on the right who have taken up the European issue, while the European elites have tried to silence debates on what kind of Europe people want to see.

Interestingly, Christianity as part of a common European heritage serves as a reference point for both concepts of Europe (Byrnes and Katzenstein 2006). The Catholic Church, for example, has always supported European integration and even modern Europe, referring to notions of human dignity and human rights as core values of a modern, open, and social Europe (Hehir 2006; Byrnes 2001). The preamble of the 2007 Lisbon Treaty quoted above supplies a perfect example of the Christian values claimed as a European heritage. The fight over a reference to God in the (failed) Constitutional Treaty showed, however, that secular Europe remains contested and may even become more controversial with Eastern enlargement.[8] Moreover, European nationalists also refer to Christianity in their efforts to build categorical boundaries against foreigners from predominantly Muslim countries. The discourse on Turkish accession in particular is loaded with references to a European Christian civilization that is not open and cosmopolitan, but nationalist and exclusionary.

Fourth, describing the Europeanization of identities and public spheres is one thing, explaining it is more difficult. No straight causal arrows link European integration directly with Europeanized identities and public spheres. On the one

---

8. The ultra-conservative Polish Radio Maryja serves as an example for such exclusionary and antimodern Catholicism.

hand, engagement in the integration process seems to matter insofar as long-term membership and elite consensus in favor of the EU correlates with Europeanized identities and public spheres. As a result, we see a cluster of countries in continental Western and Southern Europe that not only participate in the single market, the single currency, and in Schengenland, but also exhibit a similar sense of community and regular transnational exchanges in the public spheres. The original six members belong to this group, as do Italy, Portugal, and Spain (and Greece to a lesser degree). In contrast, Great Britain continues to be different and—in this sense—does not belong to a common social space of Europeanized identities and public spheres. Of course, the more countries actively engage in EU integration, the more the EU is visible and present in the daily lives of citizens. In turn, this visibility and presence leads to the EU's psychological existence as an "imagined community" (Anderson 1991).

On the other hand, identification processes follow largely national pathways, which also explain the variations in the degree of Europeanization of identities and public spheres. The meaning constructions of Europe and the EU resonate with national and even local discourses in different ways and do not lead to homogeneity and one unified European identity.[9] In this sense, the EU's slogan, "Unity in Diversity," actually captures an important truth. Nevertheless, the identity discourses in, for example, Germany, France, Spain, and Poland show that "modern Europe" resonates with national narratives, historical memories, and symbols in different ways.

Fifth, the Europeanization of identities and public discourses matters for EU politics. Although we cannot explain every single EU policy on identity grounds, elite identities and public discourses are particularly relevant in policy areas that involve core features of national sovereignty. I demonstrate this point with regard to constitutional issues, the introduction of the euro, and the emergence of a common foreign and defense policy. Identities and public discourse also matter whenever the boundaries of the EU are at stake, whether with regard to membership or to citizenship and immigration. On Eastern enlargement, a public discourse that framed Eastern enlargement in identity terms ("return to Europe") was instrumental in granting membership to Central Eastern Europe (Schimmelfennig 2003; Sedelmeier 2005). The ongoing dispute over Turkish membership is about what defines Europe and, consequently, what its boundaries are. The uneasy relationship between European modernity, secularism, and religion assumes center stage in these debates.

---

9. This finding of differential Europeanization of identities is consistent with the larger literature on Europeanization; see, for example, Cowles, Caporaso, and Risse 2001; Featherstone and Radaelli 2003; Börzel and Risse 2007.

Finally, I consider the implications of these findings for European democracy (see also Schmidt 2006). I claim that the complaints about the lack of a European demos are largely exaggerated. A European polity that the European peoples consider legitimate does not require a strong sense of collective identification. Multiple identities suffice, as long as the European project respects the heterogeneity and diversity of local as well as national communities. Moreover, the Europeanization of public spheres does not only add to the sense of community, it also serves to politicize questions of common concern for Europeans. Insofar as lively public spheres are ingredients of healthy democracies, the EU is in better shape than many of its critics suggest.

However, the more the EU moves beyond regulatory policies toward redistribution and taxing Europeans, secondary identification with Europe might reach its limits. Redistribution requires a strong sense of "solidarity among strangers" (Habermas 2006, 76) and it probably requires an identification with Europe that is deeper than a secondary identity. In this sense, if a united EU manages to weather the most severe economic and financial crisis in its history better than European nations by themselves, this will tell us more about a community of Europeans than opinion polls and speeches by politicians.

Politicization might also increase the sense of community among Europeans. But it could make governance in the EU much more cumbersome, given the competing visions of Europe as a "beacon of modernity," on the one hand, and an "exclusionary fortress," on the other. Silencing the debates—the chosen strategy of European leaders in the aftermath of the failed referenda in France and the Netherlands in 2005 and Ireland in 2008—is no solution whatsoever. It only adds to the sense of alienation that many Europeans already feel with regard to the EU. Silencing emerging debates will ensure the rise of anti-EU populism across the member states. Those who care about Europe and the EU have no choice but to continue on the path of politicization. Rather than continuing to "sell the EU" in terms of peace and prosperity, they should start debating *which Europe* and *which type of policies* the EU should pursue. There is ample room for controversy with regard to the relationship between markets and state intervention, social policies, the environment, and so forth. Debating Europe in this way might prove the only way to defend modern and cosmopolitan Europe against the increasingly forceful voices of Euroskepticism.

Plan of the Book

The book is in three parts. Parts 1 and 2 analyze the state of the art with regard to the Europeanization of identities and public spheres and try to make sense of it. I give some tentative explanations for the evolution of identities and public spheres. Part 3 turns the perspective around and asks to what extent the Europeanization of identities and public spheres actually matters for EU politics, particularly with regard to constitutional questions ("deepening"), enlargement ("widening"), and European democracy.

Since Europeanization has been given many meanings in the literature (Olsen 2002; Featherstone and Radaelli 2003; Börzel and Risse 2007), I need to clarify the term. In this book, Europeanization refers to the domestic impact of Europe and European integration. "Europeanization of (national) identities" means the extent to which references to Europe and the EU have been incorporated into national and other identity constructions. Europeanization of identities is different from "European identities." I do not claim that Europeanized identities are homogeneous or uniform across Europe and the EU. The Europeanization of French identities might look different from Europeanized identities in Poland. The same holds true for public spheres.

Social identity is an elusive concept. Chapter 1 conceptualizes collective identities, drawing upon approaches to identity formation in sociology as well as in social psychology. Social identities are collectively shared social constructions linking individuals to social groups, national or supranational imagined communities in our case. Such imagined communities need to become "real" in people's imaginations so that they can identify with them. They have to develop "psychological existence" (Castano 2004). Moreover, we all hold multiple identities, that is, we identify with several social groups and these identifications are invoked in context-dependent ways.

The chapter also discusses how collective identities can be categorized according to their substantive content and the degree to which they are contested. Identities vary with regard to their strength on a continuum between loosely coupled communities, on the one hand, and deeply held beliefs about common purpose, on the other. Collective identities also inevitably contain an "in-group/out-group" dimension that constructs boundaries between those who belong to the group and those who do not. Finally, I conceptualize identity change, which is particularly relevant to the Europeanization of identities. Identity change can happen slowly and incrementally, but it can also occur rapidly, usually following severe crises that profoundly challenge existing identities.

Chapter 2 focuses on mass public opinion and the Europeanization of citizens' identities during the past decades. A majority of Europeans identify both with their nation-state and with Europe and the EU. The main cleavage is between "exclusive nationalists," who identify only with their nation-state, and "inclusive nationalists," who also identify with Europe as a secondary identity. Although the distribution between the two groups varies widely across the EU, citizens in the new Eastern European member states do not differ much from "old Europe."

As to the substantive content of European identity, two "Europes" can be distinguished in mass public opinion. First, EU Europe represents a modern, political entity encompassing liberal values such as democracy, human rights, the rule of law, and the market economy. Modern Europe's "others" are the continent's own past of militarism and nationalism, but also xenophobia and racism. Second, "nationalist Europe" emphasizes a (Western) civilization and culture with references to a common historical heritage, strong national traditions, Christianity as its core religion, and clear geographical boundaries. Nationalist Europe's "others" are non-Christian countries such as Turkey, but also non-European immigrants and large parts of the Muslim populations in European cities.

A major problem for a collective European identity concerns the EU's lack of psychological existence in people's minds (Castano 2004). Although the EU is "real" for European elites, it is more remote for European citizens. While the EU lacks clearly defined boundaries, the European flag and the euro have recently become identity markers, thereby increasing the EU's psychological existence.

While chapter 2 focuses on European citizens, chapter 3 examines elite discourses in several EU member states to demonstrate how national identities are Europeanized (or not) through communicative practices. A survey of elite discourses in Germany, France, Spain, Poland, and Britain demonstrates how Europe blends into the narratives of national identities in various ways and relates to the particular country's history and culture. As a result, Europeanized identities still come in national colors and resonate with the various national symbols and historical and cultural memories in different ways. The Europeanization of national identities has been consensual in Germany and Spain for quite some time and is contested in France and Poland, while the dominant discourse in Great Britain remains focused on the nation-state. The identity construction of "modern Europe" dominates in Germany and Spain, while "nationalist Europe" has emerged as a countervision in France and Poland, mostly promoted by populist right-wing and Euroskeptical parties. These findings mean that Europe and the EU are no longer poorly defined identity categories, as some have argued (e.g., Breakwell 2004). Although the Europeanization of identities has not led to a uniform European identity, it has resulted in the emergence of two distinctive versions of what Europe stands for.

How can we explain the emergence of Europeanized identities on both the elite levels and in mass public opinion? Chapter 4 asks in particular whether fifty years of European integration have left their mark in strengthening the sense of imagined community among Europeans. There is little evidence for a (neo-)functionalist logic according to which those who benefit most from the EU should also identify with Europe. Rather, as Neil Fligstein has argued, Karl Deutsch's interactionist integration theory is supported by the emerging cleavage between "the Europeans," that is, the highly mobile, well-educated, and professional elites in Europe that identify most strongly with Europe, and the less-educated and less-mobile social classes that remain wedded to their nation-state (Fligstein 2008; see also Green 2007). As for elite identities in general, their Europeanization results more often than not from crisis experiences and critical junctures rather than from their exposure to the EU and to European integration.

EU membership matters insofar as older EU member states—particularly the original six—exhibit higher identification rates with Europe than newer members. The EU has had significant constitutive effects on European statehood. It essentially defines what modern statehood means in Europe. Even those who mobilize against the EU increasingly frame their opposition in European terms, defending a "nationalist Europe" against an EU open to economic, political, and cultural globalization. But there is no linear relationship between institutional effects and identity. Otherwise, British identity should have become European-ized by now. Rather, the degree to which elite identities are contested seems to be an intervening factor between the length of EU membership, on the one hand, and identification with Europe and the EU in mass public opinion, on the other (Hooghe and Marks 2005).

This latter result points to the arena in which identities are constructed and re-ified, namely public spheres. Part 2 of the book focuses on the Europeanization of public spheres. Chapter 5 parallels chapter 1 in providing a conceptual framework for thinking about transnational public spheres. Conventional wisdom has it that Europe lacks a common public sphere, because Europeans do not speak a common language and common European-wide media do not exist. I argue that neither is necessary for Europeans to be able to communicate across borders. We should not conceptualize a European public sphere as a separate entity above and beyond other public spheres. Rather, and similar to European identities, a transnational European public sphere emerges through the Europeanization of particularly na-tional public spheres. Moreover, a European public sphere is a social construct in the sense that it emerges in the process through which Europeans engage one another and debate issues of common European concern across borders.

I start from a Habermasian understanding of public spheres (Habermas 1980 [1962]). Following Klaus Eder and Cathleen Kantner (Eder and Kantner 2000), we can meaningfully speak of a Europeanization of public spheres, the more the same (European) themes are controversially debated at the same time at similar levels of attention across national public spheres, and the more similar frames of reference, meaning structures, and patterns of interpretation are used across national public spheres and media.

I add a third criterion that takes up the debate about the relationship between collective identities and public spheres. Public spheres Europeanize the more a transnational community of communication emerges in which European or other national actors participate in cross-border debates about common European problems and in which speakers and listeners recognize each other as legitimate participants in transnational discourses.

Chapters 6 and 7 use these criteria to analyze the degree of Europeanization of public spheres. Empirically, I focus on national (or regional) media, in particular newspapers. I argue in chapter 6 that the visibility of European affairs has substantially increased in the media since the 1990s. We can also observe the gradual Europeanization of public spheres with regard to common frames of reference and meaning structures, although these remain uneven. Europeans often talk about the same things when debating Europe and the EU, but national differences in the degree of Europeanization remain. A picture similar to the Europeanization of identities emerges: the most Europeanized public spheres include the original six community members as well as Southern EU members such as Spain. Great Britain—once again—remains outside Europeanized public spheres, while we lack sufficient data about Central Eastern Europe to be able to reach firm conclusions.

Things get more complex with regard to the indicators measuring the emergence of a community of communication. The data presented in chapter 7 suggest that other Europeans are regularly present and participate whenever European issues are covered and debated in national public spheres. However, most Europeanized public spheres are populated by members of national governments as well as EU officials, which suggests that there is no equal access to Europeanized public spheres. Last but not least, we can observe Europeanized communities of communication in cross-border debates about constitutional issues ("deepening") as well as enlargement ("widening"), but they are uneven and segmented. These discourse communities usually include the continental Western and Southern EU members and exclude Great Britain and—to some extent—Scandinavia, while the jury is still out with regard to Central Eastern Europe. In sum, however, the empirical findings suggest that we can indeed observe the gradual—albeit uneven and sometimes segmented—emergence of Europeanized public spheres, which also serve as sites where European identities are constructed and debated.

The final part of chapter 7 speculates about how we can explain the evidence. If the Europeanization of public spheres is a rather recent phenomenon, it followed rather than led processes of European integration. At least, the evidence is consistent with an institutionalist account according to which EU institutions and policies have become more visible and salient in the domestic politics of the member states so that media reporting indicates the politicization of EU policies. Thus, Europeanized public spheres and communities of communication reflect the emergence of a polity. This account also explains the differential Europeanization of public spheres insofar as the cluster of continental Western and Southern EU members with strongly Europeanized public spheres consists of those member states that are most actively engaged in European integration—from the single market to the single currency and borderless traffic in Schengenland.

What does the Europeanization of identities and public spheres mean, however, for the "big picture" of European politics, that is, European institution-building, EU enlargement, and European democracy? I address these questions in part 3. Chapter 8 analyzes the impact of Europeanized identities and public spheres on European institution-building. Although identities have little effects on daily policymaking in Brussels, the Europeanization of identities and public spheres matter the more constitutional issues are involved. This concerns questions about which issues should be subjected to EU policymaking and to what extent member states should give up sovereignty (the degree of supranationalization).

With regard to the attitudes of citizens, statistical analyses show that Europeanized identities have a clear and decisive impact for support for EU membership and European integration. The cleavage between "exclusive nationalists" who only identify with their nation-state, on the one hand, and "inclusive nationalists" who also identify with Europe, on the other, is most significant in this context. Moreover, Euroenthusiasm and Euroskepticism are orthogonal to the cleavages between the Right and the Left that structure most national political systems. Rather, these attitudes map onto a cultural cleavage between more cosmopolitan and more introverted and traditional values (Kriesi et al. 2008; Hooghe and Marks 2008). The clash between the two visions of Europe—"modern" versus "nationalist"—is consistent with this cleavage.

With regard to elite debates, I discuss three cases involving the transfer of major sovereignty rights to the European level: (1) the introduction of the euro; (2) debates about a European Common Foreign and Security Policy (CFSP); (3) the constitutional debates during the first decade of the twenty-first century. In each of these cases, I demonstrate two points. First, the public debate itself was largely framed in terms of identity discourse, by both supporters and opponents of the respective sovereignty transfers. Second, identity constructions not only served to legitimize the respective national positions, but these constructions correlated largely with the different national preferences expressed by governments. Although correlation does not equal causation, I show that the degree of Europeanization of elite identities provides better explanations on average for the national positions in EU treaty-making than more conventional accounts. As to the substantive content of these identities, the controversies surrounding the euro, a common European foreign and security policy, and the Constitutional Treaty were largely dominated by the vision of "modern Europe." This changed during the referenda debates in France, the Netherlands, and Ireland when the counterdiscourse of a "nationalist Europe" became more salient across the EU.

Constitutional issues are linked to collective identities, because they describe who "we" are and what is distinctive about us. But identities also demarcate the boundaries of a community and delineate who is "not us." Chapter 9 uses the controversies over EU enlargement and over immigration to demonstrate how the Europeanization of identities and public spheres has affected the EU's boundary construction. With regard to Eastern enlargement, I argue that EU decisions during the early 1990s to open membership negotiations with Central Eastern Europe (CEE) can only be understood against the background of deliberate efforts at European community-building (Schimmelfennig 2003; Sedelmeier 2005). European policymakers—in Brussels and in national capitals—adopted an identity discourse according to which the end of the cold war meant the "return to Europe" for the CEE countries. Central Eastern Europe was constructed as part of "us," the European community. Once this discourse had been established, Eastern enlargement became a question of when rather than if.

But the identity part of the Eastern enlargement story was not over when the CEE countries joined in 2004 and 2007. Eastern enlargement has changed the EU identity landscape (Byrnes and Katzenstein 2006; Checkel and Katzenstein 2009a). Although particularly West European support for Eastern enlargement was largely based on the construction of "modern Europe," Eastern accession put antisecular and antimodern ideas about Christianity back on the European agenda. As a result, the meanings of Europe and the EU have become more pluralistic—and more controversial.

This became obvious with regard to the debates about Turkish membership and immigration to which I then turn. These controversies pit the modern and secular Europeanized identity head on against a more nationalist vision of Europe and its boundaries. The meaning of Europe's Christian heritage has assumed center stage in the polarized debates about Turkish membership. Constructing the EU as a modern political community implies accepting Turkish membership if and when the country manages the transition to a consolidated democracy and market economy. In contrast, viewing Europe as a predominantly Christian civilization and culture means that the door to Turkish membership remains shut for good and that non-Christian immigrants have to be kept out. Thus, the debates about enlargement and immigration show that Europeanized identities are contested once again.

The controversies about "deepening" and "widening" have contributed to the politicization of EU affairs. I discuss the consequences for European democracy in chapter 10. First, I argue against those who claim that democracy is impossible at the EU level because it lacks a demos. As shown in parts 1 and 2, the preconditions for a European democracy are there in terms of sufficiently Europeanized identities and public spheres. There is a European polity in the making and it is increasingly politicized. Second, however, the EU suffers from an incongruence in where decisions are made—in Brussels—and where politics continues to take place—in the national capitals (cf. Schmidt 2006 and Hix 2008 on this point). The much-talked-about "democratic deficit" of the EU does not refer to the lack of a sense of community among Europeans, but rather to the insulation of EU policymaking from mass politics and political mobilization. Third, democratizing the EU means primarily to politicize EU affairs at home and to integrate them into the "normal" conflicts of domestic politics. "To bring politics back in" the EU appears inevitable and is also necessary to fix the democratic deficit. The referendum debates about the Constitutional and the Lisbon treaties and the controversies about Turkish membership and immigration are only the beginning of more to come.

The concluding chapter discusses the challenges of politicization. Politicization is inevitable given both the state of European integration and the emergence of two distinct and contested visions of Europe that also map onto an emerging cultural cleavage in mass public opinion and in party politics. Policymakers in Brussels and in the member states who care about the European Union must start "fighting for Europe" and defend the project of a modern, open, and cosmopolitan Europe against Euronationalism. Otherwise, they will lose the battle for public opinion, as a result of which EU policymaking will be seriously hampered. While a paralysis of EU policymaking will not lead to the renationalization of policies, it will make it impossible that Europe and the EU face the continuing challenges of globalization and a global economic crisis.

There appears to be a way out that politicizes EU affairs without necessarily leading to more Euroskepticism. Instead of debating whether or not the EU as such is good or bad, political parties should start arguing about *which* European policies are preferable. This would confront citizens with some real choices about the direction of EU decisions and, in this sense, bring EU politics back home. Therefore, I end the book on an optimistic note despite the challenges to European democracy.

Part I
AN EMERGING
EUROPEAN IDENTITY?

1

COLLECTIVE IDENTITIES
Conceptual and Methodological Questions

Identity is not only an elusive concept, it is also essentially contested. It has become so pervasive in the social sciences that Rogers Brubaker and Frederick Cooper concluded in 2000 that "the conceptual and theoretical work 'identity' is supposed to do...might be done better by other terms, less ambiguous, and unencumbered by the reifying connotations of 'identity'" (Brubaker and Cooper, 1). Although a different conceptual apparatus will not help avoid the theoretical and methodological pitfalls involved, Brubaker and Cooper are right that we need a clear understanding of what we mean by "identity" and how we know it when we see it. In this chapter I attempt to clarify the concept of social or collective identity. In particular, I distinguish between the subjects and the objects of identification, in other words, who—for example, elites or ordinary citizens—identifies with whom or what—for example, gender, nation, or Europe.[1] I discuss the notion of "multiple identities," which is particularly relevant in the European context, and suggest various ways in which we can think about them. The chapter then discusses the substantive content of social identities, as well as their contestedness and strength. I conclude with remarks on identity change and on problems of measurement.

---

1. I thank Jürgen Gerhards for suggesting these distinctions. See Gerhards 2003.

Social Constructivism and the Study of Collective Identities

This book is written from a social constructivist perspective (Adler 2002; Klotz and Lynch 2007). Social identities that link individuals to social groups are not presocially given or exist in some "objective reality" out there waiting to be discovered. Identities emerge in the very process by which individuals and social groups make sense of who they are and what they want. Studying social identities, therefore, requires that the self-understandings of group members are taken seriously and are integrated into the explanatory stories.

There are two ways in which social constructivism as an ontological stance is relevant to the study of social identities. The first concerns why political scientists who are primarily interested in describing and explaining political outcomes should be interested in identities at all. Questions of identity have assumed center stage in the study of world politics in general and European politics in particular. The original constructivist move questioned the tendency of rational choice to take the interests of actors for granted. Social identities have been found useful to explain these interests (March and Olsen 1998; Katzenstein 1996; Adler 2002). Moreover, social constructivists have been interested in how norms and other ideational factors not only regulate behavior but also how they define central properties of actors. No wonder that questions of identity have assumed a central role in constitutive stories—who I am explains to a large extent what I want, and what I want also affects who I am.

Second, constructivist ontology is also directly relevant to the study of identities as social constructions. I am born with a German passport, but there is nothing natural or genetic about my Germanness, even though "ius sanguinis," the citizenship of my biological ancestors, defined German citizenship laws for a long time. Similarly, my gender identity does not simply accompany my biological sex, as gender studies remind us (Tickner 2002). Rather, I have acquired the social knowledge of what it means to be male or German through socialization processes. Moreover, nobody forces me to strongly identify with my country or my gender even if everybody else identifies me as a male German.

Studying identities as social constructions that connect individuals to each other and to social groups requires that we treat them as meaning structures and interpretive frames. It also necessitates that we do not simply ascribe social identities to a group because of some similarities that they share. For example, we cannot deduce a European identity from the fact that citizens from EU member states also hold EU citizenship. Essentialist or substantialist conceptions of identity typically assume that membership in a social group constitutes that group as a community of fate, as if belonging to an ethnic group, for example, automatically leads to a particular ethnic identity and a sense of common purpose. In studying social identities, however, we have to take the self-understandings of group members seriously and make them an inherent part of the explanatory story. Only if an ethnic group also includes ethnicity in its self-understanding can we ascribe ethnic identity to it. This is the basic move of social constructivism in the social sciences (cf. Berger and Luckmann 1966; Wendt 1999).

Yet, a constructivist approach to social identities should not be confused with a particular theoretical or methodological stance. Identities can be studied using a variety of quantitative as well as qualitative methods including survey data, discourse and content analyses, and psychological experiments. Each of these instruments has its shortcomings, but which one is appropriate depends on the particular research question (see, e.g., Abdelal et al. 2009b; Klotz and Lynch 2007).

Moreover, a social constructivist approach does not imply that identities are always contested and/or permanently in flux. As I argue in the subsequent chapters, some constructions of European identity have remained remarkably stable over the decades and even precede the European Union. Social identities can also be extremely consensual and acquire qualities of a social taboo. Many ethnonationalist identities are constructed in such a way that they resemble primordial identities, even though they remain constructions. It is no wonder that ethnonationalist identities assume such strength that they can be easily mobilized for violence and civil wars against the respective out-group. I suggest, therefore, that the degrees of contestation and the strength of social identities should be treated as dimensions that can be measured empirically rather than as parts of the definition.

Finally, a social constructivist approach does not deny that rational choice is relevant to the study of identities. First, the paradigmatic warfare between constructivist and rationalist approaches is largely over, particularly in international relations (Risse 2002; Fearon and Wendt 2002). Second, in the real world, instrumental behavior driven by the logic of consequentialism and identity-based behavior driven by the logic of appropriateness often occur almost simultaneously. Instrumentally rational actors might engage in the social construction of ethnic and nationalist identities in order to mobilize support for costly conflicts and the use of force (Fearon and Laitin 2000).

Thus, an "identity versus interest" account only serves to reify both terms. Political elites, for example, legitimately pursue instrumentally defined interests; they want to retain and gain political power. At the same time, they actively construct and debate identities as one way to connect to their respective constituencies. The more significant question is, therefore, how identities and interests interact with each other. Causality may cut both ways. A change in instrumentally defined interests might well lead over time to identity changes. In this case, the causal arrows run from interests to identities. At the same time, identities define in the first place how actors view their instrumental interests and which preferences are regarded as possible, legitimate, and appropriate for enacting given identities.

At this point, however, it is necessary to take a closer look at what we mean by "social" or "collective identities."

From "I" to "We": Social Identities

A good starting point for the conceptualization of social identities derives from social psychology, in particular social identity and self-categorization theories (e.g., Abrams and Hogg 1990; Oakes, Haslam, and Turner 1994). These approaches conceptualize collective identities as the psychological link between individuals and social groups. Thus, Tajfel defines social identity as "that part of the individual's self-concept which derives from his knowledge of his membership of a social group (or groups) together with the value and emotional significance attached to that membership" (Tajfel 1981, 255).

Several components of this conceptualization are worth highlighting. Social identification processes link individuals (those who identify) to social groups, the objects of identification. Social identities are not about "I" or "Me," but about that part of "me" that belongs to a larger "we," a social group and/or a community. This implies that I cannot have a social identity on my own, but share it with a larger group. To be more precise, social identities are not only shared, they are *collectively* shared. "We" as Germans (or Rhinelanders) not only share a common identity but we also *know* that we share this identity and we know that the other members of the group know that we know. The mutual knowledge about membership in a social group is significant for the conceptualization of social identities.

Social identities not only entail cognitive components in terms of social knowledge about the properties of the group. They also contain evaluations and emotional attachments that connect to one's personal self-esteem. I not only know about my membership in a particular social group, I also have positive feelings about it. Last but not least, social identities have behavioral implications. Attachment leads to loyalty together with a sense of obligation to the group. It is this loyalty that constitutes a resource for social mobilization, collective action, and support for institutions such as the European Union (see Herrmann and Brewer 2004, 6, on this point). The stronger the sense of loyalty, the more behavioral consequences we should expect (Kantner 2006a).

However, the social groups of concern in this book are "imagined communities" (Anderson 1991). The psychological experiments that gave rise to social identity theory used groups in which individuals knew each other personally and were involved in face-to-face interactions. Social identities pertaining to gender, a nation, or a transnational entity such as the European Union relate to groups whose individual members we do not know and which we have to imagine. Yet, even imagined communities have to become "real" in peoples' minds in order to invoke feelings of attachment and loyalty. We can only identify with a group that we consider "for real," even if we do not know each member personally. Social psychologists refer to the psychological existence of an imagined community as its "entitativity" (Campbell 1958; Castano 2004).

Political and social elites might not know about the concept of entitativity, but they are very aware that an imagined community that demands loyalty from its members requires psychological existence. Nationalist rhetoric, the construction of specific events as decisive for a nation's history, the use of symbols such as flags, national anthems, and national currencies—all these are means to construct a nation-state as "real" and to reify its existence. Europe is no exception. Already in 1973, for example, the European Commission issued a "Declaration on European Identity" (European Commission 1973). Nevertheless, the lack of psychological existence is among the main reasons for the EU's troubles as an object of identification, as I argue in chapter 2.

Many "We's": Multiple Identities

The discussion so far has dealt with social identities as if individuals express a sense of belonging to only one identity group. Yet, we all belong to several social groups including various imagined communities with which we might identify and whose identities have different contents, are contested in diverse ways, and express varying degrees of strength. Individuals hold multiple identities that are invoked depending on the context in which people find themselves. Gender identities, for example, become salient when gender issues are relevant, while they recede in the background in other contexts. Identities pertaining to geographically defined communities are no exception. I can identify with my region of origin, the Rhineland, with Germany as a whole, with Europe, and with the whole world, but each of these identities is not always salient. I might feel Rhinelandish particularly when dealing with Bavarians, German when visiting Italy, and European when interacting with Americans.

That individuals hold multiple identities is not controversial. Individuals usually do not see their various social identities as being in conflict and they learn to negotiate between their identities and to invoke them in context-dependent ways. For example, we can strongly identify with our region, our nation-state, *and* feel loyalty toward the EU. European and national identities are not zero-sum propositions. Policymakers in Europe continuously reify the notion that national and European identities can go together. During state visits, the national flag usually flies alongside the European flag and this is regularly reported in the daily TV news across Europe. Some authors even argue that a unified and homogeneous European identity is not possible, but multiple, overlapping, and even conflicting European identities (Calhoun 2001). The EU motto of "unity in diversity" also celebrates the multiplicity of overlapping identities.

However, it does not tell us much that national and European identities can go together because of the multiplicity of identities. We need to know how the many "we's," the groups to which we feel attached, relate to each other. They are several ways of conceptualizing multiple identities (see Herrmann and Brewer 2004, 8–10, for the following). First, identities can be completely *separate*. In this case, there is almost no overlap in the membership of social groups to which I belong and with which I identify. I might feel attached to my university and be equally loyal to my local soccer club, but I might be the only one who belongs to both groups. The people with whom I identify in my professional life might be completely different from the groups to whom I feel attached in my private life.

Second, identities can be *cross-cutting*. In this configuration, some, but not all, members of one social group also identify with another group. Religious identities, for example, cut across gender identities. Cross-cutting identities are relevant in our context insofar as identification with Europe or the EU[2] cuts across loyalties toward one's gender, religion, or political orientation. I might identify strongly with the EU and with Catholicism, but not all my fellow Catholics feel the same way. Cross-cutting identities are probably a very common feature with regard to imagined communities and the sense of belonging.

Third, we can think about multiple identities as *nested* in each other, as concentric circles, such as layers of an onion or as Russian Matryoshka dolls. In this case, everyone in a smaller community is also part of a larger community and identifies with it. For example, survey data show that regional and national identities often go together in many federal systems. Most Rhinelanders also identify with Germany and many Germans also identify with Europe. In other words, "local identities are subsumed in national identities, and national identities subsumed in Europe-wide identities" (Herrmann and Brewer 2004, 8). This "onion model" of multiple identities implies some hierarchical relationships among the various components, distinguishing an identity core from an identity periphery. Nested identities are probably the most commonly used model for how scholars and practitioners think about the connection between national and European

---

2. Note that identification with Europe can be different from attachment to the EU. Europe and the EU are not the same in identity terms, as I will argue in chapter 2.

identities (e.g., Hooghe and Marks 2005; Citrin and Sides 2004). When Eurobarometer surveys (reported in chapter 2) ask whether people identify with "nation only," with "nation and Europe," with "Europe and nation," or with "Europe only," such questionnaires imply nested identities. But this "onion model" of multiple identities is only one of several ways in which identities can go together.

There is a fourth and less hierarchical possibility for how multiple identities are linked. They might actually *blend* into one another or intertwine. Such a "marble cake" model of multiple identities means that it is very hard to separate out the various components of one's identity. Feminist theorists talk about "intersectionality" in this context.[3] Intersectionality means that various categories of oppression such as gender, race, or class and the identity constructions that are related to them cannot simply be added on, but are intertwined and at least partly mutually reinforcing (see, e.g., Crenshaw 1994; McCall 2005; for a similar argument see Cram 2009).

To illustrate this concept of intertwined identities, a Rhinelander is often described as a particular type of comparatively tolerant and liberal Catholicism. In this case, regional and religious identities go together and blend into each other. With regard to Europe or the EU, dual identification with one's nation-state and with Europe often goes together. As I will show in chapter 3, it is impossible to describe modern Germany's elite identities without references to European integration. The "marble cake" model of multiple identities is less frequently used as the underlying framework of how multiple identities are connected. But it is consistent with a lot of the empirical evidence. Moreover, when we think about European identity as the "Europeanization of national identities" (Checkel 2001a; Risse 2001), whereby references to Europe and to the European Union are incorporated into one's sense of national belonging, conceptualizing collective identities as intertwined makes a lot of sense.

What Makes "Us" So Special? The Content of Social Identities

Social identities not only link individuals and social groups, they also have a specific substantive content (see Abdelal et al. 2009a). This content consists of the constitutive norms and rules that define the social group and its membership, its goals and social purposes, as well as the collective worldviews shared by the group. Social identities convey a sense of "we-ness," of (imagined) community usually based on collective narratives of a common fate, a common history, and

---

3. I thank participants in a discussion at the London School of Economics for alerting me to this literature.

a common culture. Representations of French identity, for example, often refer to the French Revolution, to the *Déclaration de Droits de l'Hommes et des Citoyens,* and to its republican values. Identity narratives also contain a sense of common purpose, of *differentia specifica* distinguishing the community from other communities. The preamble to the Lisbon Treaty quoted in the introduction to this book represents an attempt to describe what is special about the EU. Identity narratives also depict a set of constitutive norms that define the ingredients of group membership. The EU's 1993 Copenhagen criteria, for example, describe the EU as a community of liberal democracies and market economies governed by the rule of law and respecting human rights including minority rights. The Copenhagen criteria signify a set of constitutive norms, one that accession candidates have to comply with before they can enter membership negotiations. But Europe also has cultural meanings. Some even regard religious aspects, Christianity in this case, as the *differentia specifica* of a common European identity. It is with regard to such substantive content that EU and European identities can be distinguished (see chapters 2 and 3).

Social identities often convey a sense of purpose in terms of the ultimate goals of the group. Identities pertaining to territorial entities such as the nation-state describe visions of what are regarded as good and just political and social orders. In many cases, however, the social purpose of a group is contested. The EU is no exception. Federalist visions of a "United States of Europe" compete with ideas about an intergovernmental federation of nation-states. Some want to restrict the EU to market integration (Jachtenfuchs, Diez, and Jung 1998).

Where Does "We" End? "In-groups" and "Out-groups"

A most significant component of substantive identity constructions concerns the boundaries of the community (see, e.g., Cederman 2001). The content of an identity delineates who is "in" and who is "out." The distinction between "self " and "other," between "in-group" and "out-group" is an intrinsic part of any social identity. A group must have clear boundaries in order to differentiate itself from other communities. Imagined communities such as nation-states are no exception; quite the contrary. The clearer the boundaries of the community are, the more "real" its psychological existence becomes in peoples' self-concepts (Castano 2004; Castano et al. 2002).

Minimum group experiments have resulted in interesting findings in this context. Small groups were formed according to some randomly selected criterion. The groups were then asked to allocate resources, for example money, to members of the groups. Almost in every single instance, participants tended to favor their own group against the others, irrespective of how randomly the groups were selected (see, e.g., Tajfel 1982). Therefore, the "self/other" distinction often implies negative feelings, even hatred, with regard to the out-group. Sociological studies about identity formation come to similar conclusions (Connolly 1991; Neumann 1996). The more identities are essentialized, that is, constructed in such a way that their contents are treated as natural properties of a group, the more likely it is that communities reject the "others." The most typical example in this regard concerns the construction of ethnonationalist identities.

However, one should not read too much into small-group experiments and the finding of "in-group favoritism." Self-categorization theory in particular has refined social identity theory by adding the principle of meta-contrast (Oakes, Haslam, and Turner 1994): the greater the perceived differences *between* groups in contrast to the differences *within* one's own group, the greater a group's collective identity. The decisive feature of "self/other" or "in-group/out-group" boundary creation is *difference* rather than enmity. Strong male identities, for example, do not have to pair with hatred of women—on the contrary.

A typology of in-group/out-group distinctions in imagined communities might be helpful here. Sociologists Shmuel Eisenstadt and Bernhard Giesen distinguish between primordial, sacred, and civic identities (Eisenstadt and Giesen 1995). *Primordial* identity constructions essentialize the properties of the in-group and draw a sharp line to the equally essentialized properties of the out-group.[4] Identities built on constructions of race or ethnic properties often take on primordial features. Primordial identity constructions have two consequences. First, the in-group is evaluated much more positively than the out-group. Second, members of the out-group can never join the in-group. Racial stereotypes and ethnonationalist identities are good examples for such constructions. In the European context, cultural identities are often invoked in such a way. Those who regard Christianity and Judaism as the decisive features of Europe's cultural identity often emphasize Islam as the main European out-group. As a result, Muslims can never become "true" Europeans. The discourse about Turkish membership in the EU often contains such primordial constructions, insofar as Turkey is treated as a Muslim country in contrast to "Christian Europe."

In comparison, *sacred* identity constructions still contain strong differences between the in-group and the out-group and this metacontrast implies strong negative evaluations toward the "others." But sacred identities include the possibility that members of the out-group convert to the "right cause" or the "true

---

4. Note that primordial identities emphasizing race or ethnicity are still constructions. There is nothing natural about arguing that skin color as such has properties that lead to special privileges for white Caucasians over blacks.

faith" and, thus, become part of "us." The EU's Copenhagen criteria constitute a typical example of a sacred identity. Democracy, human rights, the rule of law, and the market economy are considered superior to other political, economic, and social orders and they are constitutive for the EU. But other countries can convert by becoming liberal democracies and opening up their economies and then gain membership in the club. In this sacred identity discourse, Turkey can become a member as long as it transforms itself into a liberal democracy and a market economy.

Interestingly enough, sacred identity constructions also contain the possibility that the in-group itself converts to the true faith or the just cause. In this case, the group's own past becomes the "other." Identity constructions pertaining to the EU often use the continent's past of wars, militarism, and nationalism as the modern Europe's "other." The same holds true for national identity constructions in countries that have experienced profound transformation processes, e.g., from authoritarian regimes to liberal democracies. Examples include Germany, Spain, Greece, and many Central Eastern European countries.

A third—civic—identity construction still emphasizes the difference between in-group and out-group, but without strong negative evaluations. The "others" are still different, but this difference is not regarded as inferior. Some national identities within the community of democracies contain civic properties. Germans, for example, regard federalism as a constitutive property of their nation-state and are rather proud about it, giving rise to strong regional identities. But this does not mean that they view the French centralized system as necessarily inferior. It is just different.

These three "self/other" distinctions are not only relevant with regard to how Europeans see the European out-group. They might also be salient for the construction of a European identity itself. The more national identities are constructed as primordial, the more difficulties people might have with identifying with Europe as a larger entity. Primordial national identities and identification with Europe as the larger entity do not go together (see the principle of meta-contrast mentioned above). Serbian nationalists, for example, strongly reject EU membership, even though their country would gain enormous material benefits by joining the union.

Are "We" One and Ready to Die? Contestation and Strength

There are two more dimensions along which identities can be measured and categorized. Social identities might be consensual, but they can also be deeply contested. Identity crises can be individual (Who am I?), but they can also affect an entire social group (Who are we?). Only the latter is of interest here. And identities can be strong or weak. I might feel attached to my local soccer club, but opt for a different one the moment it starts losing its games. Compare that to fans rooting for their club irrespective of its performance.

As to contestation, there has been a long debate among scholars with regard to whether controversy is an intrinsic element of any collective identity. On the one hand, there are scholars of nationalism such as Anthony D. Smith who argue that national identities tend to be rather stable and based on fairly persistent constructions of a historic territory, of common myths and memories. Once nation-states have been created through long and conflictual processes, elites rally around a particular meaning of the nation. National identities are constantly reified, but they are rarely contested. As a result, Smith remains skeptical about whether a European identity can be constructed in the absence of common historical myths, ethnic bonds, and a common language (see Smith 1991, 1992; also Kielmansegg 1996; Grimm 1995).

In contrast, radical social constructivists tend to conceptualize collective identities as fluid and always contested. What appears to be settled on the surface is often deeply controversial. The more elites reify national identities through reminding people of their common ancestry and common history, the more likely it is that the identity of a community is deeply contested and unclear (see Connolly 1991; Neumann 1996). Why would one reify an identity, unless it is not settled?

One can easily accept the notion that social identities are continuously negotiated, constructed, reconstructed, and reified and still maintain that the degree of contestation remains an empirical question (see Abdelal et al. 2009a, 20; Klotz and Lynch 2007, 70). There are times when collective identities are unsettled, in flux, and deeply controversial. Examples include Germany in the 1950s as well as France during the 1990s and early 2000s (see chapter 3). However, at other times collective identities might be settled and stable enough that we can almost treat them as social facts. German Europeanness, for example, has remained an uncontested element of German post–World War II national identity over the past fifty years, at least among the elites. The research task is then to identify the conditions under which identities are "free-floating," even "empty signifiers," or when they become part of the social "deep structure," as Iver Neumann put it (Neumann 2004).

The degree of contestation is also relevant to discerning the behavioral effects of identities. The more collective identities are consensual and stable, the more elites can use them for strategic purposes. For example, national policymakers often use the phrase "Europe made me do it" to legitimize tough political decisions at home and to give them the appearance of unavoidability. But this construction can only have the desired effects when and if citizens identify with Europe and consider it legitimate to follow EU rules. Moreover, as James March and Johan Olsen point out, the more material interests are contested, while collective identities remain stable, the more identities should be expected to trump interests—and vice versa (March and Olsen 1998). In the case of the euro, for example, the material benefits of a single currency were deeply contested and unclear throughout the 1990s, while collective identification with the EU among the elites in "Euroland" (the EU member states that have adopted the single currency) remained rather strong.

A further dimension of social identities that is not captured by either content or contestation is *strength*. Strength concerns the degree of loyalty that individuals are willing to invest when they identify with a social group. People might fight over what it means to be Polish (or German or European or Catholic), but the various camps might hold their particular view extremely dearly. The controversy over Turkish EU membership, for example, is ultimately about two different visions of European identity, one defined in historical, traditional, and religious terms, the other viewed as secular, modern, and political (see Byrnes and Katzenstein 2006; Bruter 2005). The debate is rather vicious, precisely because the two sides feel extremely strongly about their respective identities.

Strength of identification is, of course, very relevant with regard to the behavioral consequences of identities. Because individuals feel attached to various social groups and imagined communities, they hold multiple identities. But the multiplicity of identities does not imply that all are held in an equally strong way. Although most individuals identify with their gender, this identification might be strong or weak. The stronger and the more intense social identities become, the more behavioral consequences we should expect. The question is what price individuals are willing to pay for their feelings of loyalty and attachment to a social group. Patriotism and nationalism, for example, have been used regularly by political elites to justify the ultimate sacrifice for one's loyalty, "to die for the fatherland." Although nobody asks Europeans these days "to die for Europe," the question nevertheless remains how strong the "solidarity among strangers" is in the EU (Habermas 2006, 76; see also Castiglione 2009). For example, is identification with the EU strong enough to allow for redistributive policies and for "social Europe"? How much solidarity among Europeans is necessary to cope with the global economic and financial crisis? I will come back to this question repeatedly in the following chapters.[5]

Transforming Who Is "Us": Identity Change

If we conceptualize the emergence of a European identity as the Europeanization of other, particularly national identities that do not replace or substitute for, but

---

5. For a classification of collective identities according to strength, see also Kantner 2006a and Tietz 2002.

rather modify, existing identification patterns, we also need to think about identity change. This is contested territory among social scientists. Those arguing from a more postmodern stance tend to emphasize the fluidity of social identities and suggest that identities do not remain stable, but are constantly changing (e.g., Neumann 1996; Sylvester 1994). In contrast, psychologists stress the stability and stickiness of social identities (e.g., Fiske and Taylor 1984; overview in Stein 2002). Cognitive psychology generally argues that humans are cognitive misers and that beliefs or schemas, once they are formed, are resistant to change. Discrepant information often strengthens preexisting beliefs.

Yet, postmodern discourse theory and cognitive psychology might not be as far away from each other as the strong statements in the scholarly literature make us believe. First, the degree of contestation as such does not tell us much about identity change. We can fight over national identities without anybody changing his or her beliefs. Second, however, strength of identity might be related to the speed with which identities change. One could assume, for example, that weak collective identities change more frequently and adjust to changes in interests and circumstances more often than strong feelings of loyalty to a community. If we strongly believe in something, we need a lot of discrepant information in order to make us change our minds. Social identities should be no exception.

Sociologists as well as social psychologists suggest that we should distinguish between at least two types of identity change, namely gradual and incremental transformation, on the one hand, and rapid and radical change, on the other (Fiske and Taylor 1984). There are various explanations for gradual identity changes. They belong to the realm of institutionalist theories, but emphasize different processes. With regard to European integration, neofunctionalism argues that Europeanization would lead to identity change over time. Ernst Haas defined regional integration as "the process whereby political actors in several distinct national settings are persuaded to shift their loyalties, expectations, and political activities toward a new center, whose institutions possess or demand jurisdiction over the pre-existing nation states" (Haas 1958, 16; similarly Deutsch et al. 1957, 5–6; see Risse 2005).

Several causal mechanisms can be distinguished by which social institutions affect identity change in incremental ways (Herrmann and Brewer 2004, 13–16). The most commonly mentioned process concerns *socialization* (Checkel 2005b): frequent exposure to institutions and individual experiences with the institution and its consequences are expected to alter people's identities. The more frequently and the more intensely we interact with a social group in a positive way, the more we are likely to identify with it. With regard to imagined communities, the key factor in a socialization story should be the "psychological existence" of

a community. With regard to Europe and the EU, socialization processes leading to the Europeanization of national identities should be particularly observable among those who interact frequently with the institutions of the European
Union, that is, political and social elites (see Fligstein 2008 for this argument).
This process emphasizes how institutional structures shape peoples' identities.

In contrast, *persuasion* models focus on agency and institutional actors who
proactively promote identification processes (Johnston 2005; Checkel 2001b).
Policymakers, for example, regularly invoke national identities in order to promote and legitimize costly decisions, particularly with regard to issues of war
and peace, social welfare, and constitutional questions. Identity talk is frequently
used by political parties to connect to their electorates.[6] Similarly, ethnonationalist propaganda often invokes historical myths, narratives of national humilia-
tion, and other symbolic appeals to rally support for nationalist causes.

Theories of persuasion focus on how individuals receive such efforts at identity change, whether as processors of information and arguments (weighing the
pros and cons of particular reasons, cf. Risse 2000) or as receivers of appeals to
emotion and of threats to self-interest (Chaiken, Wood, and Eagly 1996; Perloff
1993). With regard to the Europeanization of national identities, we can infer
from these theories that ideas about Europe will be the more persuasive, the
more they resonate with national identities. Efforts at identity change will be all
the more successful the more the arguments or the appeals are compatible with
existing identities to which people can relate. Moreover, the Europeanization
of identities is not likely to lead to similar and homogenous identity narratives
across countries, since ideas about Europe and the EU are likely to resonate differently with existing identities. These theories of socialization and persuasion
are consistent with the marble cake model of multiple and intertwined identities
(see chapter 3 for empirical evidence).

But rapid and far-reaching identity changes are also possible, of course. In specific historical moments, even deeply held beliefs and convictions can undergo
profound and fast transformations. Scholars from different disciplinary backgrounds converge on the notion that profound crises—"critical junctures"—
are necessary conditions for such rapid identity changes. Psychologists point
out, for example, that even strongly held beliefs are unlikely to withstand large
and massively inconsistent information. Wars and military defeats often constitute such critical junctures for national identities, leading to profound changes.
World War II, for example, resulted in an almost complete transformation of
German national identity, leading to its thorough Europeanization. The end

---

6. I owe this point to Stefano Bartolini.

of the cold war and the transformation of the former Communist political, economic, and social systems constituted a similar critical juncture, this time in Eastern Europe. "Return to Europe" became the rallying cry of East European elites, leading to application for EU membership.

However, crises and critical junctures occur in the eyes of the beholder. They are not "objective" phenomena; they have to be perceived and constructed in such a way that they actually challenge social identities. A military defeat, for example, is certainly a traumatic event under almost any circumstances. But it has to be interpreted in a particular way in order to lead to identity change. Otherwise, it might simply reinforce given (nationalist) identities. The German military defeat in World War I culminating in the Treaty of Versailles resulted in a strengthening of nationalist and even militarist identities among the elites and in public opinion, which Adolf Hitler was then able to exploit. In contrast, the catastrophe of World War II was interpreted by the now liberal and democratic elites in such a way that it led to a thorough transformation of German identity.

Critical junctures as triggering events for rapid and profound identity change pose methodological problems. How do I know a crisis when I see one, particularly if the crisis itself is a social construction and must be interpreted as such? Although we can trace identity changes to perceived crises *after the fact,* it is difficult to predict which type of critical juncture will result in identity change.

Problems of Measurement

These considerations point to questions of measurement and methodology when studying social identities. Measuring social identities is a daunting task. How can one distinguish empirically between identities, role playing, and interests? Moreover, the stronger social identities are and the more they are taken for granted, the less they are talked about or symbolically represented. As a result, they might not show up in data at all. In contrast, social identities that are constantly reified, discussed, and referred to are probably rather contested. Europe and the EU should be no exceptions.

Historians, sociologists, political scientists, psychologists, and linguists have attempted to approach these issues from different methodological angles, using survey data (e.g., Citrin and Sides 2004; Hooghe and Marks 2005), variants of discourse and content analyses (e.g., Chilton and Wodak 2002; Meinhof 2004), and experiments (e.g., Brewer 2001; Castano 2004). Indeed, methodological pluralism appears to be appropriate when trying to measure such complex concepts as social identities (see Abdelal et al. 2009b; Klotz and Lynch 2007, chap. 4).

Each method has its own limitations with regard to the study of social identities. For example, the divide between quantitative and qualitative approaches to social identities has led to some controversies in the scholarly literature. Statistical analyses of survey data and psychological experiments often highlight the stability, resilience, and stubbornness of identities, which appear to change little despite discrepant information. In contrast, discourse analysts tend to emphasize the fluidity, malleability, and ways in which social identities are dependent on context. Some of these differences do not stem from the method chosen, but from differences in metatheoretical orientations among scholars.

However, one should not overlook the fact that different methods often focus on different aspects of the same concept. Good survey analyses, for example, measure identities as part of the collective meaning structures and repertoires that are available to individuals (Citrin and Sears 2009). But attitudes, including identities, measured in opinion polls are, of course, taken out of context. As a result, it is not surprising that statistical analyses emphasize stability over change. The identity repertoires available to individuals might be stable, but this excludes neither contestation nor context-dependent use.

In contrast, good discourse analyses measure "identity in use," that is, how social identities are activated in discursive practices and in particular contexts (e.g., Chandra 2009; Meinhof 2004). It is not surprising that such studies find identities that are contested, in flux, and vary strongly with context. Yet, what appears as fluid and forever malleable on the surface might be stable inside. "Identity change" is then a question of a changing social context in which different layers of multiple identities become salient. In sum, survey instruments and data from discourse analyses to a large extent tap into different aspects of social identities as meaning structures, on the one hand, and social practices, on the other.

What about the validity of the various data on social identities? How can we make sure that we have measured social identities and that the empirical evidence cannot be better explained by concepts such as interests or social roles? First, simplistic interest *versus* identity accounts miss the point. In such stories, interests mostly refer to what people prefer in terms of instrumental or material goals, such as power or money. If identities have any consequences at all, they should shape what individuals and groups consider as their instrumental interests. At the same time, the causal arrow might also run the other way round. For example, power-seeking elites might reconstruct identities in such a way that it suits their interests. This is the way in which many ethnonationalist identities are being constructed (Fearon and Laitin 2000). They are still social constructions, but they are used strategically for instrumental purposes (on "strategic constructions" see Finnemore and Sikkink 1998).

Second, it should be easier to discern identities and to distinguish them empirically from interests or preferences when these identities are challenged. Such challenges occur at "critical junctures," calling into question prevailing world views. Third, social identities are also challenged if and when materially and instrumentally defined interests change in such a way that they clash with given identities. What happens in such instances? Do social groups redefine their identities, or do they reconstruct their instrumental interests in view of their given identities?

The distinction between social roles and identities appears to be more problematic. At first glance, psychological approaches that focus on social identities and self-categorization do not clearly distinguish between the two. Role identities would be a subcategory of social identities. Individuals identify with a social group acquiring the skills and the social knowledge to interact with group members and with the outside world from the perspective of the in-group. This is role-playing. As a university professor, I know what is expected of me and what the rules are and, thus, I can play this role, whether I like it or not. I know the social structure and the norms—the logic of appropriateness (March and Olsen 1998)—and behave accordingly. Jeffrey Checkel calls role-playing "type I internalization" (Checkel 2005b, 804).

"Type II internalization" goes further and requires that actors not only know the rules but that they also consider them "the right thing to do," that is, they agree with the norms or evaluate them in a positive way. In other words, they identify with those norms and rules. Identifying then implies positive feelings toward the in-group, while role-playing only requires knowledge of the norms and rules of appropriateness that define the role.

What does this mean for measuring social identities and distinguishing them empirically from role-playing? It essentially requires that measurement instruments—whether opinion polls, texts interpreted by discourse analysis, or experiments—should contain data pertaining not only to the cognitive content of a social identity but also to its evaluative and emotional components. This is obvious from the definition of social identities that includes these evaluative and emotional aspects. But is not necessarily the case with regard to many empirical studies of social identities that often concentrate only on cognitive content (see the contributions in Abdelal et al. 2009b).

Summary

This chapter argued that, first, social identities are collectively shared constructions linking individuals—the subjects of identification—to social groups as the

identification objects. In our case of nation-states or Europe, the objects of identification are "imagined communities." Imagined communities need to become
"real" in people's imaginations so that they can identify with them. Second, individuals hold multiple identities, that is, they identify with several social groups
and these identifications are invoked in context-dependent ways. I then discussed
various possibilities about how to conceptualize multiple identities. They can be
completely separate from each other, cross-cutting, nested inside each other, or
intertwine (like a marble cake).

Third, as to their substantive content, collective identities can be distinguished
with regard to their

- *differentia specifica* in terms of constitutive norms, common purpose,
  shared history and culture;
- "in-group/out-group" distinction in terms of primordial, sacred, or civic
  identity constructions;
- degree of contestation on a continuum between settled and consensual, on
  the one hand, and fluid as well as deeply controversial, on the other; and
- degree of strength on a continuum between loosely coupled identities and
  deeply held collective beliefs about common purpose and vision.

Finally, I have conceptualized identity change, which is particularly relevant
to the Europeanization of identities. Identity change can happen slowly and incrementally, but it can also occur rapidly, usually following severe crises that profoundly challenge existing identities. As for incremental change, institutionalist
theories are particularly relevant here, focusing on processes of socialization as
well as persuasion.

This is the conceptual apparatus with which we can now approach the empirical material about the Europeanization of collective identities. The next three
chapters use this toolkit to discuss the state of the art.

2

MULTIPLE EUROPES

The Europeanization of Citizens' Identities

Is there an emerging European identity, and if so, does it replace, coexist with, or otherwise interact with various multiple identities of individuals? What is the substantive content of this European identity, how contested is it, and how much loyalty do people feel toward the EU? Do citizens differentiate between Europe and the EU in their identification processes? How "real" is Europe in people's minds?

This chapter focuses on ordinary citizens, while chapter 3 concentrates on elites. I summarize findings from a variety of disciplines and methodologies. Political scientists, sociologists, social psychologists, linguists, and others have used such diverse research tools as quantitative survey data, laboratory experiments, in-depth interviews, discourse analysis, and historical interpretation (see e.g. Herrmann, Risse, and Brewer 2004). Nevertheless, most of what we know about the identification of citizens with Europe and/or the EU stems from survey data and statistical analyses that have become ever more sophisticated in recent years. This poses methodological problems when we compare these data with more qualitative work, which sometimes leads to diverging findings.

I start with descriptive data on the distribution of Europeanized identities across Europe including the variation among countries. I then discuss who is more likely to identify with Europe and the EU and who is more inclined to remain exclusively attached to their nation-state. In other words, who are "the Europeans," to use a chapter title by Neil Fligstein (Fligstein 2008, chap. 5; also Green 2007)? The third part of the chapter takes a closer look at the object of identification processes, that is, to what extent people differentiate between

Europe and the EU and to what degree meanings of Europe are contested. The chapter concludes with remarks on how "real" Europe has become for its citizens. Can the EU be regarded as an imagined community?

Can There Be a European Identity?

Before dealing with the empirical evidence for European identity, I need to briefly address the question of whether a European identity as a collective sense of community beyond the nation-state is possible at all. Those denying this possibility have usually linked the problem of European identity to the question of a European demos as the precondition for a European democracy. Dieter Grimm has probably provided the most straightforward line of reasoning in this regard (Grimm 1995, 295; for a good discussion, see Kraus 2008, 21–26): a European demos in the sense of a European people does not exist, because Europeans lack a sense of collective identity. A European identity is not possible, because there is no common European language that might constitute a political community (see also Scharpf 1999; Greven 2000; Kielmansegg 1996). In addition, many scholars have argued that the absence of a European demos results from the nonexistence of a common European public sphere. I deal with this latter argument in chapters 5–7.

First, some arguments—although not Grimm's—are based on ethnocultural understandings of collective identities. I suggested in the previous chapter why essentialist understandings of collective identities cannot be sustained. Second, whether or not Europeans express a sense of imagined community is above all an empirical question, which I discuss below. I argue in particular that we do not observe the emergence of a single European identity above and beyond national identities, but rather the Europeanization of national identities whereby a sense of European community is expressed in various national colors that are largely complementary and tap into similar meanings and interpretations of what "Europe" signifies.

This leaves one relevant objection to the possibility of a European identity,[1] namely the lack of a common European language. Indeed, Europe and the EU are multilingual spaces. The EU's official language policy celebrates this diversity of linguistic competences and even uses it to promote the "unity in diversity" theme

---

1. Some have even argued that Europeans lack shared historical experiences upon which collective identities can be built. A brief look at the battlefields of European wars of the past centuries should lay this point to rest. In many cases—the French-German example being the most prominent one—the continuous invocation of a collective memory pertaining to past wars and mutual hatred has served to construct a common European identity as a means of overcoming the century-old enmity. On the attempts to construct a collective European history, see Kaelble 2009.

of European identity (Kraus 2008). But the EU with its twenty-three official languages is not alone in the world as a multilingual community. In fact, according to Wikipedia, most countries in the world are multilingual.[2] Some countries, such as Mexico, Indonesia, or Kenya, recognize many more than twenty-three languages. Are they, therefore, doomed as far as the emergence of a collective identity is concerned?

Moreover, and despite official efforts to foster linguistic pluralism, we can actually observe an emerging common language in Europe, namely English, with 43.1 percent of Europeans claiming to speak English either as their mother tongue or as a foreign language. Among the EU 15, the number increases to 51.9 percent, while only one fourth of the citizens of the new Central Eastern European member states claim to speak English. English language competence is highly correlated with education, age, mobility, and being a citizen of a smaller European country (data according to Gerhards 2008a, 2008c). This is precisely the group of people—"the Europeans"—who also identify strongly with Europe and the EU (Fligstein 2008, 148–49). If there is an emerging lingua franca in the EU, it is English—whether one likes it or not.

Finally, an interesting study by Nicole Doerr shows that multilingualism might actually foster rather than hinder a sense of community. She studied multilingualism among social movement activists at the European Social Forum and documented that the necessity to translate meanings in many different languages contributed to a greater sense of community on the European as compared to the national level. It also improved the deliberative quality of the proceedings (Doerr 2008, 2009).

Although the European Social Forum might be a special case, one should not overestimate the lack of common languages in Europe as an obstacle to identity formation. Multilingualism is not confined to the transnational level; it is quite common in many countries. In the absence of a common European language, English is gradually emerging as the EU's lingua franca. I conclude, therefore, that the main arguments against the possibility of a collective European identity are not particularly convincing. Let me now analyze the empirical data.

How Do They Go Together?
European and National Identities

It is no longer controversial among scholars and, increasingly, among policy-makers that individuals hold multiple social identities (see chapter 1). People can

---

2. http://en.wikipedia.org/wiki/List_of_multilingual_countries_and_regions.

feel a sense of belonging to Europe, their nation-state, their gender, and so forth. It is wrong to conceptualize European identity in zero-sum terms, as if an increase in European identity necessarily decreases one's loyalty to national or other communities. Europe and the nation are both "imagined communities" (Anderson 1991) and people can feel that they are part of both communities without having to choose a primary identification. Analyses from survey data suggest and social psychological experiments confirm that people who strongly identify with their nation-state may also feel a sense of belonging to Europe (Duchesne and Frognier 1995; Martinotti and Steffanizzi 1995; Castano 2004). Data on territorial identification processes show that most people simultaneously feel attached to their local, regional, and national communities and that many include Europe and even the world in their sense of belonging (Marks 1999). In 2004, two thirds of the respondents felt attached to both their nation-state and to Europe, according to a Eurobarometer poll (see Fuchs, Guinaudeau, and Schubert 2009).

For many Europeans, national and European identities go together. The evidence from survey data, particularly Eurobarometer polls, is overwhelming that a majority of Europeans express at least some identification with Europe.[3] The numbers vary during the 1990s and early 2000s between 50 percent and 60 percent (see figure 2.1). In 2004, almost 60 percent of the respondents described themselves as also being European, more than two thirds felt some attachment to Europe, and more than 70 percent were proud to be European (Eurobarometer data, quoted from Fuchs, Guinaudeau, and Schubert 2009). Although very few people exclusively identify with Europe or prioritize Europe over their nation-state, 40 percent to 50 percent on average feel attached to their nation and then to Europe. One might call this "identity lite," but even a superficial look at survey data demonstrates that a majority of Europeans feel at least somewhat attached to Europe. It is surprising, therefore, that some scholars, let alone policymakers, still cling to the conventional wisdom that "no collective European identity exists" (Katzenstein 2006, 29; but see Checkel and Katzenstein 2009b for a more nuanced statement).

As figure 2.1 suggests, however, there is not much movement over time, and this even appears to hold true for the period since the 1970s (Green 2007, 66). If we look at the aggregate numbers and the EU average, we do not see much evidence that European integration as such has led to increased identification with the EU (see chapter 4 for a discussion). The same holds true for the population in individual member states.

---

3. See, e.g., Citrin and Sides 2004; Hooghe and Marks 2004, 2005; Fligstein 2008, 140–43; Green 2007, ch. 3; Fuchs, Guinaudeau, and Schubert 2009; McLaren 2006.

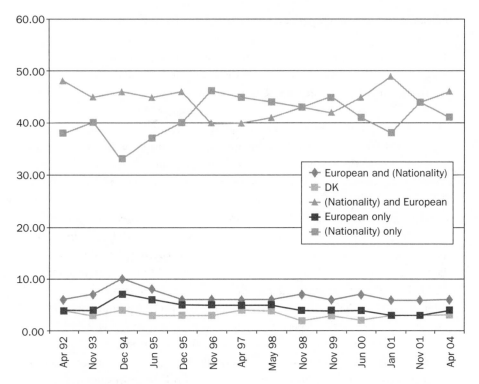

Figure 2.1. National and European identities, EU average, 1992–2004. "In the near future, will you see yourself as . . .?"
Source: Eurobarometer data, graph generated from http://ec.europa.eu/public_opinion/cf/index_en.cfm.

Among those showing some identification with Europe, "nation first and then Europe" is by far the dominant outlook. Liesbet Hooghe and Gary Marks have called this "inclusive nationalism" since people identify with their nation-state and also with Europe (Hooghe and Marks 2005). This secondary identification with Europe competes with identification with "nation only" ("exclusive nationalism") throughout the 1990s and the early 2000s. From 1992 to 1995 and from 2000 to 2004, however, "inclusive nationalists" form a plurality in the opinion polls by as much as 12 percent.

However, these average numbers overshadow the fact that identification with Europe varies enormously among member states. On the one end of the continuum, we find citizens in Luxembourg (73.4%), Italy (72.2%), France (70.3%), Spain (68.2%), and Germany (65.5%) who overwhelmingly describe themselves as Europeans, at least to some degree. As Neil Fligstein notes, majorities in four of the five most populous EU member states identify themselves with Europe (Fligstein 2008, 143). On the other end of the continuum, Great Britain is the only large member state where exclusive nationalism dominates (64.7%). Majorities in Finland (59.9%), Sweden (57.3%), Greece (55.3%), and Austria (53.0%) also identify with their nation-state only. None of these countries belong to the original six EU member states; three of them (Finland, Sweden, Austria) joined the EU only in 1995. I come back to this point in chapter 4.

On the whole, the East European countries that joined the EU in 2004 exhibit a pattern similar to those of the earlier enlargements. But citizens from the new member states do not differ dramatically compared to citizens from "old" member states. A study of dual identities in Poland confirmed and replicated the findings for the older EU members (McManus-Czubinska et al. 2003). The strongest identification with Europe among the newer EU members can be found in the island states of Cyprus and Malta; Polish citizens are somewhat below the EU average in their identification with Europe, while Czechs, Hungarians, and Lithuanians are among the most "exclusively nationalist" citizens (European Commission 2005, 96). Even Bulgarians and Romanians, who joined the EU in 2007, as well as Croatians, who have yet to become members, do not differ much from their fellow Europeans. Only the Turkish population shows a distinctive pattern, with 72 percent of the respondents identifying with Turkey only, making them the most "exclusively nationalist" in Europe.

The opinion polls presented above asked people whether they saw themselves as future Europeans and, thus, tapped directly into identity-related questions. For quite some time, Eurobarometer also has asked people for their degree of attachment to Europe, to the nation, the region, and to local communities. This question refers to emotional feelings and, thus, yields slightly different results than the question pertaining to the degree of one's Europeanness. Although attachment to one's nation-state, region, or local community has remained very high across member states (around 90%), attachment to Europe has usually stayed lower. But it substantially increased in the EU 15 during the 1990s and the early 2000s, from 49 percent on average in 1991 to 67 percent in 2004 (see Citrin and Sides 2004, 167–70; European Commission 2005, 103). More important, the number of those who felt attached to their nation-state *and* to Europe rose by almost 20 percent during the 1990s, while those expressing attachment exclusively to their nation decreased by about the same number. Although identification with Europe has not substantially increased during the 1990s and 2000s, emotional attachment apparently has. One reason for this development could be the stronger visibility of European symbols and the increased media coverage of EU affairs throughout the last two decades.

Once again, the variation among countries is substantial. Although the overall tendency toward increased dual attachment can be observed across countries (except for Greece), the greatest increases took place in Portugal and in Germany (see also Fuchs, Guinaudeau, and Schubert 2009, 13). In 2004, attachment to Europe ranged from 81 percent in Luxembourg and 76 percent in Sweden[4] to 50 percent in Great Britain and 48 percent in Greece. Citizens of the new Central Eastern European member states are not different from everybody else in that they do not form a distinct cluster, with 89 percent of the Hungarians and 84 percent of the Poles feeling at least some attachment to Europe, while only 35 percent of the Cypriots and 41 percent of the Estonians feel the same way (European Commission 2005, 104). The same Eurobarometer poll also asked people whether they felt proud to be European. Although national pride trumps European pride in all member states (86% on average for national pride in the EU 25 as compared to 68% for pride in Europe),[5] the country variation with regard to European pride is again enormous, ranging from 87 percent in Hungary to 50 percent in Great Britain (European Commission 2005, 101).[6]

Although the overall numbers are different depending on the type of question asked about identification with Europe, the general pattern remains the same. The main dividing line in contemporary Europe is not between those who identify with Europe and those who feel loyalty to their nation-state. The main cleavage is between those holding exclusive national identities, on the one hand, and those identifying with their nation-state *and* with Europe, on the other (inclusive nationalists). Even secondary identification with Europe matters enormously. Statistical analyses confirm that inclusive nationalists tend to support European integration much more strongly than those who only identify with their nation-state (see chapter 8 for details; Citrin and Sides 2004, 174–76; Fligstein 2008, 144). Moreover, exclusive identification with the nation-state is a more powerful predictor of opposition to European integration than calculations about economic costs and benefits (Hooghe and Marks 2005).

The data presented so far concern mainly Europe as an imagined community with which people can identify. Another measurement for the degree of transnational social integration and for the sense of community among strangers

---

4. Interestingly enough, although a majority of Swedes apparently feels an emotional attachment to Europe, this does not translate into a stronger sense of European identity (see above). In the case of Cyprus (see below), the opposite is the case: little attachment to Europe but strong European identity. These discrepancies support my point that the two questions tap into different attitudes with regard to a sense of belonging.

5. There is not much variation among countries with regard to national pride—except for Germany, where only 71% of the respondents express national pride. For the other EU 25 countries, national pride ranges from 98% in Ireland to 82% in Belgium and Slovakia (European Commission 2005, 100).

6. In this particular survey carried out at the end of 2004, Central East Europeans expressed particular pride in being European. This probably results from their becoming EU members earlier in the year.

refers to cross-national trust levels among Europeans. Do Europeans know each other, and do they trust each other? The answer to this question appears to be "yes, but," as a study by Jan Delhey shows (Delhey 2005, 2007). In general, Europeans are not only familiar with one another, but they also share sufficient degrees of mutual trust, measured in country dyads.[7] Trust levels remain highest among citizens of the original six EU member states and the Northern European countries that joined in the 1970s (United Kingdom, Ireland, Denmark) and in 1995 (Sweden, Finland, Austria). In contrast, the mutual trust levels among Northern and Western Europeans, on the one hand, and Southern and Eastern Europeans, on the other hand, remain significantly lower. Greeks in particular do not seem to trust the British and the Germans, while Germans and Austrians show rather low trust levels toward citizens of the new Eastern member states. As a result, trust levels among the EU 25 are much more scattered than among the Western and Northern EU members. However, there is reason for some optimism: in 1976, the country dyads for the original six members were as scattered as the country dyads for the twenty-five EU member states and accession candidates in 1997. Moreover, trust levels among Europeans have increased over time—indicating that EU membership actually matters (see chapter 4).

In sum, identification with the nation-state still runs high in Europe, and this includes old and new EU member states. The real divide is not between "nationalists" and "die-hard" Europeans, but between exclusive and inclusive nationalists who also feel attached to Europe. Europeans on average know one another and trust one another, indicating a sense of community among strangers. But a North-South divide exists in the EU with regard to both identification levels and the degree of mutual trust. Eastern enlargement has added an East-West divide in trust and partially in identification levels among EU citizens.

However, we need to discuss the implications of the rather simple insight that European and national identities go together. This fact is old news by now. The more interesting question is what the data suggest about how multiple identities go together and how they relate to each other. Chapter 1 suggested four ways in which we can think of multiple identities: identities can be separate, they can be cross-cutting, nested, or they can be intertwined. How can we interpret the data presented above?

---

7. This study was based on 1976 and 1997 Eurobarometer data and measured, for example, whether Danes not only expressed familiarity with Italians (and Germans, French, and so forth) but whether they also trusted them. In the EU 25, then, Denmark alone forms twenty-four country dyads (out of six hundred altogether). These country dyads were then put in a two-dimensional field with the familiarity scores and the trust scores forming the two axes. Hence, the more scattered the country dyads, the less Europeans know each other and the less they trust each other. See Delhey 2005 for details.

As to separate identities, those who exclusively identify with their nation-state do not have much in common with the other groups so that there is very little overlap between these groups. Exclusive nationalists form a rather distinct group of people with regard to their socioeconomic status, education, and cultural and political attitudes.

There is also support for the onion or "Russian Matryoshka doll" model of multiple identities. This model suggests a degree of hierarchy between people's sense of belonging and loyalties with regard to territorially defined spaces. Inclusive nationalism, whereby people identify with Europe as a secondary identity, is compatible with such an understanding of nested identities. In this case, loyalty to one's nation-state forms the core while attachment to Europe would be the outer layer. At least, this is how Eurobarometer polls on which these data are based have framed the question. If respondents are asked whether they identify with their nation-state first and then with Europe or vice versa, such a questionnaire implies a hierarchical understanding of nested identities.

However, the data are also consistent with the marble cake model according to which identity components blend into each other and are intertwined. First, Europe as a secondary identity of inclusive nationalists is compatible with the idea that we do not observe the emergence of separate European identities, but the *Europeanization* of national identities. Europeanization means that Europe and the EU are integrated into core understandings of one's national (or other) sense of belonging. It means that core understandings of what it means to be German, French, or Polish change and that Europe and the EU become part and parcel of these understandings. We do not cease to be Germans, French, or Polish, but become European Germans, French Europeans, or Polish in the EU. Such transformations of national identities are observable across Europe in the elite discourses (see chapter 3).

Second, the marble cake model finds indirect support in the data. If we assume a hierarchical understanding of nested identities, it would make a huge difference whether the nation-state or Europe forms the core of one's professed identity. In other words, the main dividing line in the data should be between inclusive nationalists, on the one hand, and those identifying with Europe first and their nation second, on the other hand. This is inconsistent with statistical analyses, as I discuss in more detail in chapter 8. The main cleavage with regard to attitudes toward Europe and European integration is between exclusive and inclusive nationalists rather than between the latter and "die-hard" Europeans who also identify with their nation as a secondary identity. Whether Europe forms the core of one's identity or not does not add much with regard to attitudinal or behavioral consequences. Rather, those who have integrated Europe and the EU into their sense of national belonging already exhibit cosmopolitan values and strong support for European integration. Exclusive nationalists, however, are much more likely to be xenophobic and Euroskeptic. This is exactly what the marble cake model suggests.

The finding of increasing Europeanization of national identities on average across Europe leads to two more questions. First, who are "the Europeans," i.e., those identifying with Europe, if only as a secondary identity (Green 2007; Fligstein 2008, chap. 5; Fligstein 2009)? Second, what does it mean to identify with Europe or the EU? What is the substantive content of European identity?

Who Identifies with Europe? The Europeans

Who are those identifying with Europe more strongly than others and who are the exclusive nationalists? As argued above with regard to country variation, citizenship matters. If you are Italian, Spanish, French, or German, you are more likely to belong to the group of inclusive nationalists who also identify with Europe than if you are Swedish, Finnish, or British. In general, the populations of continental Western and Southern Europe (except for Greece) feel comparatively more attached to Europe than Northern Europeans or Central Eastern Europeans.

However, where you live is far less important for your identification with Europe than who you are, how you live, and how you were brought up. First of all, there is a well-known gender gap with regard to European identity. Men are on average more likely to feel attachment to Europe than women, even though women have profited more from European integration than men with regard to equal treatment, equal pay, and gender mainstreaming (see Liebert and Sifft 2003; Nelson and Guth 2000). Material benefits, thus, do not seem to drive European identity. However, although the gender gap is significant in statistical analyses, its impact on levels of identification is less pronounced than other social attributes.

As Neil Fligstein and David M. Green show, age, education, income, and socioeconomic status in general are strong predictors for European identity (Fligstein 2008, chap. 5; Fligstein 2009; Green 2007, chap. 4). Fligstein in particular concentrates on those "Europeans" (about 10% on average) who identify more strongly with Europe than with their nation-state. If you are young, well educated, rich, and belong to the upper middle classes, chances are high that you are "European" in this strong sense of the term. Among the various indicators, education appears to be particularly relevant (Green 2007, 84). I doubt that this has to do with growing knowledge about the EU taught in civics classes across high schools in Europe, but with more general values and attitudes that accompany socialization in higher education. As to age, it remains unclear whether this is a generational or a life-cycle effect.[8] If it were the former, we should see an increase in European identity over time (Fligstein 2008, 141), yet only a modest increase can be observed.

Attachment to Europe also correlates strongly with other attitudes. Those who identify with Europe are more likely than others to hold cosmopolitan values, have positive attitudes toward immigrants, and place themselves politically more to the left than to the right on the respective scale (Green 2007, 84–85; Fligstein 2008, 145). I refer to "correlations" in this case, since I am not sure what is cause and what is effect. Although we can safely assume that European identity does not lead to higher education but rather the other way round, the direction of the causal arrows is rather unclear concerning the correlation between European identity and other values that people hold dearly. There is a high probability that these attitudes come as a bundle, that is, that Europeans with cosmopolitan values also identify with Europe as part of these attitudes.[9] Statistical data on a newly emerging cultural cleavage in Europe lends strong support to this argument. Accordingly, pro-European attitudes load heavily on the cosmopolitan end of this cleavage, while Euroskepticism is part and parcel of the nationalist end (Kriesi et al. 2008; see chapter 10 for details).

At first glance, there is a simple explanation for these results: it is all material interest and social class. Highly educated and well-to-do professionals, managers, and white-collar workers disproportionately benefit from the single market and from European integration in general, as Matthew Gabel has argued (Gabel 1998). The European political, economic, and cultural elites also profit most from the EU and it is therefore no wonder that they also identify with Europe.

If it were that simple, support for European integration could be explained by class variables, on the one hand, and perceived benefits from the EU, on the other. The two variables together should supersede identification with Europe as an explanation for supporting the EU. However, as I will show in more detail in chapter 8, statistical analyses reveal that there is an extremely strong and independent effect of the identity variable on support for European integration (see Fligstein 2008, 146–47; Hooghe and Marks 2005). In other words, class and expected benefits do not trump European identity.

Building upon Karl W. Deutsch's theory of nationalism and social communication (Deutsch 1953), Neil Fligstein offers a convincing explanation for how higher education and class lead to stronger European identity: "In essence, Europeans are going to be the people who have the opportunity and inclination to

---

8. Green does not find an age effect in his statistical analysis (Green 2007, 82).
9. On Europe as a cosmopolitan project more generally, see Beck and Grande 2004.

travel to other countries and frequently interact with people in other societies in the Europe-wide economic, social, and political fields" (Fligstein 2008, 16; also Fligstein 2009). He shows that the higher-educated social classes in Europe are also highly likely to regularly practice a second language (usually English) and to frequently travel around Europe (Fligstein 2008, 147–55). Traveling abroad is linked to positive attitudes toward the EU. Indeed, most Europeans identify the EU with the ability to freely travel, study, and work anywhere in Europe (European Commission 2006a, 73). In sum, Fligstein makes an interactionist argument that is also consistent with social psychological theories of identity: the more people interact transnationally across borders in Europe, the more they identify with Europe. Of course, well-educated young people in managerial and white-collar professions are more likely to interact regularly across European borders than less-educated blue-collar workers. In other words, the causal link between education and class, on the one hand, and the Europeanization of identities, on the other, is likely to be transnational interaction.

Data on migration, free movement in Europe, and European identity corroborate this argument. Nina Rother and Tina M. Nebe show, for example, that the more mobile people are, the more they identify with Europe (Rother and Nebe 2009). On average, "movers" are four times more likely than "stayers" to exclusively identify with Europe, and the former are also far less likely to identify only with their home state than the latter. Adrian Favell calls this group the "Eurostars," those professional, skilled, and educated people who circulate in the European knowledge economy locating and relocating between the various "Eurocities," that is, London, Paris, Berlin, Madrid, Amsterdam, Brussels, and others (Favell 2008, 2009). These are the prototypical Europeans who identify easily with Europe, their home country, and their country of residence. But Favell also shows that this group is a very small minority in Europe, since less than 2 percent of Europeans regularly live outside their country of birth. He also argues that most European societies, including the locals in the "Eurocities," form close-knit communities that make it very hard for foreigners to integrate: "Eurostars...are trying to explicitly live a post-national life; most of them find that it is a rather difficult proposition in the European Union today" (Favell 2009, 181–82).

Yet, as Favell also points out, the final test of how class and education, on the one hand, and transnational interaction, on the other, go together to create "Europeans" depends on the fate of those whom he calls the "East-West movers," that is, the postenlargement migrants from Central Eastern Europe who have moved to Britain, Ireland, and elsewhere to find jobs (Favell 2009, 182–85). To a large extent, they are highly skilled blue-collar workers (the famous "Polish plumber"). Will they become "Europeans," or will they feel rejected by the antimigration sentiments in many West European countries? And how will the global economic crisis affect their attitudes, particularly when it forces them to return home?

This brings me to the other side of the coin, to the "non-" or even "anti-Europeans." As demonstrated above, about 40 percent of the population in Europe continues to exclusively identify with their nation-state, thus outnumbering Favell's "Eurostars" by a huge margin. This group almost forms the mirror image of those identified by Green and Fligstein as "the Europeans." Exclusive nationalists are much more likely to be older, less-educated, blue-collar workers, and to have lower social status than "the Europeans." Exclusive nationalism also comes with a bundle of other attitudes, for example, hostility toward foreigners and/or immigrants who are perceived as threatening one's national culture (McLaren 2006, chap. 5). Exclusive nationalists also hold more right-wing than left-wing political attitudes.

Of course, exclusive nationalism is not the same as "anti-Europeanism." As I will explore in more detail in chapters 8 and 10, the effects of exclusive nationalist identities on support levels for European integration vary widely (Marks and Hooghe 2003, 21). However, primordial and nationalist identities in conjunction with low-skilled occupational levels are powerful sources of Euroskepticism (Hooghe, Huo, and Marks 2007; McLaren 2007a; Fuchs, Magni-Berton, and Roger 2009). This is the social basis and potential for the "sleeping giant" of "anti-EU" political mobilization by mostly right-wing populist parties across Europe (Franklin and Van der Eijk 2006; Kriesi et al. 2008).

In sum, two groups of people can be distinguished with regard to their identification levels with Europe. On the one hand, there are "the Europeans" and even a small group of "Eurostars" who strongly interact transnationally, are highly educated, have high-skilled occupational levels, and hold mostly cosmopolitan values. This group feels very much attached to Europe and the EU. On the other hand, exclusive nationalists who reject Europe and the EU have less transnational interactions, lower education levels, and work mostly in blue-collar jobs. While both groups hold strong feelings—either positive or negative—about Europe and the EU, there is a large group in the middle who identifies with Europe as a secondary identity, the inclusive nationalists. Although their (positive) attitudes toward European integration resemble those of the true "Europeans" (see chapter 8), the future of European integration in the years to come will be largely decided by this group.

Now that we have identified "the Europeans," we need to have a clearer picture of what it actually means to feel attached to Europe. Is the attachment to the EU as a political community? Does "attachment to Europe" signify identification with a larger cultural Europe or even a European civilization?

Europe or EU? Contested Identities in Mass Public Opinion

Modern Europe vs. Nationalist Europe: Competing Identity Constructions

To what extent is European identity synonymous with EU identity? This question is particularly important if we want to find out which effects European integration has had on identity changes. People might feel a sense of belonging to Europe in general, while feeling no attachment to the EU at all—and vice versa.

As David Green shows in his analysis of public opinion data from the late 1980s to the late 1990s (Green 2007, chap. 5; also Kufer 2009), respondents identify Europe with the following substantive content: peace, freedom of travel, shared cultural traditions, cultural diversity and tolerance, and religious and philosophical values. Shared cultural traditions and cultural diversity are particularly relevant for those who feel attached to Europe, "the Europeans."

Michael Bruter has demonstrated in his work that Europeans distinguish between Europe in general and the EU in particular (Bruter 2004, 2005). He points out that it makes a difference whether Europe is defined in political or cultural terms. "Culture" in this understanding encompasses history, ethnicity, civilization, heritage, and other social similarities. "Political identity" instead is more circumscribed and refers to the identification of citizens with particular political institutions such as the EU. Bruter finds that people systematically distinguish between these two dimensions. His evidence is corroborated by a Europe-wide focus group study commissioned by the European Commission. This study shows that people by and large identify "Europe" as a historical, political, and cultural space rather than as a geographically bound entity (OPTEM 2001). In contrast, when Europe is introduced in mostly territorial terms, attachment rates drop dramatically (EOS Gallup Europe 2001). In this case, comparatively more people feel attached to the "world" than to Europe. It is cultural identity that seems to form the substance of citizens' identification with Europe as a whole.

People identify the EU as a political, value, and economic community. In particular, the EU stands for the values of modernity: enlightenment, democracy, human rights, and peace. In 2007, 27 percent each named "culture" and "economy" as the two most important issues that create a sense of community among EU citizens, followed by "history" (21%) (European Commission 2007b, 64). A 2006 Eurobarometer poll asked respondents for the values that the European Union represents. The top values are human rights (38%), democracy (38%), and peace (36%), followed by the rule of law (24%) and respect for other cultures (19%) (European Commission 2007a, 28–35). The data are comparatively homogenous across member states, suggesting that the EU as a value community is relatively well defined in the perception of European citizens. Eurobarometer also regularly asks people what the European Union means to them personally. In spring 2006, 50 percent of the respondents named "freedom to travel, study, and work any-where in the EU" as the number-one item, followed by the euro (39%) and "peace" (33%) (European Commission 2006a, 73). A year later, respondents were asked what best describes the idea they have of the European Union. The two number-one items (70% each) are "democracy" and "modern," followed by "protective" (57%). The two more negative attributions—"technocratic" and "inefficient"—follow at a distance (48% and 37%). Although there is Europe-wide consensus on the first three attributions, the variation across Europe on the two negative statements is enormous, ranging from 77 percent in Greece ("technocratic") to 13 percent in Bulgaria ("inefficient") (European Commission 2007b, 75–77).

This is precisely what Bruter refers to as the European political identity. His work shows that Europeans indeed identify with the EU as a distinct civic and political entity based on universal values (Bruter 2005).[10] In this sense, the EU *is* modern Europe. Of course, the EU as modern Europe resonates with the highly mobile and well-educated political, social, and economic elites that I have de-scribed above as "the Europeans." And this identity construction is also compat-ible with deliberate attempts by EU elites to construct a postnational identity in the Habermasian sense that emphasizes democracy, human rights, the market economy, the welfare state, and cultural diversity (Habermas 1996a; Dewandre and Lenoble 1992). These values have become constitutive for the EU, since one cannot become a member without subscribing to them (the Copenhagen cri-teria). As the enlargement debates show, the self-description of the EU and the dominant discourses surrounding it have moved quite a long way toward build-ing a polity and going beyond simple market integration (Laffan 2004). Europe's political identity constitutes a "sacred" identity construction in the Eisenstadt/Giesen sense (Eisenstadt and Giesen 1995) insofar as it is seen as superior to other political orders. In sum, the substantive content of the EU's political identity—as promoted by the elites and as perceived by the larger public—refers to a modern, democratic, secular, and cosmopolitan value community.

In contrast, cultural Europe is based on a common historical and religious heritage that is broader than EU Europe. However, as I will show in more detail in the following chapters, the European cultural heritage has been used more recently to build a countervision to the modern and cosmopolitan EU Europe

---

10. Bruter uses the term "civic identity," which I find confusing because it conflates the notion with the categories introduced by Giesen and Eisenstadt as discussed in chapter 1 (Eisenstadt and Giesen 1995).

(see, e.g., Holmes 2009). To the extent that cultural Europe becomes politically salient in the discourses and debates across Europe, it is constructed as a primordial European identity, one that is based on traditional values, on a particular interpretation of Christianity and other historical traditions, and on an exclusionary rhetoric that is hostile to non-EU foreigners and immigrants. Euroskeptical parties—mostly on the political right—have started to construct their own vision of the EU based on a nationalist and primordial European identity which primarily uses cultural values as its distinctive categories. This nationalist European identity resonates in particular with those holding exclusive nationalist identities. However, it is increasingly a distinct *European* identity construction that transfers nationalist values to the European level. Exclusionary Europe represents a noteworthy kind of "nationalism" beyond the nation-state. Although it pertains to a supranational entity, the EU, it is still nationalist, because it uses the building blocks of nineteenth-century nationalism to reconstruct them on the European level. Thus, "European nationalism" taps into the sense of European cultural identity that can be found in mass public opinion, but then uses it to create a counterimage to the cosmopolitan and modern idea of Europe embraced by "the Europeans." This particular version of European nationalism also resonates with the widespread Euroskepticism that has become politically salient across the EU during the 2000s (Fuchs, Magni-Berton, and Roger 2009; Hooghe and Marks 2007; Taggart and Szczerbiak 2005/2008).

We can observe this discourse, for example, in the debates about Turkish EU membership, but also about immigration (see chapter 9). Accordingly, principled opponents of Turkish EU membership have constructed Turkey as a Muslim country that does not belong to Europe, because it does not share its cultural heritage and its Christian tradition: "Europe was built on the dual heritage of Christianity and Enlightenment. But Turkey was not" (*Le Figaro*, 27 Nov. 2002, quoted in Wimmel 2006a, 16; see also Wimmel 2006b). Christianity and enlightenment are used here as primordial constructions so that the boundary between Europe and the "others" cannot be overcome. Interestingly enough, proponents of Turkish EU membership use the same enlightenment values to construct a European "sacred identity" that is not exclusive, but inclusive. As long as Turkey adheres to the values of human rights, democracy, and the rule of law, it can be admitted to the EU.

In sum, a more political and a more cultural understanding of what Europe means can be discerned from public opinion data. Political Europe is almost identical with EU Europe and its *differentia specifica* are the modern values of peace, human rights, democracy, secularism, and cosmopolitanism. However, cultural Europe has most recently been constructed into a countervision of modern Europe, one that is nationalist, white, Christian, and exclusionary. Both visions come with their own out-groups. The more European identity politicizes, the more we will see clashes between these two alternative visions of Europe and the EU (Checkel and Katzenstein 2009b; see chapter 10).

Europe's Multiple "Others"

Identity constructions not only contain references about what is so special about the "imagined community." They also delineate the boundaries of the community by identifying in-groups and out-groups.

The narrative that portrays European integration as a modernization project of human rights, the rule of law, democracy, and the market economy constructs a particular out-group: Europe's or the particular nation-state's own past of militarism, nationalism, and economic backwardness. This construction of Europe's past as the out-group of modern European identity has dominated the elite discourses in Germany, Spain, Portugal, and, to a degree, Poland (see chapter 3 for details). German political elites have continuously referred to the German past of militarism and Nazism as the European "other" to be overcome by European integration. In the Polish discourse, Communism as well as the experiences of occupation by both the Nazis and later on the Soviet Union plays a similar role. "Return to Europe" became the rallying cry of those who wanted to leave the Communist past behind. Europe's own past is the out-group of the EU's modern political identity.

The EU's modern political identity also includes an "out-group from within": xenophobia and racism. The EU's identity of enlightenment and modernity constructs xenophobia, racism, and right-wing populism as remnants of the past and, thus, the out-group. Xenophobia and racism as the "others" of core European values resonate with those in mass public opinion who identify with Europe. Statistical analyses demonstrate that identification with Europe correlates strongly with antiracist and antixenophobic attitudes as well as support for the rights of immigrants (De Vreese and Boomgaarden 2005; Lahav 2004, chap. 5). The European-wide controversy in 2000 about the ascent to power of a right-wing populist party in Austria (the so-called Haider debate) illustrates such identity constructions. Xenophobia in general and Jörg Haider in particular were seen as the European out-group, as an enemy from within (Van de Steeg 2006; Risse and Van de Steeg 2008; see chapter 6). The issue was how European values of democracy and human rights could be upheld against the rise to power of a xenophobic party that did not distance itself sufficiently from the European Nazi past.

In contrast, those who conceive of Europe and the EU primarily in more nationalist and exclusionary terms tend to use religion in general and Christianity in particular as the demarcation lines of Europe's in-group. In this historical construction, the Christian universe encompasses Catholicism, Orthodox

Christianity, and modern Protestantism. Islam, however, is definitely out and so are the successors to the Ottoman Empire, which constitute Europe's primary "others." As a member of the European Parliament (EP) put it: "Leaving aside the cost because they [Turkey] are very backwards...[it is] Christendom, the area where Christians roughly were during the Middle Ages....We all [identified with] the Church, whether we [went] or we didn't. But Turkey is an Islamic country—it is entirely different....The real problem is that the differences between Christendom and Islam are quite big" (quoted from Lahav 2004, 161).

The antimodern vision of traditional and religious Europe also constructs an "out-group within," namely non-European immigrants, mainly from North Africa or from Turkey itself. Those who exclusively identify with their nation-state are also likely to exhibit xenophobic and anti-immigrant attitudes (De Vreese and Boomgaarden 2005). As Gallya Lahav shows, these anti-immigrant feelings of exclusive nationalists mostly pertain to non-European immigrants, not to foreigners in general (Lahav 2004, 114–15). People seem to clearly differentiate between fellow Europeans who are still part of "us" and the "others," the non-Europeans.

As in the case of EU's modern political identity, this narrative about the European out-group is only marginally connected to geographic location. Historically, the Ottoman Empire extended well into what is today the EU and covered Greece, Hungary, Bulgaria, Romania, and parts of contemporary Austria. At the same time, since Orthodox Christianity constitutes part of the in-group, ancient Constantinople (East Rome) and Byzantium belong to the European cultural heritage, while modern Istanbul apparently does not.

In short, those identifying with the EU as a modern political community tend to view the European and their own nationalist past as the main out-groups of modern Europe, while those identifying with Europe in primordial and traditional terms see non-Christians, particularly Muslims, as the most important European "others." Both groups also have their European others "within," namely racists and xenophobes in the case of a modern identity and non-European immigrants in the case of nationalist Europe.[11]

What about the United States as a potentially prominent European "other?" Unilateral foreign policies by the Bush administration during the early 2000s and the ensuing transatlantic conflicts, which culminated in the Iraq crisis of 2002–03, gave rise to the suspicion that the United States is increasingly being constructed as a European out-group, particularly by the European left. Although this book is not about the history of European anti-Americanisms (Katzenstein and Keohane 2006; Anderson, Ikenberry, and Risse 2008), it is hard to construct the United States as a generalized European "other." First, the dominant

---

11. I come back to these issues in more detail in chapters 9 and 10.

narratives in most European countries are ambivalent about the United States. On the one hand, the United States is considered part of Western civilization, of the heritage of modernity and enlightenment. Modern Europe and the EU's identity described above are part and parcel of this construction of *the West*. The history of the cold war makes it particularly difficult to construct Europe in opposition to a country that has supported European integration from the beginnings of the Marshall Plan. On the other hand, most national narratives in Europe have contained some elements of anti-Americanism almost since the United States came into being. The American frontier and cowboy mythology have always been regarded with mixed feelings, evoking sentiments against "un-civilized Americans." Conservatives add that the United States has no sense of history and of tradition so that antimodernist and anti-American feelings converge here. On the left, American (laissez-faire) capitalism and the occasionally unilateral foreign policies of a superpower have always evoked hostile feelings.

Second, it is hard to construct a generalized American out-group from these constructions without immediately provoking counterreactions in many European countries on either side of the political spectrum. There are only two specific contexts in which the EU is constructed with the United States as the "other." The first context pertains to discussions about a so-called European social model.[12] Whenever a European welfare state is being debated, it is juxtaposed against "Anglo-Saxon," that is American, "laissez-faire capitalism" (Wodak 2004). Here, U.S. capitalism constitutes a European "other." A second context in which the United States is constructed as a European "out-group" is related to foreign and security policy. The emerging narrative about the EU as a "civilian" power in foreign policy is constructed in opposition to the United States as a military superpower that prefers military over political means of conflict resolution (see chapter 8).

In sum, however, Europe and the EU have multiple "others" and the various identity discourses do not converge on a specific out-group. This is where the troubles of the EU as an imagined community begin.

The EU as an Imagined Community: Psychological Existence and Strength

How "Real" Is the EU?

As argued in chapter 1, imagined communities such as Europe have to become "real" in people's minds (Castano 2004). Nation-states employ many mechanisms

---

12. Of course, it is hard to identify a uniform European social model of a welfare state given the differences between, say, the Scandinavian welfare state, British capitalism, and the Rhinelandish social market economy.

to remind their citizens that they belong to a national community. There are symbols such as the national flag, the national anthem, the currency, passports, and particular national holidays to commemorate extraordinary moments in the nation's history. These symbols serve as identity markers. Moreover, national elites use various narratives to reify the nation-state, to celebrate historical moments, and to delineate what is so special about France, Britain, Italy, or Poland. And powerful socialization efforts in educational institutions instill a sense of belonging to a national community in the children.

This is where the EU as an imagined community appears to be in trouble. Although the EU is "real" for "the Europeans," in particular the "Eurostars," who have to deal with it in their daily lives, it is more remote for average citizens. First, there is no glorious European history to be proud of in the same way that British and French histories are narrated in a triumphant way. On the contrary, the identity of modern political Europe is being constructed against the European past of wars, nationalism, and militarism as the EU's "other."

Second, the blame game of national policymakers vis-à-vis Brussels is not particularly suitable to increasing people's sense of a European community. In the national discourses, the EU and a "faceless European bureaucracy" are often blamed for tough and costly decisions ("Brussels made me do it"), while policymakers tend to claim the more beneficial decisions for themselves. This results in negative attributions of responsibility to EU institutions in national media. A study of German media reporting on the EU showed, for example, that roughly two thirds of all attributions in which EU institutions were made responsible for particular policies were framed in negative terms, even though the overall number of such attributions was rather low (Gerhards, Offerhaus, and Roose 2009).

Third, to the extent that imagined communities need clear boundaries, the EU faces problems. The EU now has twenty-seven member states and is due to take in Croatia. In addition, all the western Balkans states are entitled to become EU members and, thus, have an accession perspective. So has Turkey. The EU's boundaries are, therefore, constantly moving. In addition, it is confusing for the average European when she leaves the EU. Under normal circumstances, I leave the imagined community of my nation-state when I have to show my passport. But this no longer serves as a marker in the EU. Schengenland constitutes the area of borderless travel in Europe where people cross borders without having to show their passports. But Schengenland does not encompass two EU members, Great Britain and Ireland, even though three *non*members—Norway, Switzerland, and Iceland—participate. As to the second most important identity marker in the EU, the single currency, only sixteen of the twenty-seven member states have adopted it (plus the nonmembers Kosovo and Montenegro). As a result, when I travel from Germany to Finland via Denmark and Sweden, I do not have to show my passport, but I have to change currency twice (to the Danish krone and the Swedish krona) before returning to the euro in Finland. Can boundaries be any "fuzzier"?

Things get worse when we consider other organizations that carry Europe in their name. The Organization for Cooperation and Security in *Europe* (OSCE) defines Europe in the broadest possible terms, covering an area from Vancouver, British Columbia, all the way to Vladivostok, Russia, with fifty-five member states altogether including the United States, Canada, Russia, and the successor states of the Soviet Union. The Council of Europe, which monitors human rights developments in Europe and includes the European Court of Human Rights (not to be confused with the European Court of Justice, the EU court), has forty-six member states and includes Bosnia-Herzegovina, Serbia, Russia, Turkey, and Ukraine (but not Belarus).

In sum, Europe and the EU, as spaces of profound and extremely legalized political organization and institutionalization, have no clear boundaries. And these borders continue to move. As a result, only 50 percent of the respondents were able to identify the statement as false that the EU had fifteen member states in 2006 (European Commission 2006a, 110). This has led Glynis Breakwell to conclude that the "EU has poor definition as a superordinate category and that, without an agreed-on 'portrait' for this identity element derived from EU categorization, there will be great diversity in the ways it is characterized by different people in different countries" (Breakwell 2004, 38; see Breakwell and Lyons 1996). Claims about the emptiness of Europe and the EU as identity categories are corroborated by findings from interviews with people along the old East-West borderline in Europe (Meinhof 2004). The interviewed did not mention Europe or the EU spontaneously, even though the significance of EU enlargement should be quite obvious to them. Does the EU, therefore, represent an "empty signifier" that means whatever those using the term think it means (Laclau 1996)?

Fortunately, the situation is not as bleak as many scholars have painted it. Since the 1990s, the EU and its institutions have made conscious efforts to develop their own symbols and identity markers. The European flag with the twelve yellow stars against a dark blue background is now ubiquitous in Europe. The same holds true for the burgundy red European passport, for the European drivers' license, and for license plates with the EU symbol on it. Europe has its own anthem, Beethoven's "Ode to Joy." Then, of course, there is the European currency, the euro. For each of these identity markers, the message conveyed to the citizens is the same: Europe and the EU are not constructed in opposition to, but are complementary to, national identities. When Europeans see the EU flag on their evening news, it usually flies alongside the respective national flags. The European passport has both the inscription "European Union" and the respective nation-state including a national symbol on its cover. Even the euro contains a conscious effort to construct dual identities. Although euro bills all look alike across the euro zone,[13] the Euro coins are Janus-faced: one side is the same everywhere and inscribes the value of the money, the other side is distinctly national. Members of the euro zone were allowed to pick national symbols of their own. The Germans put the Brandenburg gate on the backside of all their coins, while the Italians were more innovative and picked the Colosseum, Botticelli's *Birth of Venus,* Leonardo da Vinci's *Vitruvian Man,* and other national icons.

What are the effects of these conscious efforts at building a European community as a secondary identity? The answer varies quite a bit. Roughly 95 percent of the Europeans are now aware of the European flag and can correctly identify it, and the numbers have remained high throughout the 2000s (see European Commission 2007b, 79–80). Even two thirds of the Turkish respondents recognized the European flag. Eighty-five percent consider the flag a "good symbol for Europe," while 54 percent of the respondents even claim to identify with it. In other words, the European flag has achieved its standard as an identity marker.

The same holds true for the euro, but this is mainly confined to Euroland, that is, the sixteen EU member states that have adopted the single currency (Risse 2003). Between 50 percent and 60 percent of the respondents in the EU members states that have adopted the euro claim that, for them, the single currency represents the EU. These numbers are substantially higher than the numbers in the non-euro countries, except, interestingly enough, for three Southern European member states: Italy, Portugal, and Spain (see European Commission 2007b, 91). In sum, symbols of European integration have moderate effects on identification, as Michael Bruter confirms in an experimental design (Bruter 2005, 128–29).

As shown above, the overall image of the EU is quite positive. From 2000 to 2008, between 42 percent and 52 percent of the respondents held a positive image of the EU, while between 13 percent and 21 percent expressed negative feelings. Not surprisingly, only 26 percent of the British respondents held a positive view of the EU—in contrast to almost two thirds of the Romanians and the Irish (2008 data; see European Commission 2009, 47–48).

At the same time, however, only 46 percent of the respondents claim that they know how the EU works (another 46% profess ignorance, see European Commission 2006a, 109). The variation among countries is enormous, ranging

---

13. Since the members of the original euro zone could not agree on common European symbols to put on the bills, the bridges and buildings are phantasy products with some resemblance to gothic, Renaissance, and modern architecture, thus signifying the Christian heritage, enlightenment, and modernity—once again.

from 62 percent of Polish respondents expressing knowledge of the EU down to 34 percent for the neighboring Slovakians. In this case, too, citizens of the "old" member states do not differ much from the "new" ones, covering the entire spectrum. Trust levels in the European Union are also not too high. In spring 2006, 48 percent of the respondents expressed trust in the EU, while 39 percent did not trust the union. Trust levels in the EU remain rather high in the new member states (60%) and substantially increase the more respondents know about the EU (European Commission 2006a, 54–56; European Commission 2007c, 35–36). However, we need to put these numbers into perspective: only 35 percent of the respondents on average trust their national governments, while 59 percent distrust them. The only institution that reaches higher trust levels than the EU is the United Nations, which 52 percent of the respondents claim to trust (European Commission 2006a, 50). In general, these numbers appear to suggest a general suspicion by Europeans of their political institutions rather than specific feelings about the EU.

In this context, Michael Bruter has used an experimental design to test how media news about the EU affects identification levels (Bruter 2005, chap. 6). Not surprisingly, good news about the EU is good news for European identity. More important, positive media reporting about the EU strengthens people's attachment to European political institutions in particular, while identification with a cultural Europe increases only slightly as a result of positive news coverage of the EU. I will come back to the relationship between media reporting and European identity in chapters 5 and 7.

In sum, although the EU's boundaries remain blurred and confusing, it has apparently managed to increase its visibility and its psychological existence in the perception of Europeans. Above all, this means the European flag and the single currency as significant identity markers. But it also relates to the overall positive image of the EU among Europeans. As a result, the EU has become more "real" for the average Europeans during the 2000s. This is an important precondition for the emergence of an imagined European community.

Strength of European Identity

Although the "reality" of the EU as an imagined community might have increased in people's minds, it is unclear how strong identification patterns are. In particular, the question remains what kind of sacrifices those who identify with the EU are willing to make. How much "solidarity among strangers" (Habermas 2006, 76–77) can we expect in the twenty-seven EU member states? How much are people prepared to sacrifice for their fellow Europeans, particularly during times of severe economic and financial crises as in 2008–10?

Although we can see an emerging European demos with majorities of EU citizens identifying with both their nation-state and with Europe, we cannot observe a sense of European patriotism that equals patriotic feelings as pronounced as in, say, France, Britain, or Poland. In all EU member states, national patriotism outweighs European patriotism by 18 percent on average (calculated from European Commission 2005, 100–101). "Solidarity among strangers" has limits in Europe. Inclusive nationalism, with Europe as a distinct secondary identity, might suffice for supporting the EU in its current constitutional equilibrium as a multilevel governance system with the member states remaining the "masters of the treaties." Neither the EU nor most European nation-states require the ultimate sacrifice of life from their citizens anymore, having moved overwhelmingly toward professional armies. But what about redistributive welfare policies in Europe? What about European solidarity with faltering economies in times of crises? Is "European identity lite" sufficient to allow for a move toward a more social and more redistributive Europe, which might require a much stronger sense of community (see Bartolini 2005, 211–41)?

Unfortunately, we lack good data on the extent to which EU citizens are prepared to accept sacrifices for the sake of their fellow Europeans and, thus, on the strength of European identity. Some data appear to confirm the "identity lite" view, though. A study based on the European Value Survey shows that only one third of European citizens are prepared to accept the principle of nondiscrimination toward foreigners in national labor markets if jobs are scarce while the overwhelming majority would reserve jobs to their fellow countrymen under such circumstances (Gerhards 2008b). But the variation among countries is enormous. A majority of Swedish, Dutch, and Belgian citizens accept the principle of nondiscrimination even under dire economic circumstances, while only minorities in Germany and in Southern Europe are prepared to do so. Interestingly enough, citizens of the new EU member states are much more opposed to job mobility in Europe than the EU average, even though they would profit the most from it.

Another study of German public opinion by Gerhards and his team appear to confirm these results. On an abstract level, Germans overwhelmingly support the equal access of Europeans to the labor markets of EU member states as stipulated by the Single Market. However, when people are asked to put their money where their professed values are, the numbers drop considerably. Only 2 percent would give a repair job to a Polish firm that is as qualified as a German firm and charges the same price. The number increases to 25 percent if the Polish firm is 10 percent less expensive, and it jumps to 62 percent if the Poles demand half the price of the German firm, but is still equally qualified (data according to Gerhards, Lengfeld, and Schupp 2007, 39, 41). In other words, there appears to be a rather high degree of "solidarity among strangers" in the abstract, which drops considerably, however, the more citizens are asked to behave accordingly.

Summary

The empirical findings on the Europeanization of identities in mass public opinion can be summarized in three points:

1. A majority of Europeans identify with Europe as well as with their nation-state. The main cleavage in mass public opinion is between those who exclusively identify with their nation-state ("exclusive nationalists") and those who identify with Europe as their secondary identity ("inclusive nationalists"). "The Europeans" who strongly identify with Europe are the younger, the better educated, the wealthier, and the more politically informed parts of the population. Moreover, European identity is strongly correlated with cosmopolitan and other liberal values.

2. As to the substantive *content* of European identity, two Europes can be distinguished in mass public opinion. EU Europe is identified as a modern political entity encompassing liberal values such as democracy, human rights, the rule of law, and the market economy. This is the Europe that particularly the European elites and "the Europeans" hold dearly. Modern Europe's "others" are the continent's own past of militarism and nationalism, but also xenophobia and racism. In contrast, a "nationalist European identity" appears to be emerging that is based on a view of Europe in primarily cultural terms, a (Western) civilization with a common historical heritage, strong national traditions, Christianity as its core religion, and clear geographical boundaries. Traditional Europe's "others" encompass non-Christian countries such as Turkey, as well as non-European immigrants and the Muslim populations in European countries. Nationalist Europe is emerging as a countervision to the modern image of the EU. It is promoted particularly by Euroskeptical parties and supported by many exclusive nationalists.

3. Compared with well-established nation-states, the psychological existence of the EU as an imagined community is still lacking. The main problem for the EU is its unclear boundaries. However, the symbolic visibility of the EU (the flag, the euro) has increased significantly, as has media reporting. As a result, the EU has become more "real" for people in their daily lives. In addition, the strength of identification with Europe remains unclear, but the limited evidence appears to suggest an "identity lite" with little "solidarity among (European) strangers."

The available empirical evidence from quantitative as well as qualitative studies suggests that Europeans on average are divided between a majority that holds Europeanized national identities, on the one hand, and a strong minority with exclusive nationalist identities, on the other. The former view Europe and the EU primarily in modern enlightenment terms. In contrast, a less open and less cosmopolitan narrative of Europe as a distinct historical and religious (Christian) entity is increasingly constructed as an alternative discourse, one that taps into widespread cultural identification patterns. This alternative view is strongly supported by exclusive nationalists. The next chapter takes a closer look at these discourses in selected member states with the aim of investigating in more detail the substantive content of Europeanized national identities.

3

MODERN EUROPE AND ITS DISCONTENTS

The Europeanization of Elite Identities

The previous chapter argued that European citizens are increasingly divided between those who identify with Europe at least to some extent ("inclusive nationalists") and those who exclusively identify with their nation-state ("exclusive nationalists"). In parallel to this cleavage, two distinct narratives concerning European identity exist. One discourse views Europe and the EU in modern terms as a product of enlightenment and modernity, while the other constructs a xenophobic, closed, and nationalist Europe. But who is doing the constructing? Political elites as well as intellectuals are primarily responsible for developing narratives linking national histories, memories, and symbols to European history, memory, and symbols (see Giesen 1993, 1999; Kaelble 2009, on intellectuals). In the following, I concentrate on political elites, since I am primarily interested in the political effects of the Europeanization of identity constructions. Political parties, for example, not only communicate with citizens about who best represents their interests and translate them into policies, they also engage in identity politics. They construct narratives about relevant political communities. In fact, "identity talk" is often used by political parties to connect to the citizens and to mobilize political support.

This chapter looks in more detail at elite discourses with the aim at demonstrating how the Europeanization (or lack thereof) of national identities works through communicative practices. I briefly examine political debates in five countries—Germany, Spain, France, Poland, and Great Britain—to show how Europe and the EU are linked (or not) to national identity constructions in various ways. This also serves to demonstrate empirically the various ways in which multiple identities relate to each other—cross-cutting, nested, or intertwined (see chapter 1).

As to *cross-cutting identities,* "professional Europeans," that is, those who deal with the EU on a daily basis as part of their job, constitute a prime example of such overlapping feelings of community. Members of the European Parliament (MEPs), for example, appear to express both a sense of belonging to Europe and to their party groups (Laffan 2004; Wodak 2004). Although party affiliation keeps them apart, attachment to Europe is widely shared across party lines. This is particularly true for the two main party families in the EP, namely the European People's Party (Christian Democrats) and the European Socialist Party (Social Democrats). Although these two party groups are divided along the Left-Right division, they usually share a vision of greater European integration.

In many EU member states, the picture is more complex in the sense that identification processes cut across both dimensions: party identification and attachment to Europe. Take France, for example. As the French referendum campaigns on the Constitutional Treaty revealed in 2005, the two main parties—the Socialists and former Gaullists (now Union pour un Mouvement Populaire [UMP])—are each divided between Euroskeptics and Euroenthusiasts.[1] The same holds true for Great Britain, even though Euroskeptics are much stronger among the Conservatives than among members of the Labour Party. In Germany, in contrast, the major parties are more or less united in their support for and identification with Europe and the EU. These divisions among elites on the European project are significant. As Liesbet Hooghe and Gary Marks show, the deeper the elite division in a country, the more exclusively national identities go together with opposition to European integration (Hooghe and Marks 2005, 426; see chapter 4).

But we can also see the presence of *nested identities* among European elites. A prime example concerns those "professional Europeans" whose job it is to both represent their country's interests in Brussels and to work toward common European solutions. COREPER, the Committee of Permanent Representatives, for example, is composed of "Janus-faced" national representatives who try both to further their respective national interests and to work toward the common European good (Lewis 1998, 2005). As a result, we can assume that their European and national identities are separate, but nested in each other.

Another example for nested identities appears to be "the Europeans," that is, those professional elites who identify strongly with Europe and whose attitudes have been analyzed by Neil Fligstein and David Green (Fligstein 2008; Green 2007; see chapter 2). This group prioritizes Europe over their national attachment. As David Green shows, "the Europeans" have a distinctively modern view

---

1. Things are even more complex. The French "Non" campaign on the left made it quite clear that it did not oppose European integration in general.

of Europe and the EU. In their view, the EU represents both peace and prosperity, as well as tolerance, diversity, multiculturalism, and a sense of common history (see Green 2007, chap. 5). Their vision of Europe resonates strongly with the identity narrative of a modern and enlightened Europe that is overcoming the nationalist and militarist tendencies of the past. This identity narrative has been constructed by many national political elites in an attempt to Europeanize their respective national identities.

This brings me to the final way of conceptualizing multiple identities, namely the concept of intertwined identities whereby national and European components mix and blend in some sort of "marble cake" model (see also Cram 2009). If the dominant narratives about the nation include Europe as part and parcel of it, national identification and attachment to Europe go together and blend into each other. If a "good Portuguese" equals a "good European," national and European identities resonate with each other and it should not make much of a difference whether citizens identify first with their nation-state or with Europe, as long as both identities are inclusive. If elites are unified in supporting European integration, they tend to construct national identities as resonating and compatible with Europe. I illustrate this point with regard to Germany and Spain. If elites are divided, however, identity talk is less useful to mobilize support for European integration. Identities might then become equally divisive, in which case the country faces an identity crisis. France serves as an example of elite divisions over Europe and French identity that gave way to an uneasy consensus on the Europeanization of French distinctiveness, followed once again by renewed elite divisions over what Europe means. Among the new member states, Poland represents a country still undergoing a profound identity crisis, resulting in deep elite divisions. Finally, if national identity narratives are stable, but do not include Europe, elites that support European integration cannot use them to bolster their claims. Great Britain and other Euroskeptic countries are prime examples of separate identities whereby Europe does not blend into national identity narratives.[2]

Germany's Past as the "Other": A European Germany

The German case is one of thorough and profound reconstruction of national identity following the catastrophe of World War II (for the following, see Engelmann-Martin 2002; Risse and Engelmann-Martin 2002). The complete

---

2. In the following, I use data from qualitative content analyses of parliamentary debates in the cases of France, Germany, and Great Britain (Risse 2001; Marcussen et al. 1999). With regard to Spain and Poland, I draw on secondary literature.

defeat and utter destruction of the German Reich turned out to be a blessing for the new Federal Republic of Germany. The national identity of postwar Germany—West *and* East—had to be constructed in sharp contrast to its nationalist and militarist past. Nazi Germany and the German Reich in general became postwar Germany's "other." West Germany's new identity constitutes a primary example of the marble cake model of intertwined identities, demonstrating how the reconstructed national identity blends into and integrates a European identity. Thomas Mann's dictum that "We do not want a German Europe, but a European Germany" quickly became the mantra of the post–World War II (West) German elites.[3] Since the 1950s, a fundamental consensus has emerged among the political elites and has been shared by public opinion that integration into the West in general and into Europe in particular was in West Germany's vital interest (Katzenstein 1997; Diez Medrano 2003, chap. 6; Doering-Manteuffel 1999).

In the following, I briefly discuss the identity constructions of West Germany's main party elites, which have dominated the political discourse of the Federal Republic. As for East Germany, the German Democratic Republic (GDR), its Communist party elites also engaged in distancing the country from the German past (Neller 2006). At the same time, however, West German capitalism and consumerism also served as East Germany's "other." German unification in 1989 and the accession of the GDR to the West German *Grundgesetz* ("Basic Law," the German constitution) put an end to this identity construction, which nevertheless occasionally emerges in debates about *ostalgia* (nostalgia for life in the former East Germany).

In the Federal Republic after 1945, the newly founded Christian Democratic Party (CDU) immediately embraced European unification as the alternative to the nationalism of the past. Christianity, democracy, and—later on—the social market economy became the three pillars on which a collective European identity was to be based. It was sharply distinguished from both the German nationalist and militarist past and from Soviet communism and Marxism. In other words, Germany's own past as well as communism constituted the "others" in this identity construction.

The Social Democratic Party (SPD), the main opposition party to Chancellor Konrad Adenauer's policies at the time, had been the first major German party to embrace the concept of a "United States of Europe" already in its 1925 Heidelberg Program. When the party was forced into exile during the Nazi period,

---

3. "For a European Germany, against a German Europe" was the subtitle of *Deutsche Blätter,* a journal edited by Germans in exile from the Nazis in Santiago, Chile from 1943 to 1946, to which Thomas Mann frequently contributed.

the leadership embraced the notion of a democratic European federation, which would almost naturally become a Socialist order. Consequently, when the SPD was refounded in 1946, Social Democrats viewed Europe, Germany, democracy, and socialism as almost identical concepts. Kurt Schumacher, the SPD's first postwar leader and a survivor of Nazi concentration camps, strongly promoted a "Europe as a third force" concept for the new German identity. He argued vigorously against the politics of Western integration, since it foreclosed prospects for the rapid reunification of the two Germanies (Paterson 1974; Rogosch 1996). Two major elections defeats later (1953 and 1957), the SPD changed course. Party officials such as Ernst Reuter (the legendary mayor of Berlin), Willy Brandt (subsequent mayor of Berlin who later became party chairman and chancellor), Fritz Erler, Herbert Wehner, and Helmut Schmidt (Brandt's successor as chancellor) had long supported closer relations with the United States as well as German integration into the West. These party leaders supported the identity construction of a modern European Germany as part of the Western community of liberal and democratic states. The changes culminated in the 1959 Godesberg Program (Bellers 1991; Rogosch 1996). At this point, the Westernization and Europeanization of the Federal Republic's postwar identity was complete (see Doering-Manteuffel 1999).

From the 1960s onward, an almost federalist consensus ("United States of Europe") prevailed among the German political elites that comprised the main parties from the center-right to the center-left. This consensus outlasted the changes in government from the CDU to the SPD in 1969, from the SPD to the CDU in 1982, the coming into power of the so-called 1968 generation in 1998 (the "red-green" coalition of Chancellor Gerhard Schröder and Foreign Minister Joschka Fischer), as well as the subsequent change toward a "grand coalition" in 2005 with Angela Merkel as the first chancellor from East Germany. More significant, German unification in 1990 did not result in a reconsideration of German European identity as expressed and formulated by the political, economic, social, and cultural elites. Germany did not reconsider its fundamental foreign policy orientations, since Germany's commitment to European integration had long outlived the context in which it had originally emerged (Banchoff 1999; Hellmann 1996; Katzenstein 1997; Rittberger 2001). In the aftermath of unification, the German government accelerated rather than slowed down its support for further progress in European integration. The different past and different memories of East German citizens had virtually no effect on elite identity constructions (on East German identity constructions, see, e.g., Diez Medrano 2003, chap. 7; Neller 2006).

This does not mean that European issues were never controversial in German politics. However, the identity construction of a European Germany meant that debates about European issues could never reach a point where European integration as such could be called into question. The story of Germany giving up its beloved deutsche mark in favor of the euro, the single currency, is instructive in this regard (for the following, see Risse et al. 1999).[4] As I discuss in more detail in chapter 8, there was considerable domestic opposition to the single currency and mass public opinion was deeply divided. Among the political parties, the Bavarian Christian Social Union as well as some Social Democrats, among them Gerhard Schröder, expressed concerns about the euro. Yet, Chancellor Helmut Kohl managed to thwart the opposition by reminding everyone that Germany was at the forefront of European integration and that, therefore, a "good German" as a good European had to support the euro. He easily won the debate by linking the introduction of the euro to German European identity.

The German European consensus went hand in hand with a peculiar identity construction in the aftermath of World War II. The notion of what constitutes the "other" was related to European and German nationalist history. Germany's own nationalist and militarist past constituted the "other" in the process of "post-national" identity formation whereby Europeanness replaces traditional notions of national identity. Nowadays, a "good German" equals a "good European" supporting a united Europe. "Europe" in this identity construction stands for a stable peaceful order overcoming the continent's bloody past, for democracy and human rights (in contrast to European—and German—autocratic history), as well as for a social market economy including the welfare state (in contrast to both Soviet communism and Anglo-Saxon "laissez-faire" capitalism; see Bellers and Winking 1991; Katzenstein 1997).

Thus, the Europeanization of German identity embraces the modern and enlightened vision of Europe and the EU. This vision remains consensual among all major political parties to this day. The countervision of a nationalist and xenophobic "fortress Europe" has not (yet) reached German elite discourse, partly because the Christian Democrats have so far been able to fight off any populist right-wing party on the national level. It remains to be seen whether the new populist left-wing party Die Linke (The Left), a merger of West German leftist groups and remnants of the former East German communists, will start exploiting the considerable Euroskepticism in German public opinion (Dolezal 2008).

In sum, Germany represents a case of a comprehensive transformation of pre–World War II nationalism in a modern postwar identity. German European identity is also a prime example of an elite consensus that supports the vision

---

4. Note that the decision by the Kohl government in favor of a single currency was not linked to unification, as some observers have argued. As Andrew Moravcsik shows in detail, the German decision to give up the deutsche mark had been taken prior to unification (Moravcsik 1998).

of modern and enlightened Europe amalgamating with the self-image of post–World War II Germany. The reconstruction of the German identity incorporated "Europe" and the "West" into what "modern Germany" means. Although the Europeanization of German identity was contested throughout the 1950s, it became consensual afterward, partly because it suited the instrumental power interests of political elites. Although the need to distance the country from the German past of nationalism and militarism (the "European other") is starting to recede into the background, the identity construction of a European Germany has remained stable. A study comparing identity constructions of young Germans with those of senior citizens revealed virtually no difference in the degree of identification with Europe. While Europe and the EU are realities of daily life for the younger generation, the German past as the European "other" is still very relevant for older citizens (Fondermann 2006).

It is important to note that the European integration process did not create the German postwar identity. Rather, it reinforced and stabilized it by demonstrating that Germany could prosper economically and gain political clout in Europe through a policy of "self-binding" to European institutions. German Europatriotism deeply affected elite perceptions of the country's national interests and attitudes toward European integration.

Europeanization as Modernization: Spanish European Identity

Like Germany, Spain is a case of the reconstruction of national identity by incorporating Europe into understandings of what constitutes modern Spain (for details, see, e.g., Diez Medrano 2003, chap. 5; Diez Medrano and Gutiérrez 2001). As in the German case, European Spain's "other" is the country's own past of authoritarian dictatorship, by Generalissimo Francisco Franco in this case. Spain's post-Franco identity also serves to illustrate the marble cake model of intertwined identities, since Europe has been thoroughly incorporated into modern Spain's national identity.

This modern Spanish identity cannot be understood without taking into account that Franco ruled Spain for more than thirty-five years, from 1939 to 1975. While Germany was "present at the creation" of postwar European integration, Spain was not and could not enter the European Community until 1986, after its return to democracy. The emerging European Community had a profound effect on Spain, even during Franco's regime, strongly contributing to its erosion.

Franco tried to combine economic modernization and authoritarianism. The emergence of the European Economic Community made it impossible for him simply to reject Europe. Thus, he tried to walk a fine line between embracing Europe as an economic modernization project, on the one hand, and rejecting its political values, on the other. Franco encouraged identification with European economic progress (from which Spain benefited through its 1970 commercial treaty with the European Community), but claimed *"España es diferente"* (Spain is different) with regard to its political institutions (see Diez Medrano and Gutiérrez 2001; Jáuregui 1999, 276–80).

But there had always been a liberal tradition in Spanish identity constructions that equated modernization with Europeanization and the latter with democracy and human rights, that is, a genuinely anti-Franquist project. European integration provided an opportunity structure for the opposition against Franco, which linked Spain's liberal tradition to that of the modern political Europe. As Jáuregui put it, "As the legitimacy of his [Franco's] dictatorship eroded over the years, 'Europeanization' increasingly became a fundamental component of the national we-image defended and promoted by all those Spaniards who opposed the regime and demanded political change" (Jáuregui 1999, 274). Throughout Franco's regime, two identity constructions clashed. On the one hand, Spain was constructed as an immutable social hierarchy based upon the Crown, the Catholic Church, and the aristocracy, erected against the (European) forces of secularism and, during the cold war, Communism. On the other hand, Spain's future was seen in Europe, and Spanish *atraso* (backwardness) was to be overcome by entering the integration process and fully embracing political modernization (Jáuregui 1999, 274–80; Diez Medrano and Gutiérrez 2001).

When Spanish democracy was restored during the late 1970s through a negotiated transition (*transición pactada*), the latter constructions quickly achieved hegemony in the discourses of the Spanish elites. In this context, Franquism became the "other" of the new Spanish Europeanness. It was equated with backwardness and isolationism, as expressed in this quote by a Catalan civil servant: "One of Spain's problems is that changes that take place in Europe have always arrived late. If we are inside [the European Union] changes will take place at the same speed, or at least will not arrive so late" (quoted in Diez Medrano 2003, 159). Europeanization in post-Franco Spain meant to overcome this backwardness and to catch the train to modernity. Europeanization equaled both economic and political modernization. As in the German case, post-Franco Spain was constructed as incorporating the European project of modernization, not only economically but also politically with regard to human rights, the rule of law, and democracy. Entering the European Union in the mid-1980s meant a "return to Europe" in identity terms similar to the application by the Central Eastern European countries over a decade later. Spanish post-Franco identity incorporated Europe and the EU as a Western modernization project in much the same way as in Germany during the 1960s when the new German European identity assumed hegemonic status. The difference in Spain was that most post-Franquist democratic parties—whether Left or Right—joined the identity consensus (with the exception of the *Izquierda Unida,* the party of the United Left; see Ruiz Jimenez 2002). Strongly influenced by the West German Social Democrats and its Friedrich Ebert Foundation, the Spanish Socialist Party (PSOE) never adopted a "third way" rhetoric with regard to Europe, but fully embraced the concept of European integration as a Western modernization project.

Today, Spanish national identity and identification with Europe as a political and economic modernization project coexist easily. A study of attitudes toward the euro showed, for example, that the single currency was regarded as a symbol of this modernization project. In fact, support for the euro was much stronger among those Spaniards who identified with Europe than among those who expected economic gains or professed knowledge of its immediate consequences (Luna-Arocas et al. 2001). At the same time, Spanish regionalism also correlates positively with pro-European attitudes. Strong regional identities are anti-Madrid, but pro-European. Basque and Catalan nationalism are cases in point (see Ruiz Jimenez 2002).

Identification with Europe as a political and economic modernization project has become part and parcel of what is considered modern and post-Franquist Spain. European integration certainly contributed to the Europeanization of Spanish identity, since it confronted Franquist Spain with the reality and the possibilities of political modernity. This facilitated Spanish entry into the EU in 1986 insofar as the new Spanish identity was fully compatible with Europe and the EU, which then reinforced and consolidated the Spanish transition to democracy (see Pridham and Lewis 1996).

Europe as France Writ Large? The Contested Europeanization of French Identity

Europeanizing French identity has been a much tougher call than integrating Europe into the collective narratives of German and Spanish identities. The Europeanization of German and Spanish identities came about during critical junctures in which the two countries returned to democracy and, as a result, its elites had to construct new identity narratives. In both cases, Europe and European integration were quickly integrated into what it meant to be a post-Nazi German or a post-Franco Spaniard who had overcome their country's dark ages.

The French experience of the quintessential *l'état nation* (nation-state) has been different (see Hayward 2007 for a historical discussion). France could always claim to have been the birthplace of human rights and democracy as a result of which modernity as Republicanism has been deeply enshrined in national identity constructions and predated the post–World War II period (even though this narrative overlooks Napoléon and—in the twentieth century—the collaboration of the Vichy regime with the Nazis). French political elites of both the interwar and the post–World War II periods could always refer to Republican values as enshrined in the concept of *l'état nation* (see Roscher 2003 for the following). In other words, modernity, secularism, and enlightenment have been and continue to be identified with the French nation-state itself rather than Europe. It took quite some time before French national identity became ready for Europe. It is still incomplete and contested.

During the 1950s and in conjunction with the first efforts toward European integration, a national debate took place that concerned French identity and basic political orientations in the postwar era. World War II and the German occupation were traumatic experiences, as a result of which French identity became deeply problematic and contested. Most controversies focused on how to deal with Germany as the most significant French "other" at the time. As Craig Parsons has argued convincingly, three visions of France, Germany, and Europe that partially cut across party lines emerged and competed in the discourses of the French elites (Parsons 2003). A traditional nationalist group—particularly Charles de Gaulle and his supporters, but also parts of the French left—defended French sovereignty and supported a strategy of counterbalancing Germany. Others supported a confederal model of loose intergovernmental cooperation in a Europe of nation-states led by France and Great Britain that contained Germany. Only a minority of Christian Democrats (among them Robert Schumann and Jean Monnet) and Socialists (e.g., Guy Mollet) were in favor of a community model of European integration. As Mollet put it in 1947, "The only means to disinfect the German people from Nazism and to democratize it is to surround Germany in a democratic Europe" (Mollet 1947). Although Robert Schumann and political allies succeeded in winning French support for the European Coal and Steel Community (ECSC) in the early 1950s, the defeat of the treaty on the European Defense Community in the French National Assembly in 1954 showed the divisions among the political elites. French identity was deeply contested at the time, with Germany serving as the "French other."

The war in Algeria and the ongoing crisis of the Fourth Republic served as another "critical juncture" for French national identity. When the Fifth Republic came into being in 1958, its founding father, President de Gaulle, reconstructed French identity and managed to reunite a deeply divided nation around a common vision of the French role in the world: "When one is the Atlantic cape of the continent, when one has planted one's flag in all parts of the world, when one spreads ideas, and when one opens oneself to the environment, in short, when one is France, one cannot escape the grand movements on the ground" (De Gaulle 1950). De Gaulle's identity construction related to historical myths of Frenchness and combined them in a unique way. The notion of sovereignty—understood as national independence from outside interference together with a sense of uniqueness (*grandeur*)—was used to build a bridge between postrevolutionary Republican France and the prerevolutionary monarchy. This understanding of the French *l'état-nation* encompassed the identity of the nation and democracy as well as the identity of French society with the Republic. Finally, de Gaulle reintroduced the notion of French exceptionalism and uniqueness in terms of a civilizing mission for the world (*mission civilisatrice*) destined to spread the universal values of enlightenment and of the French Revolution.

Of course, these self-understandings could not easily adjust to Europe, let alone integrate Europe into the national identity constructions in a way similar to Germany or Spain. Rather, the confederal model of "*l'Europe des nations*" became the battle cry during de Gaulle's presidency with little need to Europeanize French identity. At the same time, however, the Treaty of Rome and the process of European integration created institutional facts on the ground as a result of which the traditional sovereigntist model of France in the world started clashing with the realities, even for Gaullists (Parsons 2003, chap. 4).

The specific Gaullist identity construction only remained consensual among the political elites for about another ten years after de Gaulle's resignation. Beginning in the late 1970s, Europeanization gradually transformed French identity in conjunction with two crises—the failure of President François Mitterrand's economic policies in the early 1980s and the end of the cold war in the late 1980s (Flynn 1995; Schmidt 1996; Parsons 2003, chap. 5). When Mitterrand and the Socialist Party came to power in 1981, they initially embarked on a project of creating democratic socialism in France based on leftist Keynesianism. This project utterly failed and, in 1983, Mitterrand had practically no choice but to change course dramatically if he wanted to remain in power (Bauchard 1986; Uterwedde 1988). This political change led to a deep identity crisis within the Socialist Party, which then gradually moved toward ideas once derisively labeled "Social Democratic" (see also Guérot 1996). In changing course, the party followed President Mitterrand who had defined the construction of the European Community as a central issue of his time in office: "*Tout se rejoint, notre patrie, notre Europe, l'Europe notre patrie*" (Mitterrand 1986, 15).[5] The reorientation

---

5. "Everything comes together, our fatherland, our Europe, Europe our fatherland."

of the French Socialists went hand in hand with a change in attitudes toward European integration as a whole (also Schmidt 2007).

The Parti Socialiste's move toward Europe included an effort to reconstruct French identity. The French Socialists started highlighting the common European historical and cultural heritage. They increasingly argued that the French future was to be found in Europe: "France is our fatherland, Europe is our future" (Mitterrand 1992). The French left started embracing the notion of a "European France," extending the vision of the French *mission civilisatrice* toward Europe writ large. The peculiar historical and cultural legacies of France were transferred from the "first nation-state" in Europe to the continent as a whole, because all European states were seen as children of enlightenment, democracy, and Republicanism. France was to imprint its mark on Europe. This identity construction uses traditional understandings of Frenchness and the French state and extends them to Europe. It incorporates Europe into one's own collective national identity and its understandings about sovereignty and political order. French identity is transformed but only to the degree that ideas about Europe can be incorporated into and resonate with previous visions of the state. Of course, this version of French Europeanness embraced—once again—the identity narrative of a modern, secular, and enlightened Europe.

Similar changes in the prevailing visions of European order and reconstructions of French nation-state identity took place on the French right, albeit later. The heir to Charles de Gaulle's visions, the Rassemblement pour la République (RPR, now part of the Union pour un Mouvement Populaire, UMP), provides another example of the French political elite changing course. The end of the cold war constituted the "critical juncture" in this case, leading to a severe identity crisis. When the Berlin wall came down, Germany united, and the post–cold war European security order was constructed, France—*la grande nation*—remained largely on the sidelines. As a result, parts of the political elite realized that *grandeur* and *indépendence* were illusions. The way out was Europe (Flynn 1995; Parsons 2003, chap. 7). The political debates surrounding the referendum on the Maastricht Treaties in 1992 led to identity-related discourses about the new role of France in Europe and the world after the end of the cold war. As in the 1950s, fear of German power dominated the debates. This time, however, supporters of European integration prevailed.

In a fashion similar to President Mitterrand, the French center-right gradually incorporated Europe into notions of French distinctiveness and started identifying the future of France as a nation-state with European order. As President Jacques Chirac put it in a speech at the European Parliament in 2002, "To build and perfect Europe in the 21st century is to pursue France's great adventure ... to make the great voice of France heard: it will spread afar these high standards and these Republican values to which our compatriots are so deeply attached" (quoted from Schmidt 2007, 13). Chirac used the old Gaullist identity concepts of *grandeur* and Republicanism and extended them to Europe as France writ large. Presidents Mitterrand, Chirac, and even Nicolas Sarkozy when he entered office embraced the modern vision of Europe. In contrast to Germany and Spain, however, French European identity was constructed not in opposition to the past, but as a sort of extension of French Republicanism into Europe and the EU. As Klaus Roscher has convincingly argued, it was only a matter of time before this identity construction of a French Europe rather than a European France clashed with the reality of European integration, which was no longer dominated by French grand designs, if it ever was (Roscher 2003).

However, the Europeanization of French identity has remained unsettled and contested, particularly as far as the vision of a modern and Republican Europe was concerned. Groups on both sides of the political spectrum continue to use a distinct nationalist identity discourse to this day. As Philippe Séguin, the leader of the Gaullist opposition in the referendum campaign on the Maastricht Treaties, put it in 1992: "Europe buries the concept of national sovereignty and the grand principles of the Revolution: 1992 is literally the anti-1789" (quoted in Schild 2008, 11, n. 6). On the extreme right, the populist Front National developed its own discourse on Europe and the EU. Its leader, Jean-Marie Le Pen, became one of the first on the populist Right in Europe to articulate its own vision of Europe, in stark opposition to modern and enlightened Europe (Holmes 2000, 2009). The Front National fully embraced an antimodern, sovereigntist, xenophobic, and exclusionary vision of the EU that should also preserve the different national cultures and heritages (see also Riedel 2008, 14–16). In other words, the French far-right did not simply promote an anti-EU agenda but also began early on to set a counterpoint to the modern vision of the EU articulated by the majority of French Socialists and later on by the center-right. A counternarrative emerged in the French discourse that promoted a nationalist and exclusionary Europe against the vision of modern and enlightened Europe (see chapter 10).

During the early 2000s, French identity and its relation to Europeanness remained unsettled. On the French right including large factions of the former Gaullist party and the Front National on the extreme right, "fortress Europe" as a bulwark against liberalism, multiculturalism, and cultural globalization became the main battle cry. On the French left, the Socialist Party split down the middle with a large group calling for a "social Europe" as an alternative to economic globalization. The deep divisions among the French elites about the European project became obvious during the referendum debates in 2005 on the Constitutional Treaty, which the "no" campaign ultimately won (Schild 2008; Von Oppeln 2005; Schmidt 2007; Ross 2006). Since then, French identity between a modern

European France, on the one hand, and a backward-looking "sovereign France in a fortress Europe," on the other hand, remains deeply contested. As a result, the 2007 presidential campaign between Nicolas Sarkozy and Segolène Royal was full of rhetoric about French identity and France's place in Europe and the world. The debate is far from settled. This is documented by the fact that France, under President Sarkozy, has a Ministry of Immigration, Integration, National Identity, and Supportive [sic!] Development (Développement Solidaire). If a minister is in charge of national identity, the French probably face an identity crisis.

In sum, the French case demonstrates the difficulties of incorporating Europe into identity constructions that are deeply embedded in historical memories of exceptionalism, national glory, and the nation-state. The Europeanization of French identity that gradually emerged through various critical junctures leading to identity crises—first on the left, later on the Gaullist right—led to a vision of Europe as a somewhat greater version of France. From French exceptionalism to European exceptionalism, from a French *mission civilisatrice* to a European one—these appeared to be the only ways in which French elites could make Europe resonate with French identity constructions. Although the Europeanization of French identity would have been unthinkable without European integration, it remains deeply contested. French identity is caught between two competing visions of Europe, a modern Europe as "Republican France writ large" and a "nationalist fortress Europe" that stands against the forces of multiculturalism as well as economic and cultural globalization.

Between Europe and Nationalism: Poland

"Return to Europe!" This was the battle cry of the Solidarnosc movement and its supporters from Adam Michnik to the late Pope John Paul II during the turbulent years of 1989–90 and beyond. For the first time since 1939, when the Nazis occupied the country, and since 1945, when a Communist regime was installed by the Soviet Union, Poland became fully sovereign again. In the immediate aftermath of the end of the cold war, the Polish discourse constructed Europe as the country's natural place. In fact, as Krystyna Romaniszyn and Jacek Nowak point out, "return to Europe" was put in quotation marks, since Poles believed that they formed "an integral part of the European West, at times paying the highest price, of their lives, for Europe" (Romaniszyn and Nowak 2002, 23). Why would one "return" to Europe when one always belonged to the center of the continent?

At the same time, the Polish identity discourse is well aware of the fact that Poland has been denied its rightful place in the middle of Europe for centuries

(Romaniszyn and Nowak 2002; Case 2009). Polish history is constructed in this context as one of victimization. During the nineteenth and twentieth centuries, Poland had been the victim of the surrounding powers more than once. From the Polish partitions of the eighteenth and nineteenth centuries to the occupation by the Germans during World War II and subsequent Communist rule, the historical narrative is one in which Poland has never been sovereign and able to determine its own fate. The end of the cold war represented the first opportunity in centuries in which Poland was not only free but could also make its own choices. The natural choice was Europe, which represented modernity, freedom, and democracy and, thus, the fulfillment of Polish aspirations. As in the cases of post-Nazi Germany and post-Franco Spain, the EU as a modernization project prevailed in the post-Communist Polish discourse. As a result, the new Poland had to be firmly anchored in the West, through accession to the North Atlantic Treaty Organization (NATO) and the EU. In this identity construction, the "other" of Polish European identity is Poland's past as a victim of the great powers. The similarities to German post–World War II and Spanish post-Franco identity constructions are striking. It is also significant that the Polish elites embraced the modern vision of Europe and the EU immediately after the end of the cold war. This narrative of modernity, freedom, and democracy resonated with a Romantic understanding of the Polish nation dating back to the nineteenth century, which combined a nation-state with a multiethnic society and was reminiscent of the Polish Commonwealth from the fifteenth century to the Polish partitions of the late eighteenth century (Romaniszyn and Nowak 2002).

This identity discourse dominated much of the 1990s and paved the way for the Polish application for EU membership, Polish entry into NATO, and the renewed cooperative relationship with Germany, whose subsequent governments—from Chancellors Kohl to Schröder to Angela Merkel—all worked hard to facilitate Poland's entry into the union.

Yet, there has also been a counterdiscourse that became increasingly salient during the early 2000s and is now competing with a "Poland in modern Europe" discourse.[6] This narrative also dates back to the nineteenth century, but it is characterized by an exclusive rather than an inclusive nationalism that originated at a time when the Polish state did not exist. In the nineteenth century Polish nationalism constructed Poland as an ethnic and cultural whole. This version of Polish nationalism conceives of the Polish state as a bulwark against

---

6. For the following, see Adamczyk and Gostmann 2007; Krzyzanowski 2003, 2008; Case 2009; Lipinski 2010; Hahn 2007.

foreign powers, resulting from liberation struggles against foreign occupation and deserving full sovereignty against foreign intrusion.

Thus, there are two visions of Poland: a modern, liberal Poland that forms an integral part of an equally modern Europe, on the one hand, and a nationalist Poland that has to be defended against foreign intrusion in order to preserve its culture and way of life, on the other hand. The two visions compete with each other to this day and permeate the elite debates. Interestingly enough, Polish attachment to Catholicism is orthogonal to both identity constructions. Adherents of either vision of Poland refer to Catholic values to make their claims. The Polish Catholic Church including the late Pope John Paul II strongly favored Polish EU membership, while right-wing Catholic media such as Radio Maryja or the nationalist journal *Nasz Dziennik* led the movement against EU membership.

The two visions of Polish identity are reflected in mass public opinion. In general, Polish identification with Europe is well within the range of other EU member states (see chapter 2). For example, 2004 data show that Polish public opinion ranks a little below the EU average in the degree to which people see themselves as European (if only as a secondary identity), but well above the average of the new member states. An analysis by Clare McManus-Czubinska et al. shows in detail similar features for Polish public opinion as for European public opinion in general (McManus-Czubinska et al. 2003; also Kucia 1999). The main cleavage in Polish public opinion is, once again, between those who identify exclusively with their nation-state and those who hold Europe as a secondary identity. The latter also express more modern views about political life, are more cosmopolitan, comparatively better educated, and better informed about politics. In contrast, exclusive nationalists mostly come from rural areas and belong to the poorer part of the population. They fear that the EU will not only destroy their economic livelihood but also their national identity and cultural heritage. In short, Polish mass public attitudes do not differ much from the rest of Europe.

On the level of elites, the competing identity constructions came to the fore during the two most recent debates about the EU, the controversies surrounding EU membership during the 2000s, and the most recent discussions about the Constitutional Treaty.[7] At least three camps can be distinguished here. First, "Euroenthusiasts" (Romaniszyn and Nowak 2002, 23) used the "return to Europe" narrative to make their point. For them, the EU constituted a unique opportunity to firmly anchor the new Poland in the West, to overcome the legacies of both Communism and Nazism, and to join the modern community of democratic

---

7. For the following, see Biegon 2006; Hahn 2007; Kutter 2007; Lipinski 2010; Adamczyk and Gostmann 2007; Krzyzanowski 2008.

societies. This identity discourse resembles the respective constructions of German, Spanish, and French liberal elites embracing the vision of modern Europe, but it also resonates with a liberal reading of Polish history from the nineteenth century to the present. Polish Europeanness, thus, represents another example of intertwined identities. Interestingly enough, both the Democratic Left Alliance, the successor party of the Polish communists, and the Civic Platform, which formed from the remnants of the Solidarnosc movement, embrace this vision of a modern European Poland.

A second group did not use much identity talk, but constructed Polish EU membership as an inevitable necessity given the forces of globalization. The EU would guarantee the necessary modernization of the Polish economy. The conservative Law and Justice Party of the Kaczynski brothers represents a good example of this discourse, which emphasizes Polish interests in the EU and pledges to fight hard to preserve Polish sovereignty against intrusions from Brussels. Law and Justice embraces an intergovernmental vision of Europe that closely resembles the Gaullist "Europe of fatherlands."

Third, the equally determined "no camp" primarily used the narrative of Polish nationalism as the victim of foreign powers. Poland, which had been occupied by Germany and the Soviet Union for much of the twentieth century and had paid an enormous price for its freedom, is finally a sovereign state. It should stick to its sovereignty and not surrender it to Brussels and the EU. Polish opponents of EU membership often equated "Brussels" with "Moscow" as symbols of foreign rule and domination. This identity narrative also constructed European "secularism" as incompatible with traditional Polish values, particularly Catholicism. In this identity discourse, European and Polish identities are incompatible. Self Defence, the League of Polish Families, and the Peasant Party on the right promote such an exclusionary and nationalist discourse, which strongly resembles the visions and ideas of other Euroskeptical parties across the EU (Lipinski 2010).

Although the Polish people overwhelmingly voted for EU membership in a referendum, the debate was not settled at all. Once Poland had entered the EU in 2004, the uneasy relationship between Poland and Europe reemerged again in the elite discourses surrounding the (failed) Constitutional Treaty and the Lisbon Treaty (see, e.g., Mach and Pozarlik 2008). Two identity-related issues dominated the debate. The first related to whether a reference to God should be included in the European constitution.[8] Polish Euroenthusiasts as well as nationalists saw

---

8. It is interesting to note in this context that the Polish Constitution itself—after a long struggle—referred to "both those who believe in God" as well as to "those not sharing such faith." Quoted from Kutter 2007, 10.

it as their mission to anchor Christian values in the enlarged European Union. As Polish newspaper headlines put it, "A Constitution with God" and "Polish God in Europe" (quoted in Kutter 2007, 11). The fight over references to God was labeled another "great Kulturkampf," alluding to the clash between the German Reich under Chancellor Otto von Bismarck and the Catholic Church in the late nineteenth century. Of course, the Polish attempt met with firm resistance by other—more secular—EU member states including France and finally failed. When the Constitutional Treaty was replaced by the Lisbon Treaty in 2007, the issue was put to rest. In this particular case, the Polish collective identity as a Catholic country clashed head-on with the vision of a modern and secular Europe (Ramet 2006a).

The second issue on the agenda with identity-related undertones concerned the number of Polish votes in the European Council of Ministers. The Polish government fought hard to prevent the double majority formula, which puts Poland at a slight disadvantage compared to qualified majority voting under the Treaty of Nice.[9] The justification for this attempt to retain some more votes in the EU Council of Ministers was loaded with identity arguments from the beginning. The struggle was framed as another instance of Polish fights for independence (*niepodległość*) and sovereignty against the dominance of European great powers (read: Germany). The Polish government portrayed itself as fighting the good fight on behalf of all smaller EU member states, standing up to the "French-German axis" in the EU. The slogan by a right-wing Polish member of parliament, Jan Rokita, "Nice or death!" was an attempt to further dramatize the issue, which culminated in the remark by Polish Prime Minister Jarosław Kaczynski, during the run-up to the EU Brussels summit of June 2007, that Poland would have many more votes in the Council of Ministers if the Germans had not killed millions of Poles during World War II and the Holocaust. These and other statements illustrate a Polish nationalist identity construction that connects Poland's fate as a victim of European powers, namely Germany and Russia, to its heroic struggles for freedom, understood as independence and sovereignty. Further European integration is, of course, incompatible with these expressions of nationalism.

The emerging Polish anti-EU discourse based on an exclusive nationalist identity construction, according to which European integration and Polish

---

9. According to the Lisbon Treaty, decisions in the Council of Ministers are to be taken by 55% of the member states representing at least 65% of the EU's population when qualified majority voting applies. Under the Treaty of Nice's qualified majority voting rules, each member state was allocated a certain number of votes in the Council, roughly proportionate to its population. Note, however, that the Council of Ministers almost never votes formally. Thus, the dispute about the voting rules was rather symbolic.

sovereignty as well as Catholicism are incompatible, represents the Polish version of the antimodernist and antiglobalization discourse put forward by the French conservatives and right-wing parties. In the case of the Polish conservative elites, there is not much space for even "fortress Europe." Here, loyalty to Poland and identification with Europe and the EU are incompatible and separate.

In sum, Polish post-Communist identity in the new Europe remains unsettled and deeply contested. On the one hand and similar to related identity narratives in Germany, Spain, and France, the immediate post-Communist liberal Polish identity was seen as an intrinsic part of the Europe of enlightenment and modernity to which Poland "returned." On the other hand, a Polish nationalist identity also emerged and became stronger after Poland's entry into the EU, which connected to nineteenth-century Polish nationalism and constructed Poland as the defender of independence, sovereignty, Catholicism, and cultural values against the great powers and the forces of modernity and secularism. Like France, Poland remains a case of deeply contested identities, which demonstrates once again that old and new EU member states do not differ much when it comes to identity narratives and the related conflicts.

Europe as Britain's "Other"

So far, I have discussed two cases of thorough Europeanization of national identities following regime change and ruptures with the past (Germany and Spain) and two cases (France and Poland) in which European identities remain deeply contested, with competing visions of a modern and secular EU, on the one hand, and of a nationalist Europe or old-fashioned nationalism, on the other. Each of the four countries have undergone profound identity changes since World War II. In contrast, the United Kingdom represents a case of an almost uncontested national identity that has remained remarkably stable in its resistance to Europeanization over the past fifty years. It also represents a case in which EU membership made virtually no difference for identity change (the following is based on Knopf 2003; Diez Medrano 2003, chap. 8). British identity, Englishness in particular, and European identity remain separate.

More than thirty years after entry into the European Community, Britain is still regarded as "of rather than in" Europe; it remains the "awkward partner" and "semi-detached" from Europe (Bailey 1983; George 1994). This is also true for the major divisions among and within the two main parties, the Conservatives and Labour. British views on European integration essentially range from those who objected to British entry into the EC in the first place and who now oppose further European integration (the right wing of the Conservatives, the far left of

Labour) to a mainstream group within both main parties that supports EU membership in a "Europe of nation-states." European federalists remain a minority in the political discourse and are largely confined to the Liberal Democrats (on these divisions, see also Diez 1999). The general approach has not changed since the 1950s, as expressed in a famous quote from British prime minister Winston Churchill: "Where do we stand? We are not members of the European Defence Community, nor do we intend to be merged in a Federal European system. We feel we have a special relation to both. This can be expressed by prepositions, by the preposition 'with' but not 'of'"—we are with them, but not of them. We have our own Commonwealth and Empire" (Churchill 1953, 895).

The most interesting feature of the British elite discourse with regard to identity-related issues concerns the fact that it predominantly uses *English* identity constructions that date back to the late eighteenth century, when Englishness was conceived in sharp contrast to European, namely French, culture (see Diez Medrano 2003, 215–16). Originally, this identity construction was attached to the imperial project of the British Empire. With decolonization, notions of sovereignty gradually became dominant in these discourses. "Europe" continues to be identified with the Continent and to be perceived as "the other" in contrast to Englishness. It is worth noting in this context that English identity as a "non-European" identity has to be clearly separated from other regional identities in Britain, particularly Scottish and Welsh. Not unlike Catalan identity, Scottish nationalism has been constructed in sharp contrast to English identity and, as a result, has embraced Europe and Europeanness (Keating 1996; Ichijo 2004; Jolly 2007; Kumar 2003). Nevertheless, it is striking that our analysis of parliamentary speeches in the House of Commons from the 1950s to the 1990s revealed virtually no trace of identity discourses with regard to Europe that differed from constructions of "English = British" identities (Knopf 2003; Marcussen et al. 1999).

The social construction of "Englishness" comprises meanings attached to institutions, historical memory, and symbols. Each of these components is hard to reconcile with a vision of European political order that extends beyond intergovernmentalism (Lyon 1991; Schauer 1996; Schmitz and Geserick 1996). Institutions such as the Parliament and the Crown form important elements of this collective identity. The identity-related meanings attached to these institutions center around peculiar understandings of national sovereignty. The Crown in this context symbolizes "external sovereignty," which is then related to British history as independence from Rome and the pope as well as from the European continent since 1066. Parliamentary or "internal" sovereignty represents a most important constitutional principle and relates to a seven-hundred-year-old parliamentary tradition and hard-fought victories over the king. Here, sovereignty is directly connected to understandings of what constitutes democracy. English sovereignty is, thus, directly linked to narratives about a continuous history of liberal and democratic evolution and "free-born Englishmen." As a result, British objections to transferring sovereignty to European supranational institutions are often justified on grounds that such institutions lack democratic—meaning parliamentary—accountability. If sovereignty and democratic accountability are so intimately linked, however, understandings of Europe and the EU simply do not resonate with these narratives—in contrast to French Republicanism, which was deliberately Europeanized by French elites during the 1980s and the 1990s.

How do British collective identity constructions relate to general attitudes toward the EC/EU? In this regard, the picture is fairly consistent. In the 1950s, Britain did not join the European Economic Community (EEC) and instead created EFTA, the European Free Trade Association, because it opposed the political project of European integration. It nevertheless applied for membership later, but for pragmatic rather than for principled reasons (George 1992, 40). This pragmatism has characterized British policies in the EU ever since it joined. It is not surprising, therefore, that London remained "semi-detached" and on the sidelines whenever the EU took major steps toward further integration. The Single European Act is the one and only exception, while the decisions not to join the euro, not to participate in Schengenland and the removal of border controls, to opt out of the Charter of Fundamental Rights, and the continuous British objections to the supranationalization of foreign and security policy fit the bill. Until today, the United Kingdom has in fact embraced a "Europe à la carte."

As a result, to the extent that there is a pro-EU discourse in Britain, political leaders such as Prime Ministers Tony Blair or Gordon Brown have routinely used interest, rather than identity-based, language to legitimize European policies. In the case of the single currency, for example, the idea that Britain might join the euro eventually has always been justified on strictly economic grounds—in contrast to Germany, where Chancellor Kohl linked the euro to European Germany to silence any opposition (see Risse et al. 1999). In contrast, identity narratives are left to British nationalists and Euroskeptics, which also are the dominant voices in the media (see chapters 6 and 7). There have rarely been attempts by British elites to actively construct a British identity in Europe. Europeanization of identities has not reached the British isles.

In sum, Britain is a case of separate identity. English identity seems to be hardly affected by European integration and Europe is still largely constructed as the, albeit friendly, "other." It is no wonder that British citizens regularly express fears that the EU will harm and even destroy their national identity (see Diez Medrano 2003, 238). Survey data corroborate this finding and show that British identity is negatively correlated with measurements of European identity (Cinnirella 1997). This is not to suggest that English nationalism altogether resembles the exclusionary and xenophobic nationalism that can be found among the right-wing parties on the Continent. Rather, most versions of British/English identity are firmly wedded to modern, enlightened, and multicultural visions of Britain. In this sense, they resemble pre-Europeanized French national identities. Yet, there is not much space for Europe and the EU in British identity so far.

Conclusions

These short country case studies serve to demonstrate efforts by national elites to Europeanize their respective national identities by making these narratives resonate with European symbols, historical memories, and cultural as well as political values—except for the United Kingdom. In the cases of Germany, Spain, France, and Poland, liberal political elites—both center-right and center-left—constructed intertwined and amalgamated identities (the "marble cake" model) whereby the modern and enlightened vision of Europe and the EU were incorporated into narratives about national identity. In the German and Spanish cases, it is impossible today to describe national identities without mentioning Europe. French elites have also been active over the past twenty years in making Europe resonate with French ideas about Republicanism and *grandeur*. In contrast, Polish political elites struggle over what constitutes Polishness and whether and how Europe and the EU fit in. The Europeanization of national identities usually occurred after crises and critical junctures, such as World War II (Germany), regime change (Spain and Poland), or policy failures (France). Great Britain remains the only exception of a modern, democratic, and multicultural national identity that embraces "European values" without becoming European. A Europeanization of English identity did not take place.

The analysis also showed the various "others" in European identity constructions that are embedded in national identities. In Germany, Spain, and partly in Poland, Europe's "other" is the respective country's own past of nationalism/militarism (Germany), authoritarianism (Spain), and domination by foreign powers as well as by Communism (Poland). In contrast, the French European "other" remains rather vague and consists of everything "non-French," for example, the United States with regard to notions of capitalism, but also Communism during the cold war. And continental "Europe" remains the (albeit) friendly "other" in British/English identity constructions.

Most important, two findings stand out. First, the Europeanization of national identities in the elite discourses does not result in a uniform and homogenous European identity (see Cram 2009). Europeanized identities come in national colors insofar as they resonate with and are connected to respective national symbols and historical and cultural memories in different ways.

Second, however, this does not mean that we observe as many different Europeanized identities as there are EU member states. Rather, as far as the substantive content of Europeanized identities is concerned, we see a remarkable convergence in these elite discourses. Two meanings of "Europe" and the EU stand out (see also Checkel and Katzenstein 2009a): in each of the national discourses, with the exception of Britain, Europe and the EU stand for economic and political modernization and for liberal and democratic values. This modern vision of Europe has achieved consensual status in Germany and Spain and dominates the elite discourse. However, it remains contested in France and Poland.

In contrast, political elites on the (populist) right of the political spectrum have started to articulate a countervision to "modern Europe." They promote an exclusionary and anti-globalist "fortress EU" that also protects the national sovereignty and cultural heritage of the member states. This countervision has been most prominent in France in recent years,[10] while the Polish identity discourse oscillates between purely nationalist and traditionally religious visions and an "antimodern" concept of Europe. Still, in most countries, this counterdiscourse is no longer anti-European in the sense of principled opposition to EU membership, but promotes an EU that is different from the modernization project that has informed European integration so far.

These findings are remarkable, because they mean that Europe and the EU are no longer "empty signifiers" or poorly defined identity categories in the various national debates, as some have argued (e.g., Breakwell 2004). Although the Europeanization of national identities has not led to a uniform European identity, it has resulted in the emergence of two clearly observable concepts of what Europe and the EU stand for and mean. Moreover, these very identity constructions also resonate with mass public opinion, as I tried to show in chapter 2. "Nationalist Europe" resonates with those exclusive nationalists in most member states who solely identify with their nation-state. In contrast, "modern Europe" is compatible with the identities of both "the Europeans" (Fligstein 2008, chap. 5) and those who feel attached to Europe as a secondary identity.

Finally, the five country cases differ in the degree to which Europeanized identities are settled, consensual, or contested. Three countries—Germany, Spain, and

---

10. It was also visible during the referendum debates in the Netherlands and in Ireland in 2005 and 2008–9, respectively.

Great Britain—represent countries in which one identity discourse dominates the elite debates and has remained consensual so far. In Germany and Spain, Europeanized national identities referring to the EU as a modernization program prevail. In Britain, it is "non-European Englishness" that is still dominant among the political elites.

In contrast, France and Poland represent cases in which national identities, including the extent of their Europeanization, remain contested and unsettled. In the French case, modern Europe as "France writ large" struggles with "traditional and fortress Europe." In Poland, the identity battle lines are between those promoting the modern Europe to which Poland returned after the end of the cold war, on the one hand, and those who favor an exclusionary and inward-looking religious vision, be it on the European or on the purely national level. Chapters 8–10 look at the consequences of these identity battles for the issues facing the EU today.

Chapters 2 and 3 have described the uneven Europeanization of identities on the levels of mass public opinion and of (mostly political) elites. But what explains this Europeanization of identities, including the variation in the results? Has the process of European integration had any effect on the Europeanization of identities, be it on the level of elites or mass public opinion? I will turn to this question in chapter 4.

4

EUROPEANIZATION OF NATIONAL IDENTITIES

Explanations

Chapters 2 and 3 have described the Europeanization of elite and mass identities. In a nutshell, I have argued that we can observe (1) the emergence of Europeanized identities in a plurality of mass public opinion across Europe, if only as secondary identities ("European identity lite"); (2) the Europeanization of national identities in various elite discourses whereby Europe and the EU become intertwined and amalgamated in the various national identity narratives (the "marble cake" model); and (3) two visions of Europe noticeable in both the elite discourses and in mass public opinion, namely the "sacred" identity of a modern, liberal, and secular Europe and the "primordial" identity of an exclusionary and nationalist "fortress" Europe emphasizing the Christian heritage in such a way that other religions and worldviews are excluded.

Describing the Europeanization of identities across the EU is difficult enough, but explaining it on the various levels and including cross-national and other differences represents an even more daunting task. In particular, we have to ask whether fifty years of European integration have left their mark in strengthening the sense of imagined community among European citizens and elites. I use socialization and Europeanization research to get a handle on how to account for the differential impact of Europe and the EU on identification processes.

There are two theoretical stories about identity change and institutions, as mentioned in chapter 1 (see also Herrmann and Brewer 2004). The first causal story serves as the "null hypothesis" for this chapter: rationalist institutionalism exogenizes identities and interests in the institution-building process. As a result, one would expect that institutions would have little impact on identities.

In EU studies, the most prominent approach in this regard is liberal intergovern-mentalism (e.g., Moravcsik 1998). Economic interdependence leads to changes in actors' preferences in favor of international cooperation. The preferences are aggregated by national governments, which then negotiate binding agreements and institutions to ensure credible commitments. This story leaves little space for institutional feedback effects on actors' preferences, let alone for effects on their identities.

The second—constructivist or sociological institutionalist—story endo-genizes identities, interests, and institutions. Accordingly, and over time, insti-tutions become part and parcel of the social and power structure that forms the social environment in which people act. Over time, institutions tend to have *constitutive* effects on corporate actors such as national governments and interest groups, but also on individuals. Since people act in environments structured by institutions, the latter affect their interests, preferences, and collective identities. We should then expect identities and institutions to coevolve with the causal arrows between the two pointing in both directions. The EU should be no excep-tion. It might well have been created to serve specific interests based on given identities. But this would be the beginning of the story, not the end. Over time, we would expect a complex co-transformation of the EU together with people's identities and interests.

This second causal story points to several mechanisms by which identity change occurs, as suggested in chapter 1. Identity change including the Europe-anization of identities can come about through

- *Interest change leading to identity change:* This is essentially the neofunc-tionalist explanation (Haas 1958) according to which European integra-tion gradually changes the preferences of major actors and interest groups, which then results in a transfer of loyalties to the European level.
- *Frequent interaction:* The "contact hypothesis" assumes that frequent inter-action and regular contact with others should increase the sense of commu-nity and of collective identity. Karl W. Deutsch's integration theory builds upon this interaction hypothesis according to which regular transnational contact in Europe will increase the sense of community among Europeans (Deutsch 1953; Deutsch et al. 1957).
- *Incremental socialization:* Sociological institutionalism assumes that, over time, institutions affect the socialization of individuals who gradually in-ternalize the respective norms and rules (Checkel 2005a; Johnston 2005). Jeffrey Checkel distinguishes between "type I" socialization, whereby people acquire the knowledge to follow rules without reflecting on whether the rules are appropriate or morally valid, and "type II" socialization, whereby

individuals start believing in the correctness or moral validity of the norms and rules (Checkel 2005b). Thus, "type II" socialization goes beyond the role-playing of "type I" and should affect the collective identities that link individuals to social groups. In a similar way, psychological theories of identity change emphasize that the more visible the institutions of an imagined community such as the EU become, the more this should lead to identity change. The causal mechanism emphasizes the increasing psychological existence ("entitativity"; see Castano 2004) of imagined communities, which then induce identity change.

- *Socialization through persuasion:* Socialization through persuasion emphasizes more active and conscious ways through which people change their identities. Elite efforts at identity change, for example, should be all the more successful the more they actively construct the new identities in such a way that they resonate with narratives, historical memories, and symbols to which people can relate.

- *Crises and critical junctures:* Although the causal mechanisms discussed so far emphasize incremental processes of identity change, sociologists and psychologists point to traumatic experiences and massive inconsistencies between cognitive schemas and beliefs, on the one hand, and novel information or experiences of failure, on the other, which then trigger identity change (overviews in Giesen 1993; Eder and Giesen 1999; Stein 2002). Wars, revolutions, sudden regime change, and other crisis events should lead to profound changes in the way in which people make sense of the world including their collective identities.

Unfortunately, scholars have been much better at describing the Europeanization of collective identities than at explaining it. We do not have good data, including statistical analyses, to be able to test competing hypotheses to explain the emergence of and resistance to Europeanized identities among the elites and in mass public opinion. As a result, the following remarks are meant to be suggestive rather than conclusive. In particular, the available data do not (yet) allow a rigorous test of competing hypotheses.

Interest Change and Transnational Interaction

The neofunctionalist and interest-based argument according to which those benefiting directly from European integration should also shift their loyalties toward the EU receives very little support in the data (Risse 2005). Most of the limited material resources of the EU are used up by the Common Agricultural Policy. Accordingly, farmers across Europe have been direct beneficiaries of European integration from the beginning. Women also benefit from the EU insofar as both the Commission and the European Court of Justice (ECJ) have forced member states to adopt equal opportunity policies as well as equal pay and treatment rules. Yet, there is no evidence whatsoever that farmers identify more strongly than other people with Europe. As for women, the opposite is the case, as the well-known gender gap in support levels for the EU demonstrates (Liebert and Sifft 2003; Nelson and Guth 2000).

Moreover, a special issue of *International Organization* has also disconfirmed a simplistic version of the "contact hypothesis" according to which frequent exposure to (European) institutions should lead to identity change (Checkel 2005a). Liesbet Hooghe points out in a study of EU Commission officials that socialization in Brussels has had little effect on their views of supranational norms (Hooghe 2005; Hooghe 2001). Jan Beyers's study of Council officials also demonstrates that extensive exposure to the European level did not lead to strong identification with supranational roles (Beyers 2005). In each case, identification with supranational institutions resulted from prior experiences at the *national* rather than the supranational level (similarly Trondal 2002). Service in the Commission had only a modest effect on those who joined it at a relatively young age (Hooghe 2005, 876–77). Officials quickly learned to play the roles expected of them, that is, they acquired the knowledge needed to function in a European institution (Lewis 2005). Role identities, however, constitute rather weak forms of collective identification ("type I" socialization, Checkel 2005b). National experiences, particularly in federal systems, were more significant for identification processes with European institutions. Thus, intensity of exposure to institutions as a socialization process ("contact hypothesis") might lead to role identities, but it appears to be insufficient to account for stronger forms of collective identification with Europe.

Thus, although Ernst B. Haas apparently got it wrong, Karl W. Deutsch's integration theory receives support (see Fligstein 2008, chap. 5, and Fligstein 2009 for the following). "The Europeans," that is, those who strongly identify with Europe, are mostly highly educated professionals, managers, and white-collar workers who speak several languages and travel a lot (Rother and Nebe 2009; also Green 2007). Fligstein in particular shows that frequent interaction with other Europeans and high mobility leads to higher identification levels with the EU and that this effect is independent of class variables. His findings, therefore, confirm the interaction hypothesis, namely that frequent and regular interactions with "foreigners" strengthen the sense of (transnational) community.

Fligstein's argument points to a strong, albeit indirect, effect of European integration on identity change. On the one hand, there is little evidence that frequent contact with Brussels changes identities. On the other hand, European integration over the years has been mostly about market integration and the creation of a single European economic space. The single market then enables transnational exchange and interaction, creating winners and losers from European integration. The winners are "the Europeans" mentioned above who exploit the opportunities for transnational interaction to the fullest and, as a result, strongly identify with Europe and the EU.

The flip side of Fligstein's theory concerns those who lose out in European integration, however. Older, less-educated blue-collar workers do not travel very much and have little exposure to foreigners. They also profit less from economic integration and market liberalization, and they are confronted with the pressures of globalized markets on their job security, welfare benefits, and the like. As a result, they are most likely to remain or become "exclusive nationalists" who not only identify with their nation-state but are also targets of opportunity for the increasing Euroskeptical discourse of right-wing or left-wing populist parties. If Deutsch's integration theory proves to be correct, a counterintuitive effect of European integration would then be that market integration not only creates a transnational class of "Europeans" but also strengthens the nationalist and Euroskeptical convictions of those who do not enjoy the benefits of transnational interaction. Indeed, data show that European integration has led to the emergence of a cultural cleavage between Euroenthusiasm and Euroskepticism (Kriesi et al. 2008, see chapter 10 of this book).

Incremental Socialization: (EU) Membership Matters

The account so far pertains to the attitudes of those who either identify with Europe very strongly or reject the EU equally powerfully.[1] But what about the plurality in the middle who identify with Europe and the EU as secondary identities next to national identity ("European identity lite")? I argue in the following that incremental socialization processes and the increased visibility of the EU in the mass media (see chapter 6) seem to account for these trends.

With regard to incremental socialization, figure 4.1 suggests that the length of EU membership does indeed matter. It is based on 2004 Eurobarometer data from all member states (old and new) and accession countries. It measures "net European identity," that is, the percentage of those identifying with Europe at

---

1. The subhead refers to the title of Sandholtz 1996.

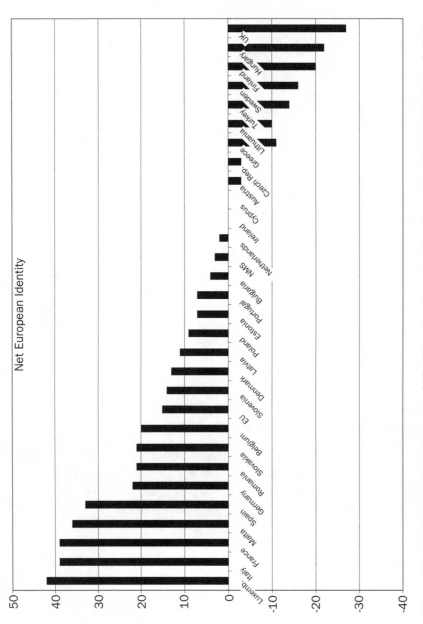

Figure 4.1. Net European identity by country, 2004. This calculation is based on the same question used in chapter 3: "In the future, do you see yourself as (Nationality only), (Nationality and European), (European and Nationality), or (European only)?" "Net European identity" is then calculated in the following way: (Nationality and European) + (European and Nationality) + (European only) – (Nationality only). See also Lahav 2004, 187. Negative numbers mean that exclusive nationalists outnumber those identifying with Europe in the respective country.

Source: Own calculations, based on European Commission 2004, B94, C48 (EU = EU 15, NMS = new member states in 2004).

least to some extent minus those identifying with their nation-state only (exclusive nationalists). The results are quite startling.

First, the average net result for the EU's fifteen member states before Eastern enlargement is much higher than the average for the ten new member states that joined in 2004 (+15 vs. +3). Among the new member states or accession candidates, only Malta (+36), Romania (+21), and Slovakia (+21) are above the EU average, while Slovenia (+14) and Latvia (+11) are slightly below. In contrast, exclusive nationalism is particularly strong in Hungary (−22), Turkey (−14), and Lithuania (−10).

Second, even more interesting, five of the six founding members of the European Economic Community are way above the EU 15 average. The one exception is the Netherlands (+2) where exclusive nationalists and those identifying with Europe almost cancel each other out. Yet, citizens of Luxembourg (+42), Italy (+39), and France (+39) show the strongest identification with Europe. Germans (+22) and Belgians (+20) are still above the EU average with regard to their European identity.[2] Among those who joined the EU later, only the Spanish show a similar degree of above average identification with Europe (+33). Thus, early membership in the European Community seems to matter.

Third, further evidence corroborates this finding, which is, of course, based on a snapshot of 2004 and does not show temporal developments. A time-series analysis by Michael Bruter appears to confirm the gradual increase in mass identification with Europe (Bruter 2005, chap. 7).[3] Once again, citizens of the original six member states stand out as showing the strongest degree of identification with Europe.

If these analyses could be further substantiated, they would disconfirm the "null hypothesis" mentioned above. The data seem to sustain the institutionalist argument that EU membership matters, leading to increasing identification with Europe over time. If so, the EU has had constitutive effects on mass public opinion in the sense that it defines what it means to be "European" these days.

However, some caveats are in order. Although original membership appears to matter quite strongly, there is no linear relationship between the duration of a country's membership in the community, on the one hand, and the identification of its citizens, on the other hand. Take figure 4.1 and compare it with the

---

2. In each of these countries, a majority holds Europe as a secondary identity ("nationality and Europe"); see chapter 2. Note, once again, that these data refer to mass public opinion, not to elite discourses.

3. There is a methodological problem, however. Bruter derives his findings by using support for European integration as the main variable. He then subtracts the variance explained by expectations of benefits ("rationalist variables"), arguing that identity forms the residual category. This is problematic, since it strongly rests on the assumption that his model is correct (Bruter 2005, appendix 3).

various enlargements of the EU. The first enlargement took place in 1973 when the United Kingdom, Ireland, and Denmark joined. Yet British citizens remain by far the most exclusive nationalists in Europe (–27) and have been so for a long time. They are even more Euroskeptical than citizens of Hungary who joined recently (–22) and of Turkey, an accession candidate (–14). Moreover, Irish (0) and Danish citizens (+13) are also located on different points of the map of European identity. A similarly diverse picture emerges with regard to Southern enlargement in 1981 (Greece: –11) and 1986 (Portugal [+7] and Spain [+33]). Finally citizens of the three countries that joined the EU in 1995—Austria (–3), Sweden (–16), and Finland (–20)—are all located way below the EU average and belong to the more Euroskeptical populations.

As a result, the data suggest as a first cut that the length of EU membership is a necessary condition for increased identification with Europe (at least "European identity lite"). But it is by no means sufficient. Institutional socialization effects might be at play, but they have to be complemented by other factors. Among them are the visibility and the "psychological existence" of the imagined community in the minds of the citizens. There are several potential and interrelated sources for the increased psychological existence of the EU: constitutional moments such as treaty-making events (Maastricht, Amsterdam, Nice, Constitutional Convention, Lisbon); the growing visibility of the EU in the media (see chapter 6); the increased visibility of symbols representing the EU, such as the European flag; and personal experience of individuals with the EU, such as the single currency or borderless travel in Schengenland.

Figure 4.2 represents the EU average of "net identification with Europe" from 1992 to 2004. The graph shows a substantial drop in identification with Europe between 1994 and 1996 as well as a gradual increase since then.

If we compare this development with the evolution of European integration, the following interpretation comes to mind: the high level of net identification with Europe in 1994 might well result from the aftermath of the Maastricht Treaties including such highly visible decisions as Economic and Monetary Union (EMU) and the single currency. The subsequent drop appears to confirm Oskar Niedermayer's observation of alternating cycles of Europeanization and nationalization in mass public opinion (Niedermayer 1995; also Lahav 2004, 187). The gradual increase from 1997 on might reflect the growing visibility of the EU with regard to the Nice Treaty in 2000, the discussion about the future of Europe following Joschka Fischer's speech in Berlin in 2000, the introduction of euro coins and bills in 2002, and the debates about Eastern enlargement.

With regard to media reporting and the use of symbols, Michael Bruter's analysis supports the hypothesis put forward by cognitive and social psychology. He conducted various experiments with French, British, and Dutch students,

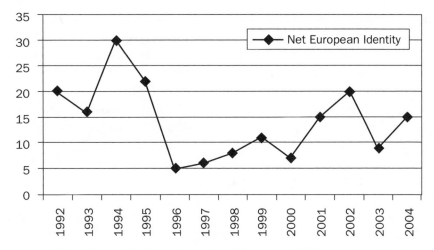

Figure 4.2. Levels of net European identity over time. See Figure 4.1 for an explanation of the calculation.
Source: Calculated from Eurobarometer data (see figure 2.1, chapter 2).

concluding that European identity has a civic/political and a cultural component (see chapter 2). His regression analyses demonstrate that both media reporting and the use of symbols such as the European flag strongly affect identification levels with Europe, in both their political and cultural components (Bruter 2005, chap. 6). "Good news" as opposed to "bad news" about Europe increases the political component of European identity by more than 20 percent, while the use of symbols has an equally strong effect on identification with Europe as a cultural entity. Bruter concludes that media reporting affects political identity more strongly than cultural identity, while the opposite is the case with regard to symbols (Bruter 2005, 127–28). Claes De Vreese and Anna Kandyla confirm this finding with regard to European foreign and security policy (CFSP) through an experimental design: presenting a common European foreign policy as an opportunity rather than a risk increases support levels for CFSP considerably (De Vreese and Kandyla 2009).

In other words, the Europeanization of public spheres increases the visibility of the EU, and seems to lead to a greater sense of community among the citizens, if only as a secondary identification. Some studies confirm that greater coverage of EU policies in national media affects attitudes toward the EU (Blumler 1983; Norris 2000; De Vreese and Boomgarden 2003, 2006). An analysis by Florian Stöckel appears to support Bruter's arguments. He used data from media content analyses in all twenty-five EU member states prior to the 2004 elections to the European Parliament (De Vreese et al. 2006) and correlated both the salience and the tone (negative or positive) of the media reporting with measurements of European identity as well as support for European integration (see Stöckel 2008). Through sophisticated statistical analyses, he demonstrated that higher visibility of the EU in the media ("salience") indeed leads to higher identification levels with the EU. At the same time, the more visible the EU becomes in the national media, the more critical people become toward EU policies and European integration. This confirms the "politicization" argument (see chapter 10). Suffice it to say here that increasing the visibility of the EU in the public sphere appears to lead to a greater sense of European community, which seems to confirm the socialization hypothesis with regard to the "psychological reality" of an imagined community.[4]

In sum, there is some evidence that EU membership is a necessary (but not sufficient) condition for the emergence of "European identity lite," whereby national and European identities go together. The same holds true for the increased visibility of the EU in the media and through symbols, which also seem to reinforce dual identities. In most member states today, for example, the European flag and national flags fly alongside each other. The euro coins also represent dual identities symbolically with a uniform European picture on one side and national symbols on the other.

Dual identities are further reinforced through active attempts by political elites at socialization through persuasion.

Socialization through Persuasion and Critical Junctures: Elite Discourses

The account so far tries to explain the differential Europeanization of identities on the level of individuals. But we still lack an account for the variation among countries reported in figure 4.1. Here, EU membership provides only a first-cut answer. I suggest that elite discourses as described in chapter 3 account for the differences.

Whether or not citizens adopt Europe as a secondary identity seems to depend a lot on the degree to which elite discourses in a country are Europeanized. Findings reported by Liesbet Hooghe and Gary Marks confirm this argument: Elite divisions over the EU in a member state are highly correlated with citizens' opposition to EU integration. This effect is particularly strong among those holding exclusively nationalist identities (Hooghe and Marks 2005).

---

4. I come back to these issues in chapters 6 and 7.

Among the original six members of the European Union, the elite discourses on European integration have been almost completely positive over the years. This is certainly true for Germany, but also for the Benelux countries and for Italy with their fairly Europeanized political elites. As a result, net European identities are way above the EU average (see figure 4.1). The same holds true for Spain, which entered the EU in the 1980s and where the elites actively Europeanized post-Franco Spanish identity. France appears to be an outlier case, since net identification with Europe is very high even though the Europeanization of elite identities has been an uneven and contested process. Here, length of EU membership might have had a stronger effect on mass-level identities than the apparent divisions among the French elites. As a study by Leah Haus shows, for example, French school curricula have been Europeanized almost completely (Haus 2007).

The cases of Great Britain and Poland are again consistent with the overall argument. British political elites never tried to reconstruct English identity and Europeanize it, even though the United Kingdom has been an EU member for more than thirty-five years. Europe and the EU remain "the other" in British discourse. The EU is also conspicuously absent in British school curricula (Haus 2007). Without an active effort of persuasion by the elites, it is little wonder that the vast majority of British citizens stick to exclusive national identities.

Poland is below the EU average, but above the average of the new member states, as far as the net European identity of its citizens is concerned (see figure 4.1). One has to note in this case, though, that the Eurobarometer poll was taken in 2004, right before Poland joined the EU. It might not yet reflect accurately the "post-membership blues" that are visible across many of the new Central Eastern European member states. Nevertheless, the Polish data are largely consistent with the contested nature of European identity in the country's elite discourses (see McManus-Czubinska et al. 2003).

As for the substantive content of the Europeanized identities that elites try to construct, we can at least observe that the dual identities of a plurality of citizens in many countries ("nation first, Europe second") correlate with the way in which Europe has been integrated into national identities in these discourses. We can observe that pro-European elites mostly construct intertwined and amalgamated identities whereby Europe and EU become part and parcel of national identity narratives. To the extent that German, Spanish, French, or Polish policymakers have actively promoted a European identity as a modernization project, it has always been integrated into the narratives of what is special about modern Germany, Spain, France, or Poland. Although I hesitate to posit causality here, this promotion of intertwined and marble cake identities is at least consistent with the fact that a plurality of citizens in these four countries hold dual identities.

This account tells a story of how elite efforts at persuasion might have affected citizen identities. But what explains the differential Europeanization of elite identities itself? Here, Europeanization research could be helpful. It tells us that European integration has a differential domestic impact and that a certain degree of "misfit" between European-level policies, processes, and ideas, on the one hand, and domestic policies, institutions, and ideas, on the other hand, is a necessary condition for the EU to have an effect at all (Börzel and Risse 2000; Cowles, Caporaso, and Risse 2001). In the case of social identities, "misfit" pertains to the degree of compatibility or incompatibility between narratives on European identity, on the one hand, and the respective narratives and constructions of national identities, on the other (Risse 2001). Of course, elites, particularly political elites, are themselves in the business of identity construction. They will try to make European and national identities resonate with each other (or not) if it suits their interests. "Misfit" or "fit" do not represent objective categories, but partly result from active strategic constructions. But we also know from persuasion research that even very clever elites cannot construct meanings from scratch, at least not under normal circumstances. Rather, active efforts at changing identities have to make sure that the new meanings and interpretations resonate with prior beliefs and cognitive schemas in order to have an effect.

What does this mean with regard to the EU and its institutions as sources of elite identity change? In general, we should expect that the EU will create identity change only in cases in which there is a medium degree of dissonance or "misfit" between European identity and national identity constructions. If there is a complete match between the meaning structures embedded in European institutions, on the one hand, and national visions and identities, on the other hand, no identity change is to be expected, since the collective identities are already Europeanized.

This explains why European integration did not cause the profound transformation of German national identity discussed in chapter 3. When the Treaty of Rome was coming into effect in the late 1950s, German political elites had already embraced European integration as national raison-d'être. In the German case, one could argue that the positive experiences with European integration reinforced Europeanized identities rather than creating them in the first place. The crisis and traumatic experiences of the defeat in World War II explain to a large degree the profound identity changes taking place in Germany. Moreover, the new (West) German leaders, from Konrad Adenauer to Kurt Schumacher and later Willy Brandt, all had their formative political experiences in the European movements of the interwar period and—to some extent—the resistance to the Nazis. For them, it was only natural that the new Germany had to become European in the sense of "modern and liberal Europe."

At the other end of the spectrum, Great Britain appears to represent a case of profound misfit and incompatibility between Englishness and Europe. As argued above, there was very little space for Europe in British and particularly English identity constructions. There was also no crisis or experience of critical juncture in the postwar period—except for the loss of the British Empire and decolonization—that would have made opting for Europe inevitable. Even the decision to join the union was justified on pragmatic grounds. European identity as a conceptual frame was not available in the domestic discourses to justify such a decision. Moreover, the British opt-outs of the single currency (Euroland) and of Schengenland ensured that the incompatibility between supranationalism and English identity could be managed so far.[5] Finally, a different identity construction has been available to British elites, namely the "special relationship" with the United States, including the references to "Anglo-America" (Vucetic 2008).[6] By definition, this created some distance to continental Europe.

The three other cases discussed in chapter 3 can be located in between the German and the British cases with regard to "misfit." In the Spanish, Polish, and French cases, (partial) identity changes among elites came about through various critical junctures: the end of the Franco era in Spain; the end of the cold war in Poland; policy failure in the early 1980s as well as the end of the cold war in France. In contrast to both Germany and Britain, European integration did exert its influence on elite identities in these three countries.

The Spanish case most closely resembles the German one. Following the regime change toward democracy, Spanish identity had to be reconstructed. At the same time, the European Community was already around and the new Spanish leaders wanted to join it by all means, for economic reasons, but also to anchor the new democracy in a supranational institution. As a result, the Europeanization of Spanish identity was almost a natural development. "Modern Europe" became integrated into the new Spanish identity (Diez Medrano 2003).

The Polish case is more complicated. On the one hand, the new Poland did not have many political options after the end of Communism than to join the EU, which exerted an enormous pull for a variety of economic, political, and security reasons. The "return to Europe" discourse during the early 1990s reflected this development and was compatible with a reorientation of Polish identity toward modern Europe. On the other hand, Polish nationalism was rather incompatible

---

5. In the Lisbon Treaty, Britain secured two more opt-outs for itself, namely from further integration in Justice and Home Affairs and from the legal effects of the EU Charter of Fundamental Rights. As a result, the only "supranationalized" policy area in which Great Britain participates remains the single market and, thus, economic integration and liberalization, which are consistent with the Anglo-Saxon model of economic policies.

6. I owe this point to John Raymond.

with European integration and with modern, particularly secular, Europe. Polish sovereignty discourse and the emphasis on Catholicism in an almost primordial sense served as a countermovement to the Europeanization of identities. As a result, Polish post-Communist identity still remains contested, particularly after EU accession had been secured and the "post-accession blues" set in.

Finally, what about France and the Europeanization of French identity during the 1980s and 1990s? In this case, the process of European integration probably had a profound impact (see Parsons 2003). Of course, French national identity had already embraced the values of modernity, enlightenment, and Republicanism long before the European Community was founded. De Gaulle's vision of the Fifth Republic was embedded in a profoundly nationalist identity construction that provided very little "space for Europe." The more European integration departed from the Gaullist concept of a "Europe of fatherlands," however, the more it became incompatible with existing French identity constructions, leading to an ever-increasing misfit between European and French identity. As argued in chapter 3, two critical junctures enabled the Europeanization of French identity, namely the profound failure of Mitterrand's nationalist economic policy during the early 1980s as well as the end of the cold war, which sidelined the *grande nation*. In this case, it was not necessary to change one's political identity to incorporate the values of modernity, but merely to supranationalize it. As a result, Europe became France writ large. Yet, the "modern France in modern Europe" discourse, which leaders from the center-right to the center-left articulated, remains contested and controversial. A counterdiscourse has emerged on the fringes of the French political spectrum, particularly on the right. It is still about Europe, but a nationalist and exclusionary Europe. As a result, French identity is still not settled.

This interpretation of the five cases seems to suggest, above all, the stickiness of national identity constructions. Elite efforts at socialization through persuasion only work in cases of a medium degree of incompatibility between European integration and national identity narratives. Moreover, the analysis points to the overriding importance of crises and critical junctures. Regime changes in Germany after World War II, in Spain after Franco, and in Poland after Communism opened windows of opportunity for elites to construct new narratives and to Europeanize national identities. In the absence of such crises, changing identities through persuasion is almost impossible, as the British case demonstrates.

Conclusions: Constitutive Effects of European Integration

This chapter asked how we can explain the Europeanization of national identities among elites and in mass public opinion. We do not have strong and empirically grounded theoretical accounts about identity change toward Europe and the EU. But the evidence is growing that more than fifty years of European integration have had constitutive effects on peoples' identities, leading to the Europeanization of national identities and to the emergence of identification with Europe as a secondary identity. However, this Europeanization of identities varies across countries (and even subregions) and is mitigated by elite discourses and narratives.

What does this say about the explanations for identity change put forward at the beginning of this chapter and in chapter 1? First, the neofunctionalist account of interest change leading to identity change and the transfer of loyalties to the European level receives only limited support. On the level of mass public opinion, there is little evidence that the perceived benefits from European integration lead to greater identification (Citrin and Sides 2004).

Second, as Neil Fligstein has argued (Fligstein 2008, chap. 5), Karl Deutsch's integration theory of community-building through interaction receives support. Here, class and transnational interaction enabled through European integration go together to create "Europeans" who strongly identify with Europe and the EU. Fligstein's analysis also explains why the losers under integration remain fixated on the nation-state and increasingly combine exclusive nationalism with Euroskepticism.

Third, incremental socialization processes are also at work. With regard to mass public opinion, the length of EU membership seems to matter, but it is mitigated by the degree to which elite discourses represent a unified picture of the EU. Moreover, the increased psychological reality of the EU in people's lives—for example, through media reporting—leads to greater identification levels.

Fourth, elite efforts at socialization through persuasion by creating narratives of dual and intertwined national and European identities correlate with majorities in mass public opinion feeling attached to their nation-state and to Europe. Moreover, Europeanization research appears to be confirmed: Europe and the EU must resonate with national narratives in order to Europeanize the latter.

Fifth, the argument that crises and critical junctures provide windows of opportunity for identity change also finds strong support. The Europeanization of identities in Germany, Spain, Poland, and France all came about through such critical junctures including the experience of failure. Great Britain confirms the argument insofar as it never experienced such a crisis with regard to the EU. This confirms the more general expectation in the literature on identity that collective identities appear to be rather sticky so that it takes major crisis experiences to change them (Abdelal et al. 2009a, b; Klotz and Lynch 2007).

What do these findings tell us about the impact of more than fifty years of European integration on identity change? I begin with the bad news for Brussels. European institutions do not seem to have a direct effect on the Europeanization of national identities, either on the mass public or on the elite level. Sending people to Brussels or exposing them to good news from the EU alone does not change identities. Rather, all these effects are mediated by media reporting, elite discourses, and the affective as well as cognitive previous experiences that people have. Conscious efforts by the authorities in Brussels to create a European identity do not seem to have much impact on identity change.

However, there is also good news for the EU. It is beyond doubt that the process of European integration has had constitutive effects on national identities. On the deepest level, the EU practically defines what statehood means in Europe (Laffan 2004; Laffan, O'Donnell, and Smith 2000). The EU as an active identity builder has successfully achieved identity hegemony in terms of determining what it means to belong to "Europe." States in Europe are increasingly defined as EU members, nonmembers, or would-be members. They are either in the EU, almost in, or remain out. There is no way that European states can ignore the EU, even such devoted nonmembers as Switzerland. There are no "neutral" states in Europe anymore vis-à-vis the EU. In short, the EU increasingly *is* Europe. As a result, it is increasingly difficult to separate European from EU identity, at least as far as political identities are concerned (Bruter 2005).

The language used by political elites is instructive in this regard. Central Eastern Europeans returned "to Europe" in the context of the EU Eastern enlargement, as if they had been outside the Continent. When Italy prepared to adopt the euro, the main slogan was "*entrare l'Europa*" (entering Europe!) as if Italy—one of the six founding members of the Community—was ever outside it (Sbragia 2001). To the extent that people identify Europe with the EU, this is a remarkable achievement of fifty years of European integration. If Europe and the EU are used interchangeably, it means that the latter has successfully occupied the social space of what it means to be European. One could then not be a "real" European without being an EU member.

The emerging counterdiscourse against the "modern, liberal, and secular Europe," which emphasizes traditional values, Christianity, and exclusionary policies, actually proves the point. Right-wing populist parties in France, the Netherlands, Ireland, and elsewhere no longer articulate a simple "anti-EU" vision and a return to the nation-state. Rather, they demand a different EU, one that defies the forces of globalization and modernization. Their exclusionary nationalism is no longer wedded to the nation-state, but encompasses the EU. To the extent that the claims and demands of the Euroskeptics (see Hooghe and Marks 2007; Taggart and Szczerbiak 2005/2008) are directed toward the EU rather than the nation-state, it suggests that European integration has had a profound impact. Not even its strongest opponents can escape the reality of the EU. To put it differently, if the political vision articulated by what used to be exclusive nationalism is increasingly framed in European rather than in national terms, this is a further sign that the EU has become a full-fledged polity, precisely because its policies and even its institutional setup are contested. (I discuss the consequences of this politicization in chapter 10.)

This is a dramatic finding. If the EU not only defines what it means to be European but its most adamant opponents also take it for granted, then the European integration process has left its mark on the deepest levels of state- and nationhood in Europe. It has done so within only fifty years and entirely peacefully. This disconfirms that community- and nation-building is inherently linked to war-making (Tilly 1975, 1985). After fifty years, the founders of the European Community would have achieved what they set out to do—to create a European peace order that redefines European statehood after centuries of war and hostility. The rise of Euroskepticism only underlines the point.

Part II

AN EMERGING EUROPEAN PUBLIC SPHERE?

5

TRANSNATIONAL PUBLIC SPHERES
Conceptual Questions

Part 1 of this book has explored the Europeanization of national identities at the levels of elite and mass opinion. In particular, I have argued that we see the emergence of collective identification with Europe as a secondary identity on the level of mass public opinion and the differential Europeanization of national identities in the elite discourses in the sense of intertwined national and European identities. Two visions of Europe are observable on either level of mass public opinion and elite discourses, namely a liberal Europe embodying the values of modernity and enlightenment, and a more traditional and exclusionary "nationalist Europe" emphasizing particularly Christian roots.

Elite discourses about Europe, however, take place in and are observed by the various public spheres. As a result, collective identities and public spheres are intimately connected in various ways. First, public spheres provide the communicative spaces where collective identities are actively constructed and reified. This is particularly salient with regard to "imagined communities" such as the nation-state or Europe. Moreover, public spheres provide the arenas where "Europe happens" and, thus, contribute to the "psychological existence" of Europe. Last but not least, we have to turn the causality around and ask whether some degree of collective identification is required for a community of communication. What are the social and cultural preconditions that enable people to communicate across borders in transnational public spheres?

Yet, before we can tackle this issue, we need to establish that transnational communication in a European public sphere is indeed possible. As in the case of European identity, a lively political and academic debate has emerged in the last fifteen years about the normative viability and the empirical possibility of a European public sphere. This discussion about the possibility of a European *Öffentlichkeit*[1] inevitably links normative and analytical perspectives (Trenz 2008a). From the normative perspective of democratic theory, most observers deem an open, pluralistic, and critical public discourse rooted in independent media crucial for providing an interface between state and society in a democratic polity. Europe should not be an exception. As a result, the debate about a European public sphere is linked to the controversy about the democratic quality of the EU and its various deficits (see chapter 10).

The normative understanding of *Öffentlichkeit* as a necessary ingredient of a democracy has implications for the analytical conceptualization of a public sphere, since it requires some indicators with regard to its communicative quality. If public spheres as the "fourth estate" are supposed to inform citizens about the political process, to monitor and critically evaluate governance, and to enable a public discourse in a democracy (McNair 2000), they must allow for meaningful communication and exchange and, thus, satisfy certain normative criteria. This has implications for the development of indicators for such public spheres, which I will discuss later in this chapter.

But how do we know a transnational public sphere (in this case European) when we see one? This chapter parallels chapter 1 in that it provides a conceptual framework for thinking about public spheres beyond the nation-state. I proceed in the following steps. First, I discuss the conventional wisdom that Europe lacks a common public sphere, because it lacks a common language, common European-wide media, and a consensus concerning the European project as a whole. In contrast, I argue that none of these components is necessary for Europeans to be able to communicate across borders. Rather, one should conceptualize a European public sphere in terms of the Europeanization and transnationalization of national public spheres—in a way similar to the Europeanization of collective identities. Moreover, communication does not require consensus; conflict and even polarization are necessary prerequisites for lively public debates.

Second, we nevertheless need a meaningful conceptualization of a transnational public sphere in order to establish its existence or non-existence in Europe. Elaborating on proposals in the literature (Eder and Kantner 2000; Kantner 2004), I argue that transborder communication emerges if and when the same issues are being discussed at the same time using similar frames of references across the various national public spheres. The last point is particularly important, since we

---

1. The German term *Öffentlichkeit* is usually translated as "public sphere." Yet, this translation does not capture the normative connotations implied in the German term. See De Vreese 2007, 4; Trenz 2008a, 1–3.

need common meaning structures and interpretive frames to prevent miscommunication. A debate without common frames of reference is impossible, even if these frames are heavily contested.

Although these are necessary conditions for transnational public spheres, they are not sufficient. At a minimum, the speakers in the various public spheres should be aware of each other, that is, mutual observation across national spheres is essential (Trenz 2002, 27). Moreover, meaningful communication across borders requires at least some degree of mutual recognition of speakers as legitimate contributors to a debate. In particular, if Europeans debate European issues *as Europeans* across borders, they should not treat each other as "foreigners" in this debate. At the same time, once they debate questions as *European issues* of common concern, they inevitably create a community of communication through discursive practice. At this point, the emergence of a transnational public sphere through communicative practices is inextricably linked to the emergence of Europeanized identities and both reinforce each other. I discuss the conceptual relationship between a European public sphere and European identity in the last part of the chapter.

A European Public Sphere? Challenging the Conventional Wisdom

For quite some time, the debate about a European public sphere was largely confined to normative reasoning in the absence of valid empirical data.[2] Grimm (1995) saw a public sphere as a precondition for a viable European democracy. Kielmannsegg (1996) argued that the EU lacks basic prerequisites to develop a "community of communication," because language differences inhibit Europeans from speaking meaningfully to each other. One of the first empirical studies on the subject came to a similar conclusion, namely that there is a European "public sphere deficit" as part of a larger democratic deficit (Gerhards 1993). These early studies established the conventional wisdom, namely that we cannot speak of a European public sphere in a meaningful way, since it lacks such necessary ingredients as

- a common language that everybody speaks and understands;
- common European-wide media that everybody watches, listens to, or reads; and
- a common European perspective (overview in Kantner 2004, 75–93).

---

2. See, e.g., Abromeit and Schmidt 1998; Grimm 1995; Kielmansegg 1996; Schlesinger 1993.

These arguments resemble the conventional wisdom about European identity, namely that Europe and the nation-state are in a zero-sum relationship. I have already dealt with the language argument (see chapter 2) and do not need to comment any further here. The second point about common European-wide media is based on the assumption that a European public sphere has to supersede national public spheres. Thus, a European public sphere is only possible above and beyond the nation-state in a separate transnational space. As Gerhards put it, "A European media system would integrate the European member states beyond the nation-states in a way similar to how the media systems in the various nation-states integrate the territorial states beyond regional entities" (Gerhards 2000, 288). By definition, the German *Frankfurter Allgemeine Zeitung* and the French *Le Monde* could never be part of the same public sphere. Because the media markets in Europe continue to be nationally organized despite some transnational media corporations such as Rupert Murdoch's company or Bertelsmann, a European public sphere would be doomed. However, it is one thing to recognize the empirical reality of nationally organized media. It is quite a different point to fall into the trap of "methodological nationalism" (Beck 1997) and conclude that the nation-state is the "natural container of the public sphere" (Trenz 2008a, 4) and that meaningful cross-border communication is therefore impossible.

Yet, these and other arguments positing the impossibility of a European public sphere can be challenged one by one. Claims about the absence of a European public sphere as well as related arguments about the nonexistence of a European collective identity are often based on essentialist notions of public spheres and collective identities. But public spheres are not a given; they are not out there waiting to be discovered by analysts. Public spheres—whether local, regional, national, or issue-specific—are social constructions in the true sense of the word. They do not preexist outside communication, but are created precisely when people speak to one another, be it in interpersonal settings or through the media. Public spheres emerge through the process by which people debate controversial issues in public. The more we debate issues, the more we engage one another in our public discourses, the more we actually create political communities (Habermas 1980 [1962]; Trenz and Eder 2004). This means that a community of communication can be constructed, deconstructed, and reconstructed through interaction. National public spheres acquire seemingly essentialist characteristics, not because they preexist prior to communication, but because they are reified daily through these communicative interactions. Once again, the similarities to the reification of "imagined communities" through processes of identity construction are striking. Why should this process stop at national borders, and why could it not also include transnational communication?

Moreover, there is no reason why we should all speak the same language and all use the same media in order to be able to communicate across borders in a meaningful way. If people attach similar meanings to what they observe in Europe, they should be able to communicate across borders irrespective of language and in the absence of European-wide media. Few people would argue that Switzerland lacks a national public sphere because of its different language communities. It is equally questionable to claim the absence of a public sphere when people read different newspapers. In fact, the opposite is true. A lively public sphere in a liberal democracy should actually be based on a pluralistic supply of media competing for the attention of citizens.

Thus, the core of this argument is not that it is impossible to translate meanings from one language to the other or that people reading *Le Monde* cannot understand those who use *Le Figaro*. The core of the argument refers to the cultural embeddedness of meanings (see Kantner 2004, 114–30, for the following). If we do not share a common lifeworld—to use Habermas's term—we cannot meaningfully communicate with each other. Indeed, we must have a common set of shared meanings at our disposal in order to understand each other and to avoid talking past each other. A radical perspective would claim that intercultural communication is impossible, since we cannot escape the inevitable cultural embeddedness of every communicative utterance.

Such a radically relativist position conceptualizes cultures as containers of meanings that are hermetically sealed from each other. But this argument makes little sense. The thought experiment about the Westerner who happens to land on an unknown island and meets indigenous peoples whose language she does not share at all, demonstrates that we can actually develop a "common language" including a common lifeworld through signs, cultural translations, and trial and error. Meaningful communication can be established even under such adverse circumstances. This does not mean that misunderstandings and communication failures resulting from cultural differences are impossible—far from it. The hermeneutic circle implies that we do not share meanings and interpretations at the beginning of our communications (Gadamer 1965). Rather, we normally assume that the other means exactly what we mean—and then we notice that this assumption is wrong. As a result, we adjust our mutual interpretations and understandings gradually by "translating" our interpretation into the cultural language of our communication partners. Mutual understanding, thus, is based on and requires the constant overcoming and translating of cultural barriers and the negotiation of difference.

In short, we can indeed assume that there are cultural differences between, say, Poles and Germans that inform the meanings they attach to communicative utterances and that these differences then lead to miscommunications and misunderstandings. But the same holds true—maybe, to lesser degrees—for, say, Bavarians and Berliners, for workers and bosses, for men and women (see Tannen 1994), and so on. To assume, however, that national cultural barriers are somehow insurmountable, while regional, class, or gender barriers are not, is hard to defend. At least, one should treat this as a matter of degree rather than principle. National public spheres are not culturally homogenous—far from it. Most national public spheres are fragmented, but few would argue, therefore, that people are unable to meaningfully communicate with one another (Eder and Kantner 2000).

Last but not least, it is unclear what is meant by the definitional requirement that a common perspective is needed to speak of a public sphere, be it European or national: "Only when there are reports about Europe, and only when these reports are written from a perspective that transcends national perspectives could a Europe of citizens emerge" (Gerhards 1993, 99). If this means that a common public sphere—whether local, national, or European—presupposes that speakers in the public space refer to the same meaning structures, I agree. However, if this argument implies that we have to discuss European themes with an eye to whether they promote or hinder European integration, or worse, that we actually agree on a common European standpoint, such a conceptualization misses the mark. There is no reason why we should expect agreement or consensus on an issue in a public sphere, be it national or transnational. Agreement about policies across boundaries cannot serve as an indicator for the existence of a public sphere nor can ideological and other cleavages serve as an indicator of its absence.

Rather, contestation and polarization are crucial preconditions for the emergence of a public sphere rather than indicators for its absence. If we agree about political issues, we are unlikely to debate them. The result is mutual silence, the opposite of a public sphere. Consensus might be the result of a discussion, but it is certainly not its starting point. In other words, the more contentious European policies and politics become and the more social mobilization occurs on European issues, the more we actually observe the emergence of a European public sphere. If political issues are not contested, if European politics remains the business of elites, the attention level of the public toward Europe and the EU will remain low. Politicization of European affairs would then be crucial to raise the salience of Europe in the national media.

However, one could easily imagine social mobilization and public debates surrounding European policies within the member states that discuss these questions solely from the various national and culturally embedded perspectives. Is joining the euro in the British, Danish, or German national interest, or not? If the debate is solely framed in these national terms, people would still debate the same question, but the frames of reference would be rather different and communication across borders would be difficult. The problem is that it is hard to communicate with each other in a meaningful way if we disagree not only over the issue in question but also over what the problem actually is. If Gerhards's plea for a "perspective that transcends national perspectives" (Gerhards 1993, 99) means that common frames of reference are required to enable meaningful transnational communication across borders, he has a point.

The discussion so far has meant to show that the conventional wisdom about the absence of a European public sphere is questionable, since it is based on exaggerated assumptions about the preconditions for effective communication across borders. But even if we relax these preconditions, we still need to have an understanding about what constitutes a transnational (European) public sphere. In the following, I take a similar stance as in the chapters on the Europeanization of identities and argue that transnational public spheres emerge through the Europeanization of national public spheres.

The Europeanization of Public Spheres: Concepts and Indicators

Over the past fifteen years, a research community has formed that studies the emergence of a European public sphere from a variety of perspectives.[3] This research mostly concentrates on mass media (and the Internet) as proxies for the existence or nonexistence of a European public sphere. Moreover, most of the empirical work is based on content analyses of so-called quality newspapers, that is, broadsheet newspapers such as the *New York Times* or *Le Monde* rather than tabloids.

This has methodological shortcomings for two reasons. First, it assumes that the mass media constitute neutral expressions and transmitters of public debates and discourses. But the mass media create their own reality; they often manipulate public opinion, or they might simply reproduce the voices of the powerful. At the same time, ordinary citizens do not have direct access to political processes, let alone to European policymaking. To the extent that they "know" Europe and the EU, they know it through the media. For most people, politics does not exist outside the media. In that sense, and irrespective of the shortcomings and manipulative tendencies of media representations of politics, the public

---

3. Overview in De Vreese 2007. See, e.g., Diez Medrano 2003; Fossum and Schlesinger 2007; Kantner 2004; Koopmans and Statham 2010; Langenbucher and Latzer 2006; Meyer 2002; Trenz 2006; Wessler et al. 2008. For the following, see also Risse and Van de Steeg 2008.

sphere is mostly "what the media make of it."[4] As a result, if one keeps in mind that the media often follow their own agenda, it is justifiable to concentrate on media representations in order to investigate the degree to which a European public sphere exists.

Second, the focus of most research on quality newspapers introduces an elite bias into these studies. We know from public opinion research that most people get their news about Europe and the EU from television, not to mention tabloids. Results based on media analysis of quality newspapers might, therefore, exaggerate the degree to which a national public sphere is Europeanized (see, e.g., Peter and De Vreese 2004; Peter, De Vreese, and Semetko 2003).

Keeping these caveats in mind, however, we know much more today about a European public sphere than we knew, say, fifteen years ago. The empirical research has also converged in its conceptual understandings of a transnational public sphere. Most significant, it has largely accepted the conclusion emanating from the above discussion, namely that we should not search for a European public sphere above and beyond national public spheres in some supranational public space. Rather, and similar to the study of collective identities, we should look for the Europeanization of public spheres: national, regional, or even local. The various studies mentioned concentrate on the degree to which national public spheres are gradually Europeanized and European issues are regularly dealt with by national media. As a result, the study of media discourses has become part and parcel of the flourishing Europeanization literature that is studying the impact of European integration on domestic policies, politics, and polities (Börzel and Risse 2007; Featherstone and Radaelli 2003).

The existing literature can be distinguished according to the role attributed to the media.[5] First, one can analyze media as political actors in their own right who contribute to and comment on European policymaking. Studies typically analyze editorials and other opinion articles in the media (e.g., Pfetsch 2004). The danger of this approach is that it often neglects the role of institutional actors such as the EU or national governments in shaping the actions on which the media then comment. After all, it is through the media that political actors communicate with the public.

Second, one can study the media—as the term implies—as observers, mediators, as well as reflections of a larger public discourse. This approach is chosen by the majority of research teams who often use frame analysis to examine particular debates concerning the degree to which issues are debated from merely national perspectives or from a common European point of view, enabling transborder

---

4. To paraphrase Alexander Wendt's famous title about anarchy and states (Wendt 1992).
5. I owe the following point to Barbara Pfetsch and Silke Adam.

communication. Of course, this perspective often overlooks the insight of the first approach, namely that the media actively select and frame the news and that they are not simply neutral transmitters of communication.

If we accept the insight that "the public sphere is what the media make of it," then both approaches are valid and complement each other. I report the various findings in chapter 6.

But we still need a clearer picture of what is meant by the Europeanization of public spheres and what would be valid indicators. Let me begin with the above-mentioned social constructivist insight that Europeanized public spheres are being constructed through social and discursive practices, creating a common horizon of reference (Kantner 2004). This is consistent with Jürgen Habermas's conceptualization of *Öffentlichkeit* (Habermas 1980 [1962]). Habermas concentrated on the emergence of arenas of semipublic reasoning and deliberation among free citizens in the saloons, coffee houses, and Masonic lodges of eighteenth- and nineteenth-century bourgeois society in Europe. These arenas constituted emerging public spheres in which private citizens challenged public authorities to legitimate themselves before the court of public opinion. Habermas's later work systematically linked the concept of a public sphere to the institutionalized opinion formation processes in a democratic political system that is governed by the rule of law (Habermas 1992). As a result, opinion formation in the public sphere no longer has to single-handedly carry the burden of ensuring that deliberation occurs in a democratic polity. Rather, it is the legal and political institutional framework of a modern democracy that ensures its deliberative quality: "Democratic procedures and institutions constitute the intersubjective framework in which public political communication gains its normative sense" (Kantner 2004, 46). In particular, these procedures and institutions serve to ensure at least two normative requirements for a public sphere in liberal democracies: (1) openness to participation and (2) the possibility of challenging public authorities to legitimate their decisions.

These two criteria from Habermas's theory of communicative action are broad enough to be compatible with other normative criteria for a democratic public sphere taken from various democratic theories.[6] First, a public sphere has to be *public,* that is, in principle it has to be open to everyone who wants to follow the discussion and actively participate (Neidhardt 1994, 7). The media, of course, are mostly open with regard to the second aspect, namely passive participation. Active participation in media discourses and debates is usually restricted to political, economic, and cultural elites. Second, public spheres are about questioning

---

6. See, for example, Ferree et al. 2002 who distinguish four models of the public sphere in modern democracies.

public authority. This aspect is linked most closely to the normative role of the media in a liberal democracy. The EU should not be an exception, since a lively public sphere constitutes a prime requirement for a democratic European polity (see chapter 10).

Both standards serve as normative yardsticks against which to measure the performance of existing public spheres. How open are the various media to contestation and to the less powerful? To what extent do they articulate challenges to public authorities rather than simply endorsing the voices of the powerful? Hans-Jörg Trenz calls this the "democracy enhancing" vs. "dumbing down" functions of the media (Trenz 2008b).

What do these normative remarks mean for the *analytical* operationalization of a Europeanized public sphere? On the one hand, if we aim too high by translating these normative standards into empirical indicators, we will probably never find a viable public sphere anywhere—whether local, national, or European—that meets these criteria. On the other hand, if we aim too low, any type of public communication will probably do and we will find democratic public spheres everywhere (see Fraser 1997, 69–98, on this problem). As I will argue in chapters 6 and 7, some of the controversies in the literature result from disagreements about the empirical yardsticks that serve as indicators for European(ized) public spheres.

In the following, I develop empirically observable indicators that function as prerequisites or as minimum conditions so that the two normative standards of openness to participation and challenges to public authorities can be met in principle. I start with Habermas's definition of a European public sphere as "a public political sphere which enables citizens to take positions at the same time on the same topics of the same relevance" (Habermas 1996b, 306). Inspired by this insight, Klaus Eder and Cathleen Kantner (2000) have formulated the following rule of thumb: there is a European debate when the same issues are discussed at the same time using the same criteria of relevance (also Kantner 2004, 132–33). These "Eder-Kantner criteria" start from the assumption that a transnational European public sphere can be built through the Europeanization of the various national media discourses.

The first indicator—the same issues at the same time—relates to the EU's *visibility* in the media (De Vreese 2007, 10). If EU affairs are not reported at all, we do not need to worry about a European public sphere any further. Moreover, the first indicator also refers to *issue cycles*. Media do not pay attention to every political question all the time, but there are high and low levels of attention. One would then simply count the number of articles on a particular theme in the various media sources across countries and then examine whether the peaks and valleys in the issue cycles of media reporting follow similar patterns. One should not exaggerate this point, though.[7] If French newspapers discuss EU member-ship for Turkey in May because of, say, a visit by the Turkish prime minister to Paris, while German media focus on the same issue later in the year, this differ-ence in timing would not per se disconfirm the existence of Europeanized public spheres. However, similar issue cycles at least ensure that cross-border commu-nication is possible.

Of course, issue cycles are probably observable for any major event anywhere in the world. A major earthquake in Japan will generate worldwide media report-ing with almost identical issue cycles. The ascending and descending slopes will probably be steeper the further away from the earthquake we move, for example, in Europe as compared to East Asia. But the observation of issue cycles alone cannot suffice to claim a common public sphere, as the example demonstrates.

This is why Eder and Kantner have introduced "same criteria of relevance" as a second indicator for a joint public sphere (also Wessler et al. 2008, 15–16). This indicator has led to different operationalizations depending on one's concept of a public sphere. On the one hand, there are those who argue that a Euro-pean public sphere requires that speakers in the sphere adopt a European rather than a national or otherwise partisan perspective (Gerhards 2000). "Same cri-teria of relevance" would then require that we debate issues from a European rather than from national or local perspectives. But how do we know a "Euro-pean perspective" when we see one? A common European perspective implies a community of communication. On the other hand, there are those who claim that "same criteria of relevance" simply means that we take notice of each other in a transnational public sphere and that we mutually observe each other. This conceptualization follows Niklas Luhmann's "mirror" analogy of a public sphere (Luhmann 1971). Accordingly, public opinion constitutes the social subsystem through which a society observes and describes itself, thereby contributing to so-cial integration (Luhmann 2000; Trenz 2006, 71–80). Communications through the media then constitute second-order observations that enable participants as well as audiences to not only observe themselves and their contributions but also the observations of others and their construction of reality. By mirroring and communicating social conflicts, the media contribute to social order in a given society. In this understanding, communication through public media does not aim at mutual understanding and public discourse, but at mutual observation.

If we operationalize this latter conceptualization of a public sphere in terms of the Europeanization of public spheres, we would have to measure to what degree national media observe political debates and conflicts in fellow European

---

7. I thank Silke Adam for alerting me to this.

countries and/or EU policymaking in "Brussels." The more news coverage of events and conflicts in other European countries takes place and the more European and EU issues are reported as compared to national or local issues, the more we would claim a Europeanization of public spheres. In a study on Spanish as compared to German media reporting of the 1998–99 corruption scandal of the EU Commission under President Jacques Santer, Hans-Jörg Trenz claimed that the public spheres had been Europeanized even though Spanish media used decidedly nationalist frames, blaming German power interests for the demise of the Commission, while German media assumed the moral high ground and portrayed Spain as un-European and corrupt (Trenz 2002, chap. 8). In this case, the two national public spheres certainly observed each other. But the Spanish media used very different frames of interpretation to comment about the conflict as compared to German newspapers. Does mutual observation suffice to claim the Europeanization of public spheres?

It is likely that U.S. media also reported about the corruption scandal on the EU Commission, probably less frequently than European newspapers, though. Does this make the United States a participant in a European public sphere? German newspapers regularly report about French domestic politics as observers and even commentators. But it makes little sense to claim that, therefore, German newspapers are part of the French public sphere.

In his later work, therefore, Trenz has fine-tuned his argument (Trenz 2006, 174–79). He still argues that a convergence of frames of reference is not necessary for a common public sphere to exist. Indeed, political debates in national public spheres often do not agree on the frame of reference under which a particular issue should be debated. In fact, many heated debates concern precisely the question of the "heading" under which a political problem should be discussed. Is the reform of public pension schemes a question of social policy or of public finances? Should immigration issues be discussed as human rights questions or as issues of social integration? Is intervention in Iraq a question of international law, of human rights, or of access to oil? Our policy responses will differ a lot depending on which frame of reference we choose. However, the more heated a public debate, the more the frames of reference will probably converge, since speakers have to relate to the interpretations of others in order to criticize them.[8]

I suggest, therefore, that a medium degree of frame convergence below the very demanding "European perspective" threshold, but above simple mutual observation, is necessary. Communication in a public sphere requires that we are aware of the different frames of interpretation under which we can discuss

---

8. I owe this point to Marianne Van de Steeg (Van de Steeg 2005, 26).

the policy problem at stake. Thus, "same criteria of relevance" should imply at a minimum that we not only observe each other in the public but that the various frames of reference are available to us so that we can understand why the contributors to a debate take a particular position. We do not have to share the frame of reference under which our communication partner discusses the issues at stake, but we need to know the frame in order to understand her position (Wessler et al. 2008, 15–16). We have to agree on what the problem is or, at a minimum, which potential interpretations of the problems exist so that we "know" what we are talking about. Otherwise, we will talk past each other. Once we know which potential interpretations of a problem exist, we can argue about which of the available frames of references are more appropriate. As Cathleen Kantner put it, "By same 'criteria of relevance,' I do not mean a 'European' perspective based on a European identity, but common interpretations of the problem that include controversial opinions on the particular question" (Kantner 2004, 58). This clarification follows the above argument that contestation and controversy are necessary ingredients for a common public sphere. We can disagree about whether the attack on Iraq was consistent with international law or not. We can even disagree about whether international law or the respect for basic human rights is more important and how we give weight to each value when discussing a particular issue. But "same criteria of relevance" requires that we agree that compliance with international law, on the one hand, and respect for basic human rights, on the other, are significant in debating questions of war and peace.

The Europeanization of public spheres does not only mean that the same themes are discussed at the same time transnationally but that the same frames of reference are available and in use in the various public spheres in Europe. The more we observe that national differences in the use of frames recede into the background, while differences between, say, conservative and leftist media become more pronounced, the more we can assume the gradual Europeanization of public spheres. Frame analysis (Gamson 1992; Snow and Bedford 1988) can be used to measure these differences and commonalities in meaning construction.

Some theoretical conceptualizations of public spheres leave it here. Availability and some convergence of frames of reference and meaning structures is all we need to enable mutual observation across borders in a transnational public sphere. A common European perspective is definitely unnecessary in such a public sphere. But is the discussion of the "same issues at the same time using the same frames of reference" enough to constitute Europeanized public spheres? Such a public sphere might meet the normative standard of openness mentioned above. But what about the challenge to public authorities, EU institutions as well as national governments involved in EU decisions in this case? Is mutual observation and using the same interpretive frames in the respective national public spheres sufficient to qualify for a transnational *Öffentlichkeit*? If public spheres are about debating issues of common concern, they are not just about *observation,* they are also about *communication.* Moreover, those who speak as well as those who listen can no longer pretend to be neutral observers in such a public sphere. Thus, if public spheres are meant to be sites of communication in a democratic polity, this inevitably raises the question of community. At this point, the question of Europeanized public spheres is inextricably linked to the issues of European identity.

Transnational Communities of Communication and Europeanized Identities

The older literature on public spheres assumed that identity is a precondition for its emergence. A community must be in place in order for us to be able to communicate with each other. Claims about the absence of an EU public sphere, therefore, usually argued that since a sufficiently strong European identity does not exist, there cannot be a public sphere (for example, Kielmansegg 1996; Offe 2003). This argument is based on the assumption that citizens enter the public sphere with a given identity and that debates in the public sphere should aim at transcending differences in identity, position, or interests (see Calhoun 2002 for a critique). If there is no collective identity, there cannot be a public sphere if it is understood as a community of communication.

I agree with this earlier literature that the concept of a public sphere is linked to questions of collective identity. However, the relationship between identities and public spheres is less troublesome from a social constructivist perspective. Social constructivists do not treat either public spheres or collective identities as given. Public spheres emerge in the process during which people debate controversial issues. Media both observe these debates and contribute to them. The more we debate issues, the more we engage one another in public discourse, and the more we leave the position of neutral observers—thereby creating and/or reifying political communities in the process. This point follows Calhoun's argument that identities are defined and redefined in the public sphere, which makes them open to change: "Participation in democratic public life is not, however, separate from the processes through which culture is produced and reproduced in modern societies; it is integral to them, and likewise part of the process by which individual and collective identities are made and remade" (Calhoun 2002, 157). In other words, public spheres constitute one of the sites where communities of communication are being constructed and reconstructed and where, as a result, collective identities emerge. Thus, Europeanized public spheres and Europeanized identities reinforce each other.

This implies that the availability of similar meaning structures and frames of reference constitutes a necessary condition for transnational communication across borders, but it is not sufficient to speak of a public sphere. Public spheres in the meaningful sense of *Öffentlichkeit* (as an ingredient of a democratic polity) require active engagement, both by the speakers and their audiences. Engaging in a debate requires listening to one another's arguments and trying to persuade one another (Habermas 1981). It certainly involves contestation, and it may or may not lead to consensus. But a community of communication in a transnational public sphere requires, at a minimum, that speakers in a public sphere recognize each other as legitimate participants in a debate. We might disagree fundamentally, but we take each other's statements seriously in a democratic polity.

Nationalists deny this legitimacy. Polarizations along national lines by definition create boundaries using national "self-other" distinctions. In the case of the EU Commission's corruption scandal, Spanish media employed this nationalist "self-other" frame: "*The* Germans are after *our* (Spanish) commissioner." In response, German media replied: "*The* Spanish don't know what the rule of law means." In these statements, the two public spheres still observed each other and they also used some common reference points. But they did not treat each other as legitimate speakers in their respective public spheres (Trenz 2002).

In contrast, during the French referendum campaign about the Constitutional Treaty in 2005, German policymakers actively participated on either side of the issue. German foreign minister Joschka Fischer made almost fifty public appearances in France to promote the "yes" vote. In contrast, German left-wing politician Oskar Lafontaine also participated in the French debate, but on the "no" side. In this case, German policymakers were treated as legitimate participants in a Europeanized French public sphere during a debate on a highly salient issue of common European concern. They were not treated as "foreigners" whose interventions constituted interference in one's domestic affairs.

The two examples show that a sense of community and of collective identification ought not to be treated as a prerequisite for a communicative discourse. Rather, as argued above, it can emerge *in the course* of a debate in the public sphere. Actively engaging in a discourse on issues of common concern can lead to collective identification processes and create a community of communication rather than presupposing it. Why should Europe be an exception? This line of thought means that "debating Europe" actually builds a community of Europeans in a transnational public sphere.[9] It constitutes Europeans *as Europeans* who no longer

---

9. My argument closely resembles that of Klaus Eder and Hans-Jörg Trenz about the reflexivity of the discourse on the EU's democratic deficit. Accordingly, debating the EU's democratic deficit is the first step to democratizing the EU (Trenz and Eder 2004).

remain neutral observers, but have to take a stance in a community of communication. This argument further implies that controversies about European policies and the subsequent politicization of the EU are good, not bad, for the sense of community and for the construction of a European polity (see chapter 10).

But how do we know a "community of communication" when we see one? Three empirical indicators are commonly used in the literature on a European public sphere. The first concerns the degree to which national media in various countries regularly observe, report, and comment about one another with regard to European affairs, thereby creating interconnectedness. Ruud Koopmans and Jessica Erbe introduced the notion of vertical and horizontal dimensions of Europeanized political communication in this context (Koopmans and Erbe 2004; also Wessler et al. 2008). *Vertical Europeanization* refers to the degree to which EU actors such as the European Commission are regularly referred to in national public spheres, while *horizontal Europeanization* concerns communicative linkages between different member states. They then distinguish between weak and strong variants of Europeanization. Weak Europeanization simply means that EU actors or actors from other member states are present in a given national public sphere, while strong Europeanization concerns the degree to which political demands are being addressed to these actors, and the extent to which EU or other national actors raise demands in a particular public sphere. In my view, only the latter version of interconnectedness qualifies as an indicator of a community of communication. What Koopmans and Erbe call "weak Europeanization" simply means that utterances of "foreign" actors are being reported in the media. However, reporting about President Bush's troubles in Iraq in German newspapers per se does not make the U.S. president a member of a (transatlantic) community of communication. This is very different from newspaper reports of the U.S. president calling upon the German government to support its policies in Iraq. The latter could be regarded as an—albeit weak—indicator for a transatlantic community of communication measured via transnational interconnectivity.

A second—and somewhat stronger—indicator for the emergence of a transnational community of communication concerns the degree to which fellow Europeans—citizens of other EU member states or EU actors themselves—are no longer treated as "foreigners," but as legitimate speakers in a common discourse. As Stefan Tobler put it, it is decisive that "competing discourse coalitions start talking to each other across different national and international arenas, thereby forming a common arena of communication" (Tobler 2002, 62; also Van de Steeg 2002). This indicator for a community of communication can be measured, for example, by focusing on the degree to which fellow European actors or members of EU institutions actively participate in national debates of common

European concern as compared to national actors from the country in which the debate is carried out. To what degree, for example, do national newspapers open their editorial or op-ed pages to fellow European or EU authors when issues of common European concern are being discussed? The more we find that other Europeans regularly participate in public discourses in the various arenas, the more we can observe a transnational community of communication.

A third indicator for an emerging community of communication refers to the development of a common European perspective on issues of European concern. This, of course, is a very strong and ambitious indicator that requires that actors in a public sphere discuss an issue from the common perspective of a community. As a result, few scholars use it as an indicator for a European public sphere and some empirical projects have rejected this notion explicitly (e.g., Koopmans and Erbe 2004; see the discussion in Kantner 2004, chap. 2).

This indicator does not refer to particular speakers or how "foreigners" are treated in a national public sphere. Rather, it concerns the content of the communication itself and involves, once again, how issues are being framed. To repeat myself, a common European perspective does not and cannot mean that speakers in a transnational public sphere adopt a neutral position above partisanship or that they agree on the issues at stake. Polarization and contestation are intrinsic to a lively public debate. "Common European perspective," therefore, means that issues are addressed as concerning "us as a community of Europeans" so that the relevant community is Europe rather than individual member states or other particular groups. In other words, the "we" in whose name speakers articulate themselves in the public sphere refers to Europe or the EU, rather than any particular group, as the relevant community. In debating a particular problem as an issue of common European concern, speakers construct a European community of communication, thereby contributing to a collective European identity.

For example, one can debate whether the single currency is in the best interests of Germany and whether, therefore, Germany should give up its cherished deutsche mark. But one can also discuss the same question from a common European perspective: To what extent does a single currency help the European economy in an era of globalization? Can we have monetary integration in Europe without economic policy coordination? The latter type of question constructs the problem in common European terms, thereby creating a community of communication and a collective identity.

Similarly, one can discuss the question of EU membership for Turkey from a distinctly nationalist perspective: What does free movement of Turkish labor mean for the national economy? But one can also discuss Turkish EU membership from a European perspective: Where are Europe's borders? Does a predominantly Muslim country belong in the EU? The latter two questions frame the issues in common European terms, irrespective of the answers. Once again, a common European perspective establishing a European community of communication should not be confused with a pro-EU, pro-integration, or otherwise substantive position on the questions at stake. The antimodern, exclusionary, and "nationalist" vision of European identity discussed in part 1 still constructs a European community of communication, as objectionable as its content might be.

One can object to these points by maintaining that articulating a problem from a European perspective already requires some minimum sense of community to begin with and that communities of communication cannot be constructed from scratch and out of thin air. This is a "chicken and egg" problem in my view. Structuration theory tells us that agency and structures are mutually constitutive of each other and that neither is ontologically prior to the other (Giddens 1984; Wendt 1987). The same holds true for the social construction of a community of communication in a European public sphere. It requires agents—speakers in this case—who actively articulate a policy problem as a *European* one of common concern for Europeans. At the same time, their sense of European community in terms of their embeddedness in a common European social structure enables them to make these claims in the first place. In this sense, Europeanized collective identities and Europeanized public spheres mutually reinforce each other.

It should also be mentioned that this conceptualization of a European community of communication does not preclude other such communities from coming into being above and beyond a Europeanized public sphere. Political issues can be constructed as questions of local, national, European, Western, or global concern, as a result of which we would be able to observe local, national, Europeanized, Westernized, or globalized public spheres. I use the terms Europeanization, Westernization, or globalization here to indicate that the transnational communities of communication beyond the nation-state usually emerge through national media systems in the absence of truly European or global media.

What are the observable implications of these conceptual statements? There are two ways of measuring the extent to which speakers in a public sphere construct a common European perspective on the issues at stake, thereby establishing a transnational community of communication. First, one can find out who the "we" is in whose name speakers communicate or to whom they refer to in their utterances (see Sifft et al. 2007) and then compare references to a European "we" with national or other "we's." However, such a measurement strategy faces methodological problems. At least, one needs to distinguish between the usage of "we" in a matter-of-fact way and a usage with an explicit identity connotation as in "it is in our supreme national interest as Germans" or "we as Europeans have an obligation to…"

Second, one can measure the degree to which policy questions are framed as issues of common European concern and of common European fate. A community of communication emerges when speakers in Europeanized public spheres not only use the same frames of references and meaning structures but also are aware across national public spheres that they are doing so. As Hans Jörg Trenz put it, "One does not only communicate about common themes in the European public sphere, but this commonality itself becomes a theme in the public sphere" (Trenz 2006, 179), thereby introducing an element of reflexivity (see, e.g., Risse and Van de Steeg 2008).

Conclusions

I have argued in this chapter that we should not conceptualize a European public sphere as a separate entity above and beyond national (or local or issue-specific) public spheres. Rather, and similarly to the conceptualization of European identity, a transnational European public sphere emerges through the *Europeanization* of various, particularly national, public spheres. Moreover, a European public sphere is not sitting out there, waiting to be discovered. Rather, it is a social construct and emerges in the process during which people engage one another and debate issues of common concern in public. Public spheres and communities of communication come into being when people argue about controversial issues.

A Habermasian understanding of *Öffentlichkeit* identifies two crucial functions of public spheres in a democratic polity, namely openness to participation and challenges to public authorities. These two standards can be used as normative yardsticks against which to measure the performance of existing public spheres including Europeanized ones.

Moving from a normative discussion to the development of empirical indicators, I referred to the "Eder/Kantner" criteria. Accordingly, we can meaningfully speak of a Europeanization of public spheres

1. the more the same (European) themes are controversially debated at the same time at similar levels of attention across national public spheres and media; and

2. the more similar frames of reference, meaning structures, and patterns of interpretation are available and in use across national public spheres and media.

To this, I have added a third criterion with three indicators that takes up the debate about the relationship between collective identities and public spheres. A public sphere that deserves its name as an essential ingredient of a democratic polity constructs a community of communication so that Europeanized identities and public spheres reinforce each other. Thus, we can speak of a transnational European public sphere

3. the more a transnational community of communication emerges in which (a) European or other national speakers regularly participate in cross-border debates, (b) speakers and listeners recognize each other as legitimate participants in transnational discourses that (c) frame the particular issues as common European problems.

It follows from these criteria and indicators that the Europeanization of public spheres is not a dichotomous variable. In other words, these indicators allow for different degrees of Europeanization. Chapters 6 and 7 use them to assess empirically to what extent we can observe the gradual Europeanization of public spheres.

6

THE GRADUAL EUROPEANIZATION OF PUBLIC SPHERES

The previous chapter addressed conceptual questions pertaining to the Europeanization of public spheres and developed criteria to measure the degree to which we can observe a Europeanization of public spheres. Chapters 6 and 7 use these criteria to survey the empirical evidence and to answer the question of to what extent public spheres are becoming Europeanized and a transnational community of communication is emerging. First, I discuss data pertaining to the visibility of EU affairs in the media as compared to national and other issues. Second, I comment on the degree to which issue cycles have become similar over time. Third, I analyze the degree to which we can observe a growing similarity in frames of reference and meaning structures. Are Europeans talking about the same things when they discuss EU issues in the public spheres?

I argue in this chapter that the visibility of EU affairs in the media has increased over time. However, the Europeanization of public spheres remains uneven with regard to both issue cycles and the similarity of meaning structures. Europeans frequently talk about the same things when they talk about Europe and the EU, but differences in the degree of Europeanization remain. The most Europeanized public spheres are observable in continental Western Europe including some Southern EU members such as Spain and Italy. The United Kingdom remains the odd one out, while we do not have sufficient data for Central Eastern Europe to allow for firm conclusions.

How Visible Is the EU in the Media?

The first requirement for Europeanized public spheres is that the EU should be visible in the media. If people cannot observe the EU, it is impossible to debate European affairs. The available data show a general trend toward increased media attention concerning the EU in the past ten to fifteen years.

However, the picture for the pre-1995 period remains unclear.[1] Jürgen Gerhards used time series data from 1951 to 1995 and tried to show that European issues mattered very little in German quality newspapers (Gerhards 2000; see Van de Steeg 2005, 145–46, for a critical discussion). Coverage of EU policies paled in comparison to both national and even international news. Of course, it is hard to generalize from one EU member state to the rest of Europe. Nevertheless, if coverage of European affairs in a traditionally pro-EU country such as Germany was rather insignificant, this should be quite sobering for claims with regard to a Europeanization of public spheres. A study by Jan-Henrik Meyer of German, French, and British newspaper coverage of five EC/EU summits between 1969 and 1991 shows a differentiated picture (Meyer 2008). Coverage fluctuated up to the 1980s, but on a low level of below one hundred articles per newspaper per summit. However, the 1991 Maastricht summit that brought about the Maastricht Treaties including monetary union received higher attention from these quality newspapers.

The data get better from the mid-1990s on. Two major projects in particular showed that the visibility of the EU has been growing. The first project at Berlin's Humboldt University analyzed news coverage of European governance and policymaking in eleven daily newspapers from six EU member states during the year 2000 (see Kantner 2006b; Trenz 2004). This research found that one third of all political news contained references to European issues—if only as a secondary theme. This is a much higher percentage than the one reported by Gerhards. Moreover, more than 90 percent of the articles covering "European" themes reported about the EU (Trenz 2006, 227).[2] In other words, the finding that the EU has occupied the meaning of what constitutes "Europe" also holds true for the media (see chapter 4).

This research group also examined the degree of intensity with which European issues were covered. Among those articles dealing with Europe at all, a little

---

1. This has partly to do with technology. Before the mid-1990s, most newspapers were only available on microfiche and, thus, were less accessible to computer aided content analyses.

2. Other European institutions such as the Council of Europe or the Organization for Security and Cooperation in Europe (OSCE) are virtually absent in the national public spheres. NATO is a different matter, since it is usually covered in a transatlantic rather than a European context.

less than half reported about the EU as their primary issue.[3] Twenty percent of the articles covered EU policies as a secondary topic in articles on foreign policy or domestic politics, while one third of the articles made at least a reference to the EU (Trenz 2006, 195–96). Among these articles, the overwhelming majority dealt with political or economic themes. The researchers also compared *European* newspapers with the *New York Times* and found substantially less coverage of the EU there. The difference between the latter and all European newspaper together was greater than the differences between European countries or between newspapers in one country. In other words, and not too surprisingly, the EU has become particularly visible in Europe.

While the Humboldt University-based team took a snapshot of EU coverage in 2000, the EUROPUB project analyzed news coverage in seven policy areas ranging from monetary policies to agriculture, immigration, and troop deployments in seven EU countries during the years 1990, 1995, and 2000–2002 (Koopmans 2004; Koopmans and Erbe 2004).[4] Not surprisingly, the EUROPUB data show that the more competences the EU has in a given issue area, the more EU actors and actors from other European countries are referred to in the media. Three policy areas stick out: European integration itself, monetary policies, and agriculture. EU actors or actors from other member states were particularly visible in the issue area of European integration (59% of the claims, Koopmans 2004, 33).

Concerning particular countries, Swiss, Spanish, and French newspapers covered EU and European actors the most (around 40% of all claims), German, Dutch, and Italian newspapers a bit less (around one third of all claims), while Great Britain seemed to have the most nationalist media. In British papers, two thirds of all actors mentioned in EU-related claims were British, only 15 percent EU and European (Koopmans 2004, 34; for similar results regarding newspaper editorials, see Pfetsch 2004; Pfetsch, Adam, and Eschner 2008).[5] The data from the Humboldt team confirm the picture. Only a little more than 10 percent of

---

3. Interestingly enough, the variation between countries did not turn out to be too significant. German, Austrian, and Spanish newspapers dealt with the EU as their primary subject in about 50% of the articles, while British, French, and Italian newspapers wavered around the 40% mark in their coverage of the EU as the primary topic.

4. EUROPUB was funded by the European Commission and led by Ruud Koopmans and Paul Statham with a research team in several EU member states (Koopmans and Statham 2010). EUROPUB covered Germany, France, Great Britain, Italy, Spain, Netherlands, and Switzerland, coding twenty-eight newspapers altogether. The study's unit of analysis was not articles, but claims, that is, political demands directed at some level of policymaking (national, European, EU, global). The researchers then coded who made the claims, to whom they were directed, or who was referred to otherwise in the claim.

5. This nationalism of the British press does not mean that European issues are not discussed in Britain. Rather, non-British actors are virtually absent in the British debates (Koopmans 2004, 23).

all political articles in the *Times* and the *Guardian* covered the EU as the primary subject, while the German *Frankfurter Allgemeine Zeitung* devoted fully one quarter of its political reporting to EU matters in 2000. At the same time, the Italian *La Repubblica* and the French *Libération* devoted 10 percent or less of their political articles to European affairs as the primary subject—in contrast to much greater coverage in *La Stampa* and *Le Monde* (Kantner 2006b, 153). In other words, the visibility of the EU is uneven across member states and sometimes within individual member states.

To come back to temporal developments, the EUROPUB data show significant increases in reporting about EU-level actors in the policy areas of European integration (from 24% in 1990 to 34% in 2002) and monetary policies (from 10% in 1990 to 26% in 2000 and 31% in 2002), reflecting the advent of the euro, while the numbers vary widely in agriculture without a clear tendency given that agriculture has been supranationalized for a long time (Koopmans 2004, 39). Research by a team based at the University of Bremen seem to confirm that European themes have increased in media reporting over time (Sifft et al. 2007; Wessler et al. 2008, chap. 3).[6] The study indicates that articles mentioning EU actors and institutions steadily increased from 8.3 percent in 1982 to about 30 percent in 2003, but still paled in comparison to national institutions and actors (about two thirds; see Wessler et al. 2008, 41). For the early 2000s, the findings are at least compatible with the studies mentioned above.[7]

These three research teams used different methodologies, but concur that European issues have become more visible in newspaper reporting across Europe. But one needs to be aware of methodological shortcomings: the team based at Humboldt University picked one year, EUROPUB chose only two years during the 1990s, and the data points selected by the Bremen-based team are each seven years apart. In the absence of time-series data, it is impossible to claim temporal developments, strictly speaking. Nevertheless, and taken together, the findings from the three studies seem to indicate increased visibility for the EU in the media discourses of the 1990s and 2000s. But this growing salience appears

---

6. The study's sampling procedure was based on eight so-called artificial weeks in 1982, 1989, 1996, and 2003 using five newspapers from five countries (Wessler et al. 2008, appendix 2). "Artificial week" refers to a sampling procedure according to which researchers select particular days over the year and then code the newspapers published on these days (e.g., a Monday in January, a Tuesday in March, a Wednesday in February, and so on). Moreover, the authors only coded "discursive articles," such as editorials, interviews, and longer reports.

7. In contrast, a study of press coverage during the 1999 European Parliament (EP) elections showed that the EU was not really present during these campaigns (Kevin 2001). The same holds true for television news coverage (Peter, De Vreese, and Semetko 2003).

to be confined to continental Western and Southern Europe[8] and includes the non-EU member Switzerland, which is, of course, strongly affected by EU policies and decisions. Great Britain, however, is not part of that trend, which serves as a first indication that Europeanization has not (yet) reached the British public sphere.

A more precise sense of temporal developments emerges from a data set on war and military interventions containing more than 450,000 newspaper articles from seven EU member states[9] and the United States covering the period from 1990 to 2005 that was put together by a team at Berlin's Freie Universität led by Cathleen Kantner and myself (Kantner, Kutter, and Renfordt 2008; Kantner 2009, for the following). Of course, this is an issue area in which the EU only recently gained competences so that one would not expect strong visibility. To discern the visibility of the EU, a corpus-linguistic analysis was carried out with a subsample of more than one hundred thousand articles focusing on military interventions (see figure 6.1).

Figure 6.1 shows, first, that the EU and EU politics are visible in 10–20 percent of the articles on average, which is rather surprising given the limited degree of EU competences in military affairs up to the late 1990s. Second, no clear pattern is visible during the early to mid-1990s. Third, however, we can observe some convergence in newspaper coverage from the late 1990s on, with a first peak in 1999, that is, during and after the Kosovo War, which also led to important EU decisions with regard to establishing the European Security and Defense Policy (ESDP). The EU's visibility then increases during the 2001–2003 period (post 9/11, Afghanistan, Iraq War) before decreasing again to the level of the mid-1990s. Fourth, the EU is mentioned surprisingly often in U.S. newspapers, particularly during the 1990s. All in all, the data disconfirm the notion that the EU is simply absent in newspaper coverage on military and security affairs.

However, an important methodological caveat is in order: the data reported so far refer to quality newspapers. Television news coverage appears to be different. A team led by Claes H. De Vreese analyzed EU coverage in television news in five countries for eleven months in 2000 (Peter, De Vreese, and Semetko 2003). The group also coded TV coverage of the EU in the weeks prior to the European Parliament elections in 1999 and 2004 for all EU member states (De Vreese et al. 2006; De Vreese 2007, 10). Overall, they found that stories about the EU accounted for less than 5 percent of the news coverage on average, increasing to about 10 percent during EU summit meetings. Although TV news coverage of

---

8. There are too few data available with regard to Central Eastern Europe to allow for even tentative conclusions.

9. Austria, France, Germany, Ireland, Netherlands, Poland, and the United Kingdom.

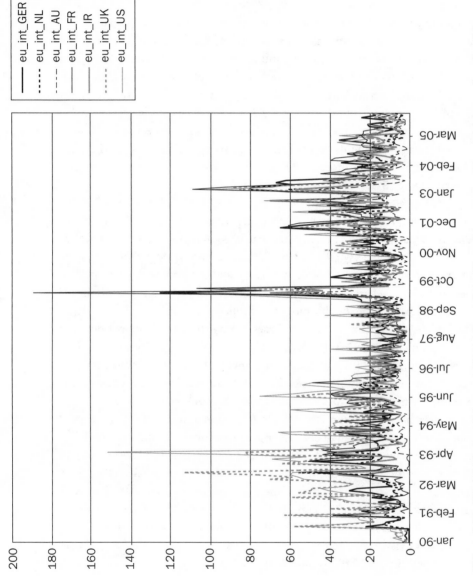

Figure 6.1. EU visibility in articles on military interventions. The y-axis measures the absolute number of articles per month per country (two quality newspapers per country except Ireland). Method: corpus-linguistic frequency analysis of references to the EU, its institutions and EU politics (altogether 24,533 articles out of N = 107,439 articles on humanitarian interventions).

Source: Kantner, Kutter, and Renfordt 2008.

the EU increased slightly from the 2000 European Parliament elections to the 2004 elections, it was still around only 10 percent on average in 2004. Peter and de Vreese conclude that "Television, it seems, has not left the nation-state" (Peter and De Vreese 2004, 18). Similar findings might hold true for the tabloid press. The EUROPUB team of Barbara Pfetsch and others showed that tabloids in Germany, Spain, and the Netherlands commented on the EU less often than quality newspapers—except, interestingly enough, for the United Kingdom where tabloids covered the EU much more frequently than the quality press (see Pfetsch, Adam, and Eschner 2008, 474).

Thus, the increased salience of EU-related issues might be confined to quality newspapers, which are mostly read by the elites including "the Europeans" (chapter 2). Since we know that most ordinary citizens get their news from TV and/or from tabloids, the higher presence of the EU in the media might only be visible to the elites and those interested in politics anyway. Nevertheless, it is no longer possible to claim that news media in general are wedded to the nation-state and ignore European politics. The data suggest a moderate degree of newspaper reporting about Europe, and this reporting includes EU level actors as well as actors from other European countries. I come back to the latter point in chapter 7.

Although it is important that European level developments no longer go unnoticed in the national newspapers, this is only the first among several necessary conditions for the Europeanization of public spheres. The EU might be more visible, but this does not imply that the same issues are discussed at the same time. I will now discuss the available data on the Europeanization of issue cycles.

Same Issues at the Same Time?

The next step is to ascertain whether or not the "same issues" are discussed "at the same time" across Europe. In a nutshell, the answer to this question is "yes, but."

There are less data available on this question than on news coverage about Europe and the EU in general. But most studies that include an analysis of issue cycles confirm that the same issues were indeed being discussed at (almost) the same time. First, Hans-Jörg Trenz investigated the "Future of Europe" debate (see Trenz 2007, 93; Trenz 2006), which started with the famous speech by German foreign minister Joschka Fischer at Berlin's Humboldt University in May 2000 and was followed by various contributions from other European foreign ministers and/or heads of states. News coverage in six EU countries[10] showed similar

10. Germany, France, Great Britain, Italy, Spain, and Austria.

highs and lows. The first peak concerned, of course, Fischer's speech and the ensuing debate, followed by another peak when French president Jacques Chirac gave his answer to Fischer at the end of June, while the Nice Summit in December 2000 led to another high point in newspaper coverage. In these cases, newspapers in all six countries increased their coverage of the debate. However, the European Convention drafting the Charter of Human Rights, which also met in September 2000, was covered extensively only by German and Spanish newspapers (maybe because its chairman was Roman Herzog, a former German Federal president, while the head of the EP delegation was a Spanish MEP).

Second, our own study of the so-called Haider debate in 2000 showed an almost identical issue cycle across Europe (see figure 6.2).[11] The first peak that concerned all newspapers in the five countries was reached in February 2000 when the EU Council of Foreign Ministers issued its so-called sanctions against the Austrian government. Another small peak occurred in July 2000, but it only concerned Italy when Jörg Haider visited the country, leading to a heated debate about whether Italians should protest against him. A final small peak was reached in September 2000 when the EU Council of Ministers cancelled its "sanctions" against Austria. Two findings stand out. To begin with, Austrian newspapers did not cover the Haider debate more extensively than other European newspapers. In February 2000, for example, the Italian newspapers *La Repubblica, Il Corriere della Serra,* and *La Nazione* as well as the French *Le Monde* carried by far the most articles on the subject. Moreover, the *New York Times* and the *Washington Post* covered the issue far less frequently compared to all other European newspapers. The Haider debate primarily concerned Europeans, while U.S. media found it less interesting.

Third, Silke Adam compared issue cycles for two debates in German and French newspapers from 2000 through 2002 (see Adam 2008, 101–2).[12] With regard to constitutional issues, she was able to confirm Trenz's findings that very similar issue cycles occurred in the two countries. A further study of German and French newspapers focusing on the 2004–5 time period comes to similar conclusions (Jentges, Trenz, and Vetters 2007). Amelie Kutter confirms these findings with regard to Polish newspapers, which she compared with the coverage of

---

11. The "Haider debate" started when a right-wing and xenophobic populist party led by Jörg Haider entered the Austrian government in February 2000 followed by a decision of the EU Council of Ministers to initiate diplomatic sanctions against Austria. The controversy mainly centered on the question of whether or not the EU was justified in meddling in the internal affairs of a member state. Our analysis focused on quality newspapers and tabloids in Belgium, France, Germany, Austria, Italy, and the United States from October 1999 to September 2000 (Risse and Van de Steeg 2008; Van de Steeg 2006).

12. Adam used a somewhat different methodology: rather than counting articles on a particular subject, she coded the claims made in these articles. See above on the EUROPUB project.

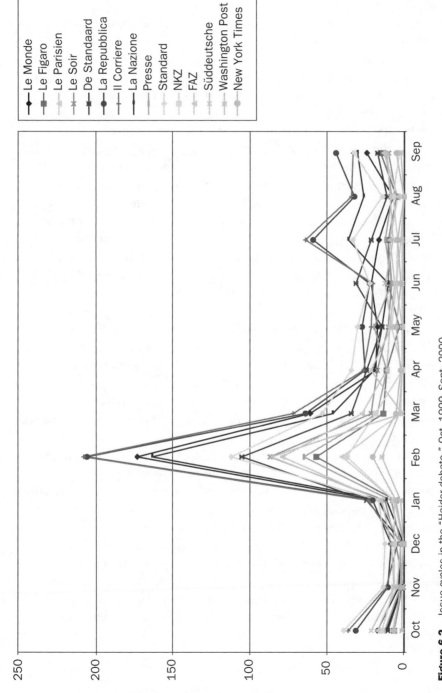

Figure 6.2. Issue cycles in the "Haider debate," Oct. 1999–Sept. 2000.

Note: The *y*-axis measures the number of articles per newspaper mentioning "Haider" as either a primary or secondary issue.

Source: Own data.

constitutional issues in French media (Kutter 2009). With regard to EU enlarge-ment, however, the highs and lows in German and French newspapers did not coincide. The enlargement debate—one of the most crucial decisions for the EU during the time period under investigation—was not very visible in the French media (Adam 2008).

Finally, the project by Cathleen Kantner et al. on news coverage relating to questions of war and peace in six EU countries and the United States also yields interesting results (see figures 6.3 and 6.4; Kantner 2009; Kantner, Kutter, and Renfordt 2008). In this case, two sampling strategies were chosen. Figure 6.3 de-picts the results of a wider sampling strategy using "military and humanitarian intervention" (and its derivatives) as well as "war" as the keywords and yielding almost half a million articles. In this case, only four peaks stick out relating to (1) the Gulf war in 1990–91, (2) the 1999 Kosovo crisis and war, (3) the inter-vention in Afghanistan in 2001, and (4) the Iraq War in 2002–03. During these four crises events, no systematic differences are observable between the amount and timing of media coverage in the six EU countries[13] and the United States.

In contrast, figure 6.4 shows the results of a corpus-linguistic frequency anal-ysis focusing on military and humanitarian interventions as well as its deriva-tives. These data yield many more peaks during the 1990s, centering on the crises in Somalia (1992–93), Rwanda (1994), Bosnia-Herzegovina (1995), and Sierra Leone (1998). Figures 6.3 and 6.4 also depict three patterns with regard to issue cycles. To begin with, issue cycles only start converging during the late 1990s, with the events surrounding the Kosovo intervention constituting the first com-mon peak among EU newspapers. Moreover, coverage of war and peace issues is generally higher in U.S. and U.K. newspapers than in the other European coun-tries, with the highs and lows following similar patterns. There is a continental (West) European pattern that also includes Ireland. German, Dutch, French, and Austrian newspapers follow rather similar issue cycles over the years.

In sum, these data show that European media have not only increased their coverage of EU policies and events, they are also by and large discussing the same issues at the same time. The increased salience of EU affairs in national newspapers as well as similarities in issue cycles indicate that the first criterion for Europeanized public spheres has been met, albeit with some qualifications. First, the findings pertain largely to quality newspapers. Second, Great Britain appears to be the exception with regard to the EU's visibility. And third, we have too few data on the new Central Eastern European members to reach firm conclusions.

---

13. Germany, Netherlands, Austria, France, Ireland, and the United Kingdom.

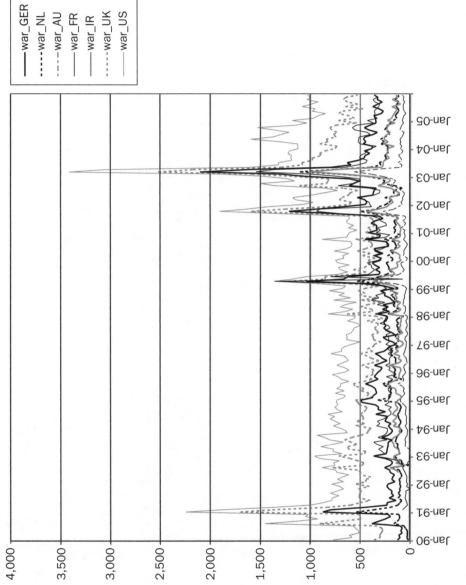

Figure 6.3. Issue cycles on wars and military interventions, 1990–2005. The y-axis measures the absolute number of articles per month per country (see figure 6.1). N = 480,847 articles on wars and military interventions.
Source: Kantner, Kutter, and Renfordt 2008; Kantner 2009.

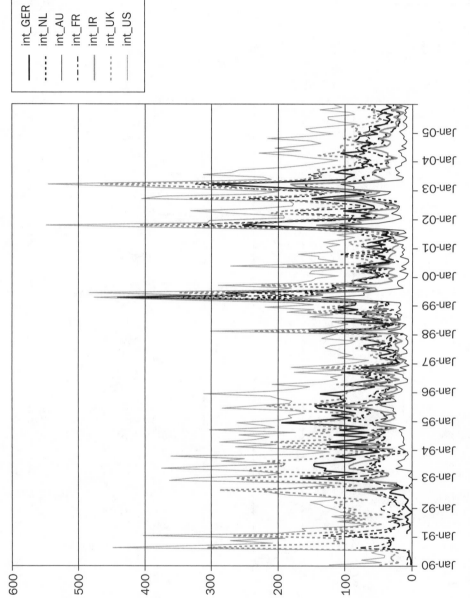

Figure 6.4. Issue cycles on military interventions only, 1990–2005. The y-axis measures the absolute number of articles per month per country (see figure 6.1). Method used: corpus-linguistic frequency analysis. N = 107,439 articles on military interventions.

Source: Kantner, Kutter, and Renfordt 2008; Kantner 2009.

With these qualifications, however, the first condition for the Europeanization of public spheres—"same issues at the same time with similar levels of attention"—can be confirmed for quality newspapers and for continental Europe. I now turn to the second criterion, namely the availability and similarity of frames of references and meaning structures with regard to European issues.

Similar Frames of Reference and Interpretations?

A common communicative space requires that we do not talk past each other, that we understand the issues at stake, and that we develop some common reference points in order to enable meaningful conversations. Fortunately, there are many studies available that have focused on such frames of reference in debates on specific European issues.[14] In general, these studies suggest that similar frames of references are available in the various national public spheres when European questions are discussed. Differences emerge with regard to the salience of particular frames and meaning structures. In many cases, general interpretative frames are widely shared (e.g., what is meant by further European integration?), while differences emerge with regard to specifics (e.g., which vision of future Europe is relevant in the respective country?). The more fine-tuned the analysis, the more researchers tend to see differences in meaning structures. In sum, we can observe the differential Europeanization of public spheres whereby certain meanings are collectively shared across countries, while others are interpreted following specific national contexts.

In the following, I concentrate on four Europe-wide debates for which we have sufficient data: (1) the so-called Haider debate in 2000, (2) the controversies on the future of European integration and the Constitutional as well as Lisbon Treaties from 2000 onward, (3) debates about EU enlargement, both with regard to Central Eastern Europe and to Turkey, and (4) discussions about European foreign and security policies. All four debates concerned central controversies about the future direction of the EU and shared a comparatively high issue salience and visibility across Europe.

---

14. In addition to the studies discussed below, see, e.g., Hodess 1998 for German and British coverage of the intergovernmental conferences in 1985 and 1990–91, Meyer 2002 for reports on the Cresson scandal that led to the fall of the Santer Commission (also Trenz 2000), and Semetko, De Vreese, and Peter 2000 for the launch of the euro.

Rule of Law or Moral Values? The "Haider Debate"

The "Haider debate" concerned the political crisis unleashed in the EU when Jörg Haider's right-wing and populist Liberal Party (Freiheitliche Partei Österreichs, FPÖ) entered the Austrian government in February 2000.[15] The EU member states agreed to impose some minor diplomatic sanctions against Austria to protest the decision to let this party, which was accused of xenophobia and Nazism, participate in the government. A European-wide debate followed on the legitimacy of the EU's intervening in the domestic politics of a member state.

Our analysis of the Haider debate[16] was based on a computer-aided qualitative content analysis of 2,160 articles from fifteen newspapers (both quality papers and tabloids) in five EU countries (France, Germany, Netherlands, Italy, and Austria) and the United States published between October 1999 and September 2000.[17] We conducted a frame analysis of the Haider debate by analyzing the dominant interpretive schema used by the various print media.

The frame analysis yielded four dominant frames:

1. "Haider, the Nazi": This frame depicts Jörg Haider as a Nazi and fascist.
2. "Haider, the xenophobe": This frame depicts Jörg Haider as a xenophobe and racist.
3. "European moral community": The EU is not just a market, but a moral community based on respect for human rights and democracy.
4. "European legal standards": The EU is primarily a legal community based on the rule of law and legal standards.

Because none of these master frames was mentioned in more than 20 percent of the coded articles, we conducted a quantitative statistical analysis. The factor analysis showed four underlying dimensions for all newspapers that loaded differently on the various frames from the content analysis:

1. "Waving the European flag": This is a visionary dimension that portrays the EU as a community of moral values and legal standards. Here, the

---

15. The following draws upon Risse and Van de Steeg 2008 and Van de Steeg 2006. See also Berkel 2006.

16. This research was funded by the German Research Foundation (Deutsche Forschungsgemeinschaft) in a joint project codirected by Bernd Giesen (University of Konstanz) and myself. I thank Valentin Rauer, Sylvain Rivet, and Marianne Van de Steeg for their cooperation.

17. France: *Le Monde, Le Figaro, Le Parisien;* Germany: *Frankfurter Allgemeine Zeitung, Süddeutsche Zeitung, Bild;* Italy: *La Repubblica, Il Corriere della Sera, La Nazione;* Belgium: *Le Soir, De Standaard;* Austria: *Die Presse, Der Standard, Neue Kronenzeitung;* United States: *New York Times, Washington Post.* Every third article in the sample based on a search strategy using "Haider" as the keyword was coded.

moral community and legal standards frames combine with support for the European "sanctions" against Austria.

Example: Italian president Carlo Azeglio Ciampi stated that "the EU is not only an alliance between states, but also a supranational entity. Now, the fact that in one of these countries…a political party may enter in government that shows understandings that are not completely respectful of the values that founded the Union, and that which I call pax Europea, well, that arouses concern." (*Il Corriere della Sera,* 2 January 2000)

2. "Upholding the law": This is the countervision to "waving the flag" insofar as it portrays the EU as a community based on clear and precise legal standards. This leads to strong opposition to European interference in a democratically elected government (as long as Austria does not break the law). This factor also loaded on frames defending Austria against accusations of being a Nazi and racist country.

   Example: "The program of the prime minister for the withdrawal of the sanctions states: The sanctions can be removed via a comprehensible system of mutual understanding and respect. The EU should develop a standard that clearly and impeccably defines how it is related to democracy, the rule of law, and human rights" (*Neue Kronenzeitung,* 17 May 2000).

3. "Haider is a Nazi": This factor loads heavily on strong evaluative frames, such as "Haider is a Nazi" or "Haider is a xenophobe" and "Austria is a Nazi country," as expressed by the author of the following article.

   Example: "Only slogans of blue—since it is the color of the FPÖ, whose liberal component is a minority today—were conspicuous because of their populist and xenophobic violence. 'Üeberfremdung' cried out the posters, without being afraid to borrow from the Nazi terminology by shouting about an 'overflow' and 'dissatisfaction' with immigrants, who are judged as 'profiteers and robbers of employment'" (*Le Soir,* 29 January 2000).

4. "Haider, the alleged Nazi": In contrast to the third factor, this one emphasizes equally strong evaluations, but not by the article's author, but by foreign actors cited in the article. In other words, this factor explicitly takes the perspective of an observer.

These factors then were submitted to linear regression analyses in order to find out how the meaning structures in the articles differed from one another. We wanted to know, for example, whether the newspaper's country of origin made a difference (e.g., Austria vs. the rest of Europe, EU member state vs. the United States), whether liberal or conservative newspapers framed the issue in different ways, or whether quality newspapers and tabloids could be distinguished in their framing.

To cut a long story short, the statistical findings regarding the similarity or differences of meaning structures were unambiguous. The main difference across variables concerned the meaning structures employed by newspapers and weeklies from EU member states, on the one hand, and those employed by the two U.S. newspapers, on the other. The conservative German *Frankfurter Allgemeine Zeitung* had more in common with the liberal French *Le Monde* and even the Austrian *Die Presse* than with the *New York Times* or the *Washington Post*.

U.S. newspapers talked significantly less about "upholding the law" in comparison to EU newspapers and reported more on "Haider, the alleged Nazi." U.S. newspapers reported on the Haider case from the perspective of distant observers. The controversy about Haider and the events in Austria were reported as happening "over there in Europe," that is, elsewhere. This observer perspective can already be seen in the headlines, for example, "Europe Moving Cautiously in Punishment for Austria" (*New York Times*, 2 April 2000), or "Report Clears Way for Europe to Drop Austrian Sanctions" (*New York Times*, 9 September 2000).

As for the European newspapers, national origin did not matter much in explaining differences in the use of particular frames. For "Upholding the law," for example, the newspaper's ideological orientation had more explanatory power than its national origins. The more conservative the newspaper, the more likely it was to use this frame, which led to a rejection of the European "sanctions." Only for "Haider is a Nazi" did the nationality of the newspapers explain more than other variables. In this case, Italian and French newspapers differed significantly from Austrian newspapers. In general, however, the European newspapers had more in common with one another than they differed. Ideological orientation mattered little (except for "upholding the law"), and, interestingly enough, the difference between quality newspapers and tabloids did not yield significant results, either.

In comparison to U.S. newspapers, European newspapers dealt with the coming to power of Haider's FPÖ as an issue that concerned not only Austrians but Europe as a whole. The media employed a common horizon of reference, even though the debate was very heated across the EU with regard to the pros and cons of the so-called sanctions. For example, the German *Frankfurter Allgemeine Zeitung* and the Austrian *Die Presse* strongly argued against the sanctions, while the Belgian *Le Soir*, the French *Le Monde*, and—surprisingly—the Austrian *Der Standard* used considerably more space for arguments in favor. However, even though the editorial positions of these newspapers were quite apparent, other opinions on the matter were fully included. In the end, both sides of the Haider debate acknowledged the values on which the European Union should be based. This was particularly true for the Austrian newspapers included in our sample. Not only did *Die Presse* and *Der Standard* disagree on the question of EU sanctions, they also did not distinguish themselves in any way from the other newspapers analyzed. The EU-wide pro-sanction camp was led by the French *Le Monde,* while the German *Frankfurter Allgemeine Zeitung* defended Austria vigorously. In this case, a transnational European public sphere emerged—via the national media. It was fundamentally a debate about European core values and their meanings (see also Trenz 2006, 265). The EU was portrayed as a community based on human rights as well as legal standards. The controversy then centered on the question which of these values had to be more significant when dealing with the coming to power of a right-wing party in a member state.

"Deepening": Europe Debates Constitutional Issues

One could object that the Haider debate was a most likely case for the emergence of Europeanized public spheres given its value-laden connotations and the lack of material interests at stake. In comparison, constitutional issues seem to be harder cases for a transnational European public sphere in light of the distinct national positions on these questions. Why should the Euroskeptical British media use similar frames as the Euroenthusiastic Italian newspapers—not to mention Eastern European or Scandinavian media? Moreover, constitutional questions in the EU concern national governments as "masters of the treaties." The main media events are intergovernmental conferences (IGCs) culminating in EU summits of heads of states and governments. This increases the likelihood that constitutional issues are discussed in distinctly national or even nationalist colors in the various public spheres.

The study by Juan Diez-Medrano provides a good starting point for the following discussion (see Diez Medrano 2003, chap. 4). Diez Medrano analyzed editorials in German, Spanish, and British newspapers and weeklies covering the time period from 1946 to 1997.[18] In general, he showed that German and Spanish journalists expressed a more positive attitude toward the EC/EU and toward European integration in general than did British editorialists. Interestingly enough, these patterns have been rather stable over time and have not been affected much by the respective country's entry into the EC or even by regime change in the case of Spain. Therefore, Diez Medrano hints at a continental (West) European positive framing of EU affairs in contrast to a British negative one.

---

18. Note, however, that his sample contained only about two hundred editorials per country for the entire time period.

Hans-Jörg Trenz analyzed German, French, British, Italian, and Spanish newspaper editorials with regard to the "Future of Europe" debate starting with Fischer's speech in Berlin in May 2000 and ending with the Nice summit in December 2000 (Trenz 2007; Trenz 2006, 297–360). The controversy was primarily seen as a French-German affair with Fischer and French president Jacques Chirac as the main protagonists, and representatives of other countries assuming observer status. All newspapers view the French-German "couple" as the engines of European integration responsible for past and present progress in the EU. Except for the British conservative press, this is evaluated positively by all newspapers. Equally interesting, the European past is portrayed as a success story of integration based on the values of a moral community.

Cleavages emerge with regard to the future. Three models for European integration form the core of the debate: a federal EU (as advocated by Fischer), a Europe of states (Tony Blair's position), and a functionally integrated Europe (with which the European Commission is identified). Although all newspaper editorials reject the latter model, the debate focuses on the federal versus the intergovernmental vision. As is to be expected, German, French, Italian, and Austrian newspapers favor Fischer's vision, while British and Spanish editorials support the intergovernmental model. Yet, and most significant in our context, the three models are present and are being evaluated in all countries, suggesting similar frames of reference. As Trenz put it, "The journalists' look at Europe is taken…through a pair of European glasses. Only the British newspapers' vision of Europe is split up by internal partisan conflicts" (Trenz 2007, 107).

The EUROPUB's analysis of newspaper editorials in seven West European countries from 2000 to 2002 confirms these results and also expands the analysis (Pfetsch, Adam, and Eschner 2008). Although using a different method (claims analysis, see above), Barbara Pfetsch and her colleagues observe a clear difference in the framing of constitutional issues between British newspapers, on the one hand, and continental European newspapers, on the other. For the latter, the main conflict lines are about, first, the federal vs. the intergovernmental model for the EU, and, second, about the prioritization of widening or deepening of the EU. Sixty-five percent to 80 percent of all conflict lines in the German, French, Spanish, and Italian newspapers cover these two dimensions (Pfetsch, Adam, and Eschner 2008, 479–80). The main difference between quality newspapers in these countries, on the one hand, and regional newspapers as well as tabloids, on the other, concerns the fact that the latter focus on the "widening vs. deepening" conflict line. Other than that, the framing appears to be similar. A more detailed analysis of debates on constitutional issues in German and French newspapers during the same time period reveals that German papers adopt rather negative views toward the EU, while the French show a much more balanced picture (Adam 2008, 2007). However, as argued in chapter 5, differences in opinions for or against the EU should not be used as indicators of the Europeanization of public spheres as long as the frames of reference are similar.

British newspapers do not care that much about institutional issues, but deal mostly with European foreign policy and with monetary issues. The debates in non-EU member Switzerland, of course, are mainly about EU membership. The findings reported by Pfetsch et al. confirm Trenz's data with regard to the future course of the EU. Newspaper editorials in continental EU countries strongly support further integration and supranationalism, and they prioritize deepening over further enlargement. British newspapers take the opposite perspective. If we take into consideration that the issue salience of European integration is also considerably lower in British newspapers, these findings seem to suggest that the United Kingdom is not only the "odd one out" with regard to the *policies* of European integration and to European *identity* (chapters 2 and 3), but also with regard to the Europeanization of *public spheres*.

Furthermore, a study led by Ruth Wodak investigated newspaper coverage surrounding the Brussels summit in December 2003 during which the Italian EU presidency failed to secure agreement on the Constitutional Treaty (Oberhuber et al. 2005). This group employed yet again a different methodology, namely critical discourse analysis (Fairclough and Wodak 1997). Nevertheless, the findings are compatible with the data from frame analysis à la Trenz and claims analysis à la EUROPUB. Wodak et al. analyzed newspapers from eight countries that not only included the usual suspects but also Poland, Sweden, and Austria. The main frame shared by all newspapers across Europe concerns the representation of the EU as a power struggle in which national interests ultimately prevail. Although this is evaluated positively or at least neutrally in the United Kingdom, Poland, and Spain (the Polish and Spanish governments vetoed a European Constitution in Brussels), French, German, Italian, Austrian, and Swedish newspapers contrast this "reality of Europe" with a European vision of common values and a common purpose. In the German case, the conservative *Frankfurter Allgemeine Zeitung* shares the views of the Euroskeptical crowd and uses very similar frames to those of the British, Spanish, or Polish newspapers.

Another common frame that is evaluated differently across Europe concerns the likely emergence of a "core Europe" of countries that prefer closer integration, leading to a split in the EU between a core and a periphery. Not surprisingly, this theme is regarded differently across the various newspapers, with no discernible pattern emerging. The same holds true for the framing of Germany and France as the "engines of integration." Although the importance of these two countries is recognized by the media across Europe, the performance of their governments is evaluated differently and there is no agreement on the issue in France and Germany itself.

Oberhuber et al. interpret their findings as disconfirming evidence for the Europeanization of public spheres, arguing that "within each country a different EU seems to be represented and different issues are debated" (Oberhuber et al. 2005, 263). I disagree with this interpretation of the data: they actually confirm the emergence of common master frames of reference with regard to constitutional issues across Europe, including the new member states. They also show—particularly with regard to France and Germany—that the main cleavages do not pit pro-integrationist countries against anti-integrationist ones, but that these lines of conflict cut across the European public space. This somewhat modifies the data by Trenz as well as by Pfetsch et al., even though the British press once again assumes a peculiar position. Finally, more so than other studies reported so far, Oberhuber et al. demonstrate the polarization in Europe when it comes to constitutional issues (see chapter 8). In my view, however, polarization and contestation are indicators of an evolving Europeanization of public spheres rather than the opposite—as long as this polarization does not strictly follow national lines. As long as Europeans use similar frames of reference, they can understand one another across borders in transnational space irrespective of the degree of contestation and polarization (see chapter 5).

This polarization about the constitutional project continued with the controversies over the ratification of the Constitutional Treaty, culminating in the two failed referendums in France and the Netherlands in 2005. Hans-Jörg Trenz and his group compared German and French news coverage of the debate on the French referendum in 2004–5 (Jentges, Trenz, and Vetters 2007). Not surprisingly, the French newspapers reported in much more politicized and polarized ways than the German papers, which were more passively observing the controversy (Germany did not have a referendum). As to "master frames" legitimizing the EU and European integration, the study found that about half of all legitimizing arguments concerned the EU as a functional problem-solving community, while the remaining arguments focused on the EU as a cosmopolitan community of universal rights, on the one hand, and a distinct historical and cultural community, on the other. These two latter frames were present in both discourses, but they were emphasized in different ways. In other words, this analysis clearly identified similar frames of reference in the two countries.

A media analysis by Ulrike Liebert and others allows us to further examine how the constitutional debate played itself out across Europe during that time period (Liebert 2007a; Meyer 2007). Moreover, this study allows for one of the first glimpses into news coverage about European politics in the new Central Eastern European member states, since, in addition to France and the

United Kingdom, it covered Poland, the Czech Republic, Latvia, and Estonia. Several results stand out. The ratification debates led to a considerable politicization and further contestation across Europe, not only in the countries where citizens had to vote on the Constitutional Treaty. Between two thirds and three fourths of all articles coded contained evaluative statements in favor of or against the Constitutional Treaty (Liebert 2007b, 254, 256). Yet, except for the Czech Republic, public involvement in the debates was rather limited in Central Eastern Europe where an elitist discourse dominated (Rakusanova 2007; Wyrozumska 2007; Evas 2007).

Two cleavages were visible during the debate: a pro- vs. anti-EU cleavage, particularly in France and the United Kingdom (less so in the new member states, interestingly enough!), on the one hand, and a pro- vs. anti-Constitutional Treaty conflict, on the other hand, which could be observed in all countries. The latter conflict centered on different issues: for example, a major debate in France concerned the question of a "social Europe" (Maatsch 2007; Jentges, Trenz, and Vetters 2007), while the Polish debate focused on the number of Polish votes in the Council of Ministers and the question of the so-called double majority (Wyrozumska 2007). In other words, we find both shared meaning structures across national public spheres and particular frames that were used only in specific national contexts.

Amelie Kutter's in-depth comparison of the constitutional debates in Polish and French quality newspapers between 2002 and 2004 confirms these findings (Kutter 2009). Both the issue salience and intensity as well as the topics covered are similar in the two countries. Differences emerge with regard to justification patterns for particular issues. Moreover, the more newspapers try to "domesticize" European issues, the more they link EU constitutional questions to symbols of national history and the national constitutional traditions. Kutter concludes that these practices successfully "translate" EU issues into domestic contexts, but—at the same time—might make transnational exchanges more difficult (Kutter 2009, chap. 4).

In sum, media analyses of debates about a European constitution that started with the "Future of Europe" controversy in 2000, continued through the deliberations of the European Convention in 2003–4, and culminated in the ratification debates on the Constitutional Treaty show increasingly politicized public spheres across Europe. We can also observe the emergence of various conflict lines focusing on the *finalité politique* (endpoint of the political integration) of the European Union (supranational vs. intergovernmental), on the European common good vs. narrowly defined national interests, and—increasingly—on the substantive content of European policies (e.g., neoliberal vs. more socially oriented policies). These cleavages are visible across the various public spheres, with different degrees of emphasis. Although there are indeed some distinctive national frames (e.g., pertaining to the number of votes in the Council of Ministers), the frames of reference and meaning structures appear to be sufficiently similar to allow for transnational European discourses. This is particularly true for continental Western Europe, where a core group of largely Europeanized public spheres is emerging. Once again, Great Britain remains an outlier in these debates, while the new Eastern European member states are apparently beginning to actively participate in these controversies. Most important, however, ten years of rather heated constitutional debates across Europe have led to a growing politicization of EU affairs, but not to a renationalization of public spheres. Rather, contestation appears to coincide with a gradual Europeanization of debates measured through increasing similarities in meaning structures. I will come back to these themes in chapters 8 and 10.

"Widening": Europe Debates Enlargement

Apart from constitutional issues, EU enlargement has been one of the most important topics in European politics since the end of the cold war (see, e.g., Schimmelfennig 2003; Sedelmeier 2005; Grabbe 2006). In the early 1990s, the EU invited the former Communist Central Eastern European countries to join. These countries entered the union in 2004 and 2007. In the late 1990s, the EU granted an accession perspective to the western Balkans, on the one hand, and to Turkey, on the other. The latter enlargements sparked widespread controversies across Europe with regard to the EU's borders, potential trade-offs between "deepening and widening," and identity-related questions as to what the EU is all about. EU enlargement also concerns an issue on which mass public opinion across the "old" EU member states has been far more skeptical all along than elite opinion, which largely supported Eastern enlargement. How are these debates reflected in the public spheres? Can we observe similar developments to those during the controversies about the future of European integration?

Marianne Van de Steeg conducted a media analysis on the coverage of Eastern enlargement from 1989 to 1998 in Germany, Netherlands, Spain, and the United Kingdom—with Switzerland as a control case (Van de Steeg 2005; also Risse and Van de Steeg 2008). Her factor analysis of the various content elements she coded yielded only two factors:

1. The enlargement as a catalyst of institutional and financial problems for the current member states. This factor loaded high on reports related to institutional reform and the financial consequences of enlargement for the budget and the agricultural, structural, and cohesion policies.

Example: "The process of enlarging the EU ... will be long and difficult. The EU has to revise its institutional and financial structure, and reform its policies in order to make this enlargement possible, while the candidates have to do their part of the homework" (*El País,* 13 March 1998).

2. A focus on Central Eastern Europe itself and the process of enlargement.

Example: "According to the Polish press, the German interior minister has made it clear that closer ties with the EC depended on the steps Warsaw takes to limit immigration" (*Guardian,* 16 February 1993).

Interestingly enough, identity-related arguments did not play a major role in Western European newspaper reporting about Eastern enlargement—in strong contrast to the controversy about Turkish membership. The absence of identity-related frames probably results from the fact that Eastern enlargement did not pose any problems in this regard. It was obvious to everyone concerned that Central Eastern Europe legitimately belonged to "Europe" and the EU and that, therefore, the end of the cold war had brought Eastern Europe "back to Europe" (see chapter 9 for a detailed analysis).

The statistical analysis then confirmed the picture that was already observable with regard to the Haider debate: the Swiss *Neue Zürcher Zeitung* differed most substantially from the newspapers and weeklies published in EU member states. The Swiss newspaper dedicated significantly more attention to the situation in the former Communist Central Eastern European countries and the process of enlargement in general. In contrast, the newspapers from EU member states did not differ much from each other and emphasized the financial and institutional consequences of enlargement. Independently of being in favor of or against Eastern enlargement, the EU-based media were more concerned than the Swiss newspaper about the necessary changes in the institutional structure of the EU, and focused on changes in the agricultural, structural, and cohesion policies to mitigate the impact of enlargement. In other words, newspapers of the "old" EU member states adopted an internal perspective with regard to enlargement, while the non-EU newspaper reported from the standpoint of being an observer and outsider. Van de Steeg's analysis documents the enlargement debates at a time (the 1990s) when they were not particularly politicized and when the "if" of Eastern enlargement was not very controversial, at least not among the political elites.

This changed during the early 2000s, the closer the accession date came. French public opinion turned out to be among the most hostile toward Eastern enlargement. In 2002, for example, 47 percent of the French were against Eastern enlargement (European Commission 2002, 85), 17 percent more than the EU average. Yet, during the same time period, French quality newspapers concealed, rather than openly debated, the conflict over Eastern enlargement. They shared the silence of the French political elites on the subject. The German media at least commented regularly, but mostly negatively, about the enlargement project (Adam 2007, 2008). Nevertheless, and particularly compared with the constitutional debates, Eastern enlargement has never been as politicized in the various public spheres—irrespective of a largely skeptical mass public opinion.

This is very different with regard to Turkish EU membership (see chapter 9). Andreas Wimmel's analysis of editorials and opinion pieces in British, French, and German newspapers on the question of Turkish membership in the EU during the fall of 2002 confirms the arguments made so far (Wimmel 2006a, 2006b). He shows a deeply polarized debate on Turkish accession, particularly in Germany and France, while British newspapers—the *Financial Times* and the *Guardian*—supported EU membership for Turkey, in line with the government of Tony Blair. Wimmel demonstrates that two frames dominated the debate about Turkey in the editorials. First, there was the controversy over the institutional consequences of Turkish membership for the EU, namely the arguments about "deepening vs. widening." This debate closely resembles the controversies surrounding Eastern enlargement and is comparable to Van de Steeg's first factor reported above. In the case of Turkish membership, the French and German newspapers used this frame to argue against accession, since it would severely strain the EU's institutional structure, while the British newspapers argued in favor of "widening" precisely because they favored a more loosely institutionalized EU. Wimmel interprets this as suggesting that different visions of the EU's *finalité politique* colored media opinions on Turkish membership.

The second frame concerned issues of culture and identity, namely the contested nature of European identity as "modern political" vs. "traditional Christian," discussed in chapters 2 and 3. This framing of the issue led to opposing recommendations in German and French newspapers. The French *Le Figaro* and the German *Frankfurter Allgemeine Zeitung* argued vigorously against Turkish membership, since this Islamic country did not belong to "Christian" Europe, while *Le Monde* and *Süddeutsche Zeitung* equally forcefully defended Europe's modern and secular identity. The EU should, therefore, keep the door open to Turkish membership. Geostrategic "realist" arguments were rarely used in the German and French press, in contrast to the British newspapers. I will come back to this in chapter 9.

In sum, the enlargement debates appear to confirm the findings reported above about constitutional issues as well as the Haider debate: we can indeed observe the gradual Europeanization of public spheres in the EU with regard to the general frames of reference and meaning structures. Although the opinions expressed on enlargement differ and often follow country-specific patterns, most frames seemed to be available across Europe. Although Eastern enlargement was not politicized and sometimes covered very little in the media, Turkish accession triggered more controversial debates in the various public spheres. This suggests that national media (including editorials) largely replicated the elite discourses on enlargement. Since Eastern enlargement was more or less consensual among the political and economic elites in the EU (see, e.g., Schimmelfennig 2003), in contrast to public opinion, the controversies did not play themselves out in the media to the extent one might have expected. In the Turkish case, however, elites were as divided as the larger publics in major EU member states. As a result, this debate showed up in the media. These findings appear to suggest that debates about Europe and the EU are very much dominated by the political elites in the media—except in cases of public referenda (as in France, the Netherlands, and Ireland with regard to the Constitutional Treaty and the Lisbon Treaty, respectively).

The External Dimension: Europe Debates Foreign and Security Policy

European foreign and security policy is a "hard" case for the emergence of Europeanized public spheres. The Haider debate, constitutional issues, and questions of EU enlargement are themes that touch the very core of what constitutes the EU as an emerging polity. If we did not find common frames of reference and similar meaning structures here, the EU would lack the essential ingredients of such a polity, namely a democratic public sphere in which questions of common concern are debated. Foreign and security policy is different. First, the EU and its member states have only recently started speaking with one voice in foreign policy and the institutional development of the Common Foreign and Security Policy (CFSP) and of the European Security and Defense Policy (ESDP) have lagged behind other policy areas (Howorth 2007; Smith 2003; Smith 2004). Second, EU attempts at establishing a common foreign policy compete both with strong national traditions and with the transatlantic security community, particularly the North Atlantic Treaty Organization (NATO). If we were to find similar developments toward the Europeanization of public spheres in this policy area, this would substantially strengthen the findings reported above.

Unfortunately, the findings from various media analyses do not allow for firm conclusions. Antje Knorr's study, for example, coded more than twenty-eight hundred articles in German, French, British, and American newspapers covering the first Gulf War in 1991, the Kosovo War in 1999, and the Iraq War in 2003 (Knorr 2006). She found that preconditions for a Europeanization of public spheres in foreign and security policy exist. In each of the cases, the frames of reference turned out to be rather similar across countries so as to enable cross-border communication. A factor analysis yielded two master frames for all three cases and across all countries and newspapers, namely "Americans strive for hegemony" and "fighting evil." Caroline Fehl's analysis of British and German newspaper reporting before and after the terrorist attacks on September 11, 2001, confirms the finding (Fehl 2005). On either side of the channel, the United States is identified with very strongly and the differences in the framing of British and German newspapers are minimal. Fehl noticed a slight difference according to the newspapers' political orientations with the reporting of the liberal *Guardian* and *Süddeutsche Zeitung* being a bit more critical of the United States than their more conservative counterparts.

However, Knorr was unable to show the emergence of a European public sphere separate from either a transatlantic public sphere or a continental European public sphere in her three cases (Knorr 2006). During the first Gulf War and during the Kosovo War, newspapers in all four countries used rather similar framing and interpretations irrespective of continent, country, or the political orientation of the media. Only during the Iraq War in 2003 did some indicators suggest the emergence of a continental European public sphere—French-German in this case—as compared to an Anglo-American one. French and German newspapers used an identity discourse to distance "Europe" from the United States. However, one should take this finding with a grain of salt given the highly controversial nature of the U.S.-led intervention in Iraq and the fact that Germany and France positioned themselves as the main critics of the Anglo-American–led war. Once again, newspapers reflected rather than actively shaped the elite discourses on the subject.

The Bremen-based team led by Hartmut Wessler analyzed newspaper editorials and other "discursive" articles in Austria, Denmark, France, Germany, and Great Britain during the crises and wars in Iraq (1991), Bosnia (1995), Kosovo (1999), and Iraq (2003) in order to discern similarities and differences (Wessler et al. 2008, chap. 6). Wessler et al. then tried to code convergence as well as divergence with regard to statements in favor of or opposed to military interventions, on the one hand, and concerning frames and patterns of justifications, on the other. They find "no evidence that the cleavage structures of public debates have converged since the 1990s" (Wessler et al. 2008, 108). But as noted in chapter 5, the degree of polarization in public debates—whether within or between countries—should not be used as an indicator for the presence or absence of transnational public spheres. With regard to frames and patterns of justifications, they found that a frame pertaining to the use of force as *a last resort* was the most widely used argument in favor of or opposed to military interventions across all four cases, while frames pertaining to human rights or international law varied widely between cases. However, no convergence of justification frames could be observed over time.[19]

A rather fine-grained analysis was conducted by Swantje Renfordt who coded German, British, and American newspapers debating UN Resolution 1441 on Iraq between November 2002 and March 2003, that is, up to the beginning of the U.S.-led intervention in Iraq (see Renfordt 2007). She found four master frames in all eight newspapers she analyzed: "law matters," "the UN matters," "Iraq poses a threat," and "U.S. foreign policy is bad." Three of these four frames were equally prominent in all three countries, suggesting a common transatlantic meaning structure. However, Renfordt showed that the "law matters" frame turned out to be a genuinely European one that was used by British and German newspapers much more often than by American ones. Irrespective of whether one supported or opposed the war in Iraq, British and German media concurred in framing the issue at stake as one involving international law.

Renfordt's dissertation built upon this study and used the data set of newspaper articles on war and military interventions in six EU countries and the United States from 1990 on developed by Cathleen Kantner et al. (Renfordt 2009; see also Kantner 2009). As mentioned above, this is the only data set available that allows developments over time to be analyzed. Renfordt's statistical analysis of more than five thousand manually coded articles covering the entire time period showed that frames pertaining to international law were by far the most significant master frames governing Western debates about war, peace, and military interventions in the post–cold war period. Everything else (national interest, sovereignty concerns, European identity, even moral principles) paled in comparison. Moreover, international law debates concerned, first, procedural issues (who legitimizes the use of force and what is the role of the UN Security Council?),[20] and, as a distant second, the relevance of international humanitarian law. Renfordt then showed that there is an increasing convergence among the countries studied over time. Differences between individual countries as well as between the ideological orientations of individual newspapers did not matter much. However, references to international law were more pronounced in European newspapers than in the U.S. media.

This legal discourse, which resonates well with the findings from the Haider debate during which the EU was interpreted as by and large a legal community,

---

19. Unfortunately, data for individual newspapers are not reported so that we do not know whether the differences between countries are more or less pronounced than the variations between newspapers and their political orientations.

20. This finding is corroborated by Wessler et al. 2008, 116–17.

appears to distinguish Europeanized public spheres from transatlantic ones. One can conclude, therefore, that we observe in foreign and security policy matters the emergence of Europeanized public spheres, not in opposition to, but embedded in a larger transatlantic discourse. Although there are still many commonalities between the United States and Europe in security affairs, some distinctive "European colors" seem to be visible.

These findings are corroborated by Cathleen Kantner's analysis which used the same data set to answer the question whether issues of European identity played a major role in these debates about military interventions (Kantner 2009). The answer is "no, but." Explicit references to a European collective identity do not seem to play a major role in controversies about foreign and security policy. However, the conflicts in the western Balkans during the 1990s (particularly Kosovo), the Afghanistan intervention in 2001, and the Iraq war in 2003 did trigger a slight increase in expressions of European identity, especially with regard to the EU as a community of values. Once again, this pattern was strongest in continental Europe.

Conclusions

What is the "big picture" for the Europeanization of public spheres with regard to the two criteria of first, visibility and similarity of issue cycles, and second, convergence of frames of reference and meaning structures? As to the first criterion, the available data suggest both a greater visibility for the EU during the 1990s and 2000s and a similarity of issue cycles.

The findings with regard to the second criterion are more ambivalent. On the one hand, a gradual Europeanization of public spheres with regard to frames of reference and interpretive structures can be observed in debates about EU constitutional issues including such value-laden questions as the Haider debate and such highly contested questions as Turkish EU membership. On the other hand, debates about Eastern enlargement as well as European foreign and security policy have not only been less politicized, but the findings from the various studies do not yet show a clear picture. With regard to foreign and security policy, a gradual Europeanization of meaning structures around legal frames seems to have emerged, not in opposition to the transatlantic sphere, but embedded in it and with a distinctive European flavor. Whether this means that the politicization of European issues not only increases the EU's visibility in the public spheres (which is obvious), but also leads to growing similarities in interpretive structures across Europe, is a hypothesis worth further testing (see chapter 10).

With regard to variation between countries as to the Europeanization of public spheres, no clear national patterns are observable with regard to individual countries—with one exception: Great Britain appears to be different and seems to have less Europeanized media than the continental West European countries including some Southern EU members such as Spain or Italy. Firm conclusions about the new East European member states are not yet possible. We might, thus, conclude with Barbara Pfetsch et al. that "the further a country is integrated into the European Union, the less parochial is its press and the stronger it takes part in a common European debate" (Pfetsch, Adam, and Eschner 2008, 465). But one should not exaggerate this point, since we can still observe both similarities and differences in the way in which European issues are being debated (see Diez Medrano 2003, 249). The general frames might be available everywhere, but they often appear in national colors.

Several methodological caveats are in order. The ambivalent results with regard to the uneven Europeanization of frames of reference are at least partly the result of the different coding methods of the various research teams—from analyzing frames (e.g., Kantner 2009; Wessler et al. 2008), focusing on claims (e.g., Koopmans and Statham 2010; Pfetsch, Adam, and Eschner 2008), and conducting linguistic discourse analysis (e.g., Oberhuber et al. 2005; Kutter 2007). In addition, there is little agreement in the literature about the baseline from which to infer a growing similarity of meaning structures. Some authors take increasing polarization and contestation as indicators of the lack of Europeanization. As argued in chapter 5, I take the opposite view. It does not matter much that the media in country X overwhelmingly reject the Lisbon Treaty, while the media in country Y support it, as long as the considerations under which the treaty is being debated remain similar.

But even if one does not use consensus or contestation as indicators for the presence or absence of a public sphere, the problem remains of how similar interpretive structures have to be in order to qualify as indicators for the Europeanization of public spheres. In general, we can observe convergence with regard to master frames such as "Europe is a legal community" or "widening or deepening," while—not surprisingly—differences occur with regard to more detailed subframes. The only way to sort these differences out methodologically would be (a) to conduct time series in order to observe temporal developments, and (b) to compare differences between individual media, on the one hand, with differences between individual countries, on the other.[21] The only data set available to allow for both comparisons is the one on foreign and security policy collected by

---

21. I thank Marianne Van de Steeg for repeatedly reminding me of these points.

Cathleen Kantner and her team in Berlin (Kantner, Kutter, and Renfordt 2008; Kantner 2009; Renfordt 2009). Some first-regression analyses demonstrate that time matters enormously and, thus, the particular context of a debate, while differences between countries and individual newspapers are almost negligible (Renfordt 2009).

With these caveats in mind, I tentatively conclude that we can disconfirm the notion that Europeans talk past each other and that they are unable to understand each other because of different languages or different orientations toward European integration. On the contrary, the findings seem to suggest that polarization and controversies lead to similar interpretations and frames of reference rather than driving communication apart. Although the Europeanization of public spheres with regard to visibility and meaning structures remains uneven, it can nevertheless be observed, at least in continental Western Europe—interestingly enough, in those countries that also show a growing Europeanization of citizen and elite identities.

But does the similarity of interpretative meaning structures lead to an emerging community of communication? The next chapter deals with this crucial question for the Europeanization of public spheres.

7

A EUROPEAN COMMUNITY
OF COMMUNICATION?

Visibility, similar issue cycles, and converging frames of reference are certainly necessary ingredients for a transnational public sphere because they enable cross-border communication in the first place. But they are not sufficient, since a lively public sphere requires that this communication actually takes place. A community of communication through Europeanized public spheres emerges if and when "foreigners" are no longer treated as such, but actively participate in debates about issues of common concern. This chapter uses the indicators developed in chapter 5 to explore the empirical evidence. I claim that we can see a community of communication in the making, but in uneven and sometimes segmented ways. The last part of the chapter discusses explanations for the Europeanization of public spheres. I argue that the Europeanization of public spheres follows rather than leads the process of European integration and that it is largely elite-driven. As is the case with the Europeanization of identities (see chapter 4), the evidence appears to confirm the expectations of sociological institutionalism, pointing to constitutive effects of European integration.

The first indicator concerns the extent to which national media in the various countries regularly observe, report, and comment about each other, thereby creating interconnectedness. The available studies suggest that this condition is usually a given, even in cases in which there is little cross-border agreement on either frames of reference or the definition of the common problem (e.g., Trenz 2000, 2002; Kantner 2004; Erbe 2005; Wessler et al. 2008, chap. 3). The second indicator is more demanding, since it requires that Europeans from other countries or

EU actors regularly participate in Europeanized public spheres and are treated as legitimate contributors to these debates.

Vertical and Horizontal Europeanization: Elites Talking to One Another

In this context, the distinction between "vertical" and "horizontal" Europeanization introduced by Ruud Koopmans and others is useful (Koopmans and Erbe 2004; Koopmans and Statham 2010). *Vertical* Europeanization refers to the extent to which EU level actors regularly participate in and contribute to national public debates while *horizontal* Europeanization concerns the degree to which actors from other European countries are present in a particular public sphere. Koopmans and Erbe also distinguish between "weak" and "strong" Europeanization whereby *weak* Europeanization is essentially identical with mutual observation, while *strong* Europeanization refers to the active participation of fellow Europeans or EU actors in a given public sphere. In the following, I concentrate on these latter data, since they can be used to measure the degree to which fellow Europeans are treated as legitimate speakers in a public sphere (interdiscursivity).

Overall, the results point to strong Europeanization whenever European issues are being debated (Koopmans and Statham 2010; Koopmans 2007). Interestingly enough, this does not seem to be a new phenomenon. A study of media coverage in Britain, Germany, and France of the 1969 EC summit in The Hague already showed a strong degree of horizontal and vertical Europeanization (Meyer 2009). For more recent periods, the EUROPUB data show with regard to vertical Europeanization that EU actors are most strongly represented—not surprisingly—in issue areas in which the EU commands substantial supranational competences, namely European integration itself (28% of all claims),[1] monetary policies (22%), and agriculture (16%; Koopmans 2004, 16). In these three policy areas, horizontal Europeanization is also rather strong. Up to 30 percent of the actors in these fields came from other European countries so that—taken together—fellow Europeans or EU actors were responsible for the majority of claims reported in national media in the issue areas of European integration and monetary policies.[2] Moreover, non-European actors were almost absent in these two policy areas. In contrast, in issue areas such as immigration and troop deployments where the

---

1. On claims analysis as used by the EUROPUB project, see chapters 5 and 6.

2. Not surprisingly, the majority of claims in the two issue areas were also targeted at the EU (Koopmans 2004, 35).

EU gained competences only recently, European and non-European actors appeared almost as frequently. With regard to security policy, U.S. actors accounted for 20 percent of the claims, making them the most cited actors in this field (for similar results, see Kantner, Kutter, and Renfordt 2008).

When European issues are being discussed or reported in the media, EU actors as well as other European actors are usually present as speakers. This finding is corroborated by Hartmut Wessler and his group who find that a bit less than 20 percent of all quoted speakers in the Austrian, Danish, French, German, and British newspaper reports analyzed are other Europeans (including EU representatives), irrespective of topic (Wessler et al. 2008, 46–49; also Sifft et al. 2007). Since they also report that only up to 10 percent of the articles in the newspapers cover EU policies, this is a very high number. Wessler et al. conclude that a "distinctly European discourse involving speakers from the EU institutions and from other European countries only takes place in the small numbers of articles which actually focus on EU policymaking" (ibid., 49). But why should we expect a European discourse when the issue at hand pertains to, say, German health care reform or to U.S. policies in Iraq? Why should non-European themes generate a European discourse? In this context, it is noteworthy that the data set developed by Cathleen Kantner et al. (see chapter 6) that covers foreign and security policy issues from 1990 to 2005 shows a slight increase over time in the degree to which the EU is treated as an international actor in its own right (Kantner, Kutter, and Renfordt 2008, 14; see also Kantner 2009).

With regard to *horizontal* Europeanization, French and German actors are most prominent in the public spheres with regard to issues of European integration. Although the "big three" (including Britain) account for the majority of horizontally Europeanized claims, actors from other EU countries are usually represented as well (Koopmans 2004, 33). Although it is not surprising that actors from the bigger European countries are more represented in Europeanized public spheres than those from smaller countries, the data do not indicate that smaller European countries are discriminated against in an emerging European public sphere.

As for individual countries, the most Europeanized EU member states—with regard to both horizontal and vertical Europeanization—are Spain, France, and Germany. The data from newspaper editorials analyzed by Barbara Pfetsch et al. confirm these findings (Pfetsch 2004; Pfetsch, Adam, and Eschner 2008). The five continental European countries in the study—Germany, France, Italy, Spain, and the Netherlands—turn out to be a rather homogenous group with between 50 percent and two thirds of fully Europeanized claims in the editorials. These findings confirm the emergence of Europeanized public spheres particularly in continental (Western) Europe (see chapter 6).

Studies of particular debates in France and Germany substantiate these over-all findings. Silke Adam's analysis of the coverage of French and German quality newspapers of the EU's Eastern enlargement and of the constitutional debates in the early 2000s show discursive cross-border exchanges in 58.2 percent to 68.6 percent of all interactions. As Adam states, "These debates truly reflect the interdependencies of a common Union as they go beyond a portrayal of internal struggles within the core EU institutions and show the multilevel governance system" (Adam 2008, 103). A similar analysis of German and French newspapers during the referendum debates on the Constitutional Treaty in 2004 and 2005 reveals a slightly different picture, however (Jentges, Trenz, and Vetters 2007). Only the German newspapers showed truly transnational interdiscursivity, while more than 50 percent of the claims reported in French papers remained within national (French) boundaries. In other words, French actors were mainly talk-ing to one another during the national referendum controversy, while German media were almost completely Europeanized.

The least Europeanized and most nationalist EU member state by far remains Great Britain, where European and EU actors together are represented only a little bit more than U.S. actors (Koopmans 2004, 34; also Statham 2007). More-over, U.K. newspaper editorials turn out to be the most nationalist in Europe (Pfetsch, Adam, and Eschner 2008). The absence of EU and European actors in British quality newspapers confirms the findings that the United Kingdom re-mains "semi-detached" from the EU (George 1992), whether we are dealing with collective identity or with public spheres.

One of the first studies of media discourses in Central Eastern Europe per-taining to the ratification debates of the Constitutional Treaty confirms the EUROPUB findings (see Liebert 2007b, 254–55). In Estonia, Latvia, the Czech Republic, and Poland, nonnational European actors represented between 57 per-cent (Czech Republic) and 41 percent (Poland) of the speakers quoted in the media. The percentage of EU institutional actors quoted in Eastern European media did not differ much from the respective numbers in France and the United Kingdom. As Liebert concludes, "Transnational communication has given foreign actors a direct voice and has led to incorporating foreign arguments—positively as well as negatively—into national public discourses" (Liebert 2007b, 254). Amelie Kutter's study of Polish and French newspapers and the constitutional debates also points to similar degrees of horizontal and vertical Europeanization (Kutter 2009).

Finally, the study of Central Eastern Europe confirms another EUROPUB finding, namely the overwhelming dominance of governmental and executive ac-tors represented in these discourses. As Koopmans points out, Europeanization—horizontal as well as vertical—almost exclusively means that national and

European members of the executive talk to each other (Koopmans 2007). Europeanized public spheres are populated by national governments or the executive branches of the EU, such as the Commission or the European Central Bank. Executive dominance is even stronger in Europeanized debates than in controversies confined to national actors. Of course, social movements in Europe have created their own issue-specific public sphere in Europe (Doerr 2008). Actors from civil society and from political parties are not very present in newspaper representations of Europeanized public spheres—including on the Internet (Koopmans and Zimmermann 2010). Although civil society actors account for more than one third of all claims in purely domestic debates, only 12 percent of all claims stem from civil society actors from other European countries (Koopmans 2007, 192–98). European-wide societal organizations and actors are not very visible in the European public sphere as represented by quality newspapers. Even European parliamentarians or parties account for only 15 percent of all claims (24% in the issue area of European integration itself). The one exception to the rule concerns the media from other European countries, which are more widely quoted than any other nonstate actors.

This finding challenges the idea that a European community of communication in the Habermasian sense allows equal access to participants (Díez Medrano 2009). Societal actors including interest associations have a minimal presence in the emerging Europeanized public spheres. If there is a European community of communication, it is mainly one in which national governments and the European Commission talk to one another. Even parliamentarians—national as well as European—are rarely represented. This does not bode well for a European democracy (see chapter 10).

To summarize the findings so far, two of the three indicators measuring a European community of communication point to Europeanized public spheres. In particular, speakers from the EU and from other European countries are regularly present in the national media when European issues are being discussed. We can, therefore, confirm that fellow Europeans are treated as legitimate speakers in Europeanized public spheres. And there is increasing evidence that the new Central Eastern European member states are developing Europeanized public spheres that are similar to their Western European neighbors. However, two caveats have to be mentioned. First, EU speakers and those from other member states populating the various public spheres are predominantly members of national governments and the European Commission. Second, the British public sphere remains the odd one out, since the developments reported here pertain more or less to continental Europe. British public opinion not only continues to be the most Euroskeptical and most nationalist with regard to collective identities (chapter 2), British elites also construct Europe and the EU as "the other" (chapter 3), and British media strengthen this picture through their nationalist reporting.

A Common Concern for European Issues?

What about Europe and the EU as issues of common concern for "us as Europeans," the third indicator for the emergence of a community of communication? This is the most ambitious indicator for a transnational public sphere (see chapter 5). If we find that actors in Europeanized public spheres take a common European perspective when debating European issues, we have to conclude that a fully developed transnational community of communication has emerged in Europe that conforms to the Habermasian ideal type of a public sphere. Such a transnational public sphere would not only represent a developed community of communication, it would also contribute to the emergence of a European identity and to the development of "solidarity among strangers" (Habermas 2006, 76; see Castiglione 2009). Unfortunately, very few attempts have been made to measure empirically the degree to which we can observe such a community in the public sphere.

Hartmut Wessler and his team, for example, studied whether "we Europeans" was used in newspaper articles. They found that "Europe" became the object of identification in only 5 percent of the cases and only in the late 1990s, while such "we" references meant the journalist's own nation-state in about 40 percent of the cases (Wessler et al. 2008, 50–51; Sifft et al. 2007, 144). As a result, the study concluded that there is no European community of communication. It remains unclear what these results mean, however. The data presented by Wessler's team, for example, pertain to all newspaper articles selected rather than to those dealing with European issues. However, once again, why should we expect references to a European "we" when the issue discussed is German health care reform?

An analysis of media reporting of various European and world events during the 1950s and 1960s in comparison with the 2005 debates on the Constitutional Treaty also shows very limited references to a "European we." During that time period, however, only one event—the 1957 Treaty of Rome—actually pertained to European questions. But almost one third of all identity references of the 2005 debate were directed at Europe and the EU (Lucht and Tréfas 2006).[3] It is very hard to reach firm conclusions on the basis of these contradictory data.

---

3. However, the 2005 debate also yields an exceptionally high degree of references to a "national we" (67%), which might result from the fact that controversies about European integration and

Fortunately, several studies have examined whether national media adopted a common European perspective when they discussed issues of common concern for Europeans.

"Widening": Debating EU Enlargement

Research by Marianne Van de Steeg on media reporting in five European countries on Eastern enlargement during the 1990s confirms at first glance that references to a national "we" are more frequently used than are those to a European or EU "we" (Van de Steeg 2005, 125–29). However, Van de Steeg also shows that there is a fair amount of variation across countries and sometimes even within countries. Two German and two British newspapers turned out to be the most nationally oriented media with few references to "we Europeans," while two Dutch and two Spanish papers referred more often to a European community of identification. Finally, the German weekly *Der Spiegel* as well as the British *Guardian* displayed both national and European identification patterns.

Moving beyond simple "we" references, Van de Steeg then investigated particular frames that constructed a common European identity as a community of fate (see also Risse and Van de Steeg 2008). She found that the enlargement discourse constructed the European Union as a positive answer to Europe's own past. In this case, Europe's past was not a single historical moment, but consisted of a series of narratives against which the new and "modern" Europe was constructed: the rivalry between the European great powers of Germany, France, and the United Kingdom that led to several wars; hegemonic Germany that tried to rule the continent and provoked two world wars; Europe divided in two by the Iron Curtain; and, more recently, the civil wars and ethnic cleansing in the Balkans. In conjunction with this complex depiction of Europe's recent past, the community that was constructed in the enlargement debate was identified with peace, security, prosperity, and unity. To quote just one example,

> Enlarging Nato is, however, a poor second to enlarging the European Union. Nato extends a brittle security to new members; only the EU offers the prosperity to make that security self-sustaining and buttress it with the political support democracies need. (*Guardian*, 15 February 1997)

The European Union was identified with these values in all media sources published in EU member states. Even the Euroskeptical *Times* criticized EU

---

supranational institution-building also led to strong reactions from those who felt threatened by the potential loss of national sovereignty and identity (Lucht and Tréfas 2006, 23).

politics while paying honor to the value of unifying Europe to overcome the old divisions, referring to the "imperative" of "bringing the new democracies into the European family" (1 July 1997).

Overall, however, identity-related frames remained in the background during the debates about Eastern enlargement. The reason was rather simple: once the cold war was over, it was not controversial that the EU had to extend to the East. That Eastern Europe belonged to "us," and, therefore, had to "return to Europe" (meaning the EU) was a given and highly consensual (for further discussion, see chapter 9).

In contrast, enlarging the EU to include the western Balkans and—even more controversial—Turkey put identity-related issues at the core of the controversy (see Wimmel 2006b). Although it did not matter for Eastern enlargement whether European identity was constructed in traditional and even religious (Christian) terms or in secular and modern meanings, the two identity constructions continue to clash head-on in the case of Turkey (see chapters 2 and 3). As a result, the controversy about Turkish membership in the EU was and is as much about Turkey as it is about the EU's core identity (see chapter 9).

"Deepening": Discussing the Future of Europe and Its Constitution

Although data pertaining to the enlargement debates do not allow for firm conclusions as to the emergence of a European community of communication, studies of the discourses surrounding the EU's future in general and the Constitutional Treaty in particular provide stronger evidence in this regard. Of course, the future of European integration represents a "most likely" case for a community of communication. If Europeans do not debate this issue from a common European perspective, what else should they discuss from a common viewpoint?

Hans-Jörg Trenz studied the "Future of Europe" debate in 2000, which was triggered by Joschka Fischer's speech and then led to the Constitutional Convention (Trenz 2006, 297–372; Trenz 2007; see chapter 6). He showed that different national preferences for a "federal" or an "intergovernmental" Europe were represented and endorsed by various national media. But these frames about the future of Europe were present in all newspapers including the British. Moreover, newspapers across Europe tried to actively construct a European "postnational" identity that is not visionary or emotional, but highly pragmatic and "based on universal principles that have been long enshrined in national constitutions" (Trenz 2007, 107). Moreover, although newspapers occasionally referred to a common European heritage and civilization and the European past

of wars and Nazism, they used the history of European integration itself as a success story upon which a European community ought to be built: "With no fixed
points derived from the past or projected toward the future, the unity of Europe
is treated as a by-product of the present practice of cooperation, as something
to be constantly in the making through common debate and dispute" (Trenz
2007, 105). This construction of a European postnational identity through the
media resembles the "unity in diversity" theme that EU policymakers advertise as
the core of European identity. Interestingly enough, European media seem to be
self-consciously aware that a European community of communication emerges
precisely through debates and controversies about a common European future.

Barbara Pfetsch's EUROPUB analysis of newspaper editorials in six EU
member states and Switzerland supports these findings (Pfetsch 2008). More
than 50 percent of the evaluative positions in the editorials were positive toward European integration—ranging from 84.5 percent in Italy to 30.7 percent
in Spain. Only British editorial positions were overwhelmingly negative toward the EU.

Florian Oberhuber et al. conducted a qualitative analysis of newspaper reporting on the 2003 Intergovernmental Conference during the Italian EU presidency
that failed to adopt the Constitutional Treaty (Oberhuber et al. 2005; see chapter 6). The EU was represented in this debate as a space where conflicting interests
meet and power struggles dominate. Various metaphors for struggle and conflict
were used. The member states were also called upon to reach a viable settlement
for their disputes, and put the common interest above their national egoisms.

Although Oberhuber et al. conclude, therefore, that a European community
of communication does not exist, one can actually interpret their data differently,
particularly if one compares them with the findings of Trenz and Pfetsch.[4] While
there was little agreement within and between the various national public spheres
about what the problem with the Constitution was and who was to blame for
the summit's failure, no distinct national perspective is discernible. Many newspapers from different countries contrast the vision of a Europe that solves common problems with the existing EU of power struggles among member states.
This, however, represents a significant indicator for an emerging polity in which
a normative ideal is used to criticize the actual functioning of the institution.
Newspaper editorials across countries construct an ideal of a European community of fate that is then compared to bickering Europeans driven by their egoistic

---

4. One problem is methodological: the results from the newspaper analysis are first aggregated
by country and only subsequently compared. This approach tends to neutralize differences within
countries and to reinforce those between countries. Such "methodological nationalism" (Zürn 2001)
emphasizes national differences.

national interests. This resembles the frequent complaints that "Europeans" do not get their act together in foreign and security policy and speak with twenty-seven different voices. The very act of negating the existence of a European community of fate actually serves to construct it in these cases. If we complain about a missing European community of communication, we start creating it.[5]

Finally, the study by Ulrike Liebert et al. on the ratification debates surrounding the Constitutional Treaty in Central Eastern Europe shows differences from, as well as some similarities to, these findings about "old Europe" (Liebert 2007a; Meyer 2007). Concerning differences, the issue salience of constitutional debates was considerably lower in Central Eastern Europe than in Western Europe, with the possible exception of the Czech Republic where President Vaclav Klaus turned out to be a prominent opponent of the Constitutional Treaty (see Rakusanova 2007). This can be explained against the background of the EU fatigue after the accession debates, on the one hand, and the dominance of "bread and butter" issues, on the other. Nevertheless, the Constitutional Treaty did generate heated debates in the Czech and Polish media. The controversy about a "federal" versus an "intergovernmental" EU was visible in both countries, particularly in conjunction with the future balance of power in an EU of twenty-seven-plus members. In addition, the Polish media also concentrated on the religious dimension of the Constitutional Treaty, namely the question of whether a reference to God should be included in the preamble (Kutter 2007; Wyrozumska 2007; Rakusanova 2007). The latter debate reverberated throughout Europe and pitted two European identity constructions against each other, the modern and secular EU Europe versus a traditional Christian (mostly Catholic) Europe (see chapters 2, 3, and 9).

In general then, the constitutional debates of the past ten years appear to show an emerging community of communication that discusses the future of European integration as an issue of common concern, irrespective of the various positions toward it. Although member states and their national media express different preferences and strongly disagree among themselves, they appear to debate these questions as concerning "us as Europeans." This finding appears to be particularly valid with regard to continental Europe and increasingly includes the new Central Eastern European members. As already mentioned, Great Britain differs as a case in which predominantly nationally focused identities and nationalist media reinforce each other. Next, I look at a particular debate in 2000 when the EU reacted to the rise to power of a right-wing populist party in Austria, the "Haider debate."

---

5. For a similar argument with regard to the EU's democratic deficit, see Trenz and Eder 2004.

Debating the EU as a Value Community

Our own study of the "Haider debate," which took place in 2000 (Van de Steeg 2006; Risse and Van de Steeg 2008; see chapter 6), confirms Trenz's argument about the reflexivity in the media's representations of European identity. Since the debate centered on the political and moral justifiability of EU "sanctions" against Austria, several identity constructions would have been possible discursively. For example, one could have constructed the incident as "Europe against Austria." In this case, we would have expected the bashing of Austria in the non-Austrian press, and an Austrian perspective portraying the country as the victim of European arrogance. Another construction would have also been possible: an attack of two big member states—Germany and France—against little Austria. In sum, the debate could have pitted the European "self" (or "other") against the Austrian "other" (or "self," depending on one's perspective).

To our surprise, neither of these constructions was prominent in the fifteen newspapers from five countries that we analyzed (including Austria itself). On the contrary, Austria was explicitly identified as belonging to the European political community. For example, "Europe with Austria, yes. Europe with Haider, no" were slogans in favor of the sanctions during a demonstration in Brussels (*Le Soir,* 21 February 2000) and in Vienna many *Viennese* chose to put up the flag of the *European Community* during the demonstrations against the ÖVP/FPÖ government (*La Repubblica,* 20 February 2000). To quote from a commentary in the *Frankfurter Allgemeine Zeitung,* which was critical of the sanctions:

> Austria remains morally the winner in the battle with its European partners. While these partners abandoned any kind of solidarity, imposed sanctions...—and thereby damaged those values and principles that they claim to want to protect—the humiliated Austria remains faithful to the Union, even up to the point that it denies itself. (*Frankfurter Allgemeine Zeitung,* 14 March 2000)

We found no signs that Europe was depicted as the out-group against which the Austrian identity was constructed, or that Austria was the out-group of a European identity. The "bad other" against which EU Europe was constructed was Haider, the personification of Nazism and xenophobia in this debate.[6] In contrast, the EU was portrayed as a community of values and principles, such as democracy, human rights, and the rule of law. Newspapers that favored the

---

6. An extremely powerful cartoon by Plantu was published by *Le Monde*. It depicted a puzzled-looking person holding the European flag in which one of the twelve stars had been replaced by a swastika. Below, Haider was portrayed as the piper who is followed by rats.

EU "sanctions" as well as newspapers that opposed them shared this image of Europe as a moral community.

The debate about Haider was a debate about what constituted the EU as a political community. Irrespective of one's view of the so-called sanctions, the EU was constructed as the new, modern, and united Europe based on human rights, democracy, and the rule of law (see chapters 2 and 3). The modern EU's "other" was Europe's own past of the Holocaust, Nazism, World War II, and xenophobia, represented by Jörg Haider and his party. In other words, the debate referred to a particular European identity that depicted core values of the European in-group against which the "other," the out-group, was positioned. Those who supported the EU "sanctions" used this identity construction to expel Haider and his followers discursively from the community as "ghosts from the past." Those who argued against the sanctions did not deny the vision of a Europe of moral and legal standards, but focused primarily on the legal issue to suggest that sanctions were an inappropriate answer to Haider. The Haider debate, thus, constructed a community of communication across Europe based on common values. The controversy was not about the Austrian "other" against the European "self," but about which part of the EU's modern core identity—human rights, cosmopolitanism, or the rule of law—should guide it in its reaction to the events in Austria.

A Community of Communication in the Making?

These transnational debates about enlargement, the "Future of Europe," the Constitutional Treaty, and about Haider and the events in Austria document instances in which Europeanized public spheres have developed gradually into a European community of communication. Questions such as "Who are we as Europeans?" "What do we want?" and "How should we treat each other as Europeans?" became relevant in each of these cases, albeit to varying degrees and sometimes exposing differences between countries. Although the various newspapers strongly disagreed with one another, the debates often developed a common European perspective. As a result, they created a transnational European public sphere in which speakers were treated as legitimate participants in the debates irrespective of their nationality or ideological orientations. During these debates, Europeanized public spheres emerged as spaces in which European identity politics plays itself out and, thus, becomes visible. By debating European issues of common concern, communities of communication emerged, constructing as well as reinforcing collective European identities.

In two of these debates, issues of a collective European identity remained consensual and, therefore, in the background and not subject to controversy. Despite all the controversies about Eastern enlargement, the future of Europe, and a European constitution, the dominant identity frames in these contexts concerned the EU as the heritage of enlightenment and modernity based on human rights, the rule of law, and democracy. The debates then concentrated on questions of what this means under the particular circumstances.

In contrast, identity constructions themselves assumed center stage during the Haider debate and the struggle over Turkish EU membership. The Haider debate concerned primarily which part of the EU's modern collective identity was to guide European practices toward Austria: human rights and cosmopolitanism, on the one hand, or the rule of law and legal standards, on the other. The debate about Turkey is even more significant in this respect, since the "modern Europe of enlightenment" clashes with traditional and backward-oriented views of Christian Europe (see chapters 8 and 9 for further discussion).

What do these findings tell us about the Europeanization of public spheres? In chapter 5, I introduced criteria and indicators for the emergence of Europeanized public spheres. Accordingly, we can meaningfully speak of European transnational communities of communication across the various public spheres and media under these conditions:

1. the more the same (European) themes are debated at the same time at similar levels of attention;
2. the more similar frames of reference and meaning structures are available and in use;
3. the more EU or other European actors participate in cross-border communication (interdiscursivity);
4. the more speakers and listeners recognize one another as legitimate participants in these cross-border debates; and
5. the more European issues are discussed as questions of common concern for Europeans.

What does the scorecard look like? The first criterion (same issues at the same time) is usually a given (see chapter 6). In particular, the available evidence suggests that European issues have gained visibility over the past fifteen years—an important precondition for Europeanized public spheres. With regard to criteria 2–4, I suggest that we can observe the gradual Europeanization of public spheres in continental Europe, encompassing the six founding members of the European Community, as well as Southern members such as Spain or Italy. When European issues are discussed, the available evidence suggests that similar interpretive frames are used and transnational cross-border communication takes place among these countries. Data with regard to the new Central Eastern European member states (as well as Scandinavia) are still sketchy, but there is increasing evidence that they do not differ much from Western Europe. However, we are also on rather safe grounds to reject the notion of a Europeanized public sphere for Great Britain. The United Kingdom remains detached from the EU when it comes to public debates, too.

It is also noteworthy that the Europeanization of public spheres stops at the EU's borders. For those cases in which we have data about media in non-EU member states such as the United States and Switzerland, the evidence suggests that they do not belong to a transnational Europeanized public sphere. Although media in both countries regularly report about Europe and the EU, they do so from an observer, not from a participant, perspective.

With regard to the last—and most demanding—indicator, firm conclusions are not (yet) possible. Concerning "most likely cases" of enlargement, constitutional questions, and the Haider debate, a transnational community of communication among the "usual suspects," that is, the original six member states as well as Southern Europe, can be observed. The jury is still out on Scandinavia and on Central Eastern Europe. And once again, British media do not participate in such a transnational community.

Several caveats are in order, however. First, most data reported in this chapter and in chapter 6 result from content analyses of quality newspapers. It remains unclear whether the Europeanization of public spheres also encompasses tabloids and regional newspapers. Data pertaining to television news and the like suggest that Europeanization has not reached electronic media (particularly De Vreese 2007). As for the internet, it does not seem to differ much from the reporting in quality newspapers, but once again, there are too few studies available (e.g. Koopmans and Zimmermann 2010).

Second, the Europeanization of public spheres encompasses mostly political, economic, and social elites who regularly contribute to and read quality newspapers. The transnationalization of discourses and its interdiscursivity are mostly confined to EU actors and national governments. Societal actors are rarely present in Europeanized discourses. Thus, public spheres and the media reflect the fact that European integration is dominated by national governments as well as executive actors in Brussels rather than by interest groups and political parties. The Europeanization of public spheres conforms even less to the ideal typical notion of a Habermasian public sphere than national public spheres do. This is particularly relevant with regard to the criterion of "equal access" to the public discourse.

Third, the data on the Europeanization of public spheres—more so than the empirical results regarding European identity (chapters 2 and 3)—often use different methodologies and, thus, are sometimes hard to compare (see chapter 6 for a discussion).

Nevertheless, and contrary to what has been written about the existence or nonexistence of a European public sphere, I suggest that we can indeed observe the—albeit unequal and sometimes segmented—emergence of Europeanized public spheres that enable transnational cross-border communication on questions of common European concern. This community of communication emerges through contestation, conflicts, and the politicization of EU questions. As a result, a European-wide "communicative space (is) in the making" (cf. the title of Fossum and Schlesinger 2007). How can this be explained?

Explaining the Evidence: The Constitutive Effects of European Integration

The following remarks are largely speculative. Although we know quite a bit descriptively about the Europeanization of public spheres and the emergence of a European community of communication, its causes are unexplored so far. In this regard, the study of the Europeanization of public spheres lags considerably behind research on the evolution of European identities (see chapter 4). I suggest, however, that similar processes might be at work.

If the findings reported above are correct, the Europeanization of public spheres and the uneven emergence of transnational communities of communication in Europe are fairly recent phenomena. They followed rather than led the processes of European integration. At least, the empirical evidence appears to be consistent with an account according to which media reporting about the EU increased over time following the growing domestic salience of EU policies and triggering as well as reflecting the politicization of EU policies in domestic politics.[7] The more salient and visible EU institutions and the rules and policies emanating from them became in the domestic politics of the member states, the more news coverage of the EU increased, leading to the emergence of Europeanized public spheres. This would explain why most available data suggest that the Europeanization of public spheres took off some time during the mid-1990s, that is, after the Single European Act and after the entry into force of the treaties of Maastricht establishing the Economic and Monetary Union. Only then did EU policies start interfering substantially with the domestic policies and

---

7. A regression analysis showed, for example, a strong and positive effect of "year of analysis" on the likelihood that newspaper articles refer to EU institutions or EU politics, suggesting temporal developments (Wessler et al. 2008, 71–72). See also Renfordt 2009.

politics of the member states, triggering public debates that were reflected by the media. These developments would also explain the findings by EUROPUB and other research that media representations of the EU concentrated on economic and market issues for quite some time and have only recently begun to focus on constitutional issues. After all, the treaties of Maastricht and even Amsterdam were still preoccupied with market-making policies—from the single market to the single currency and Schengenland, while constitutional questions only assumed center stage in EU policymaking in conjunction with the looming enlargement, that is, toward the end of the 1990s.

In a sense then, Europe and the EU started to hit home during the late 1990s by more and more affecting domestic politics in the member states. For example, the effects of the single market became visible in people's lives only during the mid-1990s, while the monetary union and the single currency assumed reality in the late 1990s. At the same time, and the closer the EU came to (Eastern) enlargement, a debate started about whether EU institutions would be able to accommodate twice the number of member states as the EU 15. This in turn led to the controversies about the future of Europe and a European constitution. This is the institutionalist part of the story. EU institutions and the ongoing integration process not only have behavioral consequences constraining how actors can pursue their interests. What we probably can observe here are the *constitutive* effects of European integration that start shaping the very process by which social and political actors define and transform their preferences and interests (on constitutive effects in general, see Kratochwil 1989; Adler 2002). The result is politicization and—through contestation and polarization—the emergence of Europeanized public spheres (see Kantner 2004 for a theoretical argument).

Moreover, the differential Europeanization of public spheres, which seems confined to continental (Western and Southern) Europe, can also be accounted for by sociological institutionalism. It is not just that "membership matters" for the Europeanization of public spheres but also that the degree of engagement in European integration might matter, too.[8] The continental Western and Southern EU member states not only encompass the six founding members but also countries that have fully embraced the various integration steps. They all share the single market, they have all adopted the euro, and they all participate in Schengenland of borderless travel. In contrast, Great Britain has opted out of both the single currency and the Schengen *acquis* (the rules and regulations covering borderless travel as well as internal security in the EU), while Sweden and Denmark have not (yet) adopted the euro. The new Central Eastern European members

---

8. I owe the following point to Barbara Pfetsch. See Pfetsch 2008; Pfetsch, Adam, and Eschner 2008.

have adopted the Schengen acquis only at the end of 2007 (except for Bulgaria and Romania), while Slovenia and Slovakia are the only new Eastern member states which are part of the eurozone. As a result, the EU, its institutions, and its norms and rules affect Western and Southern member states on the continent more strongly than they do Great Britain and the new Central Eastern European members. While this is a question of choice for the U.K., the exposure of Central Eastern Europe is changing rapidly and might even accelerate as the result of the worldwide economic and financial crisis.

As a result of these developments, the EU is more visible in the public spheres of continental Europe than it is in that of the United Kingdom. The rejection of further integration by British political elites would then be reflected in a more nationalist discourse in the British media, which only serves to reinforce "semi-detachment" of the British. By the same token, the active engagement of German (or French or Italian) elites in European integration would again be reflected in the media, leading to a (continental) European community of communication, which also strengthens Europeanized identities. If my assumption is correct, the Central Eastern European members should follow the continental Western European path to the Europeanization of public spheres (and identities) the more they integrate into the EU. Moreover, and depending on the outcome of the global economic crisis for the EU as a whole, we should then expect a further politicization of and contestation over EU policies (see chapter 10).

Of course, this institutionalist and constitutive causal story is inconsistent with a view of the media as active promoters or opponents of European integration. The media seem to play a passive role in this account, largely following the cues given by political elites rather than actively shaping the Europeanization of public spheres. I submit, however, that this picture is consistent with the findings reported above, which suggest that EU actors and national governments dominate Europeanized public spheres.

Last but not least, I come back to the starting point of the discussion on a European public sphere in chapter 5, namely the relationship between Europeanized public spheres and the emergence of a European polity. Normative democratic theory, which informed much of the earlier work on a European public sphere (see, e.g., the controversy between Jürgen Habermas and Dieter Grimm; Grimm 1995; Habermas 1994, 1996a), would suggest that a community of communication is a precondition for the emergence of a democratic polity. If we turn this normative argument into an empirical claim, we would expect that the Europeanization of public spheres would lead to a European polity. Yet, from the constructivist perspective adopted here, it makes little sense to argue over whether the emergence of a transnational public sphere in Europe predates the emergence of a polity, or the other way around. Rather, if the studies reported above indeed indicate a general trend, the emergence of Europeanized public spheres and communities of communication *constitutes* a polity or reflects the emergence of a polity. The more Europe hits home, the more European issues become politicized and part and parcel of Europeanized domestic politics, and the more a "community of strangers" emerges as a polity that is reflective of itself (Castiglione 2009, rephrasing Habermas 1996a). Contestation and politicization are then constitutive features of an emerging polity. A European polity comes into being not through the creation of prepolitical *demoi* but through Europeanized public spheres in which European issues are contested and debated. If I am correct, the French "non" and the Dutch "nej" to the Constitutional Treaty in 2005 and its reverberations throughout Europe might simultaneously signify a (legitimacy) crisis of European integration *and* the birth of a transnational polity through Europeanized public spheres and collective identities. I discuss the consequences in the remaining chapters.

Part III

CONSEQUENCES

8

"DEEPENING"
European Institution-Building

So far, I have argued in this book that, first, we can observe the—albeit uneven—Europeanization of collective identities across Europe both at the level of mass public opinion and among the elites and that these identities usually go together with other loyalties that people feel toward their national, local, or other communities. Second, at least two major identity constructions compete with each other in both elite and popular discourses, namely a "modern, enlightened, and secular Europe," on the one hand, and a traditional, introverted, and "nationalist fortress Europe," on the other hand. Third, we can observe the gradual and again uneven Europeanization of public spheres, at least in continental Europe, allowing Europeans to engage in cross-border communication and to debate issues of common European concern.

But so what? Does the Europeanization of identities and public spheres matter for European politics and policies, and if so, how does it matter? The third part of this book tries to tackle these questions. While parts 1 and 2 of the book treated identities and public spheres as "dependent variables," so to speak, I now turn the perspective around and treat identities and public spheres as potential causes rather than effects, that is, as "independent variables."

Before I get into the details, three notes of caution are in order. First, although public discourses and the way in which European issues are debated might have direct policy effects, at least domestically, we should not expect the same with regard to Europeanized identities. I can feel very proud and even nationalist as a German or French—and still disagree profoundly with individual policies of my national government. Why should Europe and the EU be different? If we want to explain EU policies with regard to the single market, public health, or the environment, we should probably not look at identities first.

Second, even in cases in which identities do have causal effects, we should not expect them to do the explanatory work single-handedly. Policymaking is a complex process—particularly in multilevel governance systems such as the EU—as a result of which the explanatory power of a single variable will likely be limited.

So, what should we assume with regard to the explanatory power of identities and public debates? We need to distinguish the constitutive from the more direct causal effects of identities on policies, politics, and polities. As to the latter, I suggest in the following chapters that we should look for the effects of identification processes and public discourses primarily with regard to issues that concern the very nature of a polity or a political community. First, identities might play a role when it comes to determining who decides what at what level of policymaking. In other words, Europeanized identities should matter with regard to constitutional questions, that is, "deepening." In the case of the EU, identification processes are expected to influence questions of which policy areas should be subjected to EU decision making (the scope of European integration) and whether member states should pool or give up sovereignty in these areas (the depth of integration) (see Börzel 2005). Moreover, identity matters with regard to who belongs to the community and who does not. Therefore, the Europeanization of identities should affect questions of citizenship and immigration as well as membership in the EU, that is, "widening" (see chapter 9). Last but not least, the Europeanization of identities and of public spheres is likely to matter with regard to the legitimacy of the EU in the eyes of its citizens and, therefore, with regard to European democracy (see chapter 10).

As to *constitutive* effects, Europeanized identities and public spheres might create the European community as an imagined community (Anderson 1991) in the first place. The more we identify with a social group or a larger social entity and the more we find others who also identify with this group, the more this group gains psychological existence ("entitativity," see Castano 2004; also chapter 1). The more we debate issues of common concern in a public sphere, the more a community of communication comes into existence (see chapters 5–7).

But discerning constitutive effects is tricky. Social constructivists remind us that agents and structures are mutually constitutive of each other (see Adler 1997, 324–25; Wendt 1999, chap. 4). Actors both create and reproduce the social structures and imagined communities in which they are embedded. At the same time, the social structures and imagined communities constitute agents insofar as they define their social identities and basic interests. The EU is no exception, as I argued in chapters 5 and 7. The most important methodological issue then concerns how to avoid circular reasoning when tackling mutual constitutiveness empirically (Checkel 1997; Klotz and Lynch 2007). One way to deal with the problem is sequencing. At time t1, one can investigate how European integration itself affects the Europeanization of identities and public spheres, thereby exerting its constitutive influence. At time t2, one then looks at how Europeanized identities and public spheres constitute an imagined European community. I deal with these constitutive effects in the following three chapters.

In this chapter I tackle the effects of identification processes with regard to European institution-building. First, I will discuss findings from mostly quantitative survey studies with regard to the relationship between Europeanized identities and support levels for membership in the union and for European integration. Second, I argue that identity discourses—both in public opinion and in the public sphere—have a discernible impact on constitutional issues in the EU. I illustrate my claims with regard to debates about the euro, the EU's foreign policy identity, and constitutionalization and treaty-making itself.

Mass Public Opinion: Identities and Support for European Integration

Mass public opinion data provide evidence that the Europeanization of collective identities matters with regard to support levels for European integration. As documented in chapter 2, the main dividing line in public opinion is between those who identify exclusively with their nation-state ("exclusive nationalists") and those who identify with their nation-state first while adding Europe as a secondary identity ("inclusive nationalists"). Jack Citrin and John Sides (2004, 174–75) showed in their data analysis that even a low degree of identification with Europe correlates with rather high support levels for EU membership, perceived benefits from EU membership, and support for faster European integration. Only 38 percent of the exclusive nationalists see EU membership as a good thing, while this percentage increases to a startling 70 percent among inclusive nationalists (2000 Eurobarometer data, see Citrin and Sides 2004, 174). A statistical analysis by Dieter Fuchs et al. confirms these findings (Fuchs, Guinaudeau, and Schubert 2009). They show that both identification with Europe and exclusive nationalism have strong effects on attitudes toward EU membership, EU enlargement, and further EU political integration, and that these effects pertain to the twenty-five member states, old and new.

A multivariate regression analysis by Liesbet Hooghe and Gary Marks (2005) confirms the significance of identity variables in accounting for support levels for European integration. They compared the effects of identity variables, economic variables on the individual and collective levels, and ideological and partisan attitudes on support levels for EU membership. If all other variables are held constant, the difference in support for EU membership between exclusive nationalists and those who identify with Europe at least to some degree is still 12.9 percent. This constitutes the strongest effect of a single variable in their model (Hooghe and Marks 2005, 432). However, their multivariate models show that economic, identity, and political variables all exercise independent effects on support for European integration. A combined model explains slightly less than 40 percent of the variance.

Other statistical analyses corroborate these findings. Using slightly different indicators, Lauren McLaren shows that both personal economic utilitarian concerns and identity-related variables tend to affect support levels for European integration (McLaren 2006, chap. 6). She confirms that exclusive nationalists tend to distrust EU institutions and to object to European integration. Moreover, concerns about a loss of national identity because of European integration appear to be unrelated to economic considerations about the costs and benefits from the EU (McLaren 2007a). Yet, one should not overestimate the effect of nationalism on these support levels. McLaren shows that almost half of those who fear a loss of national identity (48% EU-wide) still support their country's EU membership.

The variation among countries is enormous, however: 74 percent of the Irish, 63 percent of the Dutch, and 59 percent of the Spanish who think that the EU threatens their identity still support EU membership, while only 19 percent of the Austrians and 21 percent of the British who express similar fears support EU membership (McLaren 2004, 2006). Hooghe and Marks confirm these findings. They show that British citizens with exclusive national identities "have a level of support for European integration that is on average 32.4 points lower (on our 100 point scale) than those with some kind of multiple identity. In Portugal, at the other extreme, the difference is 9.7 points" (Marks and Hooghe 2003, 20–21). As usual, the attitudes of British citizens are way below the EU average, while people in most Southern European and many West European countries are above the average.

Although these data pertain to the impact of identity-related attitudes on support or rejection levels for European integration and the EU in general, similar findings are available with regard to specific EU institutions and EU policies. Matthew Gabel, for example, finds that a sense of European political identity, among other factors, significantly affects support for the European Parliament (Gabel 2003). Moreover, Europeanized identities are correlated with support for the euro. Exclusive nationalism leads to rejection of the euro, while identification with Europe strongly increases support for the single currency (Müller-Peters 1998, 2001; Risse 2003; Banducci, Karp, and Loedel 2003).

In a clever design, Joseph Jupille and David Leblang (2007) compared the degree to which economic calculations and identification processes affect attitudes toward the euro. In 2000 and 2003, respectively, Denmark and Sweden held national referenda on the adoption of the single currency that resulted in a rejection of the euro in both cases. However, the Danish case was largely about the symbolism of money, since the Danish krone is pegged to the euro and Denmark participates in the European Exchange Rate Mechanism (ERM). As a result, keeping the krone does not result in retaining an independent monetary policy. In the Swedish case, however, monetary policies were at stake, too, since the Swedish krona floated against the euro. Jupille and Leblang then showed that identity-related variables mattered in both Denmark and Sweden, accounting for the support or rejection of the euro, while economic interests had a significant impact on attitudes toward the euro only in Sweden (Jupille and Leblang 2007).

Similar results can be found with regard to foreign and security policy, another domain with considerable repercussions for the tension between supranationalism and the preservation of national sovereignty. Both interest and identity considerations have a significant impact on the propensity of citizens to support a European foreign and security policy. A study by Harald Schoen demonstrates, for example, that utilitarian considerations such as the degree of threat perception or being a citizen of a country with nuclear weapons (such as France and Great Britain) significantly influence support for the Common Foreign and Security Policy (CFSP) (Schoen 2008b). At the same time, exclusive identification with one's nation-state decreases support for the CFSP. Attachment to Europe increases support for European foreign policy only, while it has little impact on one's preparedness to favor a European defense policy or a European rapid deployment force. This latter finding suggests that those who strongly identify with the EU are reluctant to support a militarization of EU foreign policy—in line with their cosmopolitan and liberal values (Fligstein 2008).

In sum, Europeanized identities have a significant impact on support for European integration. The analyses show that identification processes and economic interest calculations are not mutually exclusive. Economic interests and identification processes seem to be independent sources of support for or rejection of European integration. The findings support the view that the heated debates between rational choice focusing on economic interest calculations, on the one hand, and social constructivism's emphasis on norms and identities, on the other, might have been exaggerated.

The good news for European integration is that it takes only a modest degree of identification with Europe to substantially increase the support level for EU membership.

Inclusive nationalists who add Europe as a secondary identity to their national identity strongly support EU membership, supranational institutions, and the EU's constitutional projects such as the single currency. In other words, the European polity does not require a demos that replaces national with European identities, but one in which national and European identities coexist.

At the same time, we should avoid overly optimistic conclusions. Although we might see an emerging European polity and increasing European sense of community, we do not observe a sense of European patriotism that equals patriotic feelings as pronounced as in, say, France, Britain, or Poland. In all EU member states, national patriotism outweighs European patriotism by 18 percent on average (calculated from European Commission 2005, 100–101). This means that "solidarity among strangers" (Habermas 2006, 76) might have limits in Europe. Inclusive nationalism with Europe as a distinct secondary identity might suffice to support the EU in its current constitutional equilibrium as a multilevel governance system in which the member states remain the "masters of the treaties."

But it remains to be seen whether "European identity lite" is sufficient to sustain European integration in the long run, particularly with regard to redistributive policies and a more "social Europe." The massive economic and financial crisis of the late 2000s serves as a wake-up call in this regard. Fortunately in this case, economic interests and sense of community work in the same direction, since the interdependent economies of the single European market cannot allow national economies such as Ireland or Hungary to go under without severe consequences for the remaining countries and their economies.

Europeans are acutely aware of this situation. In early 2009, only 14 percent on average thought that national governments could deal effectively with the economic and financial crisis, while 17 percent named the EU and 25 percent the G8 countries; however, 19 percent thought that nobody could deal with the crisis (see European Parliament 2009 for the following). As usual, the country variation was enormous: only 6 percent of the British thought that the EU could deal with the crisis, in contrast to 28 percent of Greeks. In April 2009, that is, in the midst of the economic crisis, 56 percent of the EU citizens polled perceived the EU as more of an opportunity than a threat (17%) in the context of globalization (Fondation pour l'Innovation Politique 2009). British citizens—once again—proved to be the odd ones out: only 22 percent saw the EU as an opportunity, while 56 percent took a neutral stance. Among the remaining EU countries, the variation ranged from 41 percent in Hungary and the Netherlands to 72 percent in Ireland and 70 percent in Germany.

Although 44 percent of the Europeans thought that member states tended to act individually, almost two thirds would prefer coordinated action on the EU level (European Parliament 2009, 13). Interestingly enough, support for coordinated EU action against the economic and financial crisis did not seem to correlate strongly with the severity of the crisis in individual countries. Among the hardest hit countries, support for EU coordination rather than national efforts was particularly strong in Estonia, Lithuania, Hungary, Greece, and Finland, while it was well below the EU average in Ireland, Latvia, and, of course, Britain. In other words, we cannot automatically infer from a country's economic misery a desire for better-coordinated EU policies. The same holds true for the better-off countries: their citizens do not necessarily prefer national action over EU coordination in times of severe crises.

At the same time, the data do not allow for firm conclusions with regard to the strength of "solidarity among strangers" in the EU, either. However, it is noteworthy that—except for Luxembourg and Italy—citizens from the original six Western European member states as well as from Southern Europe are all above the EU average when it comes to net support for EU coordinated action in times of crisis, while citizens from the more Euroskeptical countries as well as from Central Eastern Europe are located all over the place (see figure 8.1). Incidentally, the original six as well as Southern Europe are also those EU member states with the strongest degree of both Europeanized identities and public spheres. Maybe there is some solidarity among Europeans in times of crisis after all.

As usual, Britain is way below the EU average. The data confirm what has been documented throughout this book: a majority of British citizens are not part of the political, social, and cultural space that the EU now occupies.

Elite Discourses: Europeanized Identities and the EU's Constitutional Choices

The Europeanization of collective identities on the level of mass public opinion has discernible effects on the preparedness of EU citizens to lend diffuse support to European integration. But what about the elite level of policymakers in charge or European politics and policies, both in the member states and in the European institutions? What does the Europeanization of collective identities and of public spheres contribute to explaining the process and outcome of European integration? Does it add anything to the accounts promoted by the various theories of European integration, such as (liberal) intergovernmentalism (Moravcsik 1998), neofunctionalism (Haas 1958), or multilevel governance (Hooghe and Marks 2001; Stone Sweet, Sandholtz, and Fligstein 2001)?

As argued earlier, identity does not add much to explanatory accounts of specific EU policies or to the daily business of European institutions. Rather, one

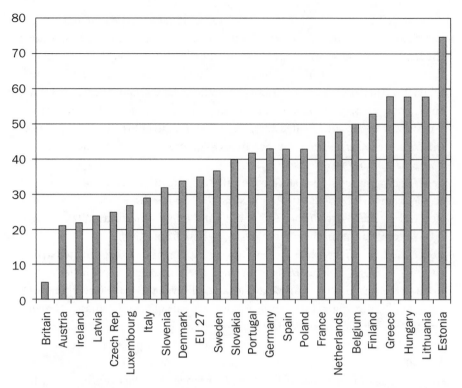

Figure 8.1. Support for EU coordinated action in economic crisis, 2009. The Eurobarometer question was: "As a citizen would you say that you would be better protected in the face of the current financial and economic crisis if (OUR COUNTRY) adopted measures and applied them individually or in a coordinated way with the other EU countries." Those opting for individual national protection were then subtracted from those opting for coordinated EU policies.
Source: European Parliament 2009, 13.

needs to focus on the so-called history-making decisions such as treaty-making (the constitutionalization process) or major integration choices such as the single market, the single currency, or foreign and security policy. Major theories of European integration can actually incorporate ideational accounts focusing on collective identities. Liberal intergovernmentalism, for example, is open to collective beliefs—whether norms or knowledge-based beliefs—as the source of domestic preferences, the theory's starting point.[1] Haas's neofunctionalism included identification processes in the very definition of integration.[2] More recent

---

1. Andrew Moravcsik has aptly called this "ideational liberalism." See Moravcsik 1997.
2. Haas defined integration as "the process whereby political actors in several distinct national settings are persuaded to shift their loyalties, expectations, and political activities toward a new

reformulations of neofunctionalism also include identification processes in their causal accounts (e.g., Hooghe and Marks 2008).

I do not attempt to add a new theory of European integration to the existing ones. Rather, I try to show that the construction of collective identities by national and European elites has to be incorporated into a causal story of how history-making decisions in the European Union have come about. In this context, two types of causal explanations can be distinguished. First, collective identities and their representations in the public spheres can be linked causally to the development of actors' preferences, whether as an alternative to accounts emphasizing material interests or as being somewhat complementary to these interests. The problem with such accounts is that it is virtually impossible to convincingly demonstrate what actors "really want" and whether they are primarily motivated by ideational rather than material factors (for an attempt with regard to France, see Parsons 2003). In most cases, we will find material as well as ideational factors at play.

A second, but weaker, explanatory account focuses on the communicative utterances of actors to discern whether (material) interest-based or identity-based arguments dominate the relevant discourses (or which combination does). Discourse matters in any causal story of political outcomes (Schmidt and Radaelli 2004). At a minimum, elite discourses in liberal democracies serve to legitimize political decisions in order to generate the domestic support necessary to sustain these choices. It makes a difference if we find that the dominant discourse refers to collective identities rather than narrowly defined material interests.

In the following, I demonstrate that identity-based arguments are regularly being used in the legitimating discourses with regard to the EU's history-making decisions. I discuss three such choices, namely the introduction of the euro during the early 1990s, the decisions to institutionalize the Common Foreign and Security Policy as well as the European Security and Defense Policy, and, finally, the constitutional decisions of the early 2000s (the "Future of Europe" debate, the Constitutional Treaty, the Treaty of Lisbon). My account concentrates mostly on the public discourses of the "big three," France, Great Britain, and Germany. These three countries not only matter most in EU treaty-making given their veto player status. They also represent crucial cases in the sense that their willingness or unwillingness to give up sovereignty in favor of supranational solutions is in need of explanation. If we can demonstrate that identity matters in these accounts, we have come quite a way to showing its significance in theories of European integration.

---

centre, whose institutions possess or demand jurisdiction over the pre-existing national states" (Haas 1958, 16; for a discussion, see Risse 2005).

To Euro or Not to Euro?

The introduction of the euro marked a major step in the process of European integration following the decision to pursue the single market.[3] The 1992 Maastricht Treaties established the Economic and Monetary Union (EMU), which went into force in 1999 followed by the introduction of euro bills and coins in 2002. Germany and France had been at the forefront of those promoting a single currency ever since the Single European Act, while Great Britain remained on the sidelines and opted out of EMU at the negotiations of the Maastricht Treaties (Moravcsik 1998, chap. 6; McNamara 1998; Verdun 2000). How is this difference in attitudes to be explained?

A first-cut answer points to economic reasons. The single currency was viewed as the logical follow-up to the European single market, which allowed for the free movement of goods, capital, labor, and services. The euro would stop the excessive currency fluctuations and protectionist pressures that could jeopardize the single market. It would eliminate transaction costs and might lead to increased investment. In sum, the euro was supposed to be the answer to the increased economic interdependence among the EU member states and to the challenges of globalization.

Yet, this reasoning cannot account for the variation in elite attitudes toward the single currency in Britain, France, and Germany. In particular, why did Britain choose not to participate in the single currency, even though its economy is as integrated with the continental European economies as any country's? Take the British government's "five economic tests" issued in 1997, for example. These tests deal with the compatibility of business cycles and economic structures, labor market flexibility, investments in Britain, the U.K.'s financial services industry, and with growth, stability, and an increase in jobs. The British government's 2003 assessment of these "tests" indicates the political rather than the economic nature of a decision to join the single currency. It even argues that the United Kingdom meets the EMU convergence criteria and that the "UK now exhibits a greater degree of cyclical convergence than some EMU members demonstrated in the run-up to the start of EMU in 1999 and remains more convergent than a number of EMU countries today."[4]

A second explanation points to geopolitical and security reasons. The end of the cold war brought the German problem back onto the European agenda. EMU can be regarded as an effort to contain German power in Europe in the aftermath

---

3. The following is based on Risse et al. 1999; Risse 2003.
4. See "HM Treasury: Executive Summary. Government Policy on EMU and the Five Economic Tests," http://www.hm-treasury.gov.uk/euro_assess03_repexecsum.htm.

of unification by firmly binding the Federal Republic to Western institutions and by preventing a German *Sonderweg*[5] (Grieco 1995). Moreover, the single currency and the European Central Bank (ECB) effectively ended the quasi hegemony of the German Bundesbank over monetary policies in Europe. However, if it was in the geopolitical interest of Germany's neighbors to opt for "binding" through institutional arrangements, then it was also in Germany's interest to retain as much national sovereignty as possible. In other words, why should the Germans have given up their cherished deutsche mark which had allowed them economic hegemony in Europe?[6]

There are as many good economic or geopolitical reasons *in favor* of the euro as there are against it. In particular, the perceived instrumental interests of actors as such do not explain the considerable *variation* in attitudes. Rather, actors' perception of their material and instrumental interests with regard to the euro were deeply influenced by their visions of European political order. Differences in the construction of collective elite identities pertaining to the nation-state and to Europe explain the controversies among the political elites in the three countries as well as the variation in attitudes.

In the case of *Germany,* its government had agreed to EMU early on and stubbornly supported the euro throughout the 1990s. The majority of the German political elite never wavered in its support for the single currency. Even more surprising was the lack of public controversy about the euro, despite the fact that a majority of German mass public opinion rejected giving up the deutsche mark. General elite support for the single currency was based on the German post–World War II European identity, whose purpose was to overcome the German nationalist and militarist past once and for all (see chapter 3; Engelmann-Martin 2002). Chancellor Kohl in particular wanted to be remembered as the one who pushed through EMU and hence made a closer European Union inevitable, preventing a return to nationalism in Europe (Banchoff 1997, 61–63). Kohl framed the single currency as *the* symbol of European integration and he deeply identified his political fate with the realization of the euro. He also labeled 1997—the year of reference for the fulfillment of the convergence criteria—as

---

5. Sonderweg refers to an alleged temptation of Germany to pursue its own nationalist path between East and West instead of remaining firmly anchored in the community of democracies. It is based on a specific reading of nineteenth-century German history of nationalism and militarism.

6. A widespread narrative of the history of EMU holds that the German government under Chancellor Kohl had agreed to the single currency as the political price to be paid for French (and others) support for German unification. This interpretation overlooks that Germany had agreed to EMU in principle long before German unification was negotiated in 1990. For details on this point, see Moravcsik 1998, 437–38.

the "key year of Europe," as *existential* for further integration. He even argued that the success of EMU was a "question of war and peace."[7] In essence, Chancellor Kohl framed the issue in German political discourse by constructing a powerful equation linking the euro to German identity:

Support for the euro = support for European integration = good Europeanness = good Germanness = rejection of the German militarist and nationalist past.

This framing of the issue served as a silencing mechanism of the political debate on EMU. It was no longer possible to argue about the pros and cons of a single currency and to weigh the policy alternatives in a neutral way. The opponents of a single currency had to make sure that they could not be regarded as "bad Germans," that is, as proponents of German nationalism. As a result, German opponents of the euro almost never declared their opposition openly, but rather demanded a postponement of the euro. They went to great lengths to show that one could be a "good German European" and still remain skeptical of a single currency.[8] Even those opposed to EMU did not dare touch the German consensus on European integration, but framed their criticism in terms of asking for a delay and/or demanding a strict application of the convergence criteria. They had to make sure that support for the deutsche mark could not be construed as an alternative to German Europeanness. Thus, in this case the Europeanization of German identity largely shaped the definition of economically defined interests.

In contrast, the *French* approach to EMU followed an interest-driven reorientation of French economic and monetary policies in conjunction with a change in French approaches to European order. These changes led to a reconstruction and Europeanization of French collective identities that the end of the cold war exacerbated and accelerated (see chapter 3).

The most important transformation of French attitudes toward both economic policies and European political order occurred among the French left in the early 1980s (see Roscher 2003). When President Mitterrand's initial attempt at leftist Keynesianism failed miserably in 1983, he had no other choice than to change course dramatically if he was to remain in power. Instrumental interests such as the desire to preserve political power led to a reconstruction of the

---

7. In a speech to the German Bundestag, see "Kohl: Bei der europäischen Währung ist Stabilität wichtiger als der Kalender," *Frankfurter Allgemeine Zeitung,* 28 May 1994.

8. For example, Gerhard Schröder in "Den besten Zeitpunkt suchen!" *Die Zeit,* 6 June 1997; Edmund Stoiber in "Es gab einmal eine europäische Bewegung in Deutschland...das ist vorbei," *Süddeutsche Zeitung,* 2 Nov. 1993; "Stoiber beharrt auf Kritik an EWU," *Süddeutsche Zeitung,* June 23, 1997; "Edmund Stoiber: Defender of a Decimal Point," *Financial Times,* 7 July 1997.

political program of the French Socialist Party and subsequently to a transformation and Europeanization of its collective identity. This new identity explains why the Parti Socialiste consistently supported EMU. President Mitterrand set the trend and his party followed.

Similar changes in the prevailing visions of European order combined with reconstructions of French nation-state identity took place on the French right in conjunction with the end of the cold war. The Gaullist Rassemblement pour la République (RPR) had adopted neoliberal discourse and monetarism (Baudouin 1990), but it was divided over EMU, with one faction leading the referendum campaign against the single currency and President Chirac. These divisions had little to do with differences over economic policies, and more to do with a split about what European integration meant. The divisions within the RPR over the single currency centered on understandings of what constituted sovereignty and how much supranationalism was compatible with it. It is not surprising that the competing visions of European order held by RPR policymakers corresponded to differing views of Frenchness. President Jacques Chirac expressed ideas about the Europeanization of French distinctiveness that were similar to those of the French left:

> The European Community is also a question of identity. If we want to preserve our values, our way of life, our standard of living, our capacity to count in the world, to defend our interests, to remain carriers of a humanistic message, we are certainly bound to build a united and solid bloc.... If France says yes [to the Treaties of Maastricht], she can better reaffirm what I believe in: French exceptionalism.[9]

This identity construction Europeanizes the Gaullist vision of the French nation-state by transferring its properties to Europe (see chapter 3). Support for and opposition to EMU in the French debate centered on competing understandings of national sovereignty and of "Frenchness." Although a majority of French political elites gradually embraced a Europeanization of French distinctiveness, a minority stuck to the old concepts of French *grandeur* and *indépendence*. This group mobilized again more than ten years later during the referendum on the Constitutional Treaty in 2005.

The *British* attitude toward the single currency remained the same over two decades. At the Maastricht summit, the British government reserved the right to decide for itself whether or not the United Kingdom would join EMU in 1999. The Labour government under Tony Blair confirmed this position and decided

---

9. Jacques Chirac, in *Libération*, 11 Sept. 1992.

that Britain would continue the "wait and see" attitude of its predecessor based on the "five economic tests" quoted above.

While the few British proponents of the euro used interest-based arguments to support their claims, conservative Euroskeptics routinely used identity-related statements to justify their opposition to EMU, such as "European monetary union will remove all characteristics of sovereignty which characterize a proud and independent nation" and "Abolish the pound and you abolish Britain."[10]

The British debate on EMU and the continuing reluctance to join the single currency must be understood with reference to a stable national identity collectively shared by the political elites (see chapter 3; Knopf 2003). The dominant discourse strengthened the opponents of the single currency who regularly used identity arguments to make their point. They feared that Britain would lose the ability to govern itself and argued against any further losses of national sovereignty. The political discourse centered around whether to join *later or never,* in sharp contrast with the debates in Germany, which concentrated on joining *now or later.*

In sum, the discourse on the euro in the three countries was framed to a large degree in terms of identity politics and political visions of European order. Supporters of the project joined a common vision of European integration as a modernization project to overcome the continent's historical divisions (Jachtenfuchs 2002; Jachtenfuchs, Diez, and Jung 1998). They used the single currency as a means to get closer to this political vision. The euro symbolized a collective European identity, while the deutsche mark, the franc, and the pound sterling were constructed as symbolic remnants of a nationalist past.

However, the three discourses represent different combinations of the ways in which identities and material interests are linked. With regard to both the British and the German cases, collective identities—Englishness as non-Europeanness, in one case, and German Europeanness, in the other—largely influenced how political elites came to see their economic interests with regard to European integration in general and EMU in particular. In these two cases, collective identities—whether national or Europeanized—do a large part of the causal work in explaining the particular ways in which the elites in both countries came to view British and German interests. In these two cases, the identities were rather clear, while the "national interests" remained vague and ambiguous. As a result, collective identities defined the range of (economic and political) choices available to actors.[11] In the French case, however, the causal arrow runs from

---

10. The first quote is from Peter Tapsell, Conservative, House of Commons, 24 March 1993, 967–68. The second quote is from Redwood 1997, 19.

11. For a theoretical discussion of the particular relationship between identities and interests, see March and Olsen 1998, 952.

interests to identities. Two "critical junctures"—the failure of Mitterrand's economic policies in 1983 and the end of the cold war in the late 1980s—profoundly challenged the perceived political and economic interests of the political elites. Policy failures triggered a reconstruction of political interests—in the mid-1980s for the French Socialists and in the early 1990s for the French Gaullists. Majorities in both parties then adjusted their collective identities accordingly and Europeanized their understandings of French distinctiveness, even though this Europeanization remains fragile, unstable, and contested to this day.

Toward a European Foreign and Defense Identity

While the euro is about giving up core features of national economic sovereignty, foreign and security policy concerns control over one's external affairs as a core prerogative of national executives. But in sharp contrast to EMU, which has been fully supranational from the beginning, foreign and security policy remains the one significant issue area in European affairs in which decisions are still made consensually and in an intergovernmental fashion.[12] The 2007 Treaty of Lisbon creates the position of a "High Representative of the Union for Foreign Affairs and Security Policy"—a European foreign minister in all but name—who will also be vice president of the European Commission. It also establishes an EU Diplomatic Service and further increased the EU's competences in CFSP/ESDP affairs. But it did not change the intergovernmental nature of CFSP/ESDP (overview in Howorth 2007). How is this to be explained, and what does identity have to do with it?

International relations theory has a ready-made explanation for the puzzle, of course. Realism (Morgenthau 1948; Waltz 1979) tells us that states are unlikely to give up external sovereignty and the ultimate decision over questions of war and peace. When the survival of the nation-state is at stake, states do not share or pool sovereignty. There are two problems with this argument. First, realism itself is indeterminate concerning these questions, since one can distinguish a version emphasizing that states primarily seek autonomy and a variant that focuses on "influence-seeking" (Baumann, Rittberger, and Wagner 2001). The refusal to extend qualified majority voting (QMV) to decisions over war and peace is consistent with the version emphasizing autonomy. But if states seek to increase their power and influence in international politics, then the unwillingness of some EU member states to give up external sovereignty in foreign and security affairs is

---

12. Note that this pertains mostly to military and defense issues. EU foreign affairs in the areas of environmental policies, human rights, development aid, and external trade are mostly subject to supranational decision making through qualified majority voting (QMV).

outright self-defeating. The less Europe speaks with one voice in world politics, the less EU member states can exert influence. The European divisions over the Iraq War in 2003 only serve to highlight the point. Europe remained divided, while the United States ruled. Moreover, and whatever the version of realism one adheres to, balancing is supposed to be the standard behavior of nation-states. Balancing in a one-superpower world, however, requires pooling resources and building alliances. From this perspective, one would expect the EU to get its act together in foreign and security affairs in order to build a counterweight to U.S. power (or against the rise of China).

Second, it is incorrect to maintain that most European states are not prepared to give up sovereignty in the realm of security and defense. Roughly two thirds of the current EU member states—including their populations—would be more than willing to supranationalize external security and national defense. And this includes many of the big member states, such as France, Germany, Spain, and Italy. In 2007, 72 percent of EU citizens favored a common European foreign and security policy, including 84 percent of Germans and 52 percent of the British (European Commission 2007b, 148). Thus, realism seems to apply only to *some* countries, such as the United Kingdom, which has opposed majority voting in the CFSP/ESDP so far.

If we want to account for the puzzle of European foreign and security policy, we must explain the variation among EU member states concerning their preparedness to supranationalize defense affairs. Rationalist or neoliberal institutionalism at least offers an interest-based account of interstate cooperation under specific conditions (e.g., Haftendorn, Keohane, and Wallander 1999 for an application to transatlantic institutions). In this context, one could posit that the stronger a country's military forces, the less it has to gain from supranational cooperation in defense affairs. Once again, the argument makes little sense, since it cannot explain the difference in attitudes between France and Germany, on the one hand, who have consistently supported moves toward supranationalizing defense affairs in the EU, and the United Kingdom, on the other. The difference in military power between the "big three" of the EU is too small to be able to account for the variation.

Interestingly enough, the only available empirical study that seeks to explain the variation concludes that federal states in Europe are more likely to prefer supranational decisions in external security and defense policies than unitary states (Koenig-Archibugi 2004; see also Hooghe 2001). Thus, domestic institutional features would explain differences in attitudes toward supranationalism in security affairs. The same member states that prefer supranationalism over intergovernmentalism in general are also prepared to supranationalize foreign and defense policies. What is less clear, though, are the causal mechanisms linking territorial structures to preferences for a common European foreign and defense policy. I suggest that the social constructions and collective understandings that come with federalism might be relevant. Countries whose elites and citizens are used to the notion that sovereignty can be divided and/or shared between various levels of governance might also be more prepared to include supranational levels of governance in these understandings.

Germany serves as a case in point. Federalism has been constitutive for the German state for centuries; the Federal Republic of Germany is based on cooperative federalism that involves the sharing of sovereignty between the central state and the *Länder*. Moreover, as argued above, German elites thoroughly Europeanized German collective identity after World War II. No wonder then that Germany supported a supranational CFSP/ESDP from the beginning. German policymakers from the center-left to the center-right were also never prepared to make a choice between NATO membership, on the one hand, and a European defense policy, on the other.

In contrast, *France* has been a centralized state for centuries so that it does not easily fit the bill linking the territorial division of power to a propensity to accept supranational solutions in defense affairs. On the one hand, it took the French government up to the Anglo-French St. Malo agreement of 1998 to recognize that a common European foreign and security policy could not be promoted as an alternative to NATO, but that it had to accept the German *sowohl als auch* ("as well as") in order to achieve progress in CFSP/ESDP. On the other hand, the issue at stake for France was not supranationalism, but the relationship between NATO and ESDP. This issue has finally been solved when France, under President Sarkozy, reentered NATO's military structure in 2009. I suggest that France's ambivalence with regard to a truly supranational European defense policy has more to do with the half-hearted Europeanization of French elite identities (see chapter 3) than with the institutional structures of the French state.

St. Malo also marked the beginning of a *British* turnaround toward ESDP, which was then enshrined in the 1999 Helsinki agreements of the European Council. In 1998, the British government of Prime Minister Tony Blair had gradually come to accept the notion that NATO and the Anglo-American "special relationship" were not endangered by closer European defense cooperation. But the British government consistently objected to any move toward supranationalism in CFSP/ESDP affairs, blocking agreement in the Constitutional Convention, in the subsequent Intergovernmental Conference, and in the negotiations leading up to the 2007 Treaty of Lisbon. It is hard to understand this stubborn British position without taking sovereignty considerations into account. The British arguments against supranational decision making in EU foreign and defense policy closely resemble British objections to the euro. But in this case, and in contrast to the single currency, Britain exerts an effective veto power.[13] Although the euro is viable with or without the British pound, a common EU defense policy requires British participation because it has one of the largest and best-trained armed forces in Europe.

In sum, it is very hard to explain the variation in member states' preferences with regard to CFSP/ESDP without reference to the differential Europeanization of elite identities. But the relationship between identity and foreign policy does not end here. The EU member states such as Germany that have long supported qualified majority voting (QMV) in foreign and security policy are also member states with mostly multilateral and cooperative foreign and security policies. They do not prefer a militarized European foreign and defense policy, but want Europe to be a "civilian power" (see Duchêne 1972 for the original concept; Maull 1990). Although a "civilian power" does not refuse to use military force under exceptional circumstances, it emphasizes cooperative security policy, multilateralism, and the rule of (international) law. This is precisely the foreign and security policy identity that the EU has tried to build from the 1990s on, even though it had the whole range of instruments available only in the early 2000s (Howorth 2007; Anderson 2008; Börzel and Risse 2009).

There is nothing peculiar about the EU promoting a particular identity in its external relations. Every great power in the history of international relations has tried to promote a certain set of values in its foreign affairs—from the Roman to the British empires, from the Soviet Union, which tried to promote Communism on a global scale, to the United States, which countered with its own vision of global democracy and capitalism.[14] The more interesting point is that the EU has started behaving like any other great power in this regard, even though its capacity to act in foreign affairs (actorness) has long been disputed (Hill 1993; Sjursen 2006a). This actorness is no longer in question, not even in the public spheres (Kantner, Kutter, and Renfordt 2008; Kantner 2009; see chapter 6).

With regard to its foreign policy identity, "the discourse of the EU as a normative power constructs a particular self of the EU" (Diez 2005, 614). Stephanie Anderson (2008) goes a step further and argues that creating a distinct foreign policy identity is the whole point about the EU's efforts in external affairs. This foreign policy identity represents the outward-looking version of the EU's modern and enlightenment identity. It emphasizes the rule of (international) law, multilateral

---

13. Of course, Britain had to agree to EMU in the Maastricht Treaties, too, even though it opted out. Such an opt-out in the case of ESDP would derail a common European defense policy, however, as a result of which British agreement to a supranationalized ESDP is necessary.

14. It is therefore misleading to call the EU a "normative power," given that promoting norms is not what distinguishes the EU from other powers in world history. On this concept, see Manners 2002, 2006.

and peaceful conflict resolution, and the promotion of human rights, democracy, and the social market economy. The 2003 "European Security Strategy," the first EU attempt to develop a comprehensive foreign and security policy strategy, is full of references linking what is constitutive for modern and democratic Europe to its vision for international affairs. It starts by celebrating the EU's role in establishing an enduring peace in Europe, as a result of which its members "are committed to dealing peacefully with disputes and to co-operating through common institutions" (European Council 2003, 1). The document extensively deals with the post–cold war and post-9/11 security threats, emphasizing that "none of the new threats is purely military; nor can any be tackled by purely military means" (European Council 2003, 7). The strategy then promotes an "international order based on effective multilateralism" (European Council 2003, 9), committing the EU to support multilateralism and the United Nations as well to further human rights, the rule of law, and democracy in its external affairs. In this regard, the document intentionally distanced itself from the Bush administration's tendencies toward unilateralism and preventive warfare.

But the EU's attempt to consciously develop its own foreign policy identity is not confined to a declaratory strategy alone. By about 2000, the EU's foreign and security policy had at its disposal the entire set of instruments necessary for the promotion of democracy and human rights as well as for postconflict peace- and state-building (Börzel and Risse 2009; see Magen, McFaul, and Risse 2009). Human rights conditionality, for example, has been integrated in all but a few of its association as well as partnership agreements with countries around the world. The European Neighbourhood Policy (ENP) toward the southern Caucasus, Central Asia, and the Mediterranean includes a set of instruments designed to promote democracy and good governance. Ironically, when the EU member states were bitterly divided over their stance toward the 2003 U.S. invasion of Iraq, the first robust EU peace-keeping mission started in the Former Yugoslav Republic of Macedonia.

However, it is one thing to suggest that the EU actively constructs a particular foreign policy identity. It is quite different to claim that the emerging EU foreign policy can be causally explained by the EU's collective identity. A whole literature criticizes the hypocritical nature of EU foreign policies which often prioritize geostrategic and security interests over human rights and democracy concerns (e.g., Youngs 2004; Bicchi 2006; Pace 2007). Moreover, others claim that multilateralism is the foreign policy identity of the weak who do not command the necessary economic and military resources to develop a more forceful foreign policy (Kagan 2003; Hyde-Price 2006).

Thus, the question boils down to whether the EU's foreign policy identity as a "civilian power" is a matter of choice or of necessity. On the one hand, the lack of qualified majority voting in foreign and defense affairs might lead to decisions based on the lowest common denominator, leaving the EU with no other choice than to behave as a "civilian power." On the other hand, while the EU's military might is no match for the United States, its combined defense expenditures of ca. two hundred billion euros is second only to the United States and exceeds the military expenditures of Russia or China. With regard to defense spending worldwide, Great Britain is no. 2, France is no. 4, and Germany is no. 6 (SIPRI 2008, appendix 5A). The EU contains two nuclear weapons powers, France and Great Britain. Finally, the EU's combined GDP constitutes the No. 1 economic power in the world, which would certainly command the economic resources to become a formidable military power. These data suggest that the EU's self-proclaimed "civilian power" identity is indeed a matter of choice rather than necessity. Of course, we cannot explain every single foreign policy decision of the EU on identity grounds. But the EU's foreign policy identity as a "civilian power" is roughly consistent with its behavior in foreign and defense matters. The lack of power capabilities cannot explain the EU's approach in world affairs, which is also inconsistent with an analysis pointing to "objective" economic or security interests. As a result, we can conclude that the EU's attempt to construct a distinct collective identity based on modern and enlightenment values indeed contributes to explaining its emerging foreign and security policy.

Constitutional Talk

Monetary affairs as well as foreign and security policy are "hard cases" in which it is likely that identity politics matters less. In contrast, constitutional affairs are expected to be closely connected to visions about the purpose of a political community. Constitutions *are* matters of collective identity insofar as they define the specific features of a polity, the rights and duties of the citizens, and the core institutions. The EU is no exception. Over time, the EU treaties have created a legal order that interferes massively in the internal affairs of the member states. Although the term "constitution" is heavily contested in the EU and has ultimately been rejected, the process of EU treaty-making can aptly be described as one of constitutionalization (for different perspectives, see Stone Sweet 2000; Weiler 1999; Rittberger and Schimmelfennig 2006). While this process has not resulted in a single legal document, the ongoing treaty-making process has led to no less than six major treaties over the past twenty years— from the 1986 Single European Act to the 1992 Maastricht Treaties, the 1997 Amsterdam Treaty, the 2000 Treaty of Nice, the (failed) Constitutional Treaty, and the 2007 Treaty of Lisbon, which incorporates the most important provisions of the failed effort.

On the one hand, this constitutionalization process itself can be described as the ongoing creation of the EU's legal and political identity. The treaties *are* the EU's identity, so to speak. On the other hand, EU treaty-making represents the battleground where EU and member states actors fight over what should be constitutive for the union. As Markus Jachtenfuchs has shown, the preferences of member state governments for treaty reform closely follow ideas enshrined in their various constitutional traditions (Jachtenfuchs 2002). Federal states such as Germany, Belgium, or Spain, for example, are generally more inclined to support supranational solutions than more unitary states such as Great Britain. Moreover, there is a strong correlation between Euroskepticism and a lack of Europeanized collective identities on the elite level, on the one hand, and opposition to further integration, on the other.

I have shown in chapters 6 and 7 how constitutional debates have led to Europeanized public spheres, particularly in continental Europe and gradually encompassing Central Eastern Europe. These debates have not only centered around similar issues and frames of reference across borders. They have also contributed to transnational communities of communication and, thus, to the emergence of Europeanized identities in the public spheres.

I now concentrate on the substantive content of these transnational debates to show how the constitutionalization process itself creates a battleground over contested visions of Europe and over the EU's political identity. Methodologically, this part of the chapter is different from the discussions of the euro and of European foreign and security policy. With regard to the single currency and to CFSP/ESDP, I have shown how the Europeanization of elite identities has influenced their preferences for European integration. Here, I demonstrate how Europeanized identities are constructed through the contestation over institutional reforms itself. Thus, the following represents a constitutive analysis rather than one that tries to causally explain specific decisions.

A good starting point is the "Future of Europe" debate triggered by the speech of German foreign minister Joschka Fischer at Berlin's Humboldt University on May 12, 2000. In this speech, Fischer suggested the creation of a European federation based on a European constitution that established the basic human and civil rights of citizens, described the power balance between European institutions, and delineated the division of competences between the European level and the member states (Fischer 2000). In his response six weeks later at the German Bundestag, French President Jacques Chirac took up the themes mentioned by Fischer. Chirac's speech contained ample references to a collective European identity centered on overcoming the European past as well as celebrating the accomplishments of European integration. Like Fischer, Chirac's European vision strongly resembled the modern, secular, and enlightened European project. He also suggested that France, Germany, and others should form an "avant-garde group" of countries that wanted to go ahead with advanced cooperation.[15]

In September 2000, British Prime Minister Tony Blair gave his account of the future of Europe in a speech at the Polish stock exchange, thereby emphasizing his commitment to EU enlargement. The speech positioned Britain "at the centre of Europe" and claimed that Europe without Britain would be both foolish and misguided. He strongly argued against visions of a European federation, which he called a "superstate": "Europe is a Europe of free, independent sovereign nations who choose to pool that sovereignty in pursuit of their own interests and the common good."[16] Blair emphasized that the future EU should keep a balance between supranational and intergovernmental institutions. Although he was not opposed to "enhanced cooperation," he was far more reluctant on this topic than Chirac.

The three speeches outlined the battleground for institutional reforms that the EU faced during the early 2000s. The three representatives of Germany, France, and Britain all used "identity-speak" to make their points and deliberately chose other European capitals to comment on the future of Europe. Even Blair identified the EU as a community of fate with Britain at its center rather than on its periphery. Fischer, Chirac, and Blair constructed their visions of Europe within the framework of a modern and enlightened European identity that is open to enlargement and embraces human rights, democracy, and the rule of law. This transnational and cross-national construction of a collective European identity narrative through the major speeches and in the public sphere then allowed for transnational contestation and debates about models of institutional reform (Trenz 2007).

The "Future of Europe" debate marked the beginning of a transnational discussion that was then channeled institutionally through the Constitutional Convention, which produced a draft Constitutional Treaty in mid-2003. The Convention itself represented an institutional innovation in EU treaty-making insofar as European and national members of parliaments rather than members of governments formed the majority (Göler 2006; Norman 2005). The Constitutional Convention yielded surprising results that previous IGCs had been unable to accomplish, namely the integration of the EC and EU treaties into a single legal personality of the EU, the "double majority"[17] in the Council of Ministers,

---

15. See Chirac's speech to the German Bundestag, http://www.bundestag.de/geschichte/gastredner/chirac/chirac1.html.

16. See "Prime Minister's Speech to the Polish Stock Exchange," http://www.number10.gov.uk/output/Page3384.asp.

17. "Double majority" means that a decision in the Council of Ministers has to be taken by at least 55% of the member states representing at least 65% of the EU's population. According to the Lisbon Treaty, it will enter into force by 2014.

or the creation of an EU "foreign minister." These institutional innovations survived the failure of the Constitutional Treaty and are now incorporated into the 2007 Treaty of Lisbon.

The Constitutional Convention represented a truly transnational effort at EU treaty-making rather than the traditional intergovernmental method. Its deliberations were more transparent than previous IGCs, thereby contributing to the creation of a European public sphere in which the problems at stake had to be formulated and the arguments had to be framed from a European rather than from national standpoints (Risse and Kleine 2007; for a contrasting perspective, see Magnette and Nicolaides 2004). When Convention delegates tried to push national interests, the institutional rules stipulated that national preferences had to be justified on the grounds of a common European purpose. The analysis of a small sample of newspaper coverage during the European Convention underscores this point: the German *Frankfurter Allgemeine Zeitung,* the French *Le Monde,* and the British *Financial Times* reported about the Convention and focused on European rather than national themes (Landfried 2004, 131–35).

The Convention's dominant discourse, as promoted by its president, former French president Valéry Giscard d'Estaing, consisted of repeated references to the EU as a community of fate that had to be made more effective and more democratic in order to enhance its problem-solving capacity (Kleine 2007; Tsebelis and Proksch 2007). European identity in its modern and enlightened version was constitutive for the Convention's discourse. The one instance of an identity clash during the Constitutional Convention serves to underline the point, namely the struggle over the reference to God in the draft constitution's preamble (see chapter 3). The Polish representatives, supported by the Holy See, favored such a move, which, of course, clashed with a secular European self-understanding according to which European values stem from various—religious and nonreligious—sources (Kutter 2007, 2009; Wyrozumska 2007). The preamble to the 2007 Treaty of Lisbon refers to "the cultural, religious, and humanist inheritance of Europe," but refrains from an explicit reference to Christianity (Council of the European Union 2008). The collective identity of the EU as a secular community that embraces the values of enlightenment, which are inspired by various humanist and religious sources, prevailed despite support for the Polish proposal by European Christian Democrats.

In general, the *"Future of Europe"* debates and the deliberations of the Constitutional Convention exemplify instances in which collective elite identities with regard to the EU remained fairly consensual and centered on the notion of a modern, secular, and enlightened Europe. However, and maybe *because* of the lack of deep controversies during the Constitutional Convention, the public visibility of the Convention's deliberations remained rather subdued (Packham

2003; Vetters 2007). Although the Convention made every effort to publicize its proceedings, it did not succeed in getting sufficient media attention to leave an imprint on the European public spheres.

This changed dramatically during the following IGC and—most importantly—during the referendum debates in France and the Netherlands in 2005. Identity politics now assumed center stage and became contested again in the European and national public spheres. Media attention shifted from focusing on the EU level to the level of member states, particularly those in which the Constitutional Treaty was strongly contested, such as Poland, France, and the Netherlands (see chapters 6 and 7). Yet, this does not imply that a renationalization of public debates took place. Across Europe, newspapers deplored the sad state of European affairs, contrasting an idealized community of fate with the reality of EU member states defending narrowly defined national interests.

The politicization during the referendum debates led to renewed contestations of European identity. Take the examples of Poland and France. In the Polish case, the debate was not so much about the reform of the European Union's institutions than about the degree to which a new member state belonged to Europe (Kutter 2007, 453; also Ramet 2006a, 137–43), that is, about Polish identity in Europe. The "reference to God" issue has already been mentioned. It was constructed as part of the common European cultural heritage that Poland would contribute to Europe. Interestingly enough, the Polish press used the notion of a Kulturkampf in this context, alluding to the nineteenth-century clash between German chancellor Bismarck and the Catholic Church under Pope Pius IX. Although the nineteenth-century Kulturkampf was directed against German Catholics (and Polish Catholics living on Prussian territory), the Polish press constructed it as a cultural fight pitting secular Europe against Polish culture.[18] The rejection of a "reference to God" in the Constitutional Treaty was then interpreted as lack of respect for Polish identity. However, the Polish Catholic Church was faced with a dilemma, since it, along with the Vatican and Pope John Paul II, had continuously supported Polish accession to the EU (Ramet 2006a, 137). The Polish Catholic Church had been at the forefront of those who had supported Polish entry into the EU as the natural place of Poland in a postcommunist world. But the EU that Poland entered was a modern and secular Europe, not the Christian Europe favored by the Catholic Church.

The fight over the "double majority" was also framed in identity terms in Poland. The slogan "Nice or death!" voiced by a right-wing politician construed vote counting in the EU as a matter of (Polish) survival (Kutter 2007, 445; see Kutter 2009; Wyrozumska 2007). This construction erroneously made Poland

---

18. I owe this point to Amelie Kutter. See Kutter 2007, 443.

into one of the smaller EU member states (even though, with its population of thirty-eight million, it is the sixth largest member state in the EU 27). The reference to Polish historical identity as a victim of the great powers—particularly Germany, whose weight in the Council was to increase through "double majority" voting—is obvious (see chapter 3). Given the invocation of historical memory, it became hard for the Polish government to accept a compromise on this issue, since postcommunist Polish identity had been constructed on the basis of regaining national sovereignty. Fortunately, German chancellor Merkel worked out a face-saving deal at the 2007 EU summit that postponed the move toward "double majority" until 2014.

The two episodes demonstrate the unsettled and contested nature of Polish European identity. The Polish consensus of "returning to Europe" by entering the EU gradually gave way to a debate about *which* Europe they were returning to. The Polish debates exemplified one of the first instances in which two alternative visions of Europe—modern, secular, and enlightened Europe vs. Christian and traditional Europe—became politically salient and clashed head-on.

The same holds true for the French debates in 2005 (Schmidt 2007; Perrineau 2005; Laurent and Sauger 2005). Although this controversy also centered on France's place in Europe, the main debate was about *which* Europe France should support. At least three different discourses were salient in the French referendum debate. First, the "pro"-campaign adopted the "Europe as France writ large" theme (see chapter 3) according to which French values of enlightenment and Republicanism are best preserved in the EU and the EU serves as a shield against globalization. As Vivien Schmidt pointed out, this elite discourse met with an increasingly disillusioned public during the referendum debate as a result of which repeating the old discourse simply was not good enough (Schmidt 2007). In particular, French public opinion was no longer convinced that the EU protects against globalization. Almost 70 percent of the French feared that the EU threatens the French model of social protection and this perception cut across one's position toward EU membership (Evans 2007). Moreover, almost 50 percent of the French felt that French national identity was threatened by European integration.

The discourses of the "no" campaign tapped right into these identity constructions. On the French right, the Front National and the conservative part of the Gaullist Union pour un Mouvement Populaire (UMP) argued that the Constitutional Treaty threatened national sovereignty and, therefore, French identity. These groupings—although not per se anti-European—adopted a discourse promoting a traditional, Christian, anti-immigrant, and exclusionary Europe. On the French left, parts of the Parti Socialiste and the Parti Communiste that opposed the Constitutional Treaty argued that the modern and secular European project required defending it more forcefully against globalization and, therefore, the Constitutional Treaty had to be rejected as a "neoliberal" project. They tried to establish that the identity of modern Europe would survive only if a more "social Europe" was established. This part of the "no" campaign, therefore, tried to tap into the attitudes of those voters who favored European integration but feared a loss of social protection. The result was a resounding "no" to the Constitutional Treaty in 2005, which sent shivers through the pro-European elites in France and elsewhere.

In sum, the discourses surrounding the French referendum cannot be understood without taking identity politics into account. What is most noteworthy about these debates is that they did not simply pit pro-Europeans against anti-Europeans. It would be wrong, for example, to interpret the "no" vote as a vote against European integration. Rather, the issues were largely about *which Europe* was supposed to solve the problems of the French nation-state. While the "yes" campaign tried to defend the traditional French view in favor of European integration, the "no" campaign assembled those who promoted an exclusionary EU protecting French workers against immigrants and even "Polish plumbers," on the one hand, and those on the left who wanted to transform the modern Europe of the single market into a more social and inclusive Europe, on the other. The French (as well as the Dutch and Irish) referendum debates foreshadowed a politicization of European politics that the political elites across Europe had always tried to avoid. I come back to this point in chapter 10.

As discussed in chapters 6 and 7, the referendums debates in France and the Netherlands also gave rise to a further Europeanization of public spheres—much more so than the Constitutional Convention itself, which was explicitly designed to do just that. Media analyses of these debates across Europe demonstrate a high degree of transnationalization. The studies also show increasing convergence in the justifications given for the European project. These findings confirm that identity-related discourses matter quite substantially when it comes to constitutional issues in the European Union—and irrespective of whether the particular constitutional project is contested in the country under consideration.

Conclusions

This chapter examined the consequences of Europeanized identities and public spheres (or lack thereof) for the "deepening" of the EU, that is, the institutional issues concerning the scope and level of European integration. With regard to mass public opinion, statistical analyses show that the Europeanization of collective identities (if only as secondary identities) has substantial effects on support levels for European integration. These studies also demonstrate that

Euroenthusiasm and Euroskepticism map onto a cultural value cleavage that is orthogonal to the traditional Left-Right cleavage along which most European party systems are organized (Kriesi et al. 2008). Finally, there is increasing evidence that the observable Europeanization of public spheres and the greater visibility of the EU in the media not only affect collective identities but can also increase Euroskepticism, particularly in cases in which the political elites are split about European integration and media reporting is overwhelmingly negative. I discuss the consequences in chapter 10.

I then examined the consequences of Europeanized identities and public spheres for "deepening" decisions. Although it is unlikely that identity politics accounts for daily policymaking in the EU, the Europeanization of identities and public spheres matters with regard to "history-making" decisions. I have demonstrated this point with regard to two major integration decisions that involve the transfer—or nontransfer—of national sovereignty to the European level, namely the introduction of the euro and the evolution of a common European foreign and defense policy. The variation in national preferences in these two policy areas can be accounted for largely by different degrees of Europeanized identities.

Finally, this chapter used the debates on the future of European integration and on the Constitutional Treaty as well as the Treaty of Lisbon in the late 1990s and early 2000s to show how these controversies by their very nature contributed to the Europeanization of identities and public spheres. The various degrees to which national elite identities have been Europeanized serve as pretty good predictors of a member state's position in the constitutional debates. More important, the transnational discourses themselves constituted a European community of communication and, thus, showed European identity "in the making." The national referenda debates in France (2005), the Netherlands (2005), and Ireland (2008 and 2009) also provided arenas for transnational communication about European issues of common concern.

As to the substantive content of identity-related discourses, the construction of a modern, secular, and liberal Europe prevailed in most elite debates surrounding the euro, a common European foreign and defense policy, and the Constitutional Treaty. "Modern Europe" was the salient identity construction in both the public spheres and among the decision-making circles (except for a brief moment when Poland tried to push the vision of a "Christian Europe"). This changed during the referenda debates in France, the Netherlands, and Ireland. Populist parties—particularly on the right—started promoting an alternative vision of Europe, an "exclusionary fortress Europe" that essentially Europeanizes exclusive nationalism. This alternative European identity construction has become even more salient during the recent discussions about EU enlargement and about EU immigration policies. I turn to these issues in the next chapter.

9

"WIDENING"
EU Enlargement and Contested Identities

The previous chapter discussed the impact of identity politics on European institution-building. "Deepening" is about what constitutes the EU as a polity and, thus, as an object of identification. It concerns the *differentia specifica* of the EU. Debates about "widening," that is, accepting new members into the union, are different. "Widening" and enlargement are about drawing the boundaries of the community. It concerns the question who is "in" and who is "out," and who can legitimately claim to be member of the community. Two issues have to be discussed in this context. The first question concerns opening the EU to new member states, that is, enlargement proper. Ever since the end of the cold war, the EU has been going through various rounds of enlargement, from Northern enlargement in 1995 (Sweden, Finland, Austria) to Eastern enlargement in 2004 and 2007 when twelve new members joined the union including most of the former Communist Eastern European countries. Thus, the EU has more than doubled in size since the end of the cold war. In addition, accession negotiations are under way with Croatia and Turkey, and the western Balkans was given a membership perspective in the late 1990s following the settlement of the wars of Yugoslav succession.[1]

I argue in this chapter that one cannot even begin to understand EU enlargement without taking identity politics into account. European identities explain to a large extent the relatively smooth processes of Eastern enlargement, since

---

1. This concerns Albania, Bosnia-Hercegovina, Kosovo, the former Yugoslav Republic of Macedonia, Montenegro, and Serbia.

there was no question that Central Eastern Europe belongs to modern Europe as represented by the EU. In sharp contrast, Turkish EU membership has remained contested from the very beginning—and identity concerns explain a large part of this controversy. Whether Turkey and the remnants of the Ottoman Empire belong to "Europe" has remained disputed for centuries.

The debate about Turkish EU membership is linked to the second issue that has become rather salient during recent years, namely debates about immigration. Immigration is not about territorial enlargement, but about "widening" with regard to citizenship and the rights of non-EU foreigners. Controversies about immigration are as much controversies about who has a legitimate claim to be accepted into the community as they are driven by economic and more material concerns. Immigration policies have become contested issues in most EU member states—and they are increasingly debated as European rather than as national questions.

Discussions about "deepening" largely concern uncontested notions of modern and liberal Europe in identity terms. More traditional and "nationalist" visions of Europe have become salient only recently in debates about the EU's institutional framework. In contrast, debates about "widening" are also controversies about what Europe and the EU are all about. Although Western European support for Eastern enlargement in particular was based on the "modern" vision of Europe and the EU, Eastern accession itself put antisecular and antimodern ideas concerning the role of Christianity back on the European agenda. More important, the controversies surrounding Turkish accession and immigration policies increasingly confront the prevailing elite ideas of modern and enlightened Europe with countervisions of an exclusionary "nationalist Europe." Hence, we can observe the return of history when "widening" is debated across the EU.

This chapter starts with an analysis of the role of identity politics concerning the EU's decision in favor of Eastern enlargement. Second, I examine the consequences of Eastern enlargement for identity politics in Europe. I then focus on the controversies about Turkish membership and the way in which identity clashes complement economic as well as geopolitical accounts. Finally, I cover European debates about immigration and show that they are as much about the "other within" as about economic and other questions.

Returning to Europe: Identity Politics and Eastern Enlargement

Why did the EU accept more than ten new member states including the former Communist Central Eastern European countries (CEEC), and why did it offer an accession perspective to the western Balkans after the wars in the late 1990s? Eastern enlargement not only represented a major challenge for the EU itself but also a puzzle for conventional, that is, rationalist, theories of European integration.

Given the enormous economic and welfare benefits that the EU as the world's largest single market has to offer, the puzzle is not so much that the CEEC and others wanted to join the union. The real issue is why the EU committed itself early on to a path to membership for Central Eastern Europe. Neither economic nor security reasons make much sense in explaining the EU's position vis-à-vis Eastern enlargement (Schimmelfennig 2003; Sedelmeier 2005; Sjursen 2006b). First, security arguments are not plausible given that the CEEC joined NATO as the dominant Western security organization almost simultaneously. Second, the economic benefits of Eastern enlargement for EU member states are distributed very unevenly. Although Germany apparently benefits (but see Zaborowski 2006), France and the Southern EU members do not. Moreover, Southern Europe has to pay the price for Eastern enlargement in terms of a smaller share of the benefits from the Common Agricultural Policy (CAP) as well as from the Structural Funds, at least in the long run. And even for Germany or Denmark, which benefit economically from Eastern enlargement, association agreements rather than membership for the CEEC would have been sufficient. In sum, from the perspective of Western European EU members, there have been few sound material reasons for accepting Eastern Europe into the union.

Yet, since its founding days, the European Community made it clear that the union was open to Central Eastern Europe:

> We must build the united Europe not only in the interest of the free nations, but also in order to be able to admit the peoples of Eastern Europe into this community if, freed from the constraints under which they live, they want to join and seek our moral support. (Robert Schuman in 1963, quoted in Sedelmeier 2005, 24)

When the Berlin wall came down in 1989, the EU immediately reaffirmed its commitment:

> The Community has taken and will take the necessary decisions to strengthen its cooperation with peoples aspiring to freedom, democracy, and progress.... The objective remains...that of overcoming the divisions of Europe. (1989 Strasbourg European Council, quoted in Sedelmeier 2005, 25)

There was no doubt that Central Eastern Europe belonged to the union. From this perspective, the cold war was a historical aberration that prevented the countries of Eastern Europe, against their will, from joining the community. Even the French, who were not among the main beneficiaries of Eastern enlargement, joined in this discourse:

> France has always known—it expressed this forcefully through the voice of General de Gaulle—that Europe's construction could not be completed until all its nations were back in its fold. (Jacques Chirac in 1996, quoted in Sedelmeier 2005, 27).

In sum, the EU and its representatives used the community discourse from the beginning to legitimize the request of the CEE countries to enter the union. The dominant discourse in Europe confirmed that Central Eastern Europe belonged to the community as "part of us" so that it became very difficult for enlargement opponents to raise objections. The enlargement discourse constructed Europe and the EU as a community of liberal values and market economies as a result of which the democratizing Central Eastern Europeans acquired an almost "natural right" to join the EU (Fierke and Wiener 1999; Neumann 2001). The 1993 European Council explicitly offered an accession perspective to Central Eastern Europe—provided that they met the "Copenhagen criteria," which enshrined the values of modern and enlightened Europe: human rights, democracy, the rule of law, and the market economy.

Frank Schimmelfennig suggested that these references to community values were mainly rhetorical devices to induce others to accept Eastern enlargement (Schimmelfennig 2003, chap. 9). However, speakers in a public sphere can successfully refer to community values in order to reach some strategic goals such as Eastern enlargement only if the audience shares these values. In other words, the collective identity of the EU as a liberal community explains the enlargement puzzle to a large extent (Sedelmeier 2005, 97–98; Sjursen 2002). Advocates of enlargement, such as the European Commission and the governments of many member states, referred to a collective European identity to persuade others to accept Eastern enlargement. Whether rhetorical or not, *commitment to community values* obliged EU member states to offer accession negotiations to the CEEC.

The identity-related discourse of European elites in support of Eastern enlargement also resonated with European public opinion. References to European values and European identity usually led to positive feelings about Eastern enlargement. In 2002–03, more than two thirds agreed about a "moral duty to re-unite Europe after the divisions of the Cold War" and concurred that new countries joining the EU was "historically and geographically natural and therefore justified" (European Commission 2003, 36). In 2006, between 62 percent and 67 percent agreed that EU enlargement reunites the European continent, expresses the EU's "solidarity to candidate or potential candidate countries," and consolidates "common European interests and values" (European Commission 2006b, 23). These attitudes correlated strongly with an elite discourse that emphasized a collective European identity and community values in order to justify EU Eastern enlargement.

Such an elite discourse was all the more necessary, since mass public opinion in general, aside from issues of European values and identity, remained rather skeptical. In early 2004, right before Central Eastern Europe entered the union, only 42 percent of people in the EU 15 supported imminent Eastern enlargement, while 39 percent opposed it, and 43 percent objected to any further enlargement of the union. Germans in particular, whose government had been among the most outspoken proponents of enlargement, were strongly opposed (56% against Eastern enlargement and 60% opposed to any further EU enlargement; see European Commission 2004, B.92–B.93). Fear of Eastern enlargement was largely connected to concerns about the economic risks of widening. In 2002–03, more than two thirds of EU citizens agreed that enlargement would be "very expensive" for their respective countries. More than 40 percent thought that enlargement would increase unemployment and result in falling standards of social welfare (European Commission 2003, 36, 68, 70).

These data strongly suggest that focusing on the EU's liberal identity was about the only way in which proponents of Eastern enlargement could connect to a largely skeptical European public. Identity talk thus became the major legitimizing tool of the political elites when they were faced with critical public opinion.

In sum, two policy consequences resulted from the identity discourse with regard to Eastern enlargement. First, references to the EU as a liberal value community silenced the considerable opposition to enlargement among the governments of member states as well as among public opinion. As Ulrich Sedelmeier put it, "EU identity ruled out opposition to the general principle of enlargement and required justifying concerns about Eastern enlargement with competing norms and legitimate goals, but not with material self-interests" (Sedelmeier 2005, 184).

Second and less obvious, the identity discourse had unanticipated consequences, particularly for the accession countries. Once the EU had accepted that Eastern Europe was part of the community and belonged to "us," the "if" of enlargement was no longer an issue and the accession talks focused on "when and how." From 1993 on at the latest, the EU had set itself on a path to enlargement. The identity-related justifications strengthened the bargaining power of the CEEC considerably in this process. Once the EU had accepted them as legitimate members of the community, it could no longer use the membership principle as such as a bargaining tool to extract concessions from Eastern Europe. As a result, the Eastern countries' bargaining power in the membership negotiations was not as weak as many observers believed (see Tulmets 2005 for details).

We should not exaggerate the impact of identity politics on the process leading to Eastern enlargement, however. The more specific the accession negotiations became, the weaker was the impact of identity talk (Sedelmeier 2005, 186). Sectoral policy paradigms rather than references to community values largely explain the outcome of accession negotiations in the various policy sectors and the degree to which the EU accommodated the interests of the candidate countries. Only on those rare occasions in which the Council of Ministers itself, rather than the Commission's general directorate or the Committee of Permanent Representatives (COREPER), became involved in the specifics of the negotiations did identity discourses matter again, silencing opposition to enlargement. This finding is consistent with the general picture of how identity matters in EU politics (see chapter 8). The more we enter the nitty-gritty of policymaking, the less we should expect community values and references to a collective identity to affect specific decisions.

Consequences of Eastern Enlargement: The Return of History

The vision of the EU as a modern, liberal, and secular community—"modern Europe"—explains to a large extent the path to Eastern enlargement in the process of remaking the European order at the end of the cold war. This vision had always resonated with the dissident cultures in Communist Poland, Hungary, Czechoslovakia, and elsewhere in their fight for freedom and human rights (Thomas 2001; for a prominent example, see Michnik 2003). Their rallying cry—"return to Europe"—connected easily with Western liberal elites who welcomed Central Eastern Europe back into the community.

But the democratic transition processes in Central Eastern Europe did not only result in Westernized and Europeanized liberal elites simply joining in the chorus of "modern Europe." Eastern enlargement also brought the return of history and religion into the EU (Mach and Pozarlik 2008). To begin with, the identity discourses in Central Eastern Europe demonstrate that collective identities in Poland, the Czech Republic, Slovakia, Hungary, and elsewhere were profoundly unsettled and contested during the tumultuous history of the 1990s and early 2000s (see chapters 3 and 8 for Poland). One of the central issues concerned the question of to what extent "returning to Europe" meant Westernization and secularization and to what extent Europe and the EU threatened historical memories as well as cultural and religious values. Part of the Eastern European discourse on joining the EU concerned pragmatic and utilitarian issues such as market access and the consequences of EU membership for the economy. Opinion poll data show that education and high income as well as liberal value orientations correlate strongly with support for EU membership (as it does in Western Europe; see Caplanova, Orviska, and Hudson 2004). But the debates also showed some profound uneasiness about Western culture (Case 2009; see Drulak 2006 for the Czech Republic and Slovakia; Kutter 2007 and Krzeminski 2001 for Poland). Polish Euroskeptics, for example, constructed the EU as a threat to Polish identity whereby anti-Europeanism connects with anti-Germanism and a long historical line is drawn from the partitions of Poland in the late eighteenth and early nineteenth centuries to Hitler's invasion of Poland in 1939 and the westward dislocation of Poland at the Yalta Conference in 1945 (Hahn 2007, 48–51). Poland is then seen as the victim of the European powers as a result of which the EU is constructed as threatening Polish sovereignty, which was regained only at the end of the cold war.

But one does not have to search at the margins of the political spectrum in Poland and elsewhere to recognize that the meaning of "Europe" is becoming more diverse with Eastern enlargement. This concerns, above all, the return of religious references to what it means to be European in the elite discourses across Europe (Byrnes and Katzenstein 2006). First, Catholicism has reentered the European discourse. I say "reentered" because one cannot even begin to tell the history of European integration without references to continental European Catholicism and the Christian Democratic parties (Kaiser 2007). Robert Schuman, Jean Monnet, Alcide de Gasperi, and Konrad Adenauer shared a Christian Democratic worldview that was deeply grounded in Catholic social teaching.

More than fifty years later, Pope John Paul II not only strongly supported Eastern enlargement against the Euroskeptical wing of the Polish Catholic Church but also promoted his own vision of Poland in Europe:

> The Church in Poland...can offer Europe as it grows in unity, her attachment to the faith, her tradition inspired by religious devotion...and certainly many other values on the basis of which Europe can become a reality endowed not only with higher economic standards but also with a profound spiritual life. ("Ecclesia in Europa," 2003, quoted in Byrnes 2006, 289)[2]

---

2. See also Ramet 2006a; Hehir 2006, 105–12.

José Casanova has called this the "great apostolic assignment" of Catholic Poland in the EU (Casanova 2006, 67–68). To be sure, this vision of a European return to Christianity is primarily directed against secularism, not against efforts at European integration. There has been no change in the attitude of the Roman Catholic Church, which has supported European community-building from the beginning. This is confirmed by public opinion data according to which Catholics tend to support European integration more strongly than Protestants (Nelson, Guth, and Fraser 2001). Yet, Eastern enlargement added a distinctive voice to those in Western Europe who have long complained that European integration embarked too much on a secular project as a result of which public voices for religion and Christianity have been silenced. Pope John Paul II and the Vatican, the Polish Catholic Church, and Catholicism in Lithuania, Hungary, and the Czech Republic have recently started attacking secularism in Europe. The controversy over the "reference to God" in the Constitutional Treaty and the 2007 Treaty of Lisbon has been among the first symbolic encounters with this new contestation.

Although European Catholicism including the Eastern European Catholic churches is at least broadly compatible with a modern and democratic vision of European identity that is based on the separation of church and state, the Orthodox churches are more ambivalent toward modern Europe. While Orthodox Greece joined the EU in 1981, Eastern enlargement has brought in three countries with a predominantly Orthodox population: Bulgaria, Romania, and Cyprus. The Greek Orthodox Church became outspoken against European integration during the late 1990s, but the various other Orthodox churches—from Russia to Bulgaria, Romania, and Serbia—have always been deeply ambivalent about the EU and are outspoken critics of secularism and the alleged moral decadence of Western Europe (Ramet 2006b; Byrnes 2006, 292–96). The Orthodox churches in Europe joined the battle for references to Christianity and the Christian God in the Constitutional Treaty, but with more religious zeal than the Catholic Church. The Orthodox vision for Europe is much more antimodern, antienlightenment, and antiliberal than Catholicism. As the Russian Metropolitan Kirill put it in 2001,

> the liberal concept, quite alien as it is to the notion of sins, includes the idea of the emancipation of human beings as they are, which actually means the release of the potential of sin in the human person.…The liberal idea stands diametrically opposed to Christianity. (quoted in Ramet 2006b, 165; see also 148–50)

Although this might be a rather extreme utterance, the various Orthodox Churches support a more exclusionary and traditional Europe that is less open to foreigners.

There are several reasons for this Euroskeptical attitude. First, Orthodox Christianity did not have to deal with the Renaissance, enlightenment, and the secular forces of modernity in the same way as Catholicism did. In contrast, Slavophilia and pan-Slavism were sometimes erected as barriers against Western liberal values. Second, and in contrast to the hierarchical as well as the transnational nature of Catholicism, autocephaly, that is, the right of each Orthodox diocese or group of dioceses to elect its own bishop, does not resonate well with European integration and the idea of pooling or even giving up national sovereignty. Over time, autocephaly has become a principle of almost absolute autonomy of the national churches (Byrnes 2006, 292), leading to a strong connection between the church and the state. Thus, to the extent that the EU has expanded eastward, it has been confronted with an antiliberal and anti-Western vision of Christianity.

It is too early to tell how Europe and the EU will cope with the return of history and religion that has resulted from Eastern enlargement. On the one hand, Europe might encounter its own version of the religious fundamentalism that has preoccupied American politics throughout much of the 1990s and the early 2000s. As a result, two versions of Christianity leading to different visions of Europe would confront the continent with its own "multiple modernities," as Peter Katzenstein put it (Katzenstein 2006, 32–33). On the other hand, the EU might also continue working as a modernization project, leading to the gradual secularization and democratization of religious forces and values in Eastern Europe, thereby helping Orthodox Christianity adapt to a more modern and liberal European identity. If the history of Southern enlargement is being repeated which originally confronted the EC/EU with similarly traditional values and attitudes, then modern Europe might carry the day (see Gerhards and Hölscher 2005 on value changes in Southern Europe following EC accession in the 1980s). It remains to be seen whether the peoples of Bulgaria, Romania, and the western Balkans will undergo such value adjustments through modernization. Greece might actually be the "proof of the pudding": while the Greek Orthodox Church has become increasingly antiliberal and anti-EU, Greek citizens are also below the EU average in their support for EU membership and identification with Europe (see figure 4.1, chapter 4).

The return of religion to European politics that has resulted from Eastern enlargement is largely confined to Christianity and its different cultural meanings. Two versions of Christianity can be distinguished in this regard, with the dividing line increasingly splitting Catholicism. On the one hand, there is the version of Christian culture roughly compatible with visions of a modern and enlightened Europe that has endorsed European integration from the very beginning. On the other hand, Eastern enlargement has brought to the fore an interpretation of

Christian values that is deeply critical of secularism and modernity and might align with a vision of an exclusionary and even nationalist Europe.

Yet, nobody denies that Christianity—whether Catholic, Protestant, or Orthodox—constitutes a fundamental part of the European historical and cultural heritage. This is very different with regard to Islam. The contested nature of what it means to be or to become European has been no more salient and no more visible in recent years than in the controversy surrounding the possibility of Turkish EU membership.

Where Does Europe End? The Controversy about Turkish Membership

It took the EU less than fifteen years after the end of the cold war to accept Central Eastern Europe as member states. In contrast, the history of Turkish-EU relations is one of slow motion. Already in 1963, Turkey signed an Association Agreement that acknowledged the final goal of membership. More than two decades later, Turkey applied for EC/EU membership in 1987. In late 1989, the European Commission accepted the Turkish request for membership in principle, but deferred negotiations. In 1996, Turkey entered a customs union with the EU. Three years later, the 1999 European Council accepted Turkish candidacy for membership. It took another five years until the 2004 European Council acknowledged that Turkey had fulfilled the Copenhagen criteria and that membership negotiations should begin in October 2005. Although accession talks with Turkey started in 2005, progress has been extremely slow. By the end of 2008, only ten of the thirty-five so-called negotiating chapters for membership covering the EU *acquis communitaire* had been opened and only one had been provisionally completed, that is, the EU Commission and Turkey had reached agreement in one issue area.[3] Major EU member states, such as Germany under Chancellor Merkel and France under President Sarkozy, remain opposed to full Turkish membership, with most center-right parties in Europe and the European People's Party (EPP), that is, the Christian Democratic bloc in the European Parliament, favoring a "privileged partnership" instead (Icener 2007b).

The cumbersome and open-ended history of Turkish-EU relations demonstrates the deep ambiguity with which both the EU and Turkey have approached the membership issue over the years—in sharp contrast to Eastern enlargement. Both Turkey and the EU in their respective discourses have constructed Turkey

---

3. Cf. http://www.abgs.gov.tr/index.php?p=65&l=2.

as a "metaphor between Europe and Asia," as Nur Bilge Criss has put it (Bilge Criss 2007). Depending where Turkey is discursively situated in this metaphor, it is either "in" Europe and, thus, eligible for EU membership, or "out." As a result, the contemporary debates about Turkish EU membership are simultaneously about who Europe and the Europeans are, that is, European identity, and about who Turkey and the Turkish are, that is, Turkish identity.

Turkey's Ambivalent Quest for Membership

Subsequent Turkish governments have continuously worked toward EU membership. Most interesting, however, it has been the moderate Islamist Justice and Development Party (AKP) that, under Prime Minister Recep Tayyip Erdogan, has worked hardest since 2002 to make Turkey comply with the Copenhagen criteria of support for democracy, the rule of law, minority rights, and the market economy as preconditions for accession talks (Avci 2006). Yet, the AKP government is faced with strong nationalist opposition, both from more radical Islamist groups and from secularist and Kemalist forces (Polat 2006). The latter include the conservative military bureaucracy, which simultaneously supports a Turkish secular and nationalist identity in the tradition of Mustafa Kemal, the founder of the Turkish Republic, and antiliberal policies to preserve military interference in Turkish domestic politics. The 2007 electoral landslide of the AKP did not calm the conservative nationalist forces.

Support for EU membership is still high among Turkish citizens, but it is not overwhelming. In 2006, 54 percent were in favor of membership, while 22 percent remained opposed with a very large number undecided (European Commission 2006b, 71). Support for membership dropped to 49 percent in 2008 (European Commission 2008, 13). Moreover, only 47 percent agree that EU enlargement consolidates common European interests and values, the lowest number among all EU member states and accession candidates (European Commission 2006b, 25). Turkish net identification with Europe is comparatively low, as figure 4.1 in chapter 4 reveals. Last but not least, the value orientations of Turkish citizens are substantially different from those of modern and liberal West Europeans, even though they have moved slightly toward accepting European normative standards in recent years (Gerhards and Hölscher 2005; Gerhards and Hans 2009, 6).

Viewed from a "modern" European perspective, the irony of the Turkish case is that moderate Islamism pushes for EU membership while at the same time trying to revoke laws that enforce secularism in Turkish society, such as the change in the law banning head scarves in Turkish universities in early 2008 (Economist 2008). At the same time, secular nationalism in Turkey is at least partly responsible for the lack of compliance with the EU's Copenhagen criteria. In other words, secularism in Turkey does not necessarily translate into postnationalist and liberal attitudes as is the case in the "modern" version of European identity, while religious fundamentalism does not equal traditional backwardness either. As M. Hakan Yavuz put it,

> the Kemalist project of identity in Turkey consisted of half-baked Westernization, radical secularization, and forced national homogenization [including the oppression of the Kurdish minority]. Islam, consequently, became an identity with which to oppose the centralizing policies of the state and its self-declared Westernization project. (Yavuz 2006, 232; also Al-Azmeh and Fokas 2007)

Moderate Islamism as represented by the AKP became the leading force opposing Kemalist secularism by fighting for religious freedom as a human rights issue consistent with the EU's Copenhagen criteria. But moderate Islamism does not simply embrace the modern vision of European identity. Rather, it is about "entering into Europe without becoming European" (Yavuz 2006, 238), at least with regard to the relationship between liberalism and secularism. As Sener Aktürk puts it, "Turkey-centric supra-national visions (Ottoman, pan-Turkic, pan-Islamist) occupy the center stage in national identity discourse," but there is no space for Europe in it (Aktürk 2007, 370; see, however, Goren and Nachmani 2007 for different views). In sum, the Europeanization of Turkey in general and of Turkish identity in particular remains deeply contested.

The Reluctant European Response

The complexities of the Turkish debate about EU membership are largely overlooked in the EU discourses about Turkey—irrespective of one's position with regard to the controversy. References to Turkish backwardness, which are often found in these debates, usually overlook that Turkey has come an extremely long way toward modernity in less than hundred years. It took European states hundreds of years and numerous bloody wars up to the triumph of absolutism in the seventeenth century to finally manage the transition from the Middle Ages to modern secularism and the separation of church and state, that is, to arrive at "Kemalism." It took (Western) Europe another two hundred years of revolutions and wars including two world wars to finally embrace democracy and human rights. The latter process, in terms of the transition to liberal democracy, has been taking place in Turkey over the past ten years or so. Last but not least, "Turkey-centric supra-national visions" do not look that different from, say, French supranational visions whereby the EU becomes French Republicanism and state-centrism writ large (see chapter 3). A critical reading of European history is virtually absent in the contemporary discourses about Turkey's membership aspirations to the EU.

Nevertheless, if the puzzle about Eastern enlargement can be solved through references to the Europeanization of (elite) identities, it is even more puzzling why the EU has entered membership negotiations with Turkey at all. To begin with, mass public opinion is strongly opposed to EU membership for Turkey and has remained so for quite some time. In 2006, 48 percent of the citizens in the EU 25 were opposed to Turkish membership, even if Turkey complied "with all the conditions set by the European Union," while only 39% were in favor (see European Commission 2006b, 71; also Gerhards and Hans 2009). Opposition to Turkish membership was strongest among citizens of the older member states. As Jürgen Gerhards and Silke Hans show, only 29.8 percent of the EU 15 supported Turkish membership, while the number increased to 43.8 percent among the ten countries (including Central Eastern Europe) that entered the EU in 2004 (Gerhards and Hans 2008, 9).

An analysis by Lauren McLaren shows that opposition to Turkish EU membership can be largely explained by identity concerns as well as material interests (see McLaren 2007b). As to the latter, the most important variable proved to be fear of Turkish mass migration into the EU, which would explain why Germans and Austrians—with their large Turkish immigrant populations—are so adamantly opposed (69% and 81%, respectively). In addition, fears of losing one's national culture, that is, identity concerns, also play a significant role in mass public opposition to Turkish EU membership (for a similar analysis with regard to Germany, see Schoen 2008a). Moreover, religion significantly affects attitudes toward Turkish membership, with Christians being strongly opposed (Gerhards and Hans 2009, 22). In contrast, rational economic self-interests, such as fear of losing one's job and income, have little affect in forming opinions toward Turkey.

In short, the EU opened membership negotiations with Turkey against a clear majority of mass public opinion. I do not suggest here that the EU cared much about public opinion during Eastern enlargement. Yet, while (Western) European citizens were at least ambivalent about Eastern enlargement, they are opposed to admitting Turkey. So, how can we explain the puzzle of opening membership negotiations with Turkey? Economic reasons do not seem to make sense, since the association agreement and the customs union are sufficient for EU member states to reap the benefits from closer economic relations with Turkey. Security concerns are at best indeterminate, too. On the one hand, many advocates of Turkish EU membership make geopolitical or geostrategic arguments. As the EU commissioner for enlargement, Olli Rehn, put it in 2004, Turkish membership has to be viewed favorably in light of

> the unique geopolitical position of Turkey at the crossroads of the Balkans, the wider Middle East, South Caucasus, Central Asia and beyond,

its importance for the security of Europe's energy supplies and its political, economic and military weight. (quoted in Lundgren 2006, 131)

Supporters of Turkish membership also argue that accepting a country with a
predominantly Muslim population would send a strong signal to the Arab world
and beyond about the EU's commitment to prevent a "clash of civilizations"
(Huntington 1996) with Islam as long as the latter accepted democracy, human
rights, and the rule of law. On the other hand, as long as Turkey is a member of
NATO, it participates in the Western security community anyway. There are also
some security risks involved with admitting Turkey to the single market and to
the free movement of people. Turkey is implicated in the illegal trafficking of
arms and drugs from the Middle East and Asia. Thus, security concerns appear
to cancel each other out in the Turkish case.

The trouble is that identity politics does not provide a much better explanation in the Turkish case. In the case of Eastern enlargement, it was never contested
that Central Eastern Europe belonged to Europe and had a legitimate right to EU
membership. In the case of Turkey, this is much more controversial. In fact, the
discourses about Turkish membership in major EU member states show a profound ambivalence about whether Turkey belongs to Europe. The debate about
Turkish membership is a discussion about the borders of Europe. Where does
Europe end, and who, as a result, has a legitimate claim to EU membership?

The debate about Turkey involves different conceptions of European identity.
To begin with, there is the modern, inclusive and liberal vision of Europe, which
has found its most significant expression in the Copenhagen criteria. Accordingly, Turkey is seen as a part of Europe as long as it respects the liberal agenda
and complies with its norms. As Olli Rehn put it in 2004:

> A Turkey where the rule of law is firmly rooted in its society and state
> will prove that, contrary to prejudices, European values can successfully
> coexist with a predominantly Muslim population. Such a Turkey will be
> a most valuable crossroads between civilisations. (quoted in Lundgren
> 2006, 137)

In a similar way, German chancellor Gerhard Schröder argued that the "European Union is a community of values....A democratic Turkey committed to
European values would serve as proof that there is no contradiction between
commitment to Islam and enlightened modern society" (in *Die Welt,* 13 Oct.
2004, quoted in Madeker 2008, 138).

The more the EU is constructed as a community that embraces human rights
and the rule of law, the more Turkey is at least eligible to become a member,
even though its use of torture and its treatment of the Kurdish minority are still

criticized. Supporters of Turkish EU membership also allude to Europe's historical heritage to which "Istanbul, the old Constantinople, [belongs as] a cradle of
our civilization" (Denis MacShane, 2004, quoted in Madeker 2008, 136). This
identity construction connects to the idea of Turkey as a bridge between East and
West, Orient and Occident, as well as Catholicism, Orthodox Christianity, and
Islam (from East Rome to Byzantium and Constantinople to Istanbul). Identity
frames that include Turkey as part of the "European self" are represented in the
public discourse by center-left politicians and by Turkish speakers. The vision
of a modern and liberal European identity constructing a democratic Turkey as
belonging to Europe also dominated debates in the European Parliament (Giannakopoulos and Maras 2005) and in the British media (Wimmel 2006a, 2006b).
In Germany, however, inclusive identity frames with regard to Turkey constitute
minority positions (Madeker 2008, 139; Wimmel 2006a, 2006b).

In contrast, an exclusionary counterdiscourse developed in the French and
German media that constructed Turkey as being outside Europe and, thus, not
eligible for membership (Von Oppeln 2005). As Madeker's quantitative and qualitative media analysis documents for the German public sphere, the construction
of an exclusionary European identity according to which Turkey constitutes the
"other" of Europe developed in the conservative press, but quickly dominated
the discourse.[4] Of course, this construction is not new: Turkey as the "other" of
European identity has a very long history going back to the Ottoman Empire and
its struggles with "Christian" Europe (Icener 2007a, chap. 5).

Opponents of Turkish EU membership use geographical, cultural, historical,
and religious arguments to construct Turkey as being outside of Europe. As for
geography, Valéry Giscard d'Estaing, the former French president and president
of the European Constitutional Convention, argued in articles published across
Europe that only 5 percent of the Turkish territory and only 7 percent of its
population live in a "European enclave," while the remaining parts are located in
Asia and Anatolia (Giscard d'Estaing 2004). Such a primordial identity construction posits a "natural" European border along the Bosporus that is then used to
exclude Turkey from Europe.

The allegedly natural boundary also serves as a cultural and historical boundary that seals Turkey off from the modern Europe of enlightenment and liberalism. As Giscard d'Estaing put it:

> The European Convention sought a clearer definition of the founda-
> tions of this entity, which include the cultural contributions of ancient

---

4. Even the liberal *Süddeutsche Zeitung* was primarily critical of Turkish EU membership in 2004
(Madeker 2008, 117).

Greece and Rome, the religious heritage pervading European life, the creative enthusiasms of the Renaissance, the philosophy of the Age of the Enlightenment and the contributions of rational and scientific thought. Turkey shares none of these. (Giscard d'Estaing 2004)[5]

The statement is remarkable insofar as it uses the historical heritage of a modern European identity as an exclusionary device. It is hard to see why other parts of the former Ottoman Empire such as Romania and Bulgaria as new EU members, as well as the western Balkans with its accession perspective, share this decidedly Western European heritage, while Turkey does not.

Although Giscard did not use Christianity as a demarcation line to exclude Turkey from the EU, others did: "Islam, which has been built in Turkey on the ruins of a Roman-Christian civilization, is completely unsuitable to revive the soul of Europe." (*Die Welt,* 10 Sept. 2004, quoted in Madeker 2008, 144). As Sabine von Oppeln points out, French and German opponents of Turkish membership on the center-right, including the German Christian Democrats and the French post-Gaullist Union pour un Mouvement Populaire (UMP), constructed a European identity based on a Christian-Carolingian understanding of Europe's cultural heritage against a more Republican European identity promoted by the French center-left (Von Oppeln 2005).[6]

The discourse on Turkish EU membership serves to emphasize two findings that I have already discussed in this book. To begin with, it constitutes yet another example of a truly transnational European discourse, thereby constructing Europe as a community of communication (see chapter 7). It is predominantly a discourse about borders and about where Europe ends, that is, about European identity, thus creating Europe as a community of fate. Two European identity constructions are pitted against each other in transnational public spheres. The first concerns the modern, inclusionary, and liberal Europe that is open to new members, including Turkey, as long as they comply with the Copenhagen criteria of democracy, human rights, the rule of law, and the market economy. A second and exclusionary identity discourse emerged in the transnational public sphere that amalgamated geographical, cultural, historical, and religious constructions to keep Turkey out once and for all time. In its most sophisticated version it even used the modern and liberal European identity in a primordial way so that others who do not share the history leading to this identity can never participate. Exclusionary Europe represents a noteworthy kind of

---

5. For similar quotes, see Madeker 2008, 142–48; Schäfer and Zschache 2008; Wimmel 2006a, 2006b.

6. For a general discussion of Islam in Europe, see Al-Azmeh and Fokas 2007.

nationalist but Europeanized identity construction (see chapter 2). It is Europeanized because it pertains to a supranational entity, the EU. It is nationalist at the same time, since it uses the exclusionary building blocks of nineteenth-century nationalism to reconstruct them on the European level.

As argued above, and in contrast to the case of Eastern enlargement, European identities vis-à-vis Turkey remain fundamentally unsettled and deeply contested. As a result, identity discourse cannot be used to explain why the EU opened membership negotiations with Turkey in 2004. This is an interesting case not foreseen in the social science literature, since neither interests nor identities are clear and well-defined in this case, and thus neither can be used to explain the outcome (March and Olsen 1998). However, it might be precisely the lack of clarity and the contested nature of identities and interests in this case that explain why the EU and Turkey have been struggling over the membership issue for decades and why the accession talks have been slow-moving so far. If this holds true, the prospects of Turkey joining the union any time soon are rather remote—apart from all the other institutional and political obstacles.

A similar picture emerges concerning the construction of European boundaries "within," that is, controversies about migration and citizenship. Once again, visions of inclusionary versus exclusionary Europe are competing with each other.

The "Others Within": Identity and Immigration

It might be unusual to deal with questions of migration and citizenship in a chapter on widening and EU enlargement. However, the treatment of immigrants not only involves questions of rights and security but also concerns the creation of boundaries. Whereas enlargement is about the outer borders of the EU, immigration refers to the inner boundaries as to who is entitled to reside within the territory, to become a member in a community, and who can claim which specific rights and duties.

Over the decades, questions of migration and immigration have become more and more politicized in Europe and the EU (Lahav 2004; Lavenex 2001). Immigration policies became more and more subject to EU regulations, particularly after the end of the Cold War. The 2007 Lisbon Treaty supranationalizes a substantial portion of immigration, refugee, and asylum policies by subjecting them to qualified majority voting. As Gallya Lahav argues convincingly, this trend toward a common EU immigration regime cannot be explained by some objective migration trend, such as increased migration flows from non-EU foreigners into the EU (Lahav 2004, chap. 2). The total number of asylum seekers into the EU peaked in 1992, but then decreased quickly and substantially, before a common European asylum policy went into force. It makes more sense to explain the trend toward an EU immigration regime as a result of spillover effects from other integrated policy areas. The movement toward a "fortress Europe" that is attempting to close its borders against non-EU citizens results from the opening of borders, borderless traffic, and the free movement of peoples inside the EU. The more the EU member states opened their borders to one another, the more they created a closed outer boundary against non-EU immigrants as well as migrants. Thus, the success of Schengenland leads almost directly to "fortress Europe." Of course, non-EU immigrants are not without rights inside the EU and enjoy some of the social benefits of European welfare states. But it is true in general that the creation of an EU citizenship by the 1992 Maastricht Treaties led to a sharp delineation of the rights enjoyed by EU citizens residing in another EU member state, on the one hand, and the rights enjoyed by non-EU foreigners, on the other hand. An Italian citizen living in Berlin who has only recently moved to Germany enjoys more political, social, and other entitlements than, say, a Turkish citizen in Berlin who was born there and whose parents had moved to Germany from Anatolia.

But this chapter is not about EU policies toward non-EU migrants and immigrants in general, but about the ways in which immigration policies interact with identity questions. Let me consider, first, how EU integration in the realm of citizenship and immigration policies has affected identity questions. More than fifteen years after the Maastricht Treaties went into force, the creation of EU citizenship has had constitutive effects on the sense of community among citizens. The boundary removal among the EU member states has led to increased perceptions that EU nationals from other countries are no longer "foreigners," but members of the community.

European Social Survey data from 2003 show some interesting findings in this regard (Hainmueller and Hiscox 2007, 411–12). Across Europe, people prefer immigrants from either richer or poorer European countries over immigrants from either richer or poorer countries outside the EU. Although the most preferred immigrants are from wealthy EU member states and the least preferred from poor non-European countries, Europeans on average like their poor neighbors more than rich non-EU citizens. In other words, common Europeanness trumps economic considerations when it comes to evaluations of immigrants (see also Lahav 2004, 90).

EU immigrants in general tend to be more highly regarded than non-EU foreigners, even if the latter come from a wealthy background. In this sense, then, we can see some limited constitutive effects on an increased sense of community among EU citizens in the sense that fellow Europeans from other EU countries are less regarded as "strangers" than non-Europeans. As Adrian Favell has argued, the "proof of the pudding" for these constitutive effects will be whether Western Europeans regard immigrants from Eastern Europe as fellow Europeans or whether they treat them in the same way as noncommunity foreigners, irrespective of their rights (Favell 2009).

If the creation of EU citizenship had some limited constitutive effects on who is regarded as "us," how do identity concerns affect attitudes toward immigrants in general? To begin with, the attitudes of Europeans toward immigrants are fairly ambivalent. Although most Europeans (above 80%) did not consider the presence of foreigners "disturbing" in their daily lives throughout the 1990s, a majority (54%) regarded immigrants and asylum seekers as a "big problem," particularly in Germany, Belgium, and France (Lahav 2004, 81–82). In 2006, only 40 percent of EU citizens agreed with the statement that immigrants contributed a lot to their country, while 52 percent disagreed (European Commission 2006a, 43). In 2008, 47 percent of EU citizens considered immigration "more of a problem" rather than "more of an opportunity" (35%), with British citizens being the most skeptical (62%) and the French among the least concerned (35%) (Transatlantic Trends 2008, 5). At the same time, almost two thirds of Europeans agreed that immigrants will improve the culture with new ideas and customs, while only 34 percent thought that immigrants take jobs away from native-born workers (Transatlantic Trends 2008, 8, 11; British citizens: 52%). Eastern Europeans as well as British citizens are particularly hostile to immigrants, while Swedish, Portuguese, Irish, and Dutch citizens are considerably more tolerant toward the presence of immigrants in their countries.

What explains these attitudes, and what role do identity concerns play in this regard? First, attitudes toward immigrants might be determined by the number of foreigners living in one's country. Austria, Belgium, Germany, the Netherlands, Spain, and Sweden have the largest numbers of foreign-born in their countries (more than 10%, see OECD 2008, table A.1.4; also Lahav 2004, 93; Fligstein 2008, 169). Apart from Belgium, two thirds to three fourths of these are non-EU foreigners. Moreover, if we add the number of national citizens with a "migration background," that is, those whose parents have immigrated, the numbers are considerably higher. In Germany, for example, this group amounts to almost 20 percent of the population, or sixteen million people (Statistisches Bundesamt Deutschland 2008). But these numbers can only partially explain hostility toward immigrants, given that Eastern European countries tend to have very limited numbers of foreign-born residents and even Great Britain is below the EU average, while public opinion in countries with large numbers of foreigners—Germany, for example—tends not to be particularly xenophobic (Hainmueller and Hiscox 2007, 412).

A second explanation concerns socioeconomic interests. Conventional wisdom holds that anti-immigration sentiments are strongly correlated with fears of labor-market competition among low-skilled and blue-collar workers. Less educated native workers are expected to lose their jobs when faced with competition from equally low-skilled immigrants. Because most economic studies show that the labor market effects of immigration in most European countries are actually rather insignificant, it would then be the perceived rather than the actual threat of economic competition that explains xenophobia. The data on Eastern European sentiments toward immigrants appear to support this account.

However, using sophisticated statistical models, Jens Hainmueller and Michael Hiscox demonstrate that fears of labor-market competition do not drive anti-immigration sentiments in Europe. Rather, they lend strong support to a third explanation, according to which

> anti-immigration sentiments are associated instead with values and beliefs that foster animosity toward foreigners and foreign cultures and that are most prevalent among less educated individuals. The data indicate that more educated respondents are significantly less racist and place far greater value on cultural diversity in society. (Hainmueller and Hiscox 2007, 437)[7]

Rather than economic concerns, education and the set of cultural values that come with it explain attitudes toward foreigners.

Yet, highly educated Europeans are also those who identify most strongly with Europe and the EU (see chapters 2 and 4). These are "the Europeans" (Fligstein 2008, chap. 5; Green 2007). Inclusive nationalists, who identify with both their own nation and with Europe, are also less xenophobic, more cosmopolitan, and multiculturally oriented than exclusive nationalists (Citrin and Sides 2004). The less educated the latter, the more they hold xenophobic attitudes. We can conclude that this is the connection between identity and attitudes toward immigration.

European cosmopolitans are, of course, also supportive of the modern, postnational, and inclusionary vision of European identity. In this sense, then, the same set of values that explain attitudes toward Turkish membership also account for feelings toward "the other within" (non-European foreigners). The values that come with "modern Europe" encompass tolerance toward people of different races, religions, and cultural backgrounds. In this view, immigrants do not represent a threat to European societies, but a potential enrichment.

---

7. For similar findings, see McLaren 2001; Kessler and Freeman 2007.

In sharp contrast, the countervision of an exclusionary and traditional "fortress Europe" of nation-states, which has recently been promoted by right-wing populist parties across the EU, is linked to hostile attitudes not only to potential Turkish accession but also to "the others within," that is, non-European immigrants. Those who promote an exclusionary vision of Europe and the EU strongly oppose the increasing visibility of Islam in Europe. And they prefer sharp restrictions on immigration (Lahav 2004, chap. 4; Lahav and Messina 2007).

In sum, attitudes toward immigration are located at the intersection of the two political cleavages that increasingly shape European politics, namely the conventional Left-Right continuum, on the one hand, and the cultural cleavage, on the other (Kriesi et al. 2008; Hooghe and Marks 2008). Anti-immigration policies are both a traditional right-wing issue and are also highly salient for exclusionary nationalists. As a result, these issues are increasingly politicized by right-wing populist parties across Europe, combining a nationalist vision of the EU and strong principled opposition to Turkish membership with xenophobic policies against non-European foreigners. I discuss the consequences in the next chapter.

Conclusions

I have argued in this chapter that the "widening" of the EU concerning both enlargement and immigration policies cannot be explained without taking identity issues into account. Interestingly enough, although the controversies about the future of European integration and the EU's institutional equilibrium are mostly about interpretations of what "modern Europe" means, identity clashes assume center stage with regard to "widening." The future of EU enlargement and of EU immigration policies is debated in Europeanized public spheres, pitting the vision of "modern and liberal" Europe against a more exclusionary and introverted concept of "nationalist" Europe (see chapters 6 and 7). The decision to open the EU to the new Central Eastern European member states was largely framed in terms of the modern identity construction. In contrast, the controversies about Turkish EU membership and about immigration policies have brought about a nationalist and exclusionary vision of Europe. To some extent, this was visible during the controversies about the French, Dutch, and Irish referenda on the Constitutional Treaty and on the Lisbon Treaty.

Debates about "widening" are always about where Europe and the EU end and, thus, about different visions of Europe. These discourses have brought history and religion back into the picture. As to the latter, two interrelated topics have to be distinguished. First, can Islam be(come) European, or is the EU a club confined to white Christians? Second, which interpretation of Christianity prevails in the end, one compatible with modern and liberal Europe or a more exclusionary one that is particularly promoted by ultra-conservative Catholics as well as Christian Orthodox churches?

In sum, the public debates about widening, EU enlargement, and immigration demonstrate that European identities are contested once again. They have also contributed to the politicization of EU affairs in transnational public spheres. I discuss the consequences for European democracy in the next chapter.

10

EUROPEAN DEMOCRACY
AND POLITICIZATION

The last two chapters dealt with the effects of Europeanized identities and public spheres on basic features of the European Union, namely constitutionalization ("deepening") and enlargement ("widening"). But one of the most important reasons that we should care about identities and public spheres (*Öffentlichkeit*) in the first place is because of concerns about democracy. Democratic theory holds that a democratic polity without a demos, without a shared sense of community among the people, is probably not viable. A polity without a demos lacks the diffuse support of the citizens for the political institutions, which is deemed necessary to generate compliance with costly rules. In the absence of a sense of community among the citizens, states are not capable of collecting taxes, of enforcing the law, of engaging in redistributive policies, or of demanding the ultimate sacrifice, the lives of citizens in the defense of their country. In this sense, a democratic polity is based on a prepolitical sense of community to ensure a minimum degree of social integration. Moreover, a community—whether prepolitical or not—also requires that people are able to communicate with one another and to debate issues of common concern. This is the link between a demos, collective identities, and public spheres. At the same time, a viable public sphere is deemed constitutive for a modern democracy.

This chapter analyzes the relationship between Europeanized identities and public spheres, on the one hand, and European democracy, on the other. I discuss the consequences of the empirical findings analyzed in this book for the democratic legitimacy of the European project. In so doing, I take an explicit normative stance, namely that (a) European integration requires a democratic polity and that (b) the EU suffers from a "democratic deficit." There is good news, bad news, and mixed news if we care about European democracy.

The good news is that Europeanized identities as "secondary identities" in the sense of inclusive nationalism (Hooghe and Marks 2005) appear to provide the degree of diffuse support necessary to ensure the viability of the EU as a multilevel polity, at least for the time being. There is enough prepolitical "solidarity among strangers," at least in the majority of EU member states. Although I discuss some of the limitations of Europeanized identities, particularly with regard to support for strong redistributive policies, the overall picture is a happy one. There is little in the data to suggest that the EU suffers from a fundamental legitimacy problem because of a lack of identification with it. Moreover, as I have argued in part 2, the Europeanization of public spheres is well under way, at least in continental Western and Southern Europe, enabling transnational communities of communication about questions of common European concern. This is big news, because it lays to rest many of the skeptical arguments about the impossibility of a European demos and a European community of communication.

But we need to be aware that the Europeanization of identities only concerns a bit more than half of the EU's citizens. Forty percent of EU citizens on average hold exclusive national identities and are deeply skeptical of European integration. The rise of Euroskeptical parties across Europe and the countervision of an exclusive and nationalist "fortress Europe" tap into these feelings of alienation. Moreover, inclusive and exclusive nationalism maps onto a cultural cleavage across Europe that is orthogonal to the traditional socioeconomic cleavage (Left vs. Right) and is becoming increasingly salient in politics (Kriesi et al. 2008).

On the whole, the much talked about "democratic deficit" of the EU does not refer to the lack of a sense of community among European citizens. Rather, it concerns the insulation of EU decision making from mass politics and political mobilization. If the EU regulates to what extent I have or do not have the right to get a job in another member state or may even lose my job because of competition from a "Polish plumber," it affects personal lives to a considerable degree. But there is incongruence in Europe between where decisions are made and where politics plays itself out. As Vivien Schmidt has described the problem of European democracy (Schmidt 2006, 5), "while the EU makes *policy without politics,* given the marginalization of national partisan politics, its member states suffer from having *politics without policy,*" because so much is decided at the European level. This is the bad news for European democracy.

The mixed news is that the politicization of European affairs—"bringing politics back in"—appears inevitable. The debates about the Constitutional Treaty and the Lisbon Treaty in France, the Netherlands, Ireland, and elsewhere as well as the controversies about "social Europe," immigration policies, and Turkish membership in the EU are only the beginning of more to come. The vision of an inclusive Europe embracing the values of enlightenment and modernity and externalizing these values through a multilateral and cooperative foreign policy is increasingly challenged by a countervision of an exclusive and nationalist Europe based on a traditional interpretation of European cultural and religious history. The rise of Euroskepticism across the EU member states, mainly promoted by right-wing populist parties (Hooghe and Marks 2007), suggests that politicization is out of the box. Euroskepticism increasingly exploits the cultural cleavage mentioned above. So far, the ruling political elites in Europe have not developed a satisfactory answer to these challenges. Continuing to silence the debates will not suffice, particularly not in a time of severe economic crisis.

I proceed in the following steps. First, I review the theoretical debates about European democracy. Second, I discuss the consequences of the empirical findings of this book for European democracy. Third, I deal with the questions of a European "democratic deficit" and the possibilities for politicization.

Is Democracy Possible beyond the Nation-State?

Before we consider the consequences of Europeanized identities and public spheres for European democracy, we have to consider whether democracy can be conceptualized at all beyond the nation-state, and, moreover, whether the EU suffers from a democratic deficit. As to the first point, some scholars challenge the very possibility of a European democracy beyond the nation-state (e.g., Grimm 1995; Kielmansegg 1996; Scharpf 1999). This reasoning closely resembles the principled arguments against European identities and public spheres discussed in chapters 1 and 5. The claim rests on the assumption that substantial social and cultural prerequisites are needed for democracy to work. In particular, an effective democratic polity requires that citizens forego "purely instrumental calculations in the distribution of benefits and entitlements between peoples, groups, and territories within the same political formation" (Bartolini 2005, 221). The more a polity engages in redistributive policies, the more it needs to be built on these prerequisites. This is what is usually called a demos, a strong sense of community and loyalty among a political group. It took centuries to build the political configurations of the European nation-state including numerous nationalist and, therefore, identity-creating wars (Bartolini 2005, chap. 2). The EU is unlikely to create such an imagined community, and thus the prepolitical social and cultural prerequisites for a strong democratic polity are missing beyond the nation-state in the EU.

Fritz W. Scharpf has developed the most sophisticated argument concerning the dire consequences of this reasoning (see, e.g., Scharpf 1999, 2007, 2009). The market-making policies of the EU including the single currency as well as decisions by the European Court of Justice, seriously infringe on the autonomous social and welfare policies of the member states, which have tried to alleviate the negative consequences of economic globalization. At the same time, the high consensus requirements at the EU level prevent member states from achieving "European solutions" for these issues about which citizens deeply care. These consensus requirements, therefore, undermine the problem-solving capacity of the European Union and, thus, its "output legitimacy" securing voluntary compliance with costly rules. Increasing the EU's "input legitimacy" through greater participatory rights for citizens is no solution, either, given the lack of a European demos: "In the two-level European polity, therefore, the EU must be seen and legitimated not as a government of citizens, but as a government of governments" (Scharpf 2009, 181). It follows that EU policies and the *acquis communitaire* not only suffer from legitimacy problems at the EU level but also increase the legitimacy deficits for the member states, which no longer have the means to mitigate the consequences of integration policies. In sum, the EU not only cannot generate its own (input) legitimacy, it also undermines the legitimacy of its member states.

Scharpf's position, while logically consistent, depends on two crucial empirical assumptions. First, that there is no European demos. Second, that European integration is primarily about the removal of barriers to the free functioning of markets. I agree with Scharpf on the second point that EU social and welfare policies lag behind the liberalization and deregulation of markets (see, however, Caporaso and Tarrow 2009). As to the first assumption, however, this book has tried to demonstrate that the prerequisites for a democratic polity do exist in the EU.

Europeanized Identities, Public Spheres, and European Democracy

To begin with, the very notion of social prerequisites for democratic polities must be put into perspective so as not to fall into the trap of essentializing political identities. Although some degree of social integration and a sense of community are certainly conditions for a democratic polity, such a community spirit does not exist outside the political process itself. Collective identities are themselves constantly reconstructed and reified in the political discourse. European identity is no exception. The more European issues of common concern are debated in transnational and Europeanized public spheres, the more a European sense of community is being created. This is what we have observed over the past fifteen to twenty years.

As argued throughout this book, we notice the gradual Europeanization of national identities—albeit with some degree of variation across countries and even though there is no "thick" European identity on a par with national identification levels. We also witness an increasing Europeanization of public spheres, allowing citizens not only to observe EU policies but also to make informed decisions about them. As a result, a European sense of community as well as a community of communication is in the making. This community does not exist above and beyond the nation-states, but has come into being through the Europeanization of national communities and, thus, matches the EU multilevel polity. This implies that its sources of democratic (input) legitimacy not only rest on diffuse support for EU institutions but also on the legitimacy of the member states' polities. It also means that the EU is not just a "government of governments," but can generate its own sources of (input) legitimacy.

Two identity constructions with regard to the European polity can be observed (see chapters 2 and 3). First, there is the modern and inclusionary vision of Europe based on human rights, democracy, and socially embedded market economies (Beck and Grande 2004). Modern Europe's social basis is the well-educated white-collar workers and the highly mobile young urban professionals whom Neil Fligstein calls "the Europeans" (Fligstein 2008, chap. 5). Moreover, slightly more than 50 percent of European citizens hold at least "inclusive national" identities, that is, they identify both with their nation-state and with Europe as a secondary identity. Europeans with dual identities support European integration by wide margins. They represent what Hanspeter Kriesi, Edgar Grande, and their team call the "integration" end of a cultural cleavage that is orthogonal to the traditional socioeconomic cleavage (Left vs. Right) in Europe (Kriesi et al. 2008; see Hooghe and Marks 2008 for a similar argument). Both groups belong to the winners from globalization and Europeanization.

A second vision of Europe is exclusionary and antimodern. Although this vision used to be simply anti-integration and anti-EU, I have argued that it no longer is. Rather, the—mostly right-wing—populist parties supporting it emphasize a "Europe of nation-states" and thus oppose supranationalism rather than the EU in general. This European countervision feeds into and provides fertile ground for Euroskepticism across the EU member states (Hooghe and Marks 2007). Euroskepticism represents the "demarcation" end of the cultural cleavage mentioned above. "Exclusionary Europe" resonates with the almost 40 percent of mass public opinion in Europe that hold exclusive nationalist attitudes. Its social basis is older, less educated, blue-collar, and poorer citizens, in other words, the losers in both globalization and Europeanization (see Fligstein 2008; Kriesi et al. 2008).

Overall, this is good news for European democracy. First, even "European identity lite," whereby European identity constitutes a secondary identity, increases diffuse support for EU institutions and for European integration to a large degree (see chapter 8). One does not have to identify strongly with the EU in order to support it. A limited sense of community on top of the sense of national belonging appears to be sufficient. European cosmopolitanism does not require giving up one's national attachments. The EU as a multilevel governance system does not need exclusive loyalties in order to generate a degree of legitimacy that allows for compliance with costly rules.

Second and somewhat counterintuitively, it is encouraging for European democracy that Euroskepticism is increasingly framed less as simply anti-European and more in terms of an alternative vision for the European polity, one that combines intergovernmentalism with nationalism on the European level. Exclusionary Europeanism constitutes a strange sort of "nationalism beyond the nation-state" in that values traditionally identified with nationalism are transferred to the European level. However, if nationalism is framed in European colors, the EU has won as a polity even among those who used to reject European integration altogether. To the extent then that the voices of the more than 40 percent exclusive nationalists become politically salient across Europe, their concerns are taken up by parties demanding "a different EU" rather than no EU at all. A "nationalist Europe" is nationalist and xenophobic, of course, but it still directs its demands to Europe.

The third encouraging sign for European democracy concerns the gradual Europeanization of public spheres, leading to a transnational public space in which issues of common European concern are being debated. Europe and the EU, its institutions and policies have gained increasing salience in the national public spheres during the past ten years—in parallel with the growing importance of European policies for national, subnational, and local rules and institutions (see chapters 6 and 7). This, of course, adds to the visibility of the EU and increases its psychological existence as an imagined community, thereby contributing to people's sense of community. Moreover, the data show that Europeans do not talk past each other when debating issues of common concern. Such transnational debates are still rare when compared with national political controversies. But, to the extent that they occur, it can be shown empirically that the frames of reference and the meaning structures do not vary much across national borders. These findings are relevant for European democracy. They challenge the notion that social ligatures such as collective identities are impossible beyond the nation-state. The earlier "permissive consensus" about European integration might have disappeared, but diffuse support for the EU prevails among majorities in most countries who identify with Europe, at least to some extent. To the extent that the EU requires a prepolitical sense of loyalty among its citizens, this

is no longer a hopeless proposition. It implies that the legitimacy of EU institutions appears to be stronger among the citizens than many scholars assume.
Data on trust levels toward the EU as compared to national governments and
parliaments support this view (see European Commission 2007b, 35–36, for the
following). Across the EU 27, 48 percent tend to trust the EU, while only 34 percent trust their national governments and 35 percent trust their national parliaments. Trust in the EU as compared to national institutions is particularly high
in Southern as well as Central Eastern Europe (and Belgium), that is, in countries
where political institutions are either not yet fully consolidated (Eastern Europe)
or face recurrent stability problems (Southern Europe and Belgium). In contrast,
pluralities among British, German, Swedish, and Finnish citizens tend to distrust
the EU. In other words, the less stable the national political institutions are in a
country, the more the people of that country tend to trust the EU, and vice versa.
On average, the EU might not face legitimacy problems that are worse than those
experienced by national institutions.

Furthermore, the Europeanization of identities and public spheres not only
strengthens the social and cultural prerequisites for European democracy, thereby
disconfirming claims about the nonexistence of a European demos, but Europeanized public spheres also add a crucial ingredient to European democracy.
Media representations and mutual observation enable citizens to make informed
decisions about Europe and the EU. In addition, transnational communities of
communication are essential for the development of democratic policymaking
beyond the nation-state. Without Europeanized public spheres to enable cross-
border communication, European politics would be next to impossible. The
emergence of Europeanized public spheres constitutes a first step in the politicization of European policies. This is very good news for European democracy.

Some caveats have to be added to this rosy picture, though. First, the Europeanization of identities and public spheres is unevenly spread across Europe, as
argued in the previous chapters. For example, although only about one third of
the Italians, the French, and the Germans exclusively identify with their country,
almost two thirds of the British and large majorities in Finland, Sweden, and
Greece do so (Fligstein 2008, 143). The Europeanization of public spheres is confined to continental Europe with the original six EU members as well as Spain
and Portugal as its core and Central Eastern Europe gradually entering the community of communication (see, e.g., Kutter 2009 on Poland). There is an emerging European demos, but one of the larger member states—Great Britain—is
clearly not part of it, and Scandinavia remains on the sidelines, too.

Second, the Europeanization of identities found in the data might suffice for
diffuse support for the EU's current institutional equilibrium. This equilibrium—
as recently confirmed by the Lisbon Treaty—holds the supranational (European

Commission, European Parliament, and European Court of Justice) and the intergovernmental institutions (Council of Ministers) in a delicate balance. As long as the EU remains a multilevel governance system, a weak sense of community as a secondary European identity might be sufficient to ensure the EU's legitimacy. Moves toward strengthening the supranational components of the EU at the expense of intergovernmental institutions might not be consistent with the present sense of community among EU citizens. Those who identify with the EU as a secondary identity in addition to their national identification support European integration at its current level. But there seems to be little demand for an even more firmly integrated Europe, let alone a United States of Europe as a federal state (rather than the current federation). And those who identify exclusively with their nation-state mostly favor a return to more intergovernmentalism, as most of the Euroskeptical parties on the populist Right demand these days.

Third and more important, it remains unclear how far the "solidarity among strangers" (Habermas 2006, 76–77; see Castiglione 2009) can be stretched to allow for costly EU policies in the security and the social policy realms. On the one hand, a common European foreign and defense policy has always enjoyed strong support among the citizens. Support levels for a common foreign policy have stayed between 63 percent and 72 percent since 1992 (European Commission 2007a, 146). On the other hand, this does not imply that Europeans are prepared to "die for the EU" or that they are even aware that the European Defense and Security Policy (ESDP) is now engaged in robust peacekeeping and peace enforcement. Most European citizens prefer a "civilian power Europe," while support for an EU force and its deployment abroad is rather limited, even among Euro-enthusiasts (Schoen 2008b). Given the European history of wars and nationalism, however, we should welcome the European reluctance to support a militarization of foreign policy. One cannot really blame Europeans for holding pacifist attitudes.

This is different with regard to potential EU moves toward redistributive policies (see chapter 8). On the one hand, demands for a "social Europe" have been a strong mobilizing force among the Left in many EU member states in the context of the recent referendum campaigns. On the other hand, many wealthy continental European countries (including Germany) have insisted on strict limitations on the free movement of labor, on immigration, and on regional and agricultural transfer payments during the accession negotiations with the new Central Eastern European member states (Sedelmeier 2005). This suggests that the propensity of rich member states to accept redistributive policies in the EU are limited. The economic and financial crisis served as a test case for the preparedness of Europeans to stand together in hard times. The results are mixed. On the one hand, the EU did manage to save member states such as Ireland and

Hungary from going under. On the other hand, the debate on the fate of the automobile company of *Opel/Vauxhall* (the European branch of General Motors) demonstrates that German taxpayers are not prepared to save jobs in Belgium or Great Britain with their money.

Finally, as to the Europeanization of public spheres, the most important caveat is probably that the emerging European community of communication is almost exclusively populated by elites rather than by civil society (on the latter, see, however, Imig and Tarrow 2001; Della Porta 2008; Doerr 2008). This is true for most public spheres in Europe. But the Europeanized public spheres suffer from a further bias toward national and European executives. To the extent that there is a lively debate, it mainly takes place among and between national governments and the European Commission. Europeanized public spheres are even more executive-centered than national public spheres (Koopmans 2004, 2007; see chapter 7). It remains unclear whether this "community of communication" extends beyond national executives and the European Commission. However, as I argue below, we currently observe more politicization, which necessarily implies the involvement of new actors in Europeanized public spheres.

In sum, however, the difficulties facing European democracy in its current state are not the result primarily of a lack of Europeanized identities and transnational public spheres. In this regard, the glass is at least half full. The more important question facing democracy in Europe concerns the incongruence between the EU level where policymaking takes place, on the one hand, and the national levels where politics is taking place, on the other hand. This leads to the question of the EU's "democratic deficit."

Does the EU Suffer from a "Democratic Deficit"?

Once we accept that the EU has to be treated as a democratic multilevel polity, the question arises of whether it suffers from what has been called a "democratic deficit." A lively scholarly debate has emerged on this question, which was initially triggered by the near-defeat of the euro in the 1992 French referendum on the Maastricht Treaties.[1] The following arguments are usually made by those who complain about a "democratic deficit':

- The inclusion of ever more policy areas into European policymaking has led to a tremendous increase in executive power both at the national level

---

1. For example, Andersen and Burns 1996; Bartolini 2005, chap. 6; Benz 1998; Eriksen and Fossum 2000; Follesdal and Hix 2006; Hix 2008; Majone 1998; Moravcsik 2002; Nicolaidis and Howse 2001; Scharpf 1999; Schmidt 2006; Schmitter 2000.

and on the level of the EU, at the expense of both the national parliaments and the European Parliament (EP). National governments and their representatives negotiate in Brussels, and their main counterpart is the European Commission, another executive body. Although the powers of the EP and the rights of national parliaments in scrutinizing EU policies have increased over the past fifteen years, the EP's budgetary powers and its power to elect the EU's executives are still rather weak compared to national parliaments.

- There are no truly "European elections" (Follesdal and Hix 2006, 535–36). Although EU citizens elect their national governments, who then negotiate in Brussels, and they also elect members of the EP, neither national elections nor EP elections have concentrated on European issues. EP elections have so far been mainly "second order national contests" (Hix 2008, 5–6).
- The preferences of citizens with regard to European policies only indirectly influence policy outcomes in Brussels. EU institutions are, therefore, rather distant from voters. The blame-shifting of national governments ("Brussels made me do it") only adds to the problem that EU institutions are often regarded as faceless bureaucratic entities that nevertheless interfere in peoples' daily lives.
- Politics is still mostly organized at the national rather than at the EU level. There are no strong Europe-wide party organizations able to mobilize around European issues. The same holds true for systems of interest representation (see Kohler-Koch 1994, 1997). Transnational interest organizations are still rather weak compared to the national levels. EU decisions are "policies without politics," while national policymaking is "politics without policies" (Schmidt 2006).

In contrast, Giandomenico Majone and Andrew Moravcsik in particular have insisted that the "democratic deficit" of the EU is vastly exaggerated (Majone 1996; Moravcsik 2002). Majone has conceptualized the EU as a regulatory state that mostly corrects market failures. Majone warns that increasing the powers of majoritarian institutions such as the EP would necessarily lead to Pareto-inefficient outcomes and regulatory deficiencies. If at all, he argues, the *ex post* review of EU decisions by courts and technical experts should be strengthened, while increasing input legitimacy would only exacerbate the problem. Moravcsik reaches similar conclusions. The EU is not a superstate, but an intergovernmental organization that concentrates on regulating cross-border economic activities. It has very limited "tax and spend" capacity and mostly leaves the redistributive policies of the European welfare states to its members. In other words, the EU deals with issues that are of little concern to voters. At the same time, the member state governments place extremely high constraints on EU institutions— and these constraints are embedded in the treaties. It is the member states that implement EU rules and regulations and that can be held accountable by the citizens. Last but not least, the continuous insulation of EU policymaking from politics increases both the efficiency and the effectiveness of EU decisions. Politicization and increasing the participatory rights of citizens with regard to EU decision-making institutions would not make the EU more democratic; it would greatly diminish its problem-solving capacity.

Majone, Moravcsik, and Vivien Schmidt agree on at least one point—that Brussels is engaged in "policies without politics"—but they part ways with regard to their normative evaluations of this. In the end, the argument about the "democratic deficit" rests on different evaluations about whether there is indeed incongruence between where mass politics and political mobilization take place and where decisions are made. From Moravcsik's liberal intergovernmentalist viewpoint, the member states remain the most important decision makers in the EU and politics continues to take place in the domestic realm. Moreover, the consequences of the EU's regulatory policies for redistributive and welfare policies in the member states remain negligible.

The more one disagrees with the intergovernmentalist account, on the one hand, and the more one is concerned about the domestic consequences of EU policies, on the other hand, the more one should worry about the "democratic deficit." The incongruence between trans- and supranational decision-making levels and the (national) levels of politics appears to be a general problem in the age of globalization and of increasing international institutionalization (Zürn 2000; Wolf 2000). But the EU's problems are particularly relevant in this regard given the extent of supranational policymaking, on the one hand, and the intrusiveness of EU policies on the domestic policies and institutions of the member states, on the other. As Fritz Scharpf has argued time and again, market-making policies have tremendous consequences for the ability of nation-states to sustain redistributive policies, for example, in the realm of social welfare and social policies (Scharpf 1999, 2009). Economic and Monetary Union and the single currency are certainly market-enabling regulatory institutions, but they deeply affect the economic policies of the member states if monetary policies can no longer be used to govern the economy. EU environmental rules are regulatory policies to begin with, but they entail very costly adjustments by the member states (Börzel 2003). As the Europeanization literature demonstrates in detail, EU policies lead to substantial political and institutional adaptations in the member states.[2] As a result, European policies might undermine the legitimacy of national polities without providing for a substitute on the EU level.

---

2. See Cowles, Caporaso, and Risse 2001; Featherstone and Radaelli 2003; Börzel and Risse 2007.

I conclude that there is indeed incongruence between where decisions are made in Europe (in Brussels) and where politics is played out (in the member states). Thus, the EU does suffer from a "democratic deficit." However, this has little to do with the widespread assertion that the EU lacks democratic representation (see Hix 2008, 72–76, on this point). EP members are directly elected by European voters—irrespective of whether European elections are truly "European" or not—and the EP has acquired considerable authority in EU decision making. The EU Commission is elected by national governments, which are themselves elected using democratic procedures—and the EP has veto power over the selection of the Commission and its president. The EU bodies with little direct accountability—the European Central Bank and the European Court of Justice—enjoy high legitimacy from European citizens, because they are regarded as being "above the fray" of ordinary politics. As a result, institutional solutions to improve the democratic and participatory quality of EU decision-making processes, while shortening the lines of accountability from voters to the EU, will not do the trick alone. For example, if the EP were to propose and to elect the Commission president directly, this would not make the EU more democratic per se. Rather, its main effect would be the politicization of EP elections, since the European party families would have to come up with their own candidates for the Commission presidency in much the same way as national parties present their candidates for chief executives in parliamentary democracies (Hix 2008, chap. 9).

The incongruence problem has negative consequences for both the EU and the national polities. For the EU, insulation from the political process necessarily leads to a lack of transparency—no matter how many websites the EU administers and no matter how many videos the EU Commission posts on YouTube. If citizens do not know who decides and who is ultimately in charge, nobody is really in charge. This constitutes at least a "responsibility deficit" (Benz 1998). As to the nation-states, their legitimacy will be undermined if citizens increasingly perceive domestic politics as largely irrelevant, because the decisions that affect their lives are taken elsewhere. So, what can be done to tackle the EU's democratic deficit?

Bringing Politics Back In: The Challenges of Politicization

In my view, there are few institutional solutions to tackle the EU's democratic deficit and most of them will not do the trick. Rather, a gradual politicization of EU affairs is necessary. By politicization, I mean that issues become subject to political debates and controversies among interest groups and political parties as well as in the various public spheres. EU policies must be debated in much the same way as we discuss the reform of health care and pension systems or the intervention in Afghanistan. In short, EU affairs must become part of "normal politics." Once again, politicization of EU affairs does not and cannot take place above and beyond the domestic politics of the member states. Rather, politicization of EU affairs means the Europeanization of EU politics in the various and interconnected public spheres. Europe and the EU have to "hit home."[3]

This politicization of European affairs in the domestic politics of various member states that are interconnected through transnational public spheres has been under way since the end of the 1990s. Indicators for such a politicization of European affairs include

- the increasing salience of European issues in the various public spheres (see chapter 6),
- the growing importance of identity politics in the debates about EU enlargement as well as constitutionalization (Checkel and Katzenstein 2009a, 2009b; see chapters 8 and 9),
- the emergence of Euroskepticism as a force to be reckoned with across Europe,[4]
- and, particularly, the controversies surrounding the (failed) French and Dutch referenda about the Constitutional Treaty in 2005 and the two Irish referenda on the Lisbon Treaty in 2008 and 2009.[5]

These trends suggest that the politicization of EU affairs, although still sporadic and uneven across the EU, is on its way and is likely to increase in the years to come. Most important, the rise of Euroskeptical populist parties is probably inevitable. The "sleeping giant," the potential for mass mobilization of anti-EU sentiments, has begun to wake up (Franklin and Van der Eijk 2006). As I have argued in this book, Euroskeptical parties have started to construct an exclusionary and xenophobic countervision to the cosmopolitan image of a modern and enlightened EU as promoted by the liberal elites (see, e.g., Riedel 2008; De Vries and Edwards 2009). Claes De Vreese and Hajo Boomgaarden have shown in this context that anti-immigration sentiments can be easily mobilized in referenda focusing on EU policies (De Vreese and Boomgaarden 2005).

---

3. Title taken from Börzel and Risse 2000.

4. See, e.g., Hooghe and Marks 2007; Marks and Steenbergen 2004; Taggart and Szczerbiak 2005/2008.

5. The Irish referendum in 2008 rejected the Lisbon Treaty, while the referendum in October 2009 accepted it—after some symbolic concessions to Ireland.

Class Cleavage Cultural Cleavage	Left	Right
Integration	Green/Alternative Parties	Liberal Parties
Demarcation	Social Democratic Parties	Christian Democratic/ Conservative Parties
	Left-wing Populist Parties	Right-wing Populist Parties

Figure 10.1.   Position of party families in the European cleavage structure.
Source: Adapted and modified from Kriesi et al. 2006, 925.

Moreover, as mentioned above, studies of European party politics and mass public opinion increasingly converge around the notion that the political cleavage structures in Europe are changing. Although the traditional socioeconomic cleavage (Left vs. Right) has remained rather stable, the cultural cleavage, which used to have religious connotations in Europe (particularly Catholicism vs. Protestantism), has been transformed into a pro- and anti-globalization cleavage, which now also includes attitudes toward the EU (Kriesi et al. 2008; Kriesi et al. 2006; similarly Hooghe and Marks 2008). The new meaning of this cultural cleavage centers around cosmopolitan and pro-integration values, on one end of the continuum, and boundary-creating, nationalist, and xenophobic attitudes, on the other end. In other words, one could map the various European party families onto a two-dimensional space (see figure 10.1).

As argued above, the two visions of Europe—cosmopolitan and modern Europe vs. nationalist and xenophobic Europe—map onto the cultural cleavage rather than the socioeconomic cleavage. However, the two major European party families—Social Democrats and Socialists, on the one hand, and Christian Democrats and Conservatives, on the other—mobilize along the traditional class cleavage of Left vs. Right. At the same time, these mass integration parties—except for the British Conservatives—have been steady supporters of European integration and of the EU for the past decades. As a result, it is very hard for them to politicize Europe and the EU in terms of pro- or anti-integration. I submit that this is a major reason why European elections have been "second order national elections" so far, because neither Socialists and Social Democrats nor Christian Democrats and Conservatives could use attitudes toward the EU for party political purposes.[6] At most, running campaigns on "pro-" or "anti"-European platforms would provoke deep divisions within the mainstream parties rather than between them. In other words, there are structural reasons why Europe and the EU have not been politicized in the domestic politics of most member states (see also Hix 2008). Although there might be an elitist consensus not to destabilize European policymaking, there are also good old-fashioned power political reasons for not rocking the boat on Europe.

Yet, if the "sleeping giant" is slowly waking up and the cultural cleavage is becoming increasingly salient in European and domestic politics, neither Socialists and Social Democrats nor Christian Democrats and Conservatives are well prepared for the politicization of EU affairs. This explains to a large degree why the failed referenda in France, the Netherlands, and Ireland in 2008 sent such shock waves throughout European governments and the EU. The immediate reaction by EU leaders and national governments was to depoliticize EU treaty- and constitution-making even further and to shield it from public scrutiny. Although the Constitutional Convention and the resulting Constitutional Treaty were originally celebrated as prime examples of a new EU transparency and the willingness of elites to open EU affairs to public deliberation (Risse and Kleine 2007), the failure of the referenda in 2005 marked a turning point. Pro-EU elites across Europe worked hard to save the Constitutional Treaty from the public and from mass politics. The 2007 German EU presidency under Chancellor Merkel succeeded in reviving the Constitutional Treaty from the ashes. Although the Germans managed to preserve about 90 percent of its content in the new Lisbon Treaty signed at the end of 2007 in Lisbon, the EU member states agreed to remove all controversial issues from the treaty including any references to what could be read as a constitution. For example, the European flag is no longer mentioned in the treaty and the new position of foreign minister is no longer called that (even though the substance of the institution has been preserved). Although the Charter of Fundamental Rights has been removed from the Lisbon Treaty, it is referred to as legally valid in Article 6.[7] These and other symbolic changes were meant to enable EU governments to claim that the Lisbon Treaty was merely an amendment to the Treaty of Nice. As a result, no referenda were

---

6. It is no wonder, therefore, that the British Conservatives who ran on a Euroskeptical platform during the 2009 EP elections, subsequently left the European People's Party of Christian Democrats.

7. This is a particularly interesting form of symbolic politics and of shielding issues from public scrutiny: Article 6 stipulates that the Charter shall have "the same legal value" as the Treaties themselves, effectively making it part of the Treaties. The British governments under Tony Blair and Gordon Brown still insisted on an opt-out so as to be able to claim that a referendum on the Lisbon Treaty was not necessary, because it was so different from the previous Constitutional Treaty and because Britain had secured additional opt-outs.

deemed necessary this time (except for Ireland). In sum, the main lesson the European elites learned from their failed effort at securing public approval for the Constitutional Treaty was to silence constitutional issues once again.

One could argue in support of this elitist approach that submitting EU treaties to national referenda is the wrong way to attempt the politicization of EU affairs. After all, what major national constitution has ever been submitted to a popular vote? Besides, public referenda on EU treaties were bound to become votes on the EU as such, subject to all kinds of populist criticism and demands. Therefore, on balance, there is something to be said in favor of the attempts by Chancellor Merkel and others to shield treaty-making from the public sphere and have it decided behind closed intergovernmental doors.

But these efforts at silencing and at depoliticization have come at a very high price. To begin with, the EU will remain visible in the national public spheres given the salience of its policies in the domestic realm. Environmental issues such as climate change, immigration policies, monetary issues, social policies, the future of the welfare state, Turkish EU membership, and foreign and security policy including military interventions outside Europe are hot political topics in most EU member states, and the EU is part and parcel of it. Leaving the cultural cleavage to be exploited politically by populist parties on the far right and the far left could turn out to be disastrous for European integration as well as for the vision of a modern and enlightened EU. I discuss the policy options in the concluding chapter of this book.

Conclusions

I have made the following points in this chapter:

1. The gradual, albeit uneven, Europeanization of identities and public spheres means that the social conditions for a European democracy exist and that the alleged lack of a European demos should no longer be of much concern.

2. Yet, the EU continues to suffer from a democratic deficit because of the incongruence of the level at which major political decisions are made that affect the lives of millions of European citizens (in Brussels), and the level at which politics and the interplay of interest groups and parties continues to take place (at home in the member states). Democratizing the EU means primarily to politicize EU affairs at home and to integrate them into domestic politics.

3. This politicization of EU affairs is already under way, given the increased salience of European issues in transnationalized public spheres and the rise

of Euroskepticism in many member states. The latter maps onto a cultural cleavage connoting pro- vs. antiglobalization attitudes, which have started to become politically significant in many member states. As a result, there are now two competing visions of Europe, cosmopolitan and modern Europe vs. nationalist and xenophobic Europe.

4. The immediate reaction of pro-European political elites to the politicization of EU affairs has so far resulted in attempts to silence these debates— for understandable reasons. However, this silencing is short-sighted, since politicization appears to be inevitable given the various trends discussed in this book.

For those who care about the EU and European integration, the task ahead is to accept the inevitable politicization of EU affairs and to contribute to it without rocking the European boat so that it ultimately sinks in rough waters. This leads to policy conclusions to which I turn in the last chapter of this book.

DEFENDING MODERN EUROPE

> *Anton43:* I participate in the European elections, because I have seen Verdun and have read about Stalingrad. Europe stands for peace, prosperity, and the commitment to forge a common future.
>
> *Tom0464:* How do I benefit from the EU as a German? A cake consisting of the richest economies in Europe [before enlargement]. . . . We now take in many more countries that do not contribute to the cake, but want to have a piece so that the individual slices become smaller and smaller. Why should I appreciate the EU?
>
> *Conni66:* I have never phoned abroad, have never flown, and don't believe in climate change. My father is a farmer, he gets less and less support from the EU. If this continues, he can close down his farm. I don't see any advantages in the EU.[1]

These are three quotes from an Internet chat held one week before the European elections in June 2009 in response to a German TV broadcast on the EU. They pretty much sum up the range of voices of ordinary citizens in Europe today. *Anton43* stands for the vision of modern and enlightened Europe that has overcome the ghosts of the past. *Tom0464* expresses the widespread notion that the wealthy member states have to pay the price for EU enlargement, while *Conni66* demonstrates the Euroskepticism of the losers from globalization and Europeanization. In this particular case, it is the perception of loss that counts rather than the actual economic situation given that most German agriculture would probably be out of business in the absence of the EU's Common Agricultural Policy (CAP).

The three voices also demonstrate two things about Europe a decade into the twenty-first century. First, people do have opinions about the EU, either in positive or in negative terms. Polarization and contestation are important

---

1. Source: http://berlindirekt.zdf.de/ZDFforum/chat/protokoll.php?channel=berlin_6&logfile=http%3A%2F%2Fchat.zdf.de%2Fchatlogs%2Fberlin_6%2F23571.html.

preconditions for the emergence of Europeanized public spheres, as argued in this book. Second, however, there is something missing between the two positions represented here, the traditional justification of the EU in terms of peace and prosperity, on the one hand, and a Euroskepticism that sees no benefits in the European project, on the other. More than sixty years after the end of World War II, references to Verdun (even earlier) and to Stalingrad (and Auschwitz, one might add) are no longer sufficient to sway skeptical voters to support the EU. There needs to be a positive discourse rather than ritualistic invocations of the past, a discourse that connects to the realities of the twenty-first century and the real benefits of European integration at a time of severe economic and financial crises (Schmidt and Radaelli 2004).

The quotes reflect the three simultaneous crises facing the EU at the end of the decade: (1) the constitutional crisis, which culminated in the three resounding "No" votes from French, Dutch, and Irish voters in the treaty referenda in 2005 and 2008 (followed, however, by an Irish "Yes" in October 2009); (2) the enlargement crisis following the extremely successful accession of the Central Eastern European countries in 2004 and 2007, a crisis that has considerably slowed down the membership perspectives and negotiations for the western Balkans and for Turkey; and (3) the worst global economic and financial crisis since the 1930s, which tested the EU's capacities for economic coordination, the single market, and the Economic and Monetary Union (EMU).

Although these crises have resulted in widespread feelings of doom and gloom across Europe, I have claimed throughout this book that the EU is in better shape than is usually assumed. First, over the past twenty years, the EU has emerged as a democratic multilevel polity. It has developed an institutional framework with a rather stable balance of supranational and intergovernmental elements that govern European economies and monetary policies, environmental policies, justice and home affairs, a growing number of social policies, and is becoming increasingly active in foreign and security policy. At the same time, we can observe the—albeit uneven—Europeanization of collective identities that corresponds to the multilevel character of the EU. Last but not least, a European transnational community of communication through the Europeanization of public spheres is not only possible but is in the making, particularly in continental Europe and increasingly is encompassing Central Eastern Europe. Although the EU polity does not and will not resemble a nation-state, its institutional, identity, and public sphere components reflect the realities of a multilevel governance system (Hooghe and Marks 2001). There is little in the data to suggest that this polity is incapable of mastering the three crises mentioned above.

Second, Europe and the EU are "hitting home." The Europeanization of domestic politics and the politicization of EU affairs are not only inevitable but also desirable from a democratic point of view. The coming fights over Europe will no longer be whether or not one supports European integration, but *which* type of EU one prefers including which policy alternatives. In this sense, the EU is about to become a "normal" part of domestic politics in the member states. Two distinct visions of Europe and the EU are on display and are becoming ever more politically salient in the public spheres. On the one hand, there is the vision of modern, liberal, and cosmopolitan Europe that embodies the values of enlightenment, such as human rights, democracy, and the market economy, that have been constitutive for the European project for the past fifty years and are still endorsed by a majority of political elites and citizens across the continent. On the other hand, antimodern nationalism increasingly represents itself as a distinct *European nationalism,* as a "fortress and exclusionary Europe" based on an essentialist interpretation of the European Christian heritage. Interestingly enough, nationalism is less connected to the nation-state as such in this construction but is extended to Europe and the EU.

These two identity constructions map onto a cultural cleavage with increasing salience in public attitudes and in party systems that pits the winners from globalization and Europeanization—"the Europeans"—against its losers (Fligstein 2009; Kriesi et al. 2008; Green 2007). This cleavage is also expressed in two identification patterns in mass public opinion. While "modern Europe" resonates with those who identify with their nation-state and with Europe (at least as a secondary identity), "nationalist Europe" is compatible with those who feel exclusively attached to their nation-state. Finally, each of these two visions comes in national colors, that is, it is linked to specific components of national identities. The various elite discourses have built Europe into the various national identity narratives, historical memories, and symbols (see chapter 3). In other words, the Polish versions of "modern Europe" and of "nationalist Europe" differ from the French interpretation whereby modern Europe is France writ large.

The cleavage itself is increasingly visible in many member states and is likely to structure the politicization of European affairs in the coming years (see chapter 10). To exploit the cleavage politically by tapping into widespread Euroskepticism and exclusive nationalist identities is also in the interest of populist forces on the far right or on the far left that are located at the "anti-EU" end of the cultural cleavage. After all, almost 30 percent of the citizens on average in the EU population might be mobilized along these lines.

No wonder then why European policymakers including the European Commission, members of the European Parliament, and national policymakers appear to fear public debates, because they are afraid of "rocking the boat." The outcomes of the 2005 and 2008 referenda in France, the Netherlands, and Ireland seem to have confirmed concerns that public controversies about the EU are a

bad idea, because it might only serve to increase Euroskepticism given the declin-
ing levels of support for European integration (Hix 2008, 55). What if rocking
the boat sinks it in the rough waters ahead for the EU?

Besides, bringing politics back in to European affairs faces real obstacles. Part
of the problem is the lack of Europe-wide transnational party as well as interest organizations. Transnational party organizations might be strengthened as
a consequence of politicization, but the emergence of strong Europe-wide parties with the potential to mobilize around European issues is unlikely given the
fragmentation of the European political space. As a result, and analogous to the
Europeanization of identities and public spheres, the politicization of European
affairs is likely to take place through the Europeanization of domestic politics.
However, as discussed in chapter 10, most mainstream political parties in Europe are organized along the Left vs. Right spectrum, which is orthogonal to the
"pro-" vs. "anti-Europe" cultural cleavage. As a result, the more the EU is subject
to domestic political contestation, the more mainstream center-left and center-
right parties might not only split apart but might also lose ground to populist
forces on the left and the right.

But there are also old-fashioned power considerations why European elites—
both at the EU level and in the national capitals—have tried to silence debates
about the EU so far. The more the EU is shielded from domestic politics, the less
policymakers have to fear from critical public opinion. It makes perfect sense
that the European Commission does not seem to endorse public controversies
over its policies—despite all the proclamations about transparency, democratic
governance, and the like. After all, the self-image of the Commission as a neutral "guardian of the treaties" above the fray of politics also enhances the Commission's power (see Hooghe 2001). The more European policies are subject to
public scrutiny, the less the Commission will be able to keep an allegedly neutral position in EU affairs. As to national policymakers, similar considerations
explain their efforts to silence debates. As long as EU policies are not politicized,
the widespread strategy of blame-shifting ("Brussels made me do it") can be
successful. It enables national policymakers to shift tough policy choices onto the
EU level and, thus, to circumvent domestic opposition. At the same time, they
can still accept praise for EU decisions that correspond to domestic preferences
("We fought hard in Brussels for our interests, and we succeeded!").

For example, to cite a recent instance during the economic crisis, when the
German government decided to heavily subsidize the rescue of the Opel auto-
motive brand and to shield it from General Motors' insolvency, it had to get the
EU's endorsement, given the European rules with regard to state aid. German
policymakers rarely mentioned this in public. However, at about the same time,
the German Karstadt department store chain, with more than fifty thousand

employees, was in serious trouble and asked for state aid, too. This time, the German government refused—and cited Brussels rules as tying its hands.

This behavior is fairly common in the EU. Jürgen Gerhards and others conducted a study on the attribution of responsibility between national governments and the EU in German and British mass media (Gerhards, Offerhaus, and Roose 2009). Almost two thirds (64.8%) of the instances in which national governments ascribe responsibility to EU actors consist of negative attributions. In other words, national governments tend to play a blame game with the EU, particularly the EU Commission. This is true even in cases in which they themselves have supported the respective decisions in the Council of Ministers.

In sum, good old-fashioned power games as well as party politics to a large extent explain why political elites in Brussels and in the national capitals are so reluctant to politicize EU affairs. But this reaction is short-sighted. If politicians do not "fight for Europe," but try to silence the debates for reasons of power politics or out of serious concern for European integration, they will lose the battle over public opinion to Euroskepticism. If the various studies on Euroskepticism and on the transformation of European party politics are correct, politicization is on its way and inevitable. The referendum debates, the controversies about Turkish EU membership, and the controversies about immigration policies suggest as much. Depoliticization efforts by EU and national elites might succeed in the short run, but the changes in cleavage structures strongly suggest that the "sleeping giant" will soon wake up again.

Leaving the politicization of EU affairs to Euroskeptical parties risks what mainstream political elites want to avoid: a further loss of popular support for European integration, leading to more and more difficulties in legitimizing EU policies before domestic audiences. Those who fear that the politicization of the EU increases the gridlock in EU policymaking might actually get what they wanted to avoid: more gridlock in the Council of Ministers and the European Council, because national governments are afraid of their domestic constituencies in light of increasingly vocal Euroskepticism. Therefore, I strongly suggest that those who identify with "modern Europe" as an open and cosmopolitan place that faces the challenges of globalization and preserves liberal policies toward both enlargement and immigration have to fight for it rather than silence debates.

Moreover, from the standpoint of normative democratic theory, politicization is good, not bad. The EU suffers from a "democratic deficit" because of "policies without politics" at the EU level and of "politics without policies" at the domestic levels (Schmidt 2006; see chapter 10). Politicization will bring politics back in to EU affairs and, hence, democratize them. Politicization also enhances the Europeanization of public spheres. Controversies, discussions, even polarized debates are necessary ingredients of vibrant public spheres in liberal democracies—as long as speakers and audiences respect one another as part of a community of communication. As argued in this book, the ingredients for the development of transnational public spheres through the Europeanization of national public spheres are there. Chances are good that controversies about EU affairs in transnational public spheres will draw Europeans further together rather than driving them apart. This is what the available evidence suggests. In contrast, silencing controversies only strengthens disillusionment with politics including European ones.

In addition, the politicization of EU affairs increases the visibility of Europe in Europeanized public spheres. In general, greater visibility for the EU in the public spheres strengthens the psychological existence of Europe in peoples' minds and, hence, facilitates identification processes. The more "real" the EU becomes, the more people can develop a sense of community. But there is a catch: one-sided politicization that leaves the issues to Euroskepticism and simultaneously continues the blame-shifting game will have the opposite effect. We know that bad news about the EU is bad news for European identity. Yet, this is not a plea for propaganda campaigns painting a rosy picture of European politics. Rather, we need serious debates and controversies about what is good for Europe and its citizens. Political communities do not emerge through bad-mouthing or silencing, but through honest controversies about better policies and better political order. The more we debate Europe and the EU in transnational public spheres, the more we construct a common sense of purpose and thus a community with which people can identify.

But what if democratizing the EU through politicization slows down European integration by leading to even more gridlock in Brussels and, thus, alienating voters even further?[2] First, if politicization leads to more informed choices and votes by the people, so be it. And if informed voters do not like what they see in the EU, this would be a normal and altogether legitimate outcome in a democratic polity. Silencing legitimate concerns and debates will only make things worse, since it creates suspicions among citizens that the elites will do what they want anyway.

Second, I am not convinced that the outcome of politicization will be more gridlock. Although a lot of attention is being paid recently to Euroskepticism, this overlooks the fact that a majority of citizens across the Continent identify with the EU as a political order (if only as "European identity lite") and that this identification leads to stable support for European integration. Moreover, those

---

2. I owe this point to a remark by Fritz W. Scharpf during a panel at the 2009 meeting of the European Union Studies Association in Los Angeles.

fighting for a modern and enlightened Europe in the public spheres have the better arguments and, thus, might actually be able to persuade citizens. I find it interesting that those in Europe who support a modern and cosmopolitan EU often do not trust their own arguments and the ability of ordinary citizens to weigh the pros and cons of a debate.

Third, I have argued that politicization is inevitable as a result of which the only question to be asked is *which* politicization about *which* topics. It is unclear, for example, whether citizens really care about whether politicians are in favor of or against the EU as such. Rather, most public opinion surveys tell us that voters care about the state of the economy, unemployment, education, health care, and the fate of their pension systems. Yet, debates about the EU are often framed in terms as if "pro-" or "anti-Europe" was still a choice. Take the 2009 elections for the European Parliament, for example. In an advertisement, the German Christian Democrats used a picture of Angela Merkel with the slogan "We have a strong voice in Europe"—as if Merkel were a candidate. In another advertisement, her French sister party—the Gaullist l'Union pour un Mouvement Populaire—used a photo of President Sarkozy with the slogan "If Europe wants, Europe can"—a reference to Barack Obama's "Yes, we can," but devoid of political content. One should not blame voters for the low turnout that results from such campaigns.

But there is a way out that politicizes EU affairs at home without necessarily leading to increased Euroskepticism or the alienation of citizens. Policymakers who are committed to European integration should not respond to Euroskeptical populist attacks with an all-out defense of the EU devoid of substance (while at the same time blaming Brussels for everything that has gone wrong at home). One should not accept a framing of EU questions according to which support for or opposition to any European policy proposal constitutes a decision in favor of or against European integration. Rather than debating whether or not the EU is good or bad, mainstream parties should start arguing about *which* European policies are preferable. There is ample room for controversies when it comes to EU policies. Here are six examples:

- How should the EU position itself in the global economic and financial crisis? What about readjusting the balance between market capitalism and state interventionism? Does the EU need stronger macroeconomic coordination on a par with monetary union? The latter has been the French position for a long time, dating back to the Maastricht Treaties, but the issues involved transcend national positions and are of common European concern.
- The dispute about "social Europe" and about the necessity to reform and preserve European welfare states has already been on the agenda of the

referendum debates in France and the Netherlands. It concerns a typical issue about which mainstream center-right and center-left parties are bound to hold diverging positions.

- The same holds true for the debate about how to reconcile environmental protection and economic well-being in the face of climate change. The EU has so far been at the forefront of favoring drastic reductions in carbon dioxide emissions in the international climate change negotiations. Nevertheless, many people fear the economic consequences for growth and employment.

- Debates about immigration policies including the integration of foreigners and second-generation immigrants in European societies are hot topics in most EU member states. Given the reality of Schengenland, there is an inevitable European dimension to the controversy. How cosmopolitan should the EU be with regard to non-EU foreigners and immigrants? There is ample room for public controversies among mainstream parties on this question.

- Reasonable people can reasonably disagree on whether Turkey should be admitted to the EU. One the one hand, even if one strongly disagrees with the view that Europe is a community of white Christians and that a mostly Muslim society does not belong to it, one can still argue that Turkish accession will overwhelm the institutional capacities of the EU. On the other hand, it will send a very strong signal to the post-9/11 world if the EU admits an Islamic country that is committed to democracy, human rights, and the rule of law. Again, there is ample room for debate here.

- Last but not least, there has not been much public debate about the future role of the EU in world affairs, including global security policy. Should the EU develop military forces of its own or should it merely complement NATO in this regard? What does "civilian power" mean in the twenty-first century? Once again, political parties could position themselves differently on these questions.

These are issues about which Europeans have ample room and opportunity to disagree about the appropriate European policies to face these challenges. They also tap as much into the traditional "Left vs. Right" cleavage as into the new cultural cleavage of "pro-" vs. "anti-globalization" that also includes attitudes toward the EU. As a result, it should be easier for mainstream parties to take controversial positions on these questions without becoming trapped in a "pro- or anti-" EU stance. It would still politicize European affairs through the Europeanization of national discourses without rocking the boat. This type of politicization would also lessen the EU's "democratic deficit" in terms of the incongruence between politics and policies. But it would keep the debates about Europe and the EU in the realm of domestic politics with its regular channels of interest mobilization and aggregation. Last but not least, citizens might enjoy these kinds of disputes, because they are relevant for real policies, albeit at the EU rather than the domestic levels. As a result, debating Europe at home might actually help raise people's interest in politics once again rather than deepening the alienation of voters from the political realm. And it would remove the topic of Europe and the EU from the fringes of the political spectrum, since populist and Euroskeptical parties have little to contribute to the substance of these questions.

However, the rise of Euroskepticism also means that liberal elites across Europe have to leave their closets and fight for their vision of a modern, enlightened, and inclusionary EU. If they fail to do so, continental Europe will end up where the United Kingdom is now, which would then seriously endanger European integration. I have documented throughout this book that Great Britain is the least Europeanized country with regard to both identities and public spheres. British political elites have never even tried to frame Europe and the EU in constitutive rather than interest terms. Moreover, they have left the identity discourse to the Euroskeptics on the right and the left—and to the tabloids. As a result, British elites who care about the EU have lost public opinion, probably for good. It is no wonder then that the United Kingdom has opted out of the single currency, Schengenland (borderless traffic), and the Charter of Fundamental Rights. That the British Conservatives have now left the mainstream center-right European People's Party in the European Parliament and have joined forces with some irrelevant parties on the fringes of the political spectrum only adds to the sad story of what has become of Britain in the EU. The consequences are clear: the third largest country in the EU does not form part of the European social space of Europeanized identities and public spheres. This is bad for the EU and—I submit—bad for the United Kingdom, too.

To conclude, politicization should be about Europeanizing domestic politics in the sense that European policies rather than European integration as such become subject to controversies in the public spheres. In light of the emerging Europeanization of public spheres, politicizing European policies is likely to lead to transnational disputes and, thus, to further create a European community of communication. Elites must learn that contestation and polarization actually strengthens the EU rather than weakening it. At the same time, those who care about the modern and enlightened vision of Europe and want to continue the tremendous success story of European integration must learn to fight for it in the public spheres. The times of the "Monnet method"—functional integration by stealth and depoliticized technocracy—are probably over for good.

As argued throughout this book, crises and critical junctures have positive effects on community-building, both with regard to identification processes and to transnational public spheres. In that sense, the current crises and the increasing politicization of European affairs will in the end be healthy for the construction of a European polity.

References

Abdelal, Rawi, Yoshiko Herrera, Alastair Iain Johnston, and Rose McDermott. 2009a. Identity as a Variable: A Guide for Social Scientists. In *Measuring Identity,* edited by Rawi Abdelal, Yoshiko Herrera, Alastair Iain Johnston, and Rose McDermott, 17–32. Cambridge: Cambridge University Press.

——, eds. 2009b. *Measuring Identity: A Guide for Social Scientists.* Cambridge: Cambridge University Press.

Abrams, Dominic, and Michael A. Hogg, eds. 1990. *Social Identity Theory.* London: Harvester Wheatsheaf.

Abromeit, Heidrun, and Thomas Schmidt. 1998. Grenzprobleme der Demokratie: Konzeptionelle Überlegungen. In *Regieren in entgrenzten Räumen: Politische Vierteljahresschrift, Sonderheft 29,* edited by Beate Kohler-Koch, 293–320. Wiesbaden: Westdeutscher Verlag.

Adam, Silke. 2007. Domestic Adaptations of Europe: A Comparative Study of the Debates on EU Enlargement and a Common Constitution in the German and French Quality Press. *International Journal of Public Opinion Research* 19, no. 4: 409–33.

——. 2008. Do Mass Media Portray Europe as Community? German and French Debates on EU Enlargement and a Common Constitution. *Javnost—The Public* 15, no. 1: 91–112.

Adamczyk, Grzegorz, and Peter Gostmann. 2007. *Polen zwischen Nation und Europa: Zur Konstruktion kollektiver Identität im polnischen Parlament.* Wiesbaden: Deutscher Universitäts-Verlag.

Adler, Emanuel. 1997. Seizing the Middle Ground: Constructivism in World Politics. *European Journal of International Relations* 3, no. 3: 319–63.

——. 2002. Constructivism in International Relations. In *Handbook of International Relations,* edited by Walter Carlsnaes, Beth Simmons, and Thomas Risse, 95–118. London: Sage.

Aktürk, Sener. 2007. Incompatible Visions of Supra-Nationalism: National Identity in Turkey and the European Union. *European Journal of Sociology* 48, no. 2: 347–72.

Al-Azmeh, Aziz, and Effie Fokas, eds. 2007. *Islam in Europe: Diversity, Identity, and Influence.* Cambridge: Cambridge University Press.

Andersen, Svein S., and Tom Burns. 1996. The European Union and the Erosion of Parliamentary Democracy: A Study of Post-Parliamentary Governance. In *The European Union: How Democratic Is It?* edited by Svein S. Andersen and Kjell A. Eliassen, 227–252. London: Sage.

Anderson, Benedict. 1991. *Imagined Communities: Reflections on the Origin and Spread of Nationalism.* London: Verso.

Anderson, Jeffrey J., G. John Ikenberry, and Thomas Risse, eds. 2008. *The End of the West? Crisis and Change in the Atlantic Order.* Ithaca: Cornell University Press.

Anderson, Stefanie. 2008. *Crafting EU Security Policy: In Pursuit of a European Identity.* Boulder, Colo.: Lynne Rienner.

Avci, Gamze. 2006. Turkey's EU Politics: Consolidating Democracy through Enlargement? In *Questioning EU Enlargement: Europe in Search of Identity,* edited by Helene Sjursen, 62–77. London: Routledge.

Bailey, Richard. 1983. *The European Connection: Implications of EEC Membership.* Oxford: Pergamon Press.

Banchoff, Thomas. 1997. German Policy towards the European Union: The Effects of Historical Memory. *German Politics* 6, no. 1: 60–76.

———. 1999. German Identity and European Integration. *European Journal of International Relations* 5, no. 3: 259–89.

Banducci, Susan A., Jeffrey A. Karp, and Peter H. Loedel. 2003. The Euro, Economic Interests, and Multi-Level Governance: Examining Support for the Common Currency. *European Journal of Political Research* 42, no. 5: 685–703.

Bartolini, Stefano. 2005. *Restructuring Europe: Centre Formation, System Building and Political Structuring between the Nation-State and the European Union.* Oxford: Oxford University Press.

Bauchard, Philippe. 1986. *La guerre des deux roses.* Paris: Grasset.

Baudouin, Jean. 1990. Le "moment néo-libéral" du RPR: Essai d'interprétation. *Revue Française de Science Politique* 6: 830–43.

Baumann, Rainer, Volker Rittberger, and Wolfgang Wagner. 2001. Neorealist Foreign Policy Theory. In *German Foreign Policy since Unification: Theories and Case Studies,* edited by Volker Rittberger, 37–67. Manchester: Manchester University Press.

Beck, Ulrich. 1997. *Was ist Globalisierung?* Frankfurt am Main: Suhrkamp.

Beck, Ulrich, and Edgar Grande. 2004. *Das kosmopolitische Europa.* Frankfurt am Main: Suhrkamp.

Bellers, Jürgen. 1991. Sozialdemokratie und Konservatismus im Angesicht der Zukunft Europas. In *Europapolitik der Parteien: Konservatismus, Liberalismus und Sozialdemokratie im Ringen um die Zukunft Europas,* edited by Jürgen Bellers and Mechthild Winking, 3–42. Frankfurt am Main: Lang.

Bellers, Jürgen, and Mechthild Winking, eds. 1991. *Europapolitik der Parteien: Konservatismus, Liberalismus und Sozialdemokratie im Ringen um die Zukunft Europas.* Frankfurt am Main: Lang.

Benz, Arthur. 1998. Ansatzpunkte für ein europafähiges Demokratiekonzept. In *Regieren in entgrenzten Räumen: PVS-Sonderheft,* edited by Beate Kohler-Koch, 345–68. Opladen: Westdeutscher Verlag.

Berger, Peter L., and Thomas Luckmann. 1966. *The Social Construction of Reality: A Treatise in the Sociology of Knowledge.* New York: Doubleday.

Berkel, Barbara. 2006. Political Parallelism in News and Commentaries on the Haider Conflict: A Comparative Analysis of Austrian, British, German, and French Quality Newspapers. *Communications* 31, no. 1: 85–104.

Beyers, Jan. 2005. Multiple Embeddedness and Socialization in Europe: The Case of Council Officials. *International Organization* 59, no. 4: 899–936.

Bicchi, Federica. 2006. 'Our Size Fits All': Normative Power Europe and the Mediterranean. *Journal of European Public Policy* 13, no. 2: 286–303.

Biegon, Dominika. 2006. Europäische Identität in Polen: Numerische Zuschreibung oder qualitative Identität? *Berliner Debatte Initial* 17, no. 6: 44–55.

Bilge Criss, Nur. 2007. Turkey as a Metaphor between Europe and Asia. In *The Importance of Being European: Turkey, the EU, and the Middle East,* edited by Nimrod Goren and Amikam Nachmani, 56–70. Jerusalem: European Forum at the Hebrew University.

Blumler, Jay G. 1983. *Communicating to Voters: Television in the First European Parliament Elections.* London: Sage.

Börzel, Tanja A. 2003. *Environmental Leaders and Laggards in Europe: Why There Is (Not) a Southern Problem.* London: Ashgate.

———. 2005. Mind the Gap! European Integration between Level and Scope. *Journal of European Public Policy* 12, no. 2: 217–36.

Börzel, Tanja A., and Thomas Risse. 2000. When Europe Hits Home: Europeanization and Domestic Change. *European Integration on-line Papers* 4, no. 15: http://eiop. or.at/eiop/texte/2000-015a.htm.

——. 2007. Europeanization: The Domestic Impact of EU Politics. In *Handbook of European Union Politics,* edited by Knud Erik Jorgensen, Mark A. Pollack, and Ben Rosamond, 483-504. London: Sage.

——. 2009. Venus Approaching Mars? The European Union's Approaches to Democracy Promotion in Comparative Perspective. In *Promoting Democracy and the Rule of Law. American and European Strategies,* edited by Amichai Magen, Thomas Risse, and Michael McFaul, 34–60. Houndmills, Basingstoke: Palgrave Macmillan.

Breakwell, Glynis M. 2004. Identity Change in the Context of Growing Influence of European Union Institutions. In *Transnational Identities: Becoming European in the European Union,* edited by Richard K. Herrmann, Thomas Risse, and Marilynn B. Brewer, 25–39. Lanham, Md.: Rowman and Littlefield.

Breakwell, Glynis M., and E. Lyons, eds. 1996. *Changing European Identities: Social Psychological Analyses of Change.* Oxford: Butterworth-Heinemann.

Brewer, Marilynn. 2001. The Many Faces of Social Identity: Implications for Social Psychology. *Political Psychology* 22, no. 1: 115–125.

Brubaker, Rogers, and Frederick Cooper. 2000. Beyond 'Identity.' *Theory and Society* 29, no. 1: 1–47.

Bruter, Michael. 2004. Civic and Cultural Components of a European Identity: A Pilot Model of Measurement of Citizens' Levels of European Identity. In *Transnational Identities: Becoming European in the European Union,* edited by Richard K. Herrmann, Thomas Risse, and Marilynn Brewer. Lanham, Md.: Rowman and Littlefield.

——. 2005. *Citizens of Europe? The Emergence of a Mass European Identity.* Houndmills, Basingstoke: Palgrave Macmillan.

Byrnes, Timothy A. 2001. *Transnational Catholicism in Postcommunist Europe.* Lanham, Md.: Rowman and Littlefield.

——. 2006. Transnational Religion and Europeanization. In *Religion in an Expanding Europe,* edited by Timothy A. Byrnes and Peter J. Katzenstein, 283–305. Cambridge: Cambridge University Press.

Byrnes, Thimothy A., and Peter J. Katzenstein, eds. 2006. *Religion in an Expanding Europe.* Cambridge: Cambridge University Press.

Calhoun, Craig. 2001. The Virtues of Inconsistency: Identity and Plurality in the Conceptualization of Europe. In *Constructing Europe's Identity—The External Dimension,* edited by Lars-Erik Cederman, 35–56. Boulder, Colo.: Lynne Rienner.

——. 2002. Imagining Solidarity: Cosmopolitanism, Constitutional Patriotism, and the Public Sphere. *Public Culture* 14, no. 1: 147–71.

Campbell, Donald T. 1958. Common Fate, Similarity, and Other Indices of the Status of Aggregates of Persons as Social Entities. *Behavioural Sciences* 3: 14–25.

Caporaso, James A., and Sidney Tarrow. 2009. Polanyi in Brussels: European Institutions and the Transnational Embedding of Markets. *International Organization* 63, no. 4: 593–620.

Caplanova, Anetta, Marta Orviska, and John Hudson. 2004. Eastern European Attitudes to Integration with Western Europe. *Journal of Common Market Studies* 42, no. 2: 271–288.

Casanova, José. 2006. Religion, European Secular Identities, and European Integration. In *Religion in an Expanding Europe,* edited by Timothy A. Byrnes and Peter J. Katzenstein, 65–92. Cambridge: Cambridge University Press.

Case, Holly. 2009. Being European: East and West. In *European Identity,* edited by Jeffrey T. Checkel and Peter J. Katzenstein, 111–31. Cambridge: Cambridge University Press.

Castano, Emanuele. 2004. European Identity: A Social-Psychological Perspective. In *Transnational Identities: Becoming European in the EU,* edited by Richard K. Herrmann, Thomas Risse, and Marilynn Brewer, 40–58. Lanham, Md.: Rowman and Littlefield.

Castano, Emanuele, Vincent Y. Yzerbyt, Marco P. Paladino, and Simona Sacchi. 2002. I Belong Therefore I Exist: Ingroup Identification, Ingroup Entitativity, and Ingroup Bias. *Personality and Social Psychology Bulletin* 28: 135–43.

Castiglione, Dario. 2009. Political Identity in a Community of Strangers. In *European Identity,* edited by Jeffrey T. Checkel and Peter J. Katzenstein, 29–51. Cambridge: Cambridge University Press.

Cederman, Lars-Erik. 2001. Political Boundaries and Identity Trade-offs. In *Constructing Europe's Identity—The External Dimension,* edited by Lars-Erik Cederman, 1–32. Boulder, Colo.: Lynne Rienner.

Chaiken, Shelly, Wendy Wood, and Alice H. Eagly. 1996. Principles of Persuasion. In *Social Psychology: Handbook of Basic Principles,* edited by E. T. Higgins and A. Kruglanski, 702–42. New York: Guilford Press.

Chandra, Kanchan. 2009. A Constructivist Dataset on Ethnicity and Institutions. In *Measuring Identity: A Guide for Social Scientists,* edited by Rawi Abdelal, Yoshiko M. Herrera, Alastair Iain Johnston, and Rose McDermott, 250–78. Cambridge: Cambridge University Press.

Checkel, Jeffrey T. 1997. International Norms and Domestic Politics: Bridging the Rationalist-Constructivist Divide. *European Journal of International Relations* 3, no. 4: 473–95.

——. 2001a. The Europeanization of Citizenship? In *Transforming Europe: Europeanization and Domestic Change,* edited by Maria Green Cowles, James A. Caporaso, and Thomas Risse, 180–97. Ithaca: Cornell University Press.

——. 2001b. Why Comply? Social Learning and European Identity Change. *International Organization* 55, no. 3: 553–88.

——, ed. 2005a. *International Institutions and Socialization in Europe.* Special issue of *International Organization* 59, no. 4. Cambridge: Cambridge University Press.

——. 2005b. International Institutions and Socialization in Europe: Introduction and Framework. *International Organization* 59, no. 4: 801–26.

Checkel, Jeffrey T., and Peter J. Katzenstein, eds. 2009a. *European Identity.* Cambridge: Cambridge University Press.

——. 2009b. The Politicization of European Identities. In *European Identity,* edited by Jeffrey T. Checkel and Peter J. Katzenstein, 1–25. Cambridge: Cambridge University Press.

Chilton, Paul, and Ruth Wodak, eds. 2002. *Focus: Identity Politics.* Special issue of *Journal of Language and Politics* 1, no. 1. Amsterdam: John Benjamins Publishing.

Churchill, Winston. 1953. Speech on 11 May. *House of Commons* 513: 895.

Cinnirella, Marco. 1997. Towards a European Identity? Interactions between the National and European Social Identities Manifested by University Students in Britain and Italy. *British Journal of Social Psychology* 36, no. 1: 19–31.

Citrin, Jack, and David O. Sears. 2009. Balancing National and Ethnic Identities: The Psychology of E Pluribus Unum. In *Measuring Identity: A Guide for Social Scientists,* edited by Rawi Abdelal, Yoshiko M. Herrera, Alastair Iain Johnston, and Rose McDermott, 145–74. Cambridge: Cambridge University Press.

Citrin, Jack, and John Sides. 2004. More than Nationals: How Identity Choice Matters in the New Europe. In *Transnational Identities: Becoming European in the EU,* edited by Richard K. Herrmann, Thomas Risse, and Marilynn Brewer, 161–85. Lanham, Md.: Rowman and Littlefield.

Connolly, William E. 1991. *Identity/Difference: Democratic Negotiations of Political Paradox*. Ithaca: Cornell University Press.

Council of the European Union. 2008. Consolidated Versions of the Treaty on European Union and the Treaty on the Functioning of the European Union [Lisbon Treaty]. Brussels: Council of the European Union, April 15.

Cowles, Maria Green, James A. Caporaso, and Thomas Risse, eds. 2001. *Transforming Europe: Europeanization and Domestic Change*. Ithaca: Cornell University Press.

Cram, Laura. 2009. Identity and European Integration: Diversity as a Source of Integration. *Nations and Nationalism* 15, no. 1: 109–28.

Crenshaw, Kimberlé. 1994. Mapping the Margins: Intersectionality, Identity Politics, and Violence against Women of Color. In *The Public Nature of Private Violence*, edited by Martha Fineman and Roxanne Mykitiuk, 93–118. New York: Routledge.

De Gaulle, Charles. 1950. Speech in Lille. *Discours et Messages* II (Dec. 11), Paris: 393.

Delhey, Jan. 2005. A Trade-off between Enlargement and Integration? An Analysis of Trust between EU Nationalities. WZB Discussion Paper. Berlin: Social Science Research Center Berlin (WZB).

——. 2007. Do Enlargements Make the European Union Less Cohesive? An Analysis of Trust between EU Nationalities. *Journal of Common Market Studies* 45, no. 2: 253–79.

Della Porta, Donatella. 2008. Another Europe: Social Movements and European Institutions. In *Back to Maastricht: Obstacles to Constitutional Reform within the EU Treaty (1991–2007)*, edited by Stefania Baroncelli, Carlo Spagnolo, and Leila Simona Talani, 383–407. Newcastle: Cambridge Scholars Publishing.

Deutsch, Karl W. 1953. *Nationalism and Social Communication*. Cambridge: MIT Press.

Deutsch, Karl W., et al. 1957. *Political Community and the North Atlantic Area: International Organization in the Light of Historical Experience*. Princeton: Princeton University Press.

De Vreese, Claes H. 2007. The EU as a Public Sphere. *Living Reviews in European Governance* 2, no. 3.

De Vreese, Claes H., Susan A. Banducci, Holli A. Semetko, and Hajo G. Boomgarden. 2006. The News Coverage of the 2004 European Parliamentary Election Campaign in 25 Countries. *European Union Politics* 7: 477–504.

De Vreese, Claes H., and Hajo G. Boomgarden. 2003. Valenced News Frames and Public Support for the EU. *Communications* 28: 361–81.

——. 2005. Projecting EU Referendums: Fear of Immigration and Support for European Integration. *European Union Politics* 6, no. 1: 59–82.

——. 2006. News, Political Knowledge, and Participation: The Differential Effects of New Media Exposure on Political Knowledge and Participation. *Acta Politica* 41: 317–41.

De Vreese, Claes H., and Anna Kandyla. 2009. News Framing and Public Support for a Common Foreign and Security Policy. *Journal of Common Market Studies* 47, no. 3: 453–81.

De Vries, Catherine E., and Erica E. Edwards. 2009. Taking Europe to Its Extremes: Extremist Parties and Public Euroscepticism. *Party Politics* 15, no. 1: 5–28.

Dewandre, Nicole, and Jacques Lenoble, eds. 1992. *L'Europe au soir du siècle: Identité et démocratie*. Paris: Editions Esprit.

Diez Medrano, Juan. 2003. *Framing Europe: Attitudes toward European Integration in Germany, Spain, and the United Kingdom*. Princeton: Princeton University Press.

——. 2009. The Public Sphere and the European Union's Political Identity. In *European Identity*, edited by Jeffrey T. Checkel and Peter J. Katzenstein, 81–107. Cambridge: Cambridge University Press.

Diez Medrano, Juan, and Paula Gutiérrez. 2001. Nested Identities: National and European Identity in Spain. *Ethnic and Racial Studies* 24: 753–78.

Diez, Thomas. 1999. *Die EU lesen.* Opladen: Leske and Budrich.

———. 2005. Constructing the Self and Changing Others: Reconsidering 'Normative Power Europe.' *Millenium* 33, no. 3: 613–36.

Doering-Manteuffel, Anselm. 1999. *Wie westlich sind die Deutschen? Amerikanisierung und Westernisierung im 20. Jahrhundert.* Göttingen: Vandenhoek and Ruprecht.

Doerr, Nicole. 2008. Listen Carefully: Democracy Brokers at the European Social Forums. PhD dissertation, Department of Social and Political Science, European University Institute, Florence.

———. 2009. Language and Democracy in Movement. *Social Movement Studies* 8, no. 2: 149–65.

Dolezal, Martin. 2008. Germany: The Dog That Didn't Bark. In *West European Politics in the Age of Globalization,* edited by Hanspeter Kriesi, Edgar Grande, Romain Lachat, Martin Dolezal, Simon Bornschier, and Timotheos Frey, 208–233. Cambridge: Cambridge University Press.

Drulak, Petr. 2006. Probably a Problem-Solving Regime, Perhaps a Rights-Based Union: European Integration in the Czech and Slovak Political Discourse. In *Questioning the EU Enlargement: Europe in Search of Identity,* edited by Helene Sjursen, 167–85. London: Routledge.

Duchêne, François. 1972. Europe's Role in World Peace. In *Europe Tomorrow: Sixteen Europeans Look Ahead,* edited by Richard Mayne, 32–47. London: Fontana/Collins.

Duchesne, Sophie, and Andre-Paul Frognier. 1995. Is There a European Identity? In *Public Opinion and Internationalized Governance,* edited by Oskar Niedermayer and Richard Sinnott, 193–226. Oxford: Oxford University Press.

Economist. 2008. Flags, Veils, and Sharia: Turkey's Future. July 19, 29–32.

Eder, Klaus, and Bernhard Giesen, eds. 1999. *European Citizenship and the National Legacies.* Oxford: Oxford University Press.

Eder, Klaus, and Cathleen Kantner. 2000. Transnationale Resonanzstrukturen in Europa: Eine Kritik der Rede vom Öffentlichkeitsdefizit. In *Die Europäisierung nationaler Gesellschaften: Sonderheft 40 der Kölner Zeitschrift für Soziologie und Sozialpsychologie,* edited by Maurizio Bach, 306–31. Wiesbaden: Westdeutscher Verlag.

Eisenstadt, Shmuel N., and Bernhard Giesen. 1995. The Construction of Collective Identity. *European Journal of Sociology* 36: 72–102.

Engelmann-Martin, Daniela. 2002. Identity, Norms and German Foreign Policy: The Social Construction of Ostpolitik and European Monetary Union. PhD dissertation, Department of Social and Political Sciences, European University Institute, Florence.

EOS Gallup Europe. 2001. Flash Eurobarometre 92 "Gouvernance." January–February. Brussels.

Erbe, Jessica. 2005. What Do the Papers Say? How Press Reviews Link National Media Arenas in Europe. *The Public* 12, no. 2: 75–92.

Eriksen, Erik O., and John Fossum. 2000. *Democracy in the European Union: Integration through Deliberation?* London: Routledge.

European Commission. 1973. Declaration on European Identity. General Report of the European Commission. Brussels: European Commission.

———. 2002. Eurobarometer 57. Spring 2002—EU 15 Report. October 21. Brussels: European Commission.

———. 2003. Flash Eurobarometer 140: Enlargement of the European Union. Brussels: European Commission.

———. 2004. Eurobarometer Spring 2004. Public Opinion in the European Union. Brussels: European Commission.

———. 2005. Eurobarometer 62, Oct.–Nov. 2004. Brussels: European Commission.

———. 2006a. Eurobarometer 65. Public Opinion in the European Union. Standard Eurobarometer. Brussels: European Commission.

———. 2006b. Eurobarometer 66. Public Opinion in the European Union. First Results. Brussels: European Commission.

———. 2007a. Eurobarometer 66. Public Opinion in the European Union. Standard Eurobarometer. Brussels: European Commission.

———. 2007b. Eurobarometer 67. Public Opinion in the European Union. Standard Eurobarometer. Brussels: European Commission.

———. 2007c. Eurobarometer 68. Public Opinion in the European Union. First Results. Brussels: European Commission.

———. 2008. Eurobarometer 69. Standard Eurobarometer. Brussels: European Commission.

———. 2009. Eurobarometer 70. Public Opinion in the European Union, First Results. Standard Eurobarometer. Brussels: European Commission.

European Council. 2003. A Secure Europe in a Better World—European Security Strategy. December 12. Brussels: European Institute for Security Studies.

European Parliament. 2009. Europeans and the Economic Crisis. Standard Eurobarometer (EB 71). Brussels: Directorate General for Communication.

Evans, Jocelyn A. J. 2007. The European Dimension in French Public Opinion. *Journal of European Public Policy* 14, no. 7: 1098–1116.

Evas, Tatjana. 2007. Elitist with a Russian Twist: Mass Media Discourses on European Constitutional Ratification in Estonia and Latvia. *Perspectives on European Politics and Society* 8, no. 3: 374–413.

Fairclough, Norman, and Ruth Wodak. 1997. Critical Discourse Analysis. In *Discourse as Social Interaction,* edited by Teun A. Van Dijk, 258–84. London: Sage.

Favell, Adrian. 2008. *Eurostars and Eurocities: Free Movement and Mobility in an Integrating Europe.* Oxford: Blackwell Publishing.

———. 2009. Immigration, Migration, and Free Movement in the Making of Europe. In *European Identity,* edited by Jeffrey T. Checkel and Peter J. Katzenstein, 167–89. Cambridge: Cambridge University Press.

Fearon, James D., and David D. Laitin. 2000. Violence and the Social Construction of Ethnic Identity. *International Organization* 54, no. 4: 845–77.

Fearon, James D., and Alexander Wendt. 2002. Rationalism v. Constructivism: A Skeptical View. In *Handbook of International Relations,* edited by Walter Carlsnaes, Thomas Risse, and Beth Simmons, 52–72. London: Sage.

Featherstone, Keith, and Claudio Radaelli, eds. 2003. *The Politics of Europeanization.* Oxford: Oxford University Press.

Fehl, Caroline. 2005. *Europäische Identitätsbildung in Abgrenzung von den USA? Eine Untersuchung des deutschen und britischen Mediendiskurses über das transatlantische Verhältnis.* Münster: LIT-Verlag.

Ferree, Myra Marx, William A. Gamson, Jürgen Gerhards, and Dieter Rucht. 2002. Four Models of the Public Sphere in Modern Democracies. *Theory and Society* 31, no. 3: 289–324.

Finnemore, Martha, and Kathryn Sikkink. 1998. International Norm Dynamics and Political Change. *International Organization* 52, no. 4: 887–917.

Fierke, Karin M., and Antje Wiener. 1999. Constructing Institutional Interests: EU and NATO Enlargement. *Journal of European Public Policy* 6, no. 5: 721–42.

Fischer, Joschka. 2000. From Confederacy to Federation: Thoughts on the Finality of European Integration. In *What Kind of Constitution for What Kind of Polity? Responses to Joschka Fischer,* edited by Christian Joerges, Yves Mény, and Joseph H. H. Weiler, 19–30. Florence: European University Institute.

Fiske, Susan, and Shelley Taylor. 1984. *Social Cognition*. New York: Random House.

Fligstein, Neil. 2008. *Euroclash: The EU, European Identity, and the Future of Europe*. Oxford: Oxford University Press.

——. 2009. Who Are the Europeans and How Does This Matter for Politics? In *European Identity*, edited by Jeffrey T. Checkel and Peter J. Katzenstein, 132–66. Cambridge: Cambridge University Press.

Flynn, Gregory, ed. 1995. *The Remaking of the Hexagon: The New France in the New Europe*. Boulder, Colo.: Westview.

Follesdal, Andreas, and Simon Hix. 2006. Why There Is a 'Democratic Deficit' in the EU: A Response to Majone and Moravcsik. *Journal of Common Market Studies* 44, no. 3: 533–62.

Fondation pour l'Innovation Politique. 2009. Perception Parlement Européen. Paris: Fondation pour l'Innovation Politique.

Fondermann, Tonia. 2006. National, Post-National, and European Identities in Germany. Master thesis, Otto Suhr Institute of Political Science, Freie Universität Berlin, Berlin.

Fossum, John Erik, and Philip Schlesinger, eds. 2007. *The European Union and the Public Sphere: A Communicative Space in the Making?* London: Routledge.

Franklin, Mark, and Cees Van der Eijk. 2006. The Sleeping Giant: Potential for Political Mobilization of Disaffection in Europe. In *European Elections and Domestic Politics: Lessons from the Past and Scenarios for the Future*, edited by Wouter Van der Brug and Cees Van der Eijk, 189–208. Notre Dame, Ind.: University of Notre Dame Press,

Fraser, Nancy. 1997. *Justice Interruptus*. London: Routledge.

Front National. 2007. Pétition Nationale: Non à la Turquie en Europe, Paris: http://www.frontnational.com/pdf/petitionturquie.pdf.

Fuchs, Dieter, Isabelle Guinaudeau, and Sophia Schubert. 2009. National Identity, European Identity, and Euroscepticism. In *Euroscepticism: Images of Europe among Mass Publics and Political Elites*, edited by Dieter Fuchs, Raul Magni-Berton, and Antoine Roger, 91–112. Opladen: Barbara Budrich Publishers.

Fuchs, Dieter, Raul Magni-Berton, and Antoine Roger, eds. 2009. *Euroscepticism: Images of Europe among Mass Publics and Political Elites*. Opladen: Barbara Budrich Publishing.

Gabel, Matthew. 1998. *Interests and Integration: Market Liberalization, Public Opinion, and European Union*. Ann Arbor: University of Michigan Press.

——. 2003. Public Support for the European Parliament. *Journal of Common Market Studies* 41, no. 2: 289–308.

Gadamer, Hans Georg. 1965. *Wahrheit und Methode*. Tübingen: J. C. B. Mohr.

Gamson, William A. 1992. *Talking Politics*. Cambridge: Cambridge University Press.

George, Stephen, ed. 1992. *Britain and the European Community: The Politics of Semi-Detachment*. Oxford: Clarendon Press.

——. 1994. *An Awkward Partner: Britain in the European Community*. 2nd ed. Oxford: Oxford University Press.

Gerhards, Jürgen. 1993. Westeuropäische Integration und die Schwierigkeiten der Entstehung einer europäischen Öffentlichkeit. *Zeitschrift für Soziologie* 22: 96–110.

——. 2000. Europäisierung von Ökonomie und Politik und die Trägheit der Entstehung einer europäischen Öffentlichkeit. In *Die Europäisierung nationaler Gesellschaften: Sonderheft 40 der Kölner Zeitschrift für Soziologie und Sozialpsychologie*, edited by Maurizio Bach, 277–305. Wiesbaden: Westdeutscher Verlag.

———. 2003. Identifikation mit Europa: Einige begriffliche: Vorklärungen. In *Entstaatlichung und soziale Sicherheit: Verhandlungen des 31. Kongresses der Deutschen Gesellschaft für Soziologie in Leipzig*, edited by Jutta Allmendinger, 467–474. Opladen: Leske and Budrich.

———. 2008a. Die Sprachkonstellation in der Europäischen Union und die Folgen für den europäischen Integrationsprozess. Unpublished manuscript. Berlin: Freie Universität Berlin, Institut für Soziologie.

———. 2008b. Free to Move? The Acceptance of Free Movement of Labour and Non-Discrimination among Citizens of Europe. *European Societies* 10, no. 1: 121–40.

———. 2008c. Transnationales linguistisches Kapital der Bürger und der Prozess der europäischen Integration. Berliner Studien zur Soziologie Europas 17. Berlin: Freie Universität Berlin, Institut für Soziologie.

Gerhards, Jürgen, and Silke Hans. 2008. Die Grenzen Europas aus der Sicht der Bürger. *Aus Politik und Zeitgeschichte* nos. 35–36: 6–13.

———. 2009. Türkei unerwünscht? Eine Untersuchung der Einstellungen der Bürger in den 27 Mitgliedsländern der EU zum Beitritt der Türkei. Berliner Studien zur Soziologie Europas 18. Berlin: Freie Universität Berlin, Institut für Soziologie.

Gerhards, Jürgen, and Michael Hölscher. 2005. *Kulturelle Unterschied in der Europäischen Union: Ein Vergleich zwischen Mitgliedsländern, Beitrittskandidaten und der Türkei.* Wiesbaden: VS Verlag für Sozialwissenschaften.

Gerhards, Jürgen, Holger Lengfeld, and Jürgen Schupp. 2007. Arbeitsmarkt in Deutschland: Hohe Akzeptanz der Chancengleichheit für europäische Bürger. *Wochenbericht des DIW Berlin* 74, no. 4: 37–42.

Gerhards, Jürgen, Anke Offerhaus, and Jochen Roose. 2009. Wer ist verantwortlich? Die Europäische Union, ihre Nationalstaaten und die massenmediale Attribution von Verantwortung für Erfolge und Misserfolge. In *Politik in der Mediendemokratie. PVS-Sonderheft*, edited by Barbara Pfetsch and Frank Marcinkowski, 529–58. Wiesbaden: VS Verlag für Sozialwissenschaften.

Giannakopoulos, Angelos, and Konstadinos Maras. 2005. Der Türkei-Diskurs im Europäischen Parlament 1996–2003. In *Die Türkei-Debatte in Europa: Ein Vergleich*, edited by Angelos Giannakopoulos and Konstadinos Maras, 21–34. Wiesbaden: VS Verlag für Sozialwissenschaften.

Giddens, Anthony. 1984. *The Constitution of Society: Outline of the Theory of Structuration.* Berkeley: University of California Press.

Giesen, Bernhard. 1993. *Die Intellektuellen und die Nation: Eine deutsche Achsenzeit.* Frankfurt am Main: Suhrkamp.

———. 1999. *Kollektive Identität: Die Intellektuellen und die Nation 2.* Frankfurt am Main: Suhrkamp.

Giscard d'Estaing, Valéry. 2004. A Better European Bridge to Turkey. *Financial Times*, Nov. 24.

Göler, Daniel. 2006. *Deliberation—Ein Zukunftsmodell europäischer Entscheidungsfindung? Analyse der Beratungen des Verfassungskonvents 2002–2003.* Baden-Baden: Nomos.

Goren, Nimrod, and Amikam Nachmani, eds. 2007. *The Importance of Being European: Turkey, the EU and the Middle East, Conference and Lecture Series.* Jerusalem: European Forum at the Hebrew University.

Grabbe, Heather. 2006. *The EU's Transformative Power—Europeanization through Conditionality in Central and Eastern Europe.* Houndmills, Basingstoke: Palgrave Macmillan.

Green, David Michael. 2007. *The Europeans: Political Identity in an Emerging Polity.* Boulder, Colo.: Lynne Rienner.

Greven, Michael Th. 2000. Can the European Union Finally Become a Democracy? In *Democracy beyond the State?* edited by Michael Th. Greven and Louis W. Pauly, 35–61. Lanham, Md.: Rowman and Littlefield.

Grieco, Joseph M. 1995. The Maastricht Treaty, Economic and Monetary Union, and the Neo-Realist Research Programme. *Review of International Studies* 21, no. 1: 21–40.

Grimm, Dieter. 1995. Does Europe Need a Constitution? *European Law Journal* 1, no. 3: 282–302.

Guérot, Ulrike. 1996. *Die PS und Europa: Eine Untersuchung der europapolitischen Programmatik der französischen Sozialisten 1971–1995.* Bochum: Universitätsverlag Brockmeyer.

Haas, Ernst B. 1958. *The Uniting of Europe: Political, Social, and Economic Forces 1950–57.* Stanford: Stanford University Press.

Habermas, Jürgen. 1980 (1962). *Strukturwandel der Öffentlichkeit: Untersuchungen zu einer Kategorie der bürgerlichen Gesellschaft.* Darmstadt: Luchterhand.

——. 1981. *Theorie des kommunikativen Handelns.* 2 vols. Frankfurt am Main: Suhrkamp.

——. 1992. *Faktizität und Geltung: Beiträge zur Diskurstheorie des Rechts und des demokratischen Rechtsstaats.* Frankfurt am Main: Suhrkamp.

——. 1994. Staatsbürgerschaft und nationale Identität. In *Projekt Europa: Postnationale Identität: Grundlage für eine europäische Demokratie,* edited by Nicole Dewandre and Jacques Lenoble, 11–29. Berlin: Scheltzky & Jeep.

——. 1996a. Der europäische Nationalstaat—Zu Vergangenheit und Zukunft von Souveränität und Staatsbürgerschaft. In Habermas, *Die Einbeziehung des Anderen,* 128–53. Frankfurt am Main: Suhrkamp.

——. 1996b. *Die Einbeziehung des Anderen.* Frankfurt am Main: Suhrkamp.

——. 2006. *The Divided West.* Cambridge: Polity Press.

Habermas, Jürgen, and Jacques Derrida. 2005. Feb. 15, or, What Binds Europeans Together: Plea for a Common Foreign Policy, Beginning in Core Europe. In *Old Europe, New Europe, Core Europe: Transatlantic Relations after the Iraq War,* edited by Daniel Levy, Max Pensky, and John Torpey, 3–13. London: Verso.

Haftendorn, Helga, Robert O. Keohane, and Celeste A. Wallander, eds. 1999. *Imperfect Unions: Security Institutions over Time and Space.* Oxford: Oxford University Press.

Hahn, Irene. 2007. *Polen und 'Europa': Europabilder und nationale Identität im Beitrittsprozess zur Europäischen Union.* Edited by Centrum im. Willy Brandta. Wroclaw: Oficyna Wydawnicza ATUT—Wroclawskie Wydawnictowo Oswiatowe.

Hainmueller, Jens, and Michael J. Hiscox. 2007. Educated Preferences: Explaining Attitudes toward Immigration in Europe. *International Organization* 61, no. 2: 399–442.

Haus, Leah. 2007. Europeanizaton, Education and National School Curricula: The Role of Historical Legacies in Explaining Policy Variation in England and France. Paper Presented at the *Biannual Meeting of the European Union Studies Association.* Montreal, Canada, May 17–19.

Hayward, Jack. 2007. *Fragmented France: Two Centuries of Disputed Identity.* Oxford: Oxford University Press.

Hehir, J. Bryan. 2006. The Old Church and the New Europe: Charting the Changes. In *Religion in an Expanding Europe,* edited by Timothy A. Byrnes and Peter J. Katzenstein, 93–116. Cambridge: Cambridge University Press.

Hellmann, Gunther. 1996. Good-bye Bismarck? The Foreign Policy of Contemporary Germany. *Mershon Review of International Studies* 40, no. 1: 1–39.

Herrmann, Richard K., and Marilynn B. Brewer. 2004. Identities and Institutions: Becoming European in the EU. In *Transnational Identities: Becoming European in the EU,* edited by Richard K. Herrmann, Thomas Risse, and Marilynn B. Brewer, 1–22. Lanham, Md.: Rowman and Littlefield.

Herrmann, Richard K., Thomas Risse, and Marilynn B. Brewer, eds. 2004. *Transnational Identities: Becoming European in the EU.* Lanham, Md.: Rowman and Littlefield.

Hill, Christopher. 1993. The Capability Expectation Gap, or Conceptualizing Europe's International Role. *Journal of Common Market Studies* 31, no. 4: 305–28.

Hix, Simon. 2008. *What's Wrong with the European Union and How to Fix It.* Cambridge: Polity Press.

Hodess, Robin. 1998. News Coverage of European Politics: A Comparison of Change in Britain and Germany. In *Europapolitische Grundverständnisse im Wandel: Analysen und Konsequenzen für die politische Bildung,* edited by Mathias Jopp, Andreas Maurer, and Heinrich Schneider, 449–472. Bonn: Europa Union Verlag.

Holmes, Douglas R. 2000. *Integral Europe—Fast Capitalism, Multiculturalism, Neofascism.* Princeton: Princeton University Press.

——. 2009. Experimental Identities (after Maastricht). In *European Identity,* edited by Jeffrey T. Checkel and Peter J. Katzenstein, 52–80. Cambridge: Cambridge University Press.

Hooghe, Liesbet. 2001. *The European Commission and the Integration of Europe: Images of Governance.* Cambridge: Cambridge University Press.

——. 2005. Many Roads Lead to International Norms, But Few Via International Socialization: A Case Study of the European Commission. *International Organization* 59, no. 4: 861–98.

Hooghe, Liesbet, Jing Jing Huo, and Gary Marks. 2007. Does Occupation Shape Attitudes on Europe? Benchmarking Validity and Parsimony. *Acta Politica* 42, nos. 2–3: 329–51.

Hooghe, Liesbet, and Gary Marks. 2001. *Multi-Level Governance and European Integration.* Lanham, Md.: Rowman and Littlefield.

——. 2004. Does Identity or Economic Rationality Drive Public Opinion on European Integration? *PSOnline www.apsanet.org* (July): 1–5.

——. 2005. Calculation, Community, and Cues. Public Opinion on European Integration. *European Union Politics* 6, no. 4: 419–43.

——, eds. 2007. *Understanding Euroscepticism.* Special issue of *Acta Politica* 42. Houndmills, Basingstoke: Palgrave Macmillan.

——. 2008. A Postfunctionalist Theory of European Integration: From Permissive Consensus to Constraining Dissensus. *British Journal of Political Science* 39, no. 1: 1–23.

Howorth, Jolyon. 2007. *Security and Defense Policy in the European Union.* Houndmills, Basingstoke: Palgrave Macmillan.

Huntington, Samuel. 1996. *The Clash of Civilizations and the Remaking of World Order.* New York: Simon and Schuster.

Hyde-Price, Adrian. 2006. 'Normative' Power Europe: A Realist Critique. *Journal of European Public Policy* 13, no. 2: 217–34.

Icener, Erhan. 2007a. Explaining European Union Enlargement: A Comparative Study of Romania and Turkey. PhD dissertation, Faculty of Arts, Humanities, and Social Sciences, Queen's University, Belfast.

——. 2007b. Privileged Partnership: An Alternative Final Destination for Turkey's Integration with the European Union? *Perspectives on European Politics and Society* 8, no. 4: 415–38.

Ichijo, Atsuko. 2004. *Scottish Nationalism and the Idea of Europe: Concepts of Europe and the Nation.* London: Routledge.

Imig, Douglas, and Sidney Tarrow, eds. 2001. *Contentious Europeans: Politics and Protest in an Emerging Polity.* Lanham, Md.: Rowman and Littlefield.

Jachtenfuchs, Markus. 2002. *Die Konstruktion Europas: Verfassungsideen und institutionelle Entwicklung.* Baden-Baden: Nomos.

Jachtenfuchs, Markus, Thomas Diez, and Sabine Jung. 1998. Which Europe? Conflicting Models of a Legitimate European Political Order. *European Journal of International Relations* 4, no. 4: 409–45.

Jáuregui, Pablo. 1999. National Pride and the Meaning of 'Europe': A Comparative Study of Britain and Spain. In *Whose Europe? The Turn towards Democracy,* edited by Dennis Smith and Sue Wright, 257–87. Oxford: Blackwell.

Jentges, Erich, Hans-Jörg Trenz, and Regina Vetters. 2007. Von der politischen zur sozialen Konstitutionalisierung Europas: Verfassungsgebung als Katalysator europäischer Vergesellschaftung? *Politische Vierteljahresschrift* 48, no. 4: 705–729.

Johnston, Alastair Ian. 2005. Conclusions and Extensions: Toward Mid-Range Theorizing and beyond Europe. *International Organization* 59, no. 4: 1013–44.

Jolly, Seth Kincaid. 2007. The Europhile Fringe? Regionalist Party Support for European Integration. *European Union Politics* 8, no. 1: 109–30.

Jupille, Joseph, and David Leblang. 2007. Voting for Change: Calculation, Community, and Euro Referendums. *International Organization* 61, no. 4: 763–82.

Kaelble, Hartmut. 2009. Identification with Europe and Politicization of the EU since the 1980s. In *European Identity,* edited by Jeffrey T. Checkel and Peter J. Katzenstein, 193–212. Cambridge: Cambridge University Press.

Kagan, Robert. 2003. *Of Paradise and Power: America and Europe in the New World Order.* New York: A. Knopf.

Kaiser, Wolfram. 2007. *Christian Democracy and the Origins of the European Union.* Cambridge: Cambridge University Press.

Kantner, Cathleen. 2004. *Kein modernes Babel: Kommunikative Voraussetzungen europäischer Öffentlichkeit.* Wiesbaden: VS Verlag für Sozialwissenschaften.

——. 2006a. Collective Identity as Shared Ethical Self-Understanding: The Case of the Emerging European Identity. *European Journal of Social Theory* 9, no. 4: 501–23.

——. 2006b. Die thematische Verschränkung nationaler Öffentlichkeiten in Europa und die Qualität transnationaler politischer Kommunikation. In *Demokratie in der Mediengesellschaft,* edited by Kurt Imhof, Roger Blum, Heinz Bonfadelli, and Ottfried Jarren, 145–60. Wiesbaden: VS Verlag für Sozialwissenschaften.

——. 2009. Transnational Identity-Discourse in the Mass Media: Humanitarian Military Interventions and the Emergence of a European Identity (1990–2006). Habilitation thesis, Otto Suhr Institute for Political Sciences, Freie Universität Berlin.

Kantner, Cathleen, Amelie Kutter, and Swantje Renfordt. 2008. The Perception of the EU as an Emerging Security Actor in Media Debates on Humanitarian and Military Interventions (1990–2006). Recon Online Working Paper 2008/19. Oslo: ARENA, University of Oslo.

Katzenstein, Peter J., ed. 1996. *The Culture of National Security: Norms and Identity in World Politics.* New York: Columbia University Press.

——, ed. 1997. *Tamed Power: Germany in Europe.* Ithaca: Cornell University Press.

——. 2006. Multiple Modernities as Limits to Secular Europeanization? In *Religion in an Expanding Europe,* edited by Timothy A. Byrnes and Peter J. Katzenstein, 1–33. Cambridge: Cambridge University Press.

Katzenstein, Peter J., and Robert O. Keohane, eds. 2006. *Anti-Americanisms in World Politics.* Ithaca: Cornell University Press.

Keating, Michael. 1996. *Nations against the State: The New Politics of Nationalism in Quebec, Catalonia and Scotland.* London: Macmillan.

Kessler, Alan E., and Gary P. Freeman. 2007. Public Opinion in the EU on Immigration from Outside the Community. *Journal of Common Market Studies* 43, no. 4: 825–50.

Kevin, Deidre. 2001. Coverage of the European Parliament Elections of 1999: National Public Spheres and Debates. *Javnost. The Public* 8, no. 1: 21–38.

Kielmansegg, Peter Graf. 1996. Integration und Demokratie. In *Europäische Integration,* edited by Markus Jachtenfuchs and Beate Kohler-Koch, 47–71. Opladen: Leske and Budrich.

Kleine, Mareike. 2007. Leadership in the European Convention. *Journal of European Public Policy* 14, no. 8: 1227–48.

Klotz, Audie, and Cecelia Lynch. 2007. *Strategies for Research in Constructivist International Relations.* Armonk, N.Y.: M. E. Sharpe.

Knopf, Hans Joachim. 2003. Britain and European Integration between 1950 and 1993: Towards a European Identity? PhD dissertation, Department of Social and Political Sciences, European University Institute, Florence.

Knorr, Antje. 2006. Europäische Öffentlichkeit und transnationale Kommunikation im sicherheitspolitischen Bereich: Eine Medienanalyse des Golf-, Kosovo- und Irak-Krieges, PhD dissertation, Fachbereich Politik- und Sozialwissenschaften, Freie Universität Berlin.

Koenig-Archibugi, Mathias. 2004. Explaining Government Preferences for Institutional Change in EU Foreign and Security Policy. *International Organization* 54, no. 1: 137–74.

Kohler-Koch, Beate. 1994. Changing Patterns of Interest Intermediation in the European Union. *Government and Opposition* 29, no. 2: 166-80.

———. 1997. Organized Interests in European Integration: The Evolution of a New Type of Governance? In *Participation in Policy-making in the European Union,* edited by Helen Wallace and Alasdair R. Young, 42–68. Oxford: Clarendon Press.

Koopmans, Ruud. 2004. The Transformation of Political Mobilisation and Communication in European Public Spheres. Integrated Report: Cross-National, Cross-Issue, Cross-Time. Berlin: Europub.com.

———. 2007. Who Inhabits the European Public Sphere? Winners and Losers, Supporters and Opponents in Europeanised Political Debates. *European Journal of Political Research* 46: 183–210.

Koopmans, Ruud, and Jessica Erbe. 2004. Towards a European Public Sphere? *Innovation: The European Journal of Social Science Research* 17, no. 2: 97–118.

Koopmans, Ruud, and Paul Statham, eds. 2010. *The Making of a European Public Sphere: The Europeanisation of Media Discourse and Political Contention.* Cambridge: Cambridge University Press.

Koopmans, Ruud, and Ann Zimmermann. 2010. Transnational Political Communication on the Internet: Comparing Search Engine Results and Hyperlink Networks to the Print Media. In *The Making of a European Public Sphere: The Europeanisation of Media Discourse and Political Contention,* edited by Ruud Koopmans and Paul Statham, 222–59. Cambridge: Cambridge University Press.

Kratochwil, Friedrich. 1989. *Rules, Norms, and Decisions.* Cambridge: Cambridge University Press.

Kraus, Peter A. 2008. *A Union of Diversity: Language, Identity, and Polity-Building in Europe.* Cambridge: Cambridge University Press.

Kriesi, Hanspeter, Edgar Grande, Romain Lachat, Martin Dolezal, Simon Bornschier, and Timotheos Frey. 2006. Globalization and the Transformation of the National

Political Space: Six European Countries Compared. *European Journal of Political Research* 45: 921–56.

——. 2008. *West European Politics in the Age of Globalization:* Cambridge: Cambridge University Press.

Krzeminski, Ireneusz. 2001. The National Identity and European Consciousness of Poles. In *National and European Identities in EU Enlargement: Views from Central and Eastern Europe,* edited by Petr Drulak, 57–68. Prague: Institute of International Relations.

Krzyzanowski, Michal. 2003. 'My European Feelings Are Not Only Based on the Fact That I Live in Europe': On the New Mechanisms in European and National Identification Patterns Emerging under the Influence of EU Enlargement. *Journal of Language and Politics* 2, no. 1: 175–204.

——. 2008. *Becoming European: Discourses of Identity and Social Change in Polish Politics after 1989.* Amsterdam: John Benjamins.

Kucia, Marek. 1999. Public Opinion in Central Europe and EU Accession: The Czech Republic and Poland. *Journal of Common Market Studies* 37, no. 1: 143–52.

Kufer, Astrid. 2009. Images of Europe—The Meaning and Perception of 'Europe' by Citizens of EU Member States. In *Euroscepticism: Images of Europe among Mass Publics and Political Elites,* edited by Dieter Fuchs, Raul Magni-Berton, and Antoine Roger, 35–53. Opladen: Barbara Budrich Publishers.

Kumar, Krishan. 2003. Britain, England, and Europe: Cultures in Contraflow. *European Journal of Social Theory* 6, no. 1: 5–23.

Kutter, Amelie. 2007. Petitioner or Partner? Constructions of European Integration in Polish Print Media Debates on the EU Constitutional Treaty. In *Discourse and Contemporary Social Change,* edited by Norman Fairclough, Guiseppina Cortese, and Patrizia Ardizzone, 433–57. Bern: Peter Lang.

——. 2009. EU Polity-Building and the Dynamics of Translation: Studying Transnational Dialogue in the Polish and French Media Debate on the EU Constitution. PhD dissertation, European University Viadrina Frankfurt/Oder, Frankfurt/Oder.

Laclau, Ernesto. 1996. Why Do 'Empty Signifiers' Matter to Politics? In Laclau, *Emancipation(s),* 36–46. London: Verso.

Laffan, Brigid. 2004. The European Union and Its Institutions as 'Identity Builders.' In *Transnational Identities: Becoming European in the EU,* edited by Richard K. Herrmann, Thomas Risse, and Marilynn Brewer, 75–96. Lanham, Md.: Rowman and Littlefield.

Laffan, Brigid, Rory O'Donnell, and Michael Smith. 2000. *Europe's Experimental Union: Rethinking Integration.* London: Routledge.

Lahav, Gallya. 2004. *Immigration and Politics in the New Europe: Reinventing Borders.* Cambridge: Cambridge University Press.

Lahav, Gallya, and Anthony M. Messina. 2007. The Limits of European Immigration Policy: Elite Opinion and Agendas within the European Parliament. *Journal of Common Market Studies* 43, no. 4: 851–875.

Landfried, Christine. 2004. Das Entstehen einer europäischen Öffentlichkeit. In *Europäische Öffentlichkeit,* edited by Claudio Franzius and Ulrich K. Preuß, 123–137. Baden-Baden: Nomos.

Langenbucher, Wolfgang R., and Michael Latzer, eds. 2006. *Europäische Offentlichkeit und medialer Wandel.* Wiesbaden: VS Verlag für Sozialwissenschaften.

Laurent, Annie, and Nicolas Sauger, eds. 2005. *Le référendum de ratification du Traité Constitutionel Européen du 29 Mai 2005: Comprendre le 'Non' Francais. Cahiers du Cevipof* 42. Paris.

Lavenex, Sandra. 2001. *The Europeanisation of Refugee Policies: Between Human Rights and Internal Security.* Aldershot, U.K.: Ashgate.

Lewis, Jeffrey. 1998. Constructing Interests: The Committee of Permanent Representatives and Decision-Making in the European Union. PhD dissertation, Department of Political Science, University of Wisconsin–Madison.

——. 2005. Socialization and Everyday Decision Making in the European Union. *International Organization* 59, no. 4: 937–71.

Liebert, Ulrike, ed. 2007a. *Europe in Contention: Debating the Constitutional Treaty.* Special issue of *Perspectives on European Politics and Society* 8, no. 3. London: Routledge.

——. 2007b. Introduction: Structuring Political Conflict about Europe: National Media in Transnational Discourse Analysis. *Perspectives on European Politics and Society* 8, no. 3: 235–60.

Liebert, Ulrike, and Stefanie Sifft. 2003. *Gendering Europeanisation.* Brussels: P.I.E.—Peter Lang.

Lipinski, Artur. 2010. Europe as a Symbolic Resource: On the Discursive Space of Political Struggles in Poland. KFG Working Paper Series 10, Berlin: Research College "The Transformative Power of Europe." Freie Universität Berlin.

Lucht, Jens, and David Tréfas. 2006. Hat Europa eine Identität? Eine zeitreihenbasierte Untersuchung der öffentlichen Kommunikation von 1951 bis 2005. fög discussion papers, DI-2006–0001. Zürich: Universität Zürich.

Luhmann, Niklas. 1971. Öffentliche Meinung. In Luhmann, *Politische Planung: Aufsätze zur Soziologie von Politik und Verwaltung,* 9–34. Opladen: Westdeutscher Verlag.

——. 2000. *Die Politik der Gesellschaft.* Frankfurt am Main: Suhrkamp.

Luna-Arocas, Roberto, Gustavo Guzmán, Ismael Quintanilla, and Minoo Farhangmehre. 2001. The Euro and European Identity: The Spanish and Portuguese Cases. *Journal of Economic Psychology* 42, no. 4: 441–60.

Lundgren, Asa. 2006. The Case of Turkey: Are Some Candidates More 'European' Than Others? In *Questioning EU Enlargement: Europe in Search of Identity,* edited by Helene Sjursen, 121–41. London: Routledge.

Lyon, David. 1991. British Identity Cards: The Unpalatable Logic of European Membership? *Political Quarterly* 62, no. 3: 377–85.

Maatsch, Sönke. 2007. The Struggle to Control Meanings: The French Debate on the European Constitution in the Mass Media. *Perspectives on European Politics and Society* 8, no. 3: 261–80.

Mach, Zdzislaw, and Grzegorz Pozarlik. 2008. Collective Identity Formation in the Process of EU Enlargement: Defeating the Inclusive Paradigm of a European Democracy? RECON Online Working Paper. Oslo: ARENA, University of Oslo.

Madeker, Ellen. 2008. *Türkei und europäische Identität: Eine wissenssoziologische Analyse der Debatte um den EU-Beitritt.* Wiesbaden: VS Verlag für Sozialwissenschaften.

Magen, Amichai, Michael McFaul, and Thomas Risse, eds. 2009. *Promoting Democracy and the Rule of Law. American and European Strategies.* Houndmills, Basingstoke: Palgrave-Macmillan.

Magnette, Paul, and Kalypso Nicolaides. 2004. The European Convention: Bargaining in the Shadow of Rhetoric. *West European Politics* 27, no. 3: 381–404.

Majone, Giandomenico. 1996. *Regulating Europe.* London: Routledge.

——. 1998. Europe's Democratic Deficit. *European Law Journal* 4, no. 1: 5–28.

Manners, Ian. 2002. Normative Power Europe: A Contradiction in Terms? *Journal of Common Market Studies* 40, no. 2: 235–58.

——. 2006. Normative Power Europe Reconsidered: Beyond the Crossroads. *Journal of European Public Policy* 13, no. 2: 182–99.

March, James G., and Johan P. Olsen. 1998. The Institutional Dynamics of International Political Orders. *International Organization* 52, no. 4: 943–69.

Marcussen, Martin, Thomas Risse, Daniela Engelmann-Martin, Hans-Joachim Knopf, and Klaus Roscher. 1999. Constructing Europe: The Evolution of French, British, and German Nation-State Identities. *Journal of European Public Policy* 6, no. 4: 614–33.

Marks, Gary. 1999. Territorial Identities in the European Union. In *Regional Integration and Democracy: Expanding on the European Experience,* edited by Jeffrey J. Anderson, 69–91. Lanham, Md.: Rowman and Littlefield.

Marks, Gary, and Liesbet Hooghe. 2003. National Identity and Support for European Integration. Discussion Paper. Berlin: Wissenschaftszentrum Berlin für Sozialforschung.

Marks, Gary, and Marco R. Steenbergen. 2004. *European Integration and Political Conflict.* Cambridge: Cambridge University Press.

Martinotti, Guido, and Sonia Steffanizzi. 1995. Europeans and the Nation-State. In *Public Opinion and Internationalized Governance,* edited by Oskar Niedermayer and Richard Sinnott, 163–89. Oxford: Oxford University Press.

Maull, Hanns W. 1990. Germany and Japan: The New Civilian Powers. *Foreign Affairs* 69, no. 5: 91–106.

McCall, Leslie. 2005. The Complexity of Intersectionality. *Signs: Journal of Women in Culture and Society* 30, no. 3: 1771–1800.

McLaren, Lauren. 2001. Immigration and the New Politics of Inclusion and Exclusion in the European Union: The Effect of Elites and the EU on Individual-Level Opinions Regarding European and Non-European Immigrants. *European Journal of Political Research* 39, no. 1: 81–108.

——. 2004. Opposition to European Integration and Fear of Loss of National Identity: Debunking a Basic Assumption regarding Hostility to the Integration Project. *European Journal of Political Research* 43, no. 6: 895–911.

——. 2006. *Identity, Interests and Attitudes to European Integration.* Houndmills, Basingstoke: Palgrave Macmillan.

——. 2007a. Explaining Mass-Level Euroscepticism: Identity, Interests, and Institutional Distrust. *Acta Politica* 42, nos. 2–3: 233–51.

——. 2007b. Explaining Opposition to Turkish Membership in the EU. *European Union Politics* 8, no. 2: 251–78.

McManus-Czubinska, Clare, William L. Miller, Radoslaw Markowski, and Jacek Wasilewski. 2003. Understanding Dual Identities in Poland. *Political Studies* 51, no. 1: 121–43.

McNair, Brian. 2000. *Journalism and Democracy: An Evaluation of the Political Public Sphere.* London: Routledge.

McNamara, Kathleen R. 1998. *The Currency of Ideas: Monetary Politics in the European Union.* Ithaca: Cornell University Press.

Meinhof, Ulrike Hanna. 2004. Europe Viewed from Below: Agents, Victims, and the Threat of the Other. In *Transnational Identities: Becoming European in the EU,* edited by Richard K. Herrmann, Thomas Risse, and Marilynn B. Brewer, 214–44. Lanham, Md.: Rowman and Littlefield.

Meyer, Christoph. 2002. *Europäische Öffentlichkeit als Kontrollsphäre: Die Europäische Kommission, die Medien und politische Verantwortung.* Berlin: Vistas.

——. 2007. The Constitutional Treaty Debates as Revelatory Mechanisms: Insights for Public Sphere Research and Re-Launch Attempts. RECON Online Working Paper, July. Oslo: ARENA, University of Oslo.

Meyer, Jan-Henrik. 2008. The Fall and Rise of the European Public Sphere, 1969–1991: Path Dependent Responses to European Integration. In *Europa Vicina e Lontana: Idee e Percorsi Dell'Integrazione Europea,* edited by Federica Di Sarcina, Laura Grazi, and Laura Schichilone, 317–340. Florence: Centro Editoriale Toscano.

——. 2009. Transnational Communication in the European Public Sphere. In *The History of the European Union: Origins of a Trans- and Supranational Polity 1950–1972*, edited by Wolfram Kaiser, Brigitte Leucht, and Morten Rasmussen, 110–28. London: Routledge.

Michnik, Adam. 2003. What Europe Means for Poland. *Journal of Democracy* 14, no. 4: 128–136.

Mitterrand, François. 1986. *Réflexions sur la politique extérieure de la France— introduction à vingt-cinq discours*. Paris: Fayard.

——. 1992. *Le Monde,* Sept. 4.

Mollet, Guy. 1947. *Le Populaire,* Sept. 18.

Moravcsik, Andrew. 1997. Taking Preferences Seriously: A Liberal Theory of International Politics. *International Organization* 51, no. 4: 513–53.

——. 1998. *The Choice for Europe: Social Purpose and State Power from Rome to Maastricht*. Ithaca: Cornell University Press.

——. 2002. In Defence of the 'Democratic Deficit': Reassessing Legitimacy in the European Union. *Journal of Common Market Studies* 40, no. 4: 603–24.

Morgenthau, Hans J. 1993 (1948). *Politics among Nations*. Brief edition, revised by Kenneth W. Thompson. New York: McGraw-Hill.

Müller-Peters, Anke. 1998. The Significance of National Pride and National Identity to the Attitude toward the Single European Currency: A Europe-Wide Comparison. *Journal of Economic Psychology* 19: 701–19.

——. 2001. *Psychologie des Euro: Die Währung zwischen nationaler Identität und europäischer Integration*. Lengerich: Pabst Science Publishers.

Neidhardt, Friedhelm. 1994. Öffentlichkeit, öffentliche Meinung, soziale Bewegungen. In *Öffentlichkeit, öffentliche Meinung, soziale Bewegungen,* edited by Friedhelm Neidhardt, 7–41. Opladen: Westdeutscher Verlag.

Neller, Katja. 2006. *DDR-Nostalgie: Dimensionen der Orientierungen der Ostdeutschen gegenüber der ehemaligen DDR, ihre Ursachen und politischen Konnotationen*. Wiesbaden: VS Verlag für Sozialwissenschaften.

Nelson, Brent F., and James L. Guth. 2000. Exploring the Gender Gap: Women, Men, and Public Attitudes toward European Integration. *European Union Politics* 1, no. 3: 191–217.

Nelson, Brent F., James L. Guth, and Cleveland R. Fraser. 2001. Does Religion Matter? Christianity and Public Support for the European Union. *European Union Politics* 2, no. 2: 191–217.

Neumann, Iver B. 1996. Self and Other in International Relations. *European Journal of International Relations* 2, no. 2: 139–74.

——. 2001. European Identity, EU Expansion, and the Integration/Exclusion Nexus. In *Constructing Europe's Identity—The External Dimension,* edited by Lars-Erik Cederman, 141-164. Boulder, Colo.: Lynne Rienner.

——. 2004. Deep Structure, Free-Floating Signifier, or Something in Between? Europe's Alterity in Putin's Russia. In *Identity and Global Politics: Empirical and Theoretical Elaborations,* edited by Patricia Goff and Kevin Dunn, 9–26. Houndmills, Basingstoke: Palgrave Macmillan.

Nicolaidis, Kalypso, and Robert Howse, eds. 2001. *The Federal Vision: Legitimacy and Levels of Governance in the United States and the European Union*. Oxford: Oxford University Press.

Niedermayer, Oskar. 1995. Trends and Contrasts. In *Public Opinion and Internationalized Governance,* edited by Oskar Niedermayer and Richard Sinnott, 53–72. Oxford: Oxford University Press.

Norman, Peter. 2005. *The Accidental Constitution: The Making of Europe's Constitutional Treaty*. Brussels: EuroComment.

Norris, Pippa. 2000. *A Virtuous Circle: Political Communication in Postindustrial Societies.* Cambridge: Cambridge University Press.

Oakes, Penelope J., S. Alexander Haslam, and John C. Turner. 1994. *Stereotyping and Social Reality.* Oxford: Oxford University Press.

Oberhuber, Florian, Christoph Bärenreuter, Michal Krzyzanowski, Heinz Schönbauer, and Ruth Wodak. 2005. Debating the European Constitution: On Representations of Europe/the EU in the Press. *Journal of Language and Politics* 4, no. 2: 227–71.

OECD. 2008. International Migration Outlook—2008 Edition. Paris: OECD.

Offe, Claus. 2003. Is There, Or Can There Be, a 'European Society'? In *Demokratien in Europa: Der Einfluss der europäischen Integration auf Institutionenwandel und neue Konturen des demokratischen Verfassungsstaates,* edited by Ines Katenhusen and Wolfram Lamping, 71–90. Opladen: Leske and Budrich.

Olsen, Johan P. 2002. The Many Faces of Europeanization. *Journal of Common Market Studies* 40, no. 5: 921–52.

OPTEM. 2001. Perceptions de l'Union Européenne: Attitudes et attentes à son égard; Etude qualitative auprès du public des 15 Etats membres et de 9 pays candidats à l'adhesion. March. Versailles: Commission Européenne.

Pace, Michelle. 2007. The Construction of EU Normative Power. *Journal of Common Market Studies* 45, no. 5: 1041–64.

Packham, Kathrin. 2003. Motor einer europäischen Öffentlichkeit? Der Konvent in der Medienberichterstattung der Mitgliedstaaten. In *Verfassungsexperiment: Europa auf dem Weg zur transnationalen Demokratie?* edited by Ulrike Liebert, Josef Falke, Kathrin Packham, and Daniel Allnoch, 255–78. Münster: Lit Verlag.

Parsons, Craig. 2003. *A Certain Idea of Europe.* Ithaca: Cornell University Press.

Paterson, William E. 1974. *The SPD and European Integration.* Glasgow: Glasgow University Press.

Perloff, Richard. 1993. *The Dynamics of Persuasion.* Hillsdale, N.J.: Erlbaum Associates.

Perrineau, Pascal, ed. 2005. *Le vote Européen 2004–2005: De l'élargissement au Référendum Francais.* Paris: Sciences Po.

Peter, Jochen, and Claes H. De Vreese. 2004. In Search of Europe: A Cross-National Comparative Study of the European Union in National Television News. *Harvard Journal of Press Politics* 9, no. 4: 3–24.

Peter, Jochen, Claes H. De Vreese, and Holli A. Semetko. 2003. EU Politics on Television News: A Cross-National Comparative Study. *European Union Politics* 4, no. 3: 305–27.

Pfetsch, Barbara. 2004. The Voice of the Media in European Public Sphere: Comparative Analysis of Newspaper Editorials. The Transformation of Political Mobilisation and Communication in European Public Spheres. Berlin: Europub.com.

———. 2008. Agents of Transnational Debate across Europe. *Javnost—The Public* 15, no. 4: 21–40.

Pfetsch, Barbara, Silke Adam, and Barbara Eschner. 2008. The Contribution of the Press to Europeanization of Public Debates: A Comparative Study of Issue Salience and Conflict Lines of European Integration. *Journalism* 9, no. 4: 465–92.

Polat, Necati. 2006. Identity Politics and the Domestic Context of Turkey's European Union Accession. *Government and Opposition* 41, no. 4: 512–33.

Pridham, Geoffrey, and Paul G. Lewis, eds. 1996. *Stabilising Fragile Democracies: Comparing New Party Systems in Southern and Eastern Europe.* London: Routledge.

Rakusanova, Petra. 2007. The Constitutional Debate: A One Man Show? Vaclav Klaus and the Constitutional Discourse in the Czech Republic. *Perspectives on European Politics and Society* 8, no. 3: 342–73.

Ramet, Sabrina P. 2006a. Thy Will Be Done: The Catholic Church and Politics in Poland since 1989. In *Religion in an Expanding Europe,* edited by Timothy A. Byrnes and Peter J. Katzenstein, 117–47. Cambridge: Cambridge University Press.

——. 2006b. The Way We Were—and Should Be Again? European Orthodox Churches and the "Idyllic Past." In *Religion in an Expanding Europe,* edited by Timothy A. Byrnes and Peter J. Katzenstein, 148–75. Cambridge: Cambridge University Press.

Redwood, John. 1997. *Our Currency, Our Country: The Dangers of European Monetary Union.* London: Penguin Books.

Renfordt, Swantje. 2007. *Auf dem Weg zu einer europäischen Öffentlichkeit? Eine Medienanalyse europäischer und amerikanischer Debatten über den Irak-Krieg 2003.* Saarbrücken: VDM Verlag Dr. Müller.

——. 2009. An Emerging International Law Script in the Media: Evidence from a Longitudinal, Cross-National Analysis of Western Media Debates about Military Interventions, 1990–2005. PhD dissertation, Fachbereich Politik- und Sozialwissenschaften, Freie Universität Berlin.

Riedel, Sabine. 2008. *Nationalismus im EU-Parlament: Parteien, Standpunkte und Gegenstrategien vor den Europawahlen 2009.* SWP-Studie, S 37. Berlin: Stiftung Wissenschaft und Politik.

Risse, Thomas. 2000. 'Let's Argue!' Communicative Action in International Relations. *International Organization* 54, no. 1: 1–39.

——. 2001. A European Identity? Europeanization and the Evolution of Nation-State Identities. In *Transforming Europe: Europeanization and Domestic Change,* edited by Maria Green Cowles, James A. Caporaso, and Thomas Risse, 198–216. Ithaca: Cornell University Press.

——. 2002. Constructivism and International Institutions: Toward Conversations across Paradigms. In *Political Science: The State of the Discipline,* edited by Ira Katznelson and Helen V. Milner, 597–623. New York: W. W. Norton.

——. 2003. The Euro between National and European Identity. *Journal of European Public Policy* 10, no. 4: 487–503.

——. 2005. Neo-Functionalism, European Identity, and the Puzzles of European Integration. *Journal of European Public Policy* 12, no. 2: 291–309.

Risse, Thomas, and Daniela Engelmann-Martin. 2002. Identity Politics and European Integration: The Case of Germany. In *The Idea of Europe: From Antiquity to the European Union,* edited by Anthony Pagden, 287–316. Cambridge: Cambridge University Press.

Risse, Thomas, Daniela Engelmann-Martin, Hans Joachim Knopf, and Klaus Roscher. 1999. To Euro or Not to Euro: The EMU and Identity Politics in the European Union. *European Journal of International Relations* 5, no. 2: 147–87.

Risse, Thomas, and Mareike Kleine. 2007. Assessing the Legitimacy of the EU's Treaty Revision Methods. *Journal of Common Market Studies* 45, no. 1: 69–80.

Risse, Thomas, and Matthias Leonhard Maier. 2003. Thematic Network: Europeanization, Collective Identities, and Public Discourses (IDNET). Final report, February. Florence: European University Institute.

Risse, Thomas, and Marianne Van de Steeg. 2008. The Emergence of a European Community of Communication: Insights from Empirical Research on the Europeanization of Public Spheres. Unpublished manuscript, Berlin: Otto Suhr Institute of Political Science, Freie Universität Berlin.

Risse-Kappen, Thomas. 1994. Ideas Do Not Float Freely: Transnational Coalitions, Domestic Structures, and the End of the Cold War. *International Organization* 48, no. 2: 185–214.

Rittberger, Berthold, and Frank Schimmelfennig, eds. 2006. *Die Europäische Union auf dem Weg in den Verfassungsstaat.* Frankfurt am Main: Campus.

Rittberger, Volker, ed. 2001. *German Foreign Policy since Unification: An Analysis of Foreign Policy Continuity and Change.* Manchester: Manchester University Press.

Rogosch, Detlef. 1996. *Vorstellungen von Europa: Europabilder in der SPD und bei den belgischen Sozialisten 1945–1957.* Hamburg: Kraemer.

Romaniszyn, Krystyna, and Jacek Nowak. 2002. Poland: State, Nation Formation, and Europe. EURONAT Project: Representations of Europe and the Nation in Current and Prospective Member-States: Media, Elites, and Civil Society. Florence: Robert Schuman Centre for Advanced Studies, European University Institute.

Roscher, Klaus. 2003. The Europeanisation of French Distinctiveness: European Integration and the Reconstruction of Nation-State Concepts in Political Discourse. PhD dissertation. Florence: Department of Social and Political Sciences, European University Institute.

Ross, George. 2006. Danger, One EU Crisis May Hide Another: Social Model Anxieties and Hard Cases. *Comparative European Politics* 4, no. 4: 309–30.

Rother, Nina, and Tina M. Nebe. 2009. More Mobile, More European? Free Movement and EU Identity. In *Pioneers of European Integration: Citizenship and Mobility in the EU,* edited by Adrian Favell and Ettore Recchi. Cheltenham, U.K.: Edward Elgar.

Ruiz Jimenez, Antonia Maria. 2002. Nation and Europe in Spanish Public Discourse: A Comparative Analysis of Press, TV, and Parties. November. Madrid: UNED University.

Sandholtz, Wayne. 1996. Membership Matters: Limits of the Functional Approach to European Institutions. *Journal of Common Market Studies* 34, no. 3: 403–29.

Sbragia, Alberta. 2001. Italy Pays for Europe: Political Leadership, Political Choice, and Institutional Adaptation. In *Transforming Europe: Europeanization and Domestic Change,* edited by Maria Green Cowles, James A. Caporaso, and Thomas Risse, 79–98. Ithaca: Cornell University Press.

Schäfer, Mike S., and Ulrike Zschache. 2008. Vorstellungen über die EU in der öffentlichen Debatte: Eine Analyse deutscher Pressekommentare zum EU-Beitritt der Türkei. Berliner Studien zur Soziologie Europas 12. Berlin: Institut für Soziologie, Freie Universität Berlin.

Scharpf, Fritz W. 1999. *Governing in Europe: Effective and Democratic?* Oxford: Oxford University Press.

———. 2007. Reflections on Multilevel Legitimacy. MPIfG Working Paper. Cologne: Max Planck Institute for the Study of Societies.

———. 2009. Legitimacy in the Multilevel European Polity. *European Political Science Review* 1, no. 2: 173–204.

Schauer, Hans. 1996. *Europäische Identität und demokratische Tradition.* Munich: Olzog.

Schild, Joachim. 2008. Französische Europapolitik in einer verunsicherten Geselllschaft: Soziale Identitäten, europapolitische Präferenzen und Europadiskurse seit den 1980er Jahren. Arbeitspapiere zur Europäischen Integration, Trier: Universität Trier/Politikwissenschaft—Europäische Akademie Otzenhausen.

Schimmelfennig, Frank. 2003. *The EU, NATO, and the Integration of Europe: Rules and Rhetoric.* Cambridge: Cambridge University Press.

Schlesinger, Philip R. 1993. Wishful Thinking: Cultural Politics, Media, and Collective Identities in Europe. *Journal of Communication* 43, no. 2: 6–17.

Schmidt, Vivien A. 1996. *From State to Market? The Transformation of French Business and Government.* Cambridge: Cambridge University Press.

———. 2006. *Democracy in Europe: The EU and National Polities.* Oxford: Oxford University Press.

———. 2007. Trapped by Their Ideas: French Elites' Discourses of European Integration and Globalization. *Journal of European Public Policy* 14, no. 7: 992–1009.

Schmidt, Vivien A., and Claudio M. Radaelli. 2004. Policy Change and Discourse in Europe: Conceptual and Methodological Issues. *West European Politics* 27, no. 2: 183–210.

Schmitter, Philippe C. 2000. *How to Democratize the European Union…And Why Bother?* Lanham, Md.: Rowman and Littlefield.

Schmitz, Petra L., and Rolf Geserick. 1996. *Die Anderen in Europa: Nationale Selbst- und Fremdbilder im europäischen Integrationsprozeß.* Bonn: Europa-Union Verlag.

Schoen, Harald. 2008a. Die Deutschen und die Türkeifrage: Eine Analyse der Einstellungen zum Antrag der Türkei auf Mitgliedschaft in der Europäischen Union. *Politische Vierteljahresschrift* 49, no. 1: 68–91.

———. 2008b. Identity, Instrumental Self-Interest and Institutional Evaluations: Explaining Public Opinion on Common European Policies in Foreign Affairs and Defence. *European Union Politics* 9, no. 5: 5–29.

Sedelmeier, Ulrich. 2005. *Constructing the Path to Eastern Enlargement: The Uneven Policy Impact of EU Identity.* Manchester: Manchester University Press.

Semetko, Holli A., Claes H. De Vreese, and Jochen Peter. 2000. Europeanised Politics—Europeanised Media? European Integration and Political Communication. *West European Politics* 23, no. 4: 121–41.

Sifft, Stefanie, Michael Brüggemann, Katharina Kleinen-von-Königslow, Bernhard Peters, and Andreas Wimmel. 2007. Segmented Europeanization: Exploring the Legitimacy of the European Union from a Public Discourse Perspective. *Journal of Common Market Studies* 45, no. 1: 127–55.

SIPRI, ed. 2008. *SIPRI Year Book 2008: Armaments, Disarmament, and International Security.* Oxford: Oxford University Press.

Sjursen, Helene. 2002. Why Expand? The Question of Legitimacy and Justification in the EU's Enlargement Policy. *Journal of Common Market Studies* 40, no. 3: 491–513.

———. 2006a. The EU as a 'Normative' Power: How Can This Be? *Journal of European Public Policy* 13, no. 2: 235–51.

———, ed. 2006b. *Questioning EU Enlargement: Europe in Search of Identity.* London: Routledge.

Smith, Anthony D. 1991. *National Identity.* London: Penguin Books.

———. 1992. National Identity and the Idea of European Unity. *International Affairs* 68, no. 1: 55–76.

Smith, Karen E. 2003. *European Foreign Policy in a Changing World.* Cambridge: Polity Press.

Smith, Michael E. 2004. *Europe's Foreign and Security Policy: The Institutionalization of Cooperation.* Cambridge: Cambridge University Press.

Snow, David A., and Robert D. Bedford. 1988. Ideology, Frame Resonance, and Participant Mobilization. In *International Social Movement Research: From Structure to Action: Comparing Social Movement Research across Cultures,* edited by Bert Klandermans, Hanspeter Kriesi, and Sidney Tarrow, 197–218. Greenwich, Conn.: JAI Press.

Statham, Paul. 2007. Political Communication, European Integration, and the Transformation of National Public Spheres: A Comparison of Britain and France. In *The European Union and the Public Sphere: A Communicative Space in the Making?* edited by John Erik Fossum and Philip Schlesinger, 110–34. London: Routledge.

Statistisches Bundesamt Deutschland. 2008. Leichter Anstieg der Bevölkerung mit Migrationshintergrund: Pressemitteilung 105. March 11. Wiesbaden: Statistisches Bundesamt Deutschland.

Stein, Janice Gross. 2002. Psychological Explanations of International Conflict. In *Handbook of International Relations,* edited by Walter Carlsnaes, Thomas Risse, and Beth A. Simmons, 292–308. London: Sage.

Stöckel, Florian. 2008. The European Public Sphere, the Media, and Support for European Integration. Diploma thesis Berlin: Otto Suhr Institut für Politikwissenschaft, Freie Universität Berlin.

Stone Sweet, Alec. 2000. *Governing with Judges: Constitutional Politics in Europe.* Oxford: Oxford University Press.

Stone Sweet, Alec, Wayne Sandholtz, and Neil Fligstein, eds. 2001. *The Institutionalization of Europe.* Oxford: Oxford University Press.

Sylvester, Christine. 1994. *Feminist Theory and International Relations in a Postmodern Era.* Cambridge: Cambridge University Press.

Taggart, Paul, and Aleks Szczerbiak, eds. 2005/2008. *Opposing Europe? The Comparative Party Politics of Euroscepticism, Volumes 1 and 2.* Oxford: Oxford University Press.

Tajfel, Henri. 1981. *Human Groups and Social Categories: Studies in Social Psychology.* Cambridge: Cambridge University Press.

———. 1982. *Social Identity and Intergroup Relations.* Cambridge: Cambridge University Press.

Tannen, Deborah. 1994. *Gender and Discourse.* Oxford: Oxford University Press.

Thomas, Daniel C. 2001. *The Helsinki Effect: International Norms, Human Rights, and the Demise of Communism.* Princeton: Princeton University Press.

Tickner, J. Ann. 2002. Feminist Perspectives on International Relations. In *Handbook of International Relations,* edited by Walter Carlsnaes, Thomas Risse, and Beth Simmons, 275–91. London: Sage.

Tietz, Udo. 2002. *Die Grenzen des 'Wir': Eine Theorie der Gemeinschaft.* Frankfurt am Main: Suhrkamp.

Tilly, Charles. 1975. *The Formation of the National States in Western Europe.* Princeton: Princeton University Press.

———. 1985. War Making and State Making as Organized Crime. In *Bringing the State Back In,* edited by Peter B. Evans, Dietrich Rueschemeyer, and Theda Skocpol, 169–187. Cambridge: Cambridge University Press.

Tobler, Stefan. 2002. Transnationale Kommunikationsverdichtungen im Streit um die internationale Steuerpolitik. *Berliner Debatte Initial* 13, nos. 5–6: 57–66.

Transatlantic Trends. 2008. *Transatlantic Trends 2008.* http://www.gmfus.org/trends/archive.html#2008.

Trenz, Hans-Jörg. 2000. Korruption und politischer Skandal in der EU: Auf dem Weg zu einer europäischen politischen Öffentlichkeit. In *Die Europäisierung nationaler Gesellschaften:* Sonderheft 40, *Kölner Zeitschrift für Soziologie und Sozialpsychologie,* edited by Maurizio Bach, 332–59. Wiesbaden: Westdeutscher Verlag.

———. 2002. *Zur Konstitution politischer Öffentlichkeit in der Europäischen Union: Zivilgesellschaftliche Subpolitik oder schaupolitische Inszenierung?* Baden-Baden: Nomos.

———. 2004. Media Coverage on European Governance: Exploring the European Public Sphere in National Quality Newspapers. *European Journal of Communication* 19, no. 3: 291–319.

———. 2006. *Europa in den Medien: Die europäische Integration im Spiegel nationaler Öffentlichkeit.* Frankfurt am Main: Campus.

———. 2007. 'Quo vadis Europe?' Quality Newspapers Struggling for European Unity. In *The European Union and the Public Sphere: A Communicative Space in the Making?* edited by John Erik Fossum and Philip Schlesinger, 89–109. London: Routledge.

———. 2008a. In Search of the European Public Sphere: Between Normative Overstretch and Empirical Disenchantment. RECON Online Working Papers. Oslo: ARENA, University of Oslo.

——. 2008b. Understanding Media Impact on European Integration: Enhancing or Restricting the Scope of Legitimacy of the EU? *European Integration* 30, no. 2: 291–309.

Trenz, Hans-Jörg, and Klaus Eder. 2004. The Democratizing Dynamics of a European Public Sphere: Towards a Theory of Democratic Functionalism. *European Journal of Social Theory* 7, no. 1: 5–25.

Trondal, Jarle. 2002. Beyond the EU Membership—Non-Membership Dichotomy? Supranational Identities among National EU Decision-Makers. *Journal of European Public Policy* 9, no. 3: 468–87.

Tsebelis, George, and Sven-Oliver Proksch. 2007. The Art of Political Manipulation in the European Convention. *Journal of Common Market Studies* 45, no. 1: 157–86.

Tulmets, Elsa. 2005. La Conditionnalité dans la Politique d'Elargissement de l'Union Européenne à l'Est: Un Cadre d'Apprentissages et de Socialisation Mutuelle? PhD. dissertation, Paris and Berlin: Institut Politiques de Paris—Freie Universität Berlin.

Uterwedde, Henrik. 1988. *Die Wirtschaftspolitik der Linken in Frankreich: Programme und Praxis 1984–87.* Frankfurt am Main: Campus.

Van de Steeg, Marianne. 2002. Rethinking the Conditions for a Public Sphere in the European Union. *European Journal of Social Theory* 5, no. 4: 499–519.

——. 2005. The Public Sphere in the European Union: A Media Analysis of Public Discourse on EU Enlargement and on the Haider Case. PhD dissertation. Florence: Department of Social and Political Sciences, European University Institute.

——. 2006. Does a Public Sphere Exist in the European Union? An Analysis of the Content of the Debate on the Haider Case. *European Journal of Political Research* 45, no. 4: 609–34.

Verdun, Amy. 2000. *European Responses to Globalization and Financial Market Integration: Perceptions of EMU in Britain, France, and Germany.* Houndmills Basingstoke: Palgrave Macmillan.

Vetters, Regina. 2007. Konvent + Verfassung = Öffentlichkeit? Momente europäischer Öffentlichkeit in der Berichterstattung deutscher, britischer und französischer Printmedien in der Verfassungsdebatte. PhD dissertation. Berlin: Fachbereich Politik- und Sozialwissenschaften, Freie Universität Berlin.

Von Oppeln, Sabine. 2005. Die Debatte über den Türkei-Beitritt in Deutschland und Frankreich. *Leviathan* 33, no. 3: 391–411.

Vucetic, Srdjan. 2008. The Anglo-Sphere. A Genealogy of Racialized Identity in International Relations. PhD dissertation. Columbus, Ohio: Department of Political Science, Ohio State University.

Waltz, Kenneth. 1979. *Theory of International Politics.* Reading, Mass.: Addison-Wesley.

Weiler, Joseph H. H. 1999. *The Constitution of Europe.* Cambridge: Cambridge University Press.

Wendt, Alexander. 1987. The Agent-Structure Problem in International Relations Theory. *International Organization* 41, no. 3: 335–70.

——. 1992. Anarchy Is What States Make of It: The Social Construction of Power Politics. *International Organization* 88, no. 2: 384–96.

——. 1999. *Social Theory of International Politics.* Cambridge: Cambridge University Press.

Wessler, Hartmut, Bernhard Peters, Michael Brüggemann, Katharina Kleinen von Königslow, and Stefanie Sifft. 2008. *Transnationalization of Public Spheres.* Houndmills, Basingstoke: Palgrave Macmillan.

Wimmel, Andreas. 2006a. Beyond the Bosphorus? Comparing German, French, and British Discourses on Turkey's Application to Join the European Union. Political Science Series. Wien: Institut für Höhere Studien.

——. 2006b. *Transnationale Diskurse in Europa: Der Streit um den Türkei-Beitritt in Deutschland, Frankreich und Großbritannien.* Frankfurt am Main: Campus.

Wodak, Ruth. 2004. National and Transnational Identities: European and Other Identities Constructed in Interviews with EU Officials. In *Transnational Identities: Becoming European in the EU,* edited by Richard K. Herrmann, Thomas Risse, and Marilynn B. Brewer, 97–128. Lanham, Md.: Rowman and Littlefield.

Wolf, Klaus Dieter. 2000. *Die Neue Staatsräson—Zwischenstaatliche Kooperation als Demokratieproblem in der Weltgesellschaft.* Baden-Baden: Nomos.

Wyrozumska, Aleksandra. 2007. Who Is Willing to Die for the Constitution? The National Debate on the Constitutional Treaty in Poland. *Perspectives on European Politics and Society* 8, no. 3: 314–41.

Yavuz, M. Hakan. 2006. Islam and Europeanization in Turkish-Muslim Socio-political Movements. In *Religion in an Expanding Europe,* edited by Timothy A. Byrnes and Peter J. Katzenstein, 225–55. Cambridge: Cambridge University Press.

Youngs, Richard. 2004. Normative Dynamics and Strategic Interests in the EU's External Identity. *Journal of Common Market Studies* 42, no. 2: 415–35.

Zaborowski, Marcin. 2006. More Than Simply Expanding Markets: Germany and EU Enlargement. In *Questioning EU Enlargement: Europe in Search of Identity,* edited by Helene Sjursen, 104–20. London: Routledge.

Zürn, Michael. 2000. Democratic Governance beyond the Nation-State: The EU and Other International Institutions. *European Journal of International Relations* 6, no. 2: 183–221.

——. 2001. Politik in der postnationalen Konstellation: Über das Elend des methodologischen Nationalismus. In *Politik in eine rentgrenzten Welt,* edited by Christine Landfried, 181–203. Cologne: Verlag Wissenschaft und Politik.

Index

Adenauer, Konrad, 66, 98, 210
Afghanistan War, 131, 136, 154, 238
Amsterdam, Treaty of (1997), 94, 172, 196
Anglo-American perspective, 141, 142, 152,
    153, 170, 193
Austria. *See also* Haider, Jörg, and Haider
    Debate
  citizens' identities in, 42, 44
  Europeanization of public sphere in, 129n3,
    132*f*, 133n10, 134, 135f, 136n13, 137f,
    138*f*, 140, 142–45, 152, 159
  FPÖ, 2n2, 3, 140–42, 167
  institution-building and identity in, 180
  Northern enlargement of EU to include, 204
  Turkish membership, opposition to, 216

Balkans, western, 2, 4, 56, 148, 154, 163, 164,
    204, 206, 212, 219, 244
Belgium, 60, 93, 97, 134n11, 135*f*, 142, 197, 222,
    232, 234
benefits. *See* material interests
Blair, Tony, 83, 144, 150, 189–90, 193,
    198, 240n7
blended identities, 25
borderless traffic (Schengenland), 3–4, 7,
    56–57, 83, 94, 172–73, 221, 250, 251
Bosnia-Herzegovina, 136, 204n1
Brandt, Willy, 67, 98
Britain. *See* United Kingdom
Brown, Gordon, 83, 240n7
Bruter, Michael, 50, 51, 58, 59, 93–95
Bulgaria, 173, 211, 219

Catholic Church, 6, 199, 200, 210–12
Central Eastern Europe
  citizens' identities in, 42, 43, 44, 46, 48–49
  common perspective, development of,
    143, 146–47
  community of communication in, 160
  Constitutional Treaty, debate on ratification
    of, 147, 166
  crisis situations, support for concerted action
    in, 183
  enlargement of EU to include, 7, 14, 102,
    148–51, 164, 204–13, 244

Europeanization of identity and public
    spheres in, 5, 127, 170, 172–73, 232
  identity politics of, 28, 32–33, 205–9
  immigration issues, 48–49, 60, 222
  Iraq War and identity of, 2–3
  length of engagement in integration process
    in, 7, 12
  "post-membership blues" in, 97
  return of religion and history to EU with,
    209–13
  trust levels in, 44, 232
  visibility of EU in media, 131n8
Charter of Fundamental Rights, 83, 99n5, 240,
    251
China, 192, 196
Chirac, Jacques, 74–75, 134, 144, 189, 197–98, 207
Christian Democrats, 64, 66, 67, 68, 72, 219,
    239–40, 249
Christianity. *See* religious undertones in Euro-
    pean identity
Churchill, Winston, 82
Ciampi, Carlo Azeglio, 141
citizens' identities, 9–10, 37–62, 245
  common European language, lack of, 38–39
  demographic differences, 46–49
  enlargement and immigration issues, 48–49,
    207–8
  European versus EU identity, 50–55, 61
  Europeanization of national identities revealed
    in, 38, 45
  exclusive nationalism, 41–46, 41*f*, 49, 52, 54,
    61, 62
  imagined communities, psychological exis-
    tence of, 38, 40, 53, 55–61
  inclusive nationalism, 41, 41*f*, 43–46, 49,
    60, 61
  institution-building and, 179–83
  multiple "others" and, 53–55, 61
  mutual trust levels, 44, 59
  national and European identities, coexistence
    of, 39–46, 41*f*, 61
  political and cultural, 50–53, 61
  possibility of a European/EU identity, 38–39
  variation between states/over time, 41–43,
    41*f*, 42, 46